History of England

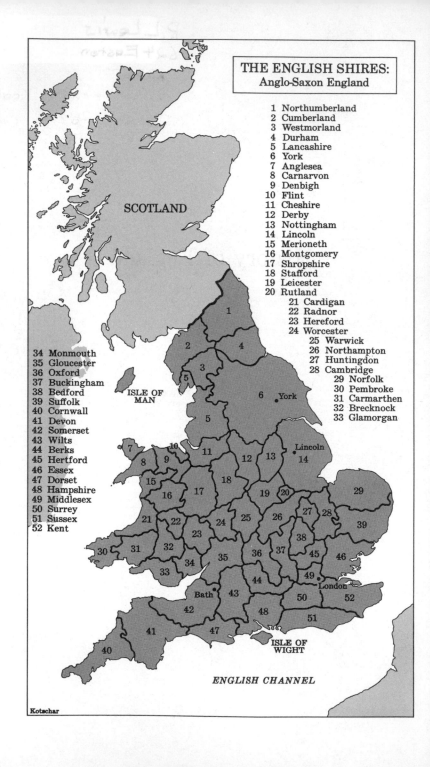

THE ENGLISH SHIRES:
Anglo-Saxon England

1 Northumberland
2 Cumberland
3 Westmorland
4 Durham
5 Lancashire
6 York
7 Anglesea
8 Carnarvon
9 Denbigh
10 Flint
11 Cheshire
12 Derby
13 Nottingham
14 Lincoln
15 Merioneth
16 Montgomery
17 Shropshire
18 Stafford
19 Leicester
20 Rutland
21 Cardigan
22 Radnor
23 Hereford
24 Worcester
25 Warwick
26 Northampton
27 Huntingdon
28 Cambridge
29 Norfolk
30 Pembroke
31 Carmarthen
32 Brecknock
33 Glamorgan
34 Monmouth
35 Gloucester
36 Oxford
37 Buckingham
38 Bedford
39 Suffolk
40 Cornwall
41 Devon
42 Somerset
43 Wilts
44 Berks
45 Hertford
46 Essex
47 Dorset
48 Hampshire
49 Middlesex
50 Surrey
51 Sussex
52 Kent

SCOTLAND

ISLE OF MAN

York

Lincoln

London

Bath

ISLE OF WIGHT

ENGLISH CHANNEL

Kotschar

COLLEGE OUTLINE SERIES

History of England

Second Edition

Harold J. Schultz

BARNES & NOBLE, Inc.
New York
Publishers · Booksellers · Since 1873

L. C. Catalogue Card Number: 79-153052

SBN 389 00044 2

Second Edition, 1971

Reprinted, 1972

Manufactured in the United States of America

About the Author

Harold J. Schultz is Chairman of the Department of History at Stetson University. A native of Canada, he received his training in British and Commonwealth History at the University of Michigan (M.A.) and the Commonwealth-Studies Center of Duke University (Ph.D.). In 1966 Dr. Schultz lectured in a Summer Program at the University of Sussex, England, and he was a Visiting Fellow at Regent's Park College, Oxford University, during 1969-1970. In 1967 he received a Fulbright Grant for a Summer Seminar in Africa. Dr. Schultz is the author of *English Liberalism and the State: Individualism or Collectivism?* and co-author of *The Politics of Discontent.*

Preface

Spinoza wrote, "I have made a ceaseless effort not to ridicule, nor to bewail, nor to scorn human actions, but to understand them." This is, indeed, the function—and fascination—of historiography. But one of the problems that plagues the serious student of history is its complexity, for there is little that is neat or orderly in the record of human affairs. History moves through the unique, the concrete, and the individual; and therefore it is as complex, and as colorful, as the world of characters who make up its cast.

To make thorough historical investigation most meaningful, however, an overview of the period or people in question is valuable in order to observe the major themes and events and ask the crucial questions—how did these things come about, and why—so that the relationship of men and ideas and events may be sensed. Perhaps by viewing the salient issues and events in the history of England, the student will obtain an historical framework to aid his understanding of the British people and their manner of life.

Certainly an understanding of the British achievement is essential to understanding many of the institutions and ideas of our own world. For the inhabitants of this small island kingdom have left a legacy that extends far beyond the shores of the British Isles. Such varied achievements as the parliamentary system, the concept of *rex sub lege*, common law, Shakespearean drama, the Anglican, Methodist, Presbyterian, and Congregational churches, the game of football, the industrial revolution, the writ of habeas corpus, the Pax Britannica, and the Commonwealth of Nations are all part of this legacy.

The English-speaking world, in particular, is indebted to the mother country for many of its institutions and traditions and, equally important, for millions of English emigrants who transplanted these ideas of a free society in the colonies. The United States was the largest of these transplantations.

Almost half of the span of American history is essentially British

Colonial history, and A. L. Rowse, the noted Elizabethan historian, in observing that the United States has picked up England's mantle of leadership of the free world, argues that "America is, after all, the greatest achievement of the English people."

It is hoped, therefore, that this College Outline will serve both as a digest of English history and as an interpretation of this heritage and achievement.

I cannot hope to do justice to the many individuals who contributed, either in their teaching or in their counsel, to the shaping of this book. To Harvey Graveline, of the Barnes & Noble editorial staff, I am particularly indebted. His patience, careful criticisms, and countless suggestions spurred my efforts in this project. Also to my wife, Carolyn, I should like to express my gratitude for her constant encouragement and reviving cups of coffee late at night.

H.J.S.

Contents

History of England

Chapter 1 ⮧ The Foundations of England

The early history of England is essentially a chronicle of invasions. Long before recorded British history began with the Roman invaders, wave after wave of warlike settlers landed on English shores. Here the migrants mingled with other tribes so that the Britons became the most mongrel of races. These early invaders came because the island lay so invitingly open to invasion. After the last of these migrant settlers, the Celts, had subdued the island, the Roman legions, in turn, subdued the Celts.

An Island People

Central to the history and character of the British people is the geographical location of Britain. Its location, twenty-one miles from the Continent, makes England part of Europe, but with a separate and insular identity. "Thus, in early times, the relation of Britain to the sea was passive and receptive; in modern times, active and acquisitive. In both it is the key to her story." [1]

The Land and Its Resources. The physical formation, climate, and minerals of the country tempted the early invaders to settle, and explain the paths of settlement they followed. Not having mastered nature, the successive invaders claimed the rich and accessible lowlands of southern and eastern Britain and drove the earlier inhabitants to the north and west.

The Islands. The five thousand British Isles, dominated by the major islands of Britain (labeled *Britannia* by Julius Caesar) and Ireland, cover approximately 120,000 square miles, with the area of England totaling less than half this amount (50,331 square miles). Presumably man first came to Britain in the Old Stone Age when the land was still joined to the Continent. With the closing of the Ice Ages, the receding glaciations transformed the physical surface of the land and left it an island. But the early connection with the Continent meant that the flora and fauna of Britain were closely identified with the flora and fauna of northern Europe.

---

[1] G. M. Trevelyan, *History of England* (Garden City, New York: Doubleday, 1953), I, p. 12.

Geographical Features. The physical map of Britain will show why England was so accessible from the Continent, for the land slopes downward from the highlands to the north and from the craggy coast of the Atlantic to the low, flat plains of the southeast. Because of the general slope of land from north to southeast most English rivers have their outlets on the south and the east coasts. Invaders moved inland by following the Trent, the Welland, the Nen, and the Thames rivers to the Midlands. Later, these rivers doubled as main arteries of trade. In the southwest the Severn River served the same dual function for the area of the Welsh border. As the invaders reached the highlands of the north and west, they halted, and these inhospitable regions became the haven for the displaced older cultures. Consequently, the Scottish Highlands, Wales, and Cornwall were inhabited by the older stocks; and to this day, they are commonly called the "Celtic fringe."

Climate. In the third millennium before Christ the first agriculturalists crossed the Channel and revolutionized the existing society of cave-dwelling hunters by introducing a new way of life: they bred cattle, sowed grain, and later developed a flint-mining industry. The more temperate climate of England after the Ice Ages was well suited to the growing of crops, because the prevailing winds from the southwest follow the Gulf Stream and keep England at a warmer and more equable temperature than its latitude would ordinarily permit. Although the rainfall is moderate, the oceanic climate produces fog, mist, and haze so that visitors, from Tacitus to modern tourists, write about the wretched weather.

Natural Resources. The temperate climate, coupled with a fairly rich soil, promoted the growing of barley and wheat. Good harbors and the long, irregular coastline encouraged fishing and ocean trade. In fact, the trade of the Levant with Britain antedated the Celtic conquest, and Mediterranean traders had long heard exaggerated tales of British gold and pearls. Copper and tin were found in abundance. By smelting the two metals together, the inhabitants manufactured bronze, and so marked the close of the lengthy Stone Age. Later, conveniently located deposits of coal and iron would support England's industrial revolution.

Prehistory of Britain. In Britain, as elsewhere, the story of man and his society can be traced through the various stone and metal ages. Man moved westward in Europe and arrived in Britain during the Paleolithic (Old Stone) Age. Since each succeeding period or "age" was also a transplanting from the Continent, Britain became largely a recipient of cultural change in the period of prehistory.

The Stone Ages. From stone and bone tools and skeletal remains it is surmised that Homo sapiens first appeared in Britain by a land bridge some 250,000 years ago. In the New Stone Age, long-headed agriculturalists, probably from the Iberian peninsula, crossed the Channel and set up mixed farming in southern England side by side with the older hunting communities. A thousand years later (around 2000 B.C.) these peaceful and mild-mannered settlers were attacked in turn by tall, powerful, round-headed warriors from Europe who overran all of habitable Britain. They brought with them metal implements and thereby introduced a new age of Bronze.

The Beaker Folk. The latest invaders were designated as the Beaker Folk after the shape of the drinking vessels which they fashioned out of clay. These newcomers possessed a mastery of metal workmanship that was reflected in the variety of weapons and tools they produced. They wore woolen and linen clothes, greatly admired jewelry, but had little interest in farming. Where the earlier immigrants (Iberians) had worshipped Mother Earth, the Beaker Folk worshipped the Sun in temples open to the sky. Stonehenge, a circular grouping of massive stones, remains to this day a fascinating and impressive monument of the period.[2] Other immigrants followed and by 1500 B.C. the blending of traditions established the distinctive Wessex culture in Britain: an age of Bronze, an organized religion and priesthood, and a tribal structure centered around a kinglike chief and a slowly evolving aristocracy.

The Celtic Invaders. The last of the early invaders were the Celts, the first of the conquerors about whom the Romans wrote. With the Celts came the higher civilization of the Iron Age.

Celtic Origins. The word "Celt," in terms of British identity, is more a matter of civilization and language than of race. Threatened by rival groups, the Celtic-speaking tribes of France and western Germany migrated to the British Isles to obtain relief from continental conflicts. During the last century before Christ, bands of Celtic invaders, armed with battle-axes and double-edged swords, landed on the south and east coasts and moved inland.

Celtic Society. The invaders wove cloth, shaved their bodies, and made agriculture and grazing important industries for the first time. Communities of farmers lived in either hut villages or protected homesteads, and the clan became the center of their social organization. Over the years Celtic culture advanced as the tribes

---

[2] The hypothesis that Stonehenge was originally planned as an astronomical observatory is offered by Gerald S. Hawkins (with John B. White) in *Stonehenge Decoded* (Garden City, New York: Doubleday, 1965).

became expert in working tin, bronze, and iron; their pottery and their metal helmets indicate a growing interest and ability in the decorative arts and in ornamentation. The south Britons had a gold coinage similar to that of Macedon, and their tribal leaders led a revelrous life, enriched with imported wines and luxury goods. At least the Celts were not just primitive savages, painted with blue dye, and beyond the pale of civilization as was once thought.

Celtic Religion. Druidism originated in England and spread to Gaul and Ireland. The druids were an organized caste of priests who exercised great power. They preached a religion of fear and immortality, worshipped various nature gods in sacred groves, and offered human sacrifices. Druid priests commanded prestige and served as judges and leaders of tribal opinion.

Celtic Britain and Gaul. Druidism, trade, and racial affinity were three of the ties between Britain and Gaul. The link became even more direct in 75 B.C. when the Belgic tribes of Gaul claimed southeast Britain (modern-day Kent, Middlesex, and Hertfordshire) as their kingdoms. These Gallic Celts dispersed the native Celts from the best lands of the southeast and were the first tribe to face the next invader, Caesar.

Roman Conquest and Consolidation

In contrast to the earlier Celt or later Saxon invaders, the Romans came to Britain to rule and exploit the island as part of a world empire, not to disperse the inhabitants and settle in their place. The Roman objectives in this new method of conquest produced quite different results. Roman rule became urban and efficient, but remained alien, and therefore only temporary in its effects.

The Roman Conquests. The annexation of Britain was scarcely a primary objective of Roman expansion, for the British Isles marked the fringe of civilization to those who ruled in imperial Rome. However, when the Romans decided to conquer and colonize Britain, their superior military and political organization was decisive.

The Invasions of Julius Caesar, 55-54 B.C. Two attacks on Britain were made by Julius Caesar during his conquest of Gaul. Certainly one of his reasons was to punish the South Britons who were providing aid to their kinsmen in North Gaul. No doubt, too, Caesar's popularity and position would be enhanced by another victory that would provide tribute and slaves for his supporters in Rome and booty for his soldiers. His first expedition (55 B.C.) was a military failure. After a skirmish with Kentish tribesmen near Dover he withdrew, but returned the next year with five legions. This time Caesar won several battles against Cassivelaunus (king of the Belgic tribe of the Catuvellauni), forded the Thames, and penetrated inland approximately to where London now stands. The Britons sued for peace, and Caesar granted a treaty on easy terms because, with renewed disturbances in Gaul, he was content with hostages and a promise of yearly tribute. The Romans then departed from Britain without making a permanent occupation. Caesar, lured on by larger stakes in Rome, crossed the Rubicon to his final triumph and tragedy.

Results of Caesar's Invasion. Caesar described his conquest graphically in his commentaries *On the Gallic Wars,* but his sortie into Britain had few permanent results except to increase trade between Britain and the Latinized province of Gaul. Roman traders and settlers now entered Britain peacefully and spread Roman culture and influence. Caesar's invasion also proved that the Romans could conquer Britain at their convenience if they were ready to devote time and men to that purpose. Almost a hundred years passed before it was convenient to do so.

The Coming of Claudius. While Rome was preoccupied with more immediate matters, Britain remained unmolested until 43 A.D., when Emperor Claudius ordered Aulus Plautius to invade the island. The decision was made because the emperor was anxious for glory and irritated by a revolt in Gaul instigated by the druids; and also because his Gallic origins increased his interest in conquering Britain. The British defenders, who were led by Caractacus, a son of Cunobelinus (Shakespeare's "Cymbeline"), displayed a vigorous but disunited resistance. Tacitus later commented upon this fact: "Our greatest advantage in coping with tribes so powerful is that they do not act in concert. Seldom is it that two or three states meet together to ward off a common danger. Thus, while they fight singly, they all are conquered." [3] Claudius himself came for a brief period to command the legions. Within three years Plautius reduced the divided Britons to guerrilla reprisals and brought southeast Britain under Roman rule. But when the legions reached the Welsh mountains and the northern moors they, like every other successful invader, encountered stubborn opposition.

Later Roman Conquests. During the governorships of Scapula (47-54 A.D.) and Suetonius (59-61 A.D.) the Roman occupation was

---

[3] *The Complete Works of Tacitus* (translated by Alfred Church and William Brodribb; New York: Random House, 1942), p. 684.

extended northward and westward. While Suetonius was suppressing the druids at their sacred center of worship in Anglesey, the Iceni under Queen Boudicca revolted (61 A.D.). The Iceni and their neighboring tribes attacked the Romans and the Britons who fraternized with them in the towns of Colchester, London, and Verulamium, in retaliation for the Roman confiscation of their property and the public outrages committed against their queen and her daughters. Tens of thousands were massacred in the uprising. Governor Suetonius returned with his legionnaires and crushed the revolt in a crucial battle; Boudicca took poison, and Roman vengeance was inflicted upon the rebellious Britons. In 78 A.D. Agricola became the new governor, completed the conquest of Wales, and extended Roman rule into Scotland after his victory at Mons Graupius. More is known of Agricola's able leadership and administration than of any other governor because Tacitus, his son-in-law, was Rome's most famous historian. Before Agricola was called back to Rome he was able to pacify the south of England by his conciliatory statesmanship; elsewhere in Britain military expansion almost ceased. The Roman garrison was reduced to three legions located at strategic centers near the frontiers—Caerleon and Chester on the border of Wales and at York in the north.

Military Consolidation. A rebellion in Scotland quickly swept away Agricola's gains and prevented Roman rule from triumphing in Scotland. In 122 A.D., to protect northern England from barbarian raids, Emperor Hadrian ordered a wall built from the Tyne river to Solway Firth. This famous wall roughly divided England from Scotland (see map, p. 7). A later emperor, Antonius Pius, extended Roman control northward and constructed a second fortification, the Antonine Wall, in 143 A.D. However, the Romans overextended their resources and the northern tribes overran both walls. Not until Emperor Severus strengthened the fortresses and frontiers (208-211 A.D.) did a semblance of peace prevail in the north. These northern wars were the price Rome paid during these two centuries for the protection and peace of southern England.

Pax Romana

Under Roman rule the Britons began to live in towns and traveled from town to town on stone highways. Romanization also introduced to the British Isles the atmosphere of the Mediterranean world with its Latin tongue, its country villas, and its new faith, Christianity. But Roman rule did not teach the Britons how to

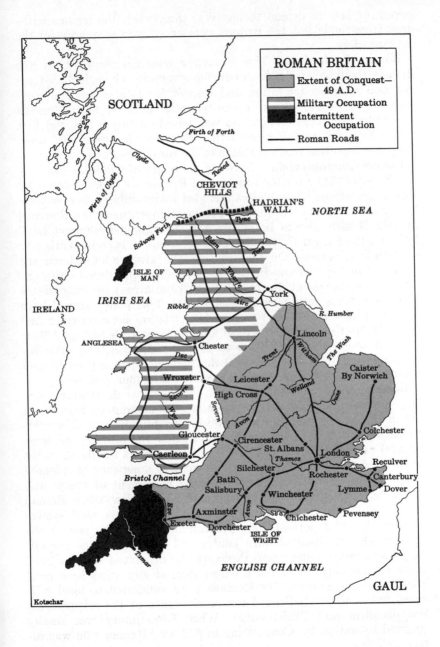

ROMAN BRITAIN

Extent of Conquest—
49 A.D.
Military Occupation
Intermittent
Occupation
Roman Roads

SCOTLAND

Firth of Forth

Clyde

Firth of Clyde

Tweed

CHEVIOT
HILLS

HADRIAN'S
WALL

NORTH SEA

Solway Firth

Tyne

Eden

ISLE OF
MAN

IRISH SEA

Wharfe

Ribble

Aire

York

R. Humber

IRELAND

Lincoln

Witham

The Wash

ANGLESEA

Dee

Chester

Trent

Caister
By Norwich

Wroxeter

Leicester

Welland

Severn

High Cross

Ouse

Severn

Wye

Avon

Gloucester

Cirencester

Colchester

Caerleon

St. Albans

London

Reculver

Bristol Channel

Exe

Bath
Salisbury

Silchester

Thames

Rochester

Canterbury

Winchester

Lymme

Dover

Axminster

Avon

Chichester

Pevensey

Exeter

Dorchester

ISLE OF
WIGHT

Tamar

ENGLISH CHANNEL

GAUL

Kotschar

govern or how to defend themselves; thus, when the legions withdrew from the island, the Britons were once again easy prey for the next invaders.

Roman Institutions. The Roman conquerors imposed on the Britons their imperial administrative structure which included racial and religious toleration and respect for local chiefs and customs as long as no political opposition was involved. Since Romans were convinced that civilization was based on urban life, the first thing they did was to build cities. But outside these city walls Roman civilization remained alien to the rural tribesmen.

Roman Administration. Between the reigns of Claudius (43 A.D.) and Severus (211 A.D.) the province of Britain was administered by Roman governors whose duties included maintaining peace, collecting taxes, and providing justice. For local government the Romans, like the British later in India and Africa, employed "indirect rule" by permitting loyal Celtic chiefs to continue to exercise authority over their tribesmen. On the frontiers the army administered the area, but in the Romano-British south, several privileged cities enjoyed self-government. In the cantons (tribal areas) the magistrates in Roman togas were usually local chiefs. This policy served both to Romanize the Celt and to minimize friction between ruler and ruled. In later years, after several ambitious generals had used their position and legions in Britain to defy the emperor, and after increasing raids from the Scots and the Picts had jeopardized Roman defenses, Britain was divided into two, and then four, provinces.

Roman Achievements. Roman contributions to Britain were largely material. They built towns and established such features of urban life as forums, public baths, indoor plumbing, and amphitheaters. Towns were originally constructed for military or commercial purposes, but served equally as the centers for the diffusion of Latin civilization. Joining these towns was a network of splendid stone highways that permitted the rapid movement of troops and commerce. Many modern British roads still follow these Roman routes. The new city of London at the hub of this road system became the chief port of entry for commerce with the rest of the empire. The tradition of town houses and country estates (or villas) was another innovation. Probably the urbanized Britons lived more comfortably under the Romans than at any other time until the nineteenth century. The Romans were indifferent to local religions unless these challenged the omnipotence of the emperor (as did druidism and Christianity). When Christianity was finally granted toleration by Constantine in 313 A.D., Roman rule was already weakening, and Romanized Britain remained essentially pagan. Christianity did gain strength in Wales, however, and was the only institution to survive the departure of the Romans.

Roman Withdrawal. By the fourth century, the declining power of the Roman Empire encouraged the Picts, the Scots, and raiders from northern Europe to harass Roman outposts in Britain and to force the Romans to draw in their defensive borders. As the empire became paralyzed by political factionalism and weakened by barbarian attacks from the East, Roman legions evacuated Britain to fight elsewhere and never returned. The last Roman soldier left the island in 407 A.D., and Britain, which had been defended by Rome for nearly four hundred years, had to fend helplessly for itself. Invaders now entered England with ease and killed or displaced the Romanized Britons of the south and east. The conquest was made easier by the revival of intertribal warfare among the Celts. Celtic culture remained in Wales and Cornwall for the same reason that it survived the Roman invasion—by existing in such an inhospitable area that any invader was deterred. In England, only the roads continued in use to remind the invading Saxons of Rome; in Wales, a Celtic version of Christianity prospered; every other memory of Rome vanished. Perhaps, therefore, the greatest fact in the Roman occupation is "a negative fact—that the Romans did not succeed in permanently Latinizing Britain as they Latinized France." [4]

---

[4] Trevelyan, *History of England*, I, p. 30.

Chapter 2 ↫ Anglo-Saxon Supremacy

The Anglo-Saxon settlement established the fundamental character of Englishmen more than any other influx of immigrants, for it brought about more permanent results in racial composition than either the Celtic and Roman conquests that preceded, or the Norman invasion that was to follow. From the Anglo-Saxons England received its name, its language, its largest ethnic group, its shires, and, for the first time, political unity as a single kingdom, even though it lacked the necessary machinery for making the king powerful enough to govern his kingdom effectively.

The Coming of the Invaders

The British Isles are so situated that they are equally accessible to the civilizations of north and south Europe. Taking advantage of the Roman retreat from the island, the barbarian tribes of northwestern Germany initially terrorized and eventually settled in Britain. These Nordic invaders came in small bands under several chieftains and lacked any kind of unified command; but the cumulative effect was to erase a superior Roman civilization and replace it with a barbaric settlement.

The Northern Invaders. The Anglo-Saxons conquered the Britons in a fashion quite different from that of the Roman legionnaires. Instead of a disciplined army of occupation the Nordic warriors crossed the Channel in shallow boats on sporadic forays and were followed years later by migrant clans of settlers. The conquest was never carried out systematically, and the invaders found it much easier to fight the Britons than to live peacefully together.

Anglo-Saxon Origins. The three dominant Nordic tribes that made these successful sorties into Britain were the Angles, the Saxons, and the Jutes. Hailing from the Jutland peninsula and northern Germany, they shared a common love of the sea and traced the descent of their kings from the god Woden. Unlike their neighboring Germanic tribes they had not traded or fought with the Romans nor had they come under the influence of Roman civilization or Christianity. They had kept intact their Germanic culture with its rugged code of justice and loyalty to a chief or military leader. Although the tribesmen were usually farmers, they were more widely known as sailors of great skill whose zest for piracy and warfare made them the terror of more civilized neighbors. When the southward invasion of the Roman Empire was preempted by other Germanic groups, these tribes took to the sea in their longboats and made Britain their prize.

The Nature of the Invasion. The Anglo-Saxon conquest continued intermittently for two centuries; however, literary records of the invasions are fragmentary at best. The Venerable Bede supports the traditional claim that the invasions began in the middle of the fifth century when two Jutish leaders, Hengist and Horsa, were invited to help the Britons defend themselves against repeated attacks by the Picts and the Scots from the north. Other details are provided by the Welsh monk Gildas in a tract, written in the first part of the sixth century, in which he bemoans the suffering and massacre of his countrymen at the hands of the Saxon invaders. However, we do know that the invaders first came for plunder; later, they moved inland and decided to settle. About 500 A.D. the Britons temporarily halted the invasion with a victory at Mons Badonicus—probably under the Romano-Briton general, Arthur (the legendary King Arthur of the Round Table). For the most part, the gradual Saxon infiltration of the civilized southeast encountered no great resistance. The disunited Britons lacked spirit and strategy in facing the invaders from the south and the Scots and Picts from the north. The outcome was the replacement of the Roman-Celtic culture of central England with the rough barbarism of the Anglo-Saxon; the Britons were either killed or enslaved, or fled overseas. However, the new invaders, like their Roman predecessors, did not triumph in the Celtic fringe. Particularly in central England were Roman cities reduced to ruins since the Anglo-Saxons continued their open countryside style of living. Once settled, the Anglo-Saxons broke yet another Roman pattern—involvement with continental affairs.

The Heptarchy. Lacking a tradition of national unity or a single leader to unify their conquests, the marauding tribes carved out separate kingdoms in England. Gradually seven kingdoms (the heptarchy) emerged from the welter of rival claimants. Kent was occupied by the Jutes, the three kingdoms of Essex, Sussex, and Wessex were settled by the Saxons, and the Angles claimed East Anglia, Mercia, and Northumbria.

Political Unification. At times a common overlord known as a *Bretwalda* (Britain-ruler) imposed temporary unity over these kingdoms. Kent was the first dominant kingdom, especially during the reign of King Ethelbert (552?-616). Northumbria succeeded Kent as the leading state in the early seventh century and was superseded by Mercia and Wales in 632. Offa II, the last of the Mercian overlords, ruled from 757 to 796 during which time he

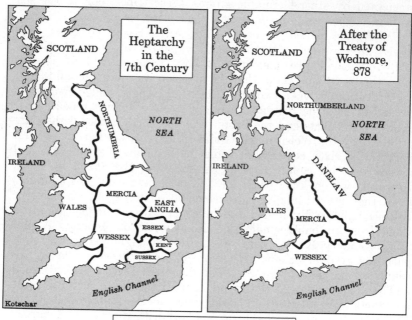

ANGLO-SAXON ENGLAND

extended his kingdom north and west, codified laws, and won recognition from the pope and Charlemagne. Since Offa conquered Wessex and established supremacy over all England south of the Humber, he is often considered the first overlord to be recognized as "king of the whole of the land of the English." With his death the Mercian supremacy of two hundred years passed in 802 to Wessex under King Egbert (775?-839). Egbert defeated the Mercians, and his son Ethelwulf continued the consolidation of Wessex; but even before Egbert's death the Danes were making their first raids along the English coast.

The Return of Christianity

Christianity did not desert the British Isles with the Roman legions. The Celtic Christian faith, although detached from Rome, remained vital in Wales through the years of Saxon encroachments. In 597 Latinized Christianity returned to England and eventually triumphed over both the Celtic church and the pagan religion of the Saxons. With the Roman church reestablished, England once again made contact with the language, law, and administrative organization of Mediterranean civilization.

The Christian Faith. The new message from the Mediterranean world and from the Celtic island of Iona was undoubtedly foreign to the Nordic tradition. Instead of a warrior's religion that reflected such traits of their culture as physical valor and feasts for fearless heroes, Christianity spoke of love, repentance, and redemption; it suggested great hope, yet, at the same time, great fear of the afterlife; it also made man contemplate the meaning and purpose of life. The ascendancy of the Christian Faith was more complete than the Saxon religion, because the latter had remained largely an expression of ethnic traditions.

Celtic Christianity. For two hundred years Christianity in Britain was almost severed from Roman influence. During this time the Celtic (Welsh and Irish) church prospered in adversity; Christianity frequently was the badge of distinction separating the Celts from their pagan attackers. The new faith with its ascetic idealism and consummate dedication grew rapidly in the fifth and sixth centuries. From 432 to 461 Saint Patrick of Britain converted Ireland and founded a church more famous for the high degree of learning of its monasteries than for its episcopal organization. An Irish monk, Saint Columba, brought the faith to western Scotland in the next century. Missionaries set out from his monastery on the island of Iona in the Irish Sea to convert the Picts in Scotland, and later won converts in England and on the Continent. In 617 Oswald of Northumbria became a Christian during his exile in Iona and, after becoming king in 634, assisted Celtic missionaries to introduce the Christian Faith to all Northumbria.

Roman Christianity. In 597 Pope Gregory I, as part of his plan to convert the conquerors of the Roman Empire, sent the Benedictine monk, Augustine, to Britain with forty missionaries. King Ethelbert of Kent cordially received the missionary party, since his Frankish wife was already a Christian. Within a year the monks converted Ethelbert and made his capital, Canterbury, the seat of the archbishopric—a position it still holds today. In the seventh century Christianity, assisted on several occasions by Christian princesses who won their husbands to the faith, gradually enlarged its influence in the heptarchy. When a king became a Christian, he would usually decree that Christianity was the official religion of his kingdom. Thus by the middle of the seventh century most of England had been converted to either Celtic or Roman Christianity, and the conflict between paganism and Christianity was replaced by a rivalry between two types of Christianity.

Synod of Whitby, 664. Although the Celtic church survived and prospered outside the pale of Roman Catholicism, it differed with the Roman church on several matters of polity and theology. It preferred, for example, a decentralized or autonomous church organization, a simpler liturgy, and a different date for Easter; the Celtic clergy even shaved their heads in a contrary manner. When the rivalry could not be reconciled and the conflict left King Oswy of Northumbria with a divided church (and citizenry) in his kingdom, an ecclesiastical conference was summoned to settle the matter. Impressed by the political and cultural advantages of identifying his faith with the Latin world, Oswy decided in favor of the Roman communion. The Celtic churchmen gradually withdrew to Iona leaving the Roman church to organize England.

The Roman Church in England. Five years after the Synod of Whitby, Theodore of Tarsus became the new Archbishop. His organizing and administrative abilities were manifested in the precedents and reforms that shaped the organization of the English church. He doubled the number of bishoprics, set up regular church councils, and laid the groundwork for the modern parish system. By providing counsel to rulers and offering the one basis for unity among feuding kingdoms, the power of the clergy increased. Under Theodore's successors the church flourished both in missionary enterprise and in the dissemination of culture. It sent missionaries to the Continent and established schools in England whose graduates provided moral leadership and scholarly achievement. The caliber of scholarship is exemplified by the "father of English history," the Venerable Bede (673-735), whose writings caught the unity of the English as a people and, also, as part of a greater unity—the Church Universal. By the eighth century English scholarship was at least the equivalent of that in western Europe, and Christianity had again brought Britain back into the mainstream of western civilization.

Alfred the Great and the Danish Threat

Often considered the greatest Englishman in early history, Alfred well deserved the compliment. Scholar, educator, and national hero he saved England from another submersion by Nordic invaders. His successful defense against the Danes preserved the identity of Anglo-Saxon England, strengthened the Christian Faith, won political pre-eminence for Wessex, and paved the way for the partial assimilation of the English with the Danish invaders.

The Danish Conquest. In 797 the English experienced pirateering and pillage similar to that which they had inflicted on the Britons three hundred years earlier. The invaders were Norsemen (or Vikings) who hailed from Scandinavia. Their attacks on England were part of the great Viking expansion reaching from Russia to Greenland; the terror of their raids scourged European coasts for over two hundred years. In England Viking attacks changed in the middle of the ninth century from piracy to settlement as a large army of conquest landed and moved inland.

The English Resistance. The Vikings usually pillaged wealthy English monasteries along the coast and then made fierce sorties inland from the east and south coasts. With good cause the English prayed, "From the fury of the Northmen, O Lord, deliver us"; and yet, they were not demoralized as the Britons had been by the Anglo-Saxon raids. The kings of Wessex repulsed the invaders on several occasions; but when the Vikings' annual raids changed to settlement, the English could not withstand them. By 871, only Wessex was free from Viking control.

Alfred of Wessex. In 871, Alfred, the youngest son of King Ethelwulf, succeeded his brother, Ethelred, as king of Wessex. Already a military veteran at the age of twenty-two, Alfred halted the Danish advance that year, and a temporary truce was concluded while the Danes organized the rest of England. After repeated attacks in 876 and 878 Wessex was finally overrun by the Danes, and Alfred escaped only by hiding in the swamps of Somerset.

Peace of Chippenham, 878, and Guthrum's Peace, 886. Rallying his scattered supporters, Alfred decisively defeated the Vikings and their leader, Guthrum, at Edington—the turning point in the war. The treaty of peace made at Chippenham imposed two demands on the Vikings: Guthrum must accept baptism as a Christian, and the Danes must retire from Wessex. Additional battles with the Danes followed as more Danish invaders arrived and joined their kinsmen against Alfred. It was during this time that Alfred built England's first navy, erected strategic fortifications in his kingdom, and remodeled the local militia (or *fyrd*) into active and reserve units. After seizing London in 886, Alfred was recognized by all the English as their national leader. That same year he concluded another treaty with Guthrum which divided England between Danes and Saxons, with the Danish north and east identified as the *Danelaw.*

Peacetime Leadership. Alfred's achievements do not end with his outstanding generalship. Viking raids had undermined law and order and had destroyed monasteries and churches; schooling and Christianity were in decline. The King showed his wide-ranging interests by fostering a religious and literary revival. He hired the few scholars available to teach in his court school and expected royal officials to follow suit by educating themselves and, then, those around them. Alfred also translated important books from Latin into English, adding prefaces that revealed artistry and scholarship. It was his conception that stimulated the writing of the *Anglo-Saxon Chronicle* which recorded the narrative of England to his time. Alfred kept in constant contact with Rome, where he had spent part of his childhood, and with leaders on the Continent. He was Saxon England's greatest lawgiver, and toward the end of his reign he issued a code of laws for the Anglo-Saxon kingdoms. He was also responsible for rebuilding London as a garrisoned town and strengthening the shire as the unit of local government.

Anglo-Saxon Society and Institutions

The Anglo-Saxon tribes had transplanted their Germanic institutions to England, but these practices did not unify the English people as much as the church and the monarchy. The church provided a common faith and parish organization, and whatever political unity was realized invariably was a consequence of the individual abilities of the monarch, for the king was the government of England. Socially, inequality was recognized as a fact of life; each freeman had his rights, but these rights differed from class to class.

Political Organization. The gradual appearance of some semblance of national unity was the most striking political feature of the period. From dozens of tribal kings there emerged a single kingdom depending largely for survival on the personal power of the king. This movement toward unity and centralization produced an administrative structure so inadequate that only complete remodeling (by the Normans) could insure its survival. However, local government introduced in this period became an integral part of English constitutional history.

Kingship. At the center of government stood the king who wielded full, but by no means absolute, power; treason against him was the most serious of all crimes. Royal power and prestige grew as the kingdom enlarged its boundaries and as the church found it expedient to support the monarchy. The trend toward centralization was kept in check by limited revenue, a small staff, and the jealous guarding of local patriotism. Aside from the *Danegeld* (a direct land tax on the whole kingdom), the king had few rights to tax. He derived his revenue largely from rents on his estates or from fees and fines, and, in addition, he had the right to exact personal work or services from his subjects.

The Witan. The Crown was usually inherited, but in practice the leading noblemen selected the new king from any member of the royal family. Most of these nobles, along with influential bishops and court officials, were members of the *witan*, which was an advisory council selected by the king. The witan served as the highest court in the land and assisted the king in framing decrees. Since only a royal summons could call the witan into session, it could not serve as a regular check on the power of the king; however, the king's consultation with this body helped to set a precedent for the demands of consultive bodies in later centuries. Detailed administration was usually handled through the local government.

Local Government. (a) The largest unit was the *shire* (called county after the Norman Conquest). Some shires marked the boundaries of early kingdoms, such as Kent; others took the name of the town which administered their areas, as Worcestershire. The chief official in the shire was the *ealdorman*, who was originally the king's representative, but his office later became hereditary and more autonomous. A more direct agent of the king was the *shire reeve* (sheriff) who collected rents from crown lands. When the king's powers grew under the Normans, so did the sheriff's, at the expense of the local earl. The third official was the *bishop*. (b) Each shire was divided into several *hundreds*. Their boundaries may have been based originally on one hundred "hides" or men. Each hundred, like the shire, had its own assembly or *moot*, and was presided over by the *hundred reeve*. Freemen elected the leaders of the hundred and participated in the sessions of the *hundred moot* which handled the bulk of local court cases. (c) The next division was the *tun* or village. Urban life was not characteristic of the Anglo-Saxons, and the township was more of an agricultural community than a modern town. Village inhabitants met to draw lots for land and to deal with common agricultural matters, but probably handled no legal or political business. (d) The last division was the *borough*. In the later Anglo-Saxon period the kings built fortresses in strategic or populous areas, and in these centers a market and a borough court of justice became common. The borough was created by a charter from the landlord who was usually the king. The charter confirmed many privileges, one of the most valuable being the right of borough residents to collect their own taxes and pay the king a lump sum. The rise of the boroughs reflected both the increasing influence of the king and a revival of town life.

Law and Justice. The Saxon code of law was personal and elementary. The principle of "an eye for an eye" was in force, with the responsibility resting with the injured person, or his kinsmen, to exact private revenge on the offender. Over the centuries this code was modified by the influence of Christianity and the laws of the kings so that the injured party or his family accepted a cash payment or *bot* in lieu of physical retaliation on the offender; in the case of homicide *wergeld* was the fine paid to relatives of the deceased. An elaborate tariff or price list developed for various injuries (the price for the loss of the big toe was twenty shillings; five for the little toe) and for each social class. If a *churl* [1] killed an earl the compensation was from three to ten times greater than if an earl killed a churl. The motive for the crime or the way in which any injury occurred were not considered important.

The Courts. Judicial procedures were an important feature of the shire moot and the hundred moot, although cases too important or controversial for the lesser courts were tried in the witan. The shire court usually met twice a year; the sheriff, earl, and bishop served as officials, and all freemen were eligible to attend. Since laws were largely custom rather than statute, a defendant stated his case and the court decided what criminal charge, if any, applied and what penalty operated in that particular shire for such an offense. The hundred court met monthly and settled local civil and criminal cases with no provision for an appeal.

Trials. Each case opened with both plaintiff and defendant swearing their complaint or denial under oath. Trial was by compurgation or ordeal. In compurgation the defendant declared his innocence before man and God with a number of compurgators (character witnesses) swearing that his oath was true. In most criminal cases, or if the defendant lacked friends, the trial was by ordeal. This method operated on the premise that God would miraculously intervene to protect the innocent from injury or death. The three most common ordeals were by hot water, hot iron, and cold water. If the defendant was found guilty and lacked money to make a cash settlement, he was usually outlawed, mutilated, or executed; jails were unknown.

---

[1] A man who was in the lowest rank of freemen below an earl or thane.

Property Law. The basic form of landholding was *folkland*—cultivated land held in common by families of the local community. Folkland could pass from father to son, but the family could not dispose of it. The church introduced *bookland*, a second form of landholding, which transferred to the grantee, not the land, but the right to have authority over it as the king formerly had. *Laenland* was a temporary transfer to a renter of the rights that the king had originally granted to the lender.

Social Classes. The Anglo-Saxons arrived in England with a rather fluid social hierarchy developed from military origins; in England the inequality between classes increased. The king and the earls, hereditary nobility, composed the aristocracy. Gradually a lesser class of free servants, known as *thanes* or *thegns*, emerged and were frequently rewarded with land gifts in payment for their military service to the king. Beneath the thane was the *churl* (*ceorl*) who was a freeman and small landholder or artisan. Churls were liable for military service in the fyrd, but could move about freely. *Serfs* were personally free but bound to the land and the service of their lord. In time, many churls became serfs because they lost their land or gave it to a lord in return for protection. The lowest class was the *thrall* or slave who most likely had lost his freedom by defeat in war or legal punishment. Thus even before the Norman conquest the pattern for a feudal society was beginning to take shape.

Economic Organization. Almost all these classes lived in small agricultural villages; not until the Danish settlement and the rise of trade in the tenth and eleventh centuries did towns become important again. Farming villages generally consisted of the thatched huts of farm workers, the great house of the local lord, a mill, and a church. The villagers had common pasture and meadows and cultivated their arable land by means of the two- or three-field open-strip system. Economically, the communal village was virtually self-sufficient, and its daily routine was seldom unsettled except by war or pestilence. Land continued to be the basis of wealth although at the end of the Anglo-Saxon period commerce began to increase in the newly fortified centers, the *boroughs*. Some industry developed, particularly in the decorative arts, but the overwhelming majority of Englishmen continued to earn their living from the soil.

The Church and Society. Christianity helped modify the coarseness of early Saxon life, but the church was unable to ameliorate the despondency or desolation resulting from the Viking invasions. Too often the monks were more concerned with personal salvation

and separation from the world than with help for the laity.
Dunstan (925?-988), abbot of Glastonbury and later archbishop of
Canterbury, was the first outstanding churchman to reform and re-
vitalize monastic and religious life in England. His friendship with
King Edgar placed royal authority behind his efforts at reform, and
the effects of the revival were felt for two centuries. Although
frequently the double standard of Christian profession and unchris-
tian practice among the clerics weakened the witness of the faith,
churchmen made a crucial contribution in nurturing and preserving the learning and literature of the age. Clerics copied and illumi-
nated books, established and taught in the few schools, and made
Latin literature available.

Anglo-Saxon Literature. The Venerable Bede was probably the
outstanding scholar of the Old English period. His forty books
covered a variety of theological and historical subjects; his most
admired work, the *Ecclesiastical History of the English Nation*,
provided an excellent account of the early history of England. His
standard of scholarship was continued by Alcuin (735-804) who
left York to head Charlemagne's palace-school, and by Alfred the
Great who wrote translations from Latin into West Saxon. Early
English poetry and prose is also indebted to Christian writers. The
epic poem *Beowulf* (composed *circa* 750?) tells the story of a
pagan Saxon hero who valiantly defies men and dragons with
equanimity. Aldhelm (640?-709), the Bishop of Sherborne, was a
noted Latin scholar and lover of English songs. His contemporary,
Caedmon, the first English poet known by name, was a North-
umbrian monk who introduced Old Testament themes in his poems.
In the eighth century Cynewulf's four religious poems are the
most imaginative of Old English verse. After the Danish invasion the revival of prose was best represented in the vernacular
homilies of Aelfric (*c.* 955-*c.* 1020). He also provided a readable
English version of the first seven books of the Bible and composed
textbooks for the teaching of Latin. *The Anglo-Saxon Chronicle*,
which spans five centuries of early English history, was the cumulative work of numerous monks in different monasteries. Alfred the
Great is believed to have greatly stimulated the writing of this
Chronicle. The one towering figure of the Anglo-Saxon period
remains Alfred the Great who combined the best qualities of
scholar, churchman, and ruler.

From Alfred to Edward the Confessor

After Alfred's death the leadership of the House of Wessex continued strong under his son and grandson only to decay and suffer

eclipse because of the second wave of Danish invaders. This time the Danes conquered all of England and restored political unity to the country. Following the death of Canute, Edward the Confessor, the last undisputed Anglo-Saxon king, ruled England in an undistinguished fashion and prepared the way for the Norman conquest.

The Second Danish Invasion. The pattern of co-existence that emerged between the Dane and the Saxon under the aegis of the House of Wessex collapsed with the invasions of the tenth century. The defeated English ransomed themselves by the payment of the Danegeld in exorbitant sums. This payment of the Danegeld introduced direct taxation in England and "hastened the decline of the freeholder into the serf." [2]

The Rise and Fall of the House of Wessex. For seventy-five years the able successors of Alfred the Great extended the power and boundaries of Wessex. His son, Edward the Elder (899-924), conquered all the lands south of the Humber. Edward's son, Aethelstan (924-939), defeated the Scots and Picts, recovered the Danelaw, and claimed the title, "Ruler of all Britain." Like his grandfather Aethelstan was an outstanding ruler. Under King Edgar (959-975) Wessex reached its zenith of power and prosperity; but decline was rapid after his death and further confounded by the return of the Danes.

Ethelred the Unready, 978-1016. The reign of Edgar's second son, Ethelred, was an unrelieved disaster. Erratic, cruel, and lazy he was completely unprepared to defend England against the Danish invasion. He tried to buy off the Danes in 991 with an extravagant payment of the Danegeld. In 1003 he ordered a massacre of all Danes in his kingdom, which, in turn, brought bloody retribution by the Danish king, Sweyn, and forced Ethelred to flee to the safety of his inlaws in Normandy. In 1016 both Ethelred and his much abler son, Edmund Ironside, died and the English were left without a leader. Having no other choice, the Saxon witan selected Canute, son of Sweyn, as king of England in the following year.

King Canute, 1017-35. The young King soon adapted to English customs and changed from a pirateering pagan to a skillful, Christian monarch. When Canute added Norway to his English and Danish thrones, it looked as if a Scandinavian confederacy was in the making; however, his early death in 1035 cut short any such ambitions—for his empire died with him. His two sons, Harold and Harthacnut, wrangled for the English throne for the next seven

---

[2] G. M. Trevelyan, *History of England* (3rd ed., London: Longmans, 1945), p. 96.

years, but neither was competent enough to win the respect of the English before they died. After this wearying experience with the two worthless sons of Canute, the witan elected Edward, son of Ethelred the Unready, to the throne, and with his reign England shifted its centuries of association from the Scandinavians of the Nordic world to their descendants, the Normans, on the French coast.

Edward the Confessor and the Normans. Half Norman by birth, Edward had spent most of his life in Normandy before attaining the English throne at the age of forty. A religious and retiring figure, he brought with him to England his Norman ideas and friends but gave more attention to the church than to the government. The favoritism of this kindly "French monk" toward Norman colleagues aroused the hostility of the Anglo-Saxon nobles. Godwin, earl of Wessex, who led the protest, was successful in marrying his daughter to the King and in displacing Norman influence with his own. When Godwin died in 1053, his four sons manipulated affairs at court with typical Saxon cunning; the most powerful of them, Harold, succeeded his father as earl of Wessex. However, King Edward had other favorites: William, duke of Normandy, and Harold's younger brother, Tostig, earl of Northumbria. Although Edward finally named Harold as his successor and the witan confirmed the decision on the death of the King, other aspirants disputed the claim and prepared to challenge Harold for the Crown. The foremost challenger was William of Normandy.

Chapter 3 ·ᴈ The French Kings

Under the Norman and Angevin rulers (1066-1399) previous Scandinavian ties were severed and replaced by a new liaison with the Continent. In these years England was dominated by a French-speaking nobility and a Latin-speaking clergy. Paradoxically, under this foreign leadership, England developed distinctive institutions which imitated no foreign models, but instead blended into a new synthesis the old Saxon traditions and the new Norman feudalism and administration. Attachment to the Continent brought England a more effective political and military system; but it also meant that English kings became embroiled in French affairs, often at the expense of the country's interests.

The Norman Conquest

William, duke of Normandy, made careful preparations to make good his claim to the English throne, and, aided by fortuitous circumstances, he defeated Harold, Godwin's son, and became king by conquest. The ruling Normans never displaced the Anglo-Saxons as the latter had done with the Britons, for the Normans were too few in number. Nevertheless, they destroyed the old English nobility and maintained their minority rule by a strong central government, by the military technique of mounted knights, and by the security of fortified castles.

Norman Rule. The Norman conquest, unlike the easy yoke imposed on the English lords by Canute, proved to be severe in consequence. William confiscated Saxon estates and gave them to his followers. A monarchy based on political feudalism was transplanted from Normandy where the Duke had already established the most centralized and best administered state in Europe. This political feudalism rested on the fealty exacted from Norman nobles in return for land holdings granted by the King.

William's Claim to the Throne. On the death of Edward the Confessor William claimed the English throne on the grounds that Edward had promised to make him his heir, that Harold, when shipwrecked on the Normandy coast in 1064, had given him a sacred oath of support, and that by Viking descent he was related to the English royal family—he was the first cousin once removed of King Edward. In addition, Pope Alexander II sanctioned William's designs; thus strengthened by these assertions, the Duke recruited an army of about seven thousand and offered his recruits the blessing of the pope and the promise of English estates.

The Invasion of 1066. King Harold moved his troops to the south coast to meet the anticipated invasion of the Duke of Normandy on the channel coast. Hardrada, king of Norway, another claimant to the throne, landed in Northumbria with the aid of Tostig, King Harold's brother. Harold rushed north and repulsed the invaders at Stamford Bridge near York, killing Harold Hardrada and Tostig. While King Harold was triumphing in the north, William landed unopposed at Pevensey on the south coast. With no respite Harold returned to the south without reinforcements and met William's army near Hastings on October 14. In a pitched battle that lasted through the day, the disciplined Norman archers at last broke through the stubborn defense of the English *housecarls* or regulars. Victory became decisive when the King's two brothers were slain, and a random arrow struck down Harold. The Duke then cautiously moved on toward London, subduing Romney, Dover, and Canterbury enroute. When no help was forthcoming from the northern earls, the people of London submitted, and William, the last successful foreign invader of England, was crowned in Westminster Abbey on Christmas.

William the Conqueror. For the next five years William crushed local resistance and was merciless in punishing the northern rebellions. The lands of the rebels were confiscated and given to his followers. Fortified castles were built in the countryside, beginning with the Tower of London. Once again, the disunity of England proved its undoing, for the revolts never won more than regional support and only succeeded in weakening the English nobility. William was equally firm in repudiating the political claims of the papacy. When Pope Gregory VII claimed England as a papal fief, William replied with the Triple Concordat which made royal permission necessary before any papal power could be exercised in England. As long as the church's demands did not jeopardize his political authority, William permitted the establishment of ecclesiastical courts and helped Lanfranc, the new Archbishop of Canterbury, increase the administrative centralization of the church.

Results of the Conquest. Although William retained Anglo-Saxon customs that did not conflict with his rule, he was instrumental in introducing many features that fundamentally altered

English life: a reformed church which governed its affairs more fully; a political feudal system based on landholding; a substantial centralizing of royal power; an increase of commercial activity with the Latin world; and the adoption of the language and the manners of the French court. Consequently, there began the five-century involvement of the kings of England with the French empire.

Anglo-Norman Feudalism

William brought with him the political and economic practices of his native Normandy and fastened them on the more loosely structured English society. However, the system came too late to have the stifling effects on the English nation that it had on parts of the Continent. Norman feudalism saved England from the more immediate dangers of anarchy and civil war and gave the country the means of coping with its greatest flaw—a lack of national unity and administration.

A Pyramid of Power. William operated on the principle, never claimed by Anglo-Saxon kings, that all the land belonged to him. In theory this meant that no tenant or vassal should be more powerful than the king, but in practice they often were more powerful than the king, especially on the Continent. As a case in point, the Duke of Normandy was far more powerful than his lord, the King of France, and defied him with impunity. Therefore, in structuring political feudalism in England, William made sure that no vassal could treat him as he had treated his liege lord. He scattered the holdings of his vassals so they could not form consolidated fiefs, such as he held in Normandy or as Earl Godwin had possessed under Edward the Confessor. He also retained the fyrd as a counterforce to the nobility. By this more centralized structure he overcame the great liability of continental feudalism—that the parts were greater than the whole.

Origins of Feudalism. The roots of feudalism can be traced to the vast villas of Roman days and the half-free *coloni* who worked the land but were not free to leave it. In the eighth century Charlemagne had granted tracts of land to followers and promised them immunity from royal administration. These privileges, known as *immunities,* had weakened the central government. With Charlemagne's death and the collapse of his empire there grew up over the next two hundred years an improvised system of land tenure based on military service. This feudal system emerged to meet two immediate needs: local protection from the menace of

Viking raids, since the king was no longer able to guarantee the safety of his subjects, and enlistment of the services of nobles and fighting men. Rival rulers had little money with which to purchase allegiance, but they had much land at their disposal when the empire was divided after Charlemagne's death. Therefore, they offered grants of land in return for allegiance and military support. The feudal arrangement became, in essence, a political, military, and social relationship between the king and his subjects in which landholding was the determining factor of rank.

Lord and Vassal. Feudalism was also a contractual relationship on a personal basis between lord (the donor of a *demesne* or parcel of land) and vassal (the recipient). In England William kept for himself one-fourth of the estates that he confiscated, gave one-fourth to the church, and parcelled out the remaining land to the barons of his conquering army on the conditions of feudal tenure. As their liege lord William guaranteed his vassals protection and justice. In return they swore their allegiance (homage and fealty) to him and promised to supply annually a specified number of knights for forty days of military service. They were further obligated to entertain the King (or the lord to whom they owed their fealty) on visits, to attend his court, and to pay certain fees, such as bearing the expense of knighting the lord's oldest son, or paying the cost of his daughter's marriage, or ransoming the lord if he became a captive. To strengthen his hold over the barons, William permitted no castles to be built without royal consent, and in the Oath of Salisbury he demanded prime allegiance, not only from his tenants-in-chief, but from all vassals. This centralization of power was likewise reflected in the continuation of the Danegeld and in an elaborate census of the ownership and wealth of the kingdom. Royal commissioners traveled to every shire to take this statistical survey for purposes of taxation, and their meticulous findings were recorded in the famous Domesday Book of 1086.

William and Local Government. Although William, as conqueror, remodeled and increased the powers of the central government, he retained many Anglo-Saxon institutions, rather than expose his new subjects unnecessarily to strange laws and customs. His Great Council preserved the function of the Saxon witan, and the fyrd was a useful check on the increasing strength of the barons. The machinery of local government continued to function in the shires where royal authority now penetrated effectively for the first time through the office of the sheriff. The sheriff replaced the earl as the official representative of the King. In this way royal power was no longer distant and indirect, but near at hand and influential in each community, since the King gave the sheriffs full administration of local government and control of the local militia. When William died in 1087, he left England "its first powerful and well-articulated system of government." [1] Even if William was a stern ruler who imposed feudal centralization by force, he was not an absolute ruler, and he did provide more order and security in England than was customary up to this time.

The Manor. The manor was the economic unit of feudalism. As an agricultural unit it was the part (or the whole) of the fief that the vassal retained for personal use, and, like its Anglo-Saxon model, it was practically self-sufficient, with a village, common fields, mill, and blacksmith shop. A major change from Anglo-Saxon days was the reduction of freemen; the Domesday survey classified 84 per cent of the rural population as serfs. The manorial relationship between lord and serf was most unequal. In return for some meager protection and facilities the serf spent most of the day tilling his lord's land or performing other obligations for him; even a percentage of a serf's produce was claimed by the lord. The serf was bound to the soil by law and could not leave the manor without the lord's consent. Any disputes between the serf and the lord were tried in the manorial court presided over by the lord's steward.

The Reigns of William II, Henry I, and Stephen

William I entrusted to his sons a monarchy whose controlling influence was exerted through feudal tenure and baronial service, central administration, and local government. These three pillars of sovereignty were tested by the three monarchs that followed King William. In spite of these turbulent years the power of the barons was checked, public finances systematized, and justice reformed— all attesting to the growing stability of the English monarchy.

Centralization and Disruption. At first, the tendency under William II and Henry I was to increase royal authority. Then under the weak and indecisive Stephen, the barons exploited the situation to break free from royal control, and for nineteen years England was convulsed by baronial rivalries and warring factions.

William II, 1087-1100. King William had bequeathed Normandy to his eldest son, Robert, left the English crown to his second son (and favorite), William Rufus, and gave five thousand marks to his youngest son, Henry. Because many Norman nobles in England favored the weaker Robert, William had to put down a rebellion

---

[1] F. G. Marcham, *A History of England* (New York: Macmillan, 1950), p. 68.

supporting Robert before he could secure his throne. William II
was an able ruler but brutal and crude in an age of public piety.
During this era of the crusades he openly despised the clergy and
disregarded conventional morality. Greedy for church lands, William prevented new appointments to vacant bishoprics and abbeys
and quarreled bitterly with Archbishop Anselm over the respective
authority of church and state. When Anselm insisted on going to
Rome to obtain the pallium from the pope, the King objected and
confiscated the Archbishop's estates. The argument was temporarily resolved, but the church-state controversy plagued future
reigns as well. However, King William persevered unfalteringly in
military exploits that proved his inherited soldierly character. He
suppressed two revolts in England and invaded the Welsh and Scottish borders. In this way, he kept intact his father's conquest and
made it possible for his brother to reunite England and Normandy.

Henry I, 1100-1135. When William II died without a son, the
nobles agreed to recognize his younger brother, Henry. To hold
their support, Henry promised in his coronation charter to abide
by the laws of Edward the Confessor and William I and to halt all
extortionate methods of collecting money from the nobles and the
church. To strengthen further his position, he recalled Archbishop
Anselm from exile and married Edith-Matilda, the nearest blood
kin of the royal house of Wessex. The year after his coronation
Henry repulsed an invasion attempt by Robert and then reciprocated by attacking Normandy and defeating Robert at Tinchebrai
in 1106—a revenge, said the English, for Hastings. Normandy
thereby came under Henry's rule, and the rest of his reign was
relatively tranquil. In 1107 the uneasy Compromise of Bec was
arranged with the church on the matter of lay investiture. The
compromise provided that the episcopate should be elected in the
presence of the king and do homage to him for their ecclesiastical
lands; however, it stipulated that the church would invest the bishops with the spiritual symbols of their office.

Central Government under Henry I. After subduing Normandy,
King Henry took advantage of his peaceful reign to reshape the
central administration. His flair for organization produced law and
order and filled the treasury. From the Great Council the King
selected a small group of administrators, the *curia regis*, and gave
them specialized roles. One councilor became justiciar, or chief
minister, and was given authority to act in the name of the King.
Second in importance was the chancellor who was responsible for
the legal and secretarial duties of the Government. The office of
treasurer increased in power, and an account was demanded of all

receipts and expenditures. Disputes over tax cases were soon held in a special session of the *curia regis* called the exchequer, which took its name from the fact that royal accounting was first calculated on a chequered cloth. The staff of the exchequer advised the court, drafted writs issued from the exchequer, and audited the accounts of crown revenue. In time the Exchequer Court became a separate common law court. To raise more money, Henry allowed the barons to make a money payment (*scutage*) in place of contributing knights as required by the feudal code. He also increased the business of the royal courts (at the expense of the shire and hundred courts) by sending itinerant judges on circuit, and thus turned the local courts into royal courts. The multiplicity of courts and jurisdictions invited royal intervention and permitted royal justice to reach into the local hamlet.

Stephen versus Matilda, 1135-54. Henry's hopes for his dynasty were jeopardized when his only legitimate son, William, drowned in 1120 crossing the Channel. He made the barons swear allegiance to his daughter, Matilda, and then promptly had her married to Geoffrey of Anjou without the barons' consent. On Henry's death the barons chose his nephew, Stephen of Blois, as King, and a disputed succession began. Stephen was mild and chivalrous but utterly unable to rule his kingdom. Only by increasing concessions to the barons and to the church was he able to maintain his title. The country was wracked by civil war and lawlessness for "nineteen long winters," until the warring factions signed the treaty of Wallingford (1153), providing for Matilda's son, Henry, to succeed Stephen. The next year Stephen died.

Henry II and the Common Law

When Henry II, the first of eight Angevin or Plantagenet kings, came to the throne at the age of twenty-one, he was in control of an impressive empire on the Continent. The extent of his possessions meant that Henry was in England only thirteen of the thirty-five years of his reign. Despite his wide-ranging interests his attention to England's legal system made his reign important in the development of the fundamental features of Common Law.

Restoration of Royal Power. King Henry had inherited from his parents Normandy, Touraine, and Maine. At nineteen he married Eleanor of Aquitaine who had divorced King Louis VII of France to wed him. She brought as her dowry Aquitaine and Toulouse. To these possessions, totaling nearly half of France, Henry added the overlordship of Wales and Scotland. Later, in

1171, he conquered southeastern Ireland. But before he could consolidate or control this empire, Henry had to restore order and authority in England where royal power had dangerously eroded in Stephen's reign. Henry regained crown lands by revoking the royal grants of lands and offices that had been made during Stephen's reign and ordered the demolition of hundreds of unlicensed castles. Within two years the redheaded and terrible-tempered King had restored law and order, helped greatly by the object lesson that Stephen's misrule had made on his subjects.

Royal Revenue. To maintain his vast holdings Henry II needed increased revenues. To secure more income he restored the exchequer to the position of prominence it held under Henry I, extended scutage to the lay nobles and hired mercenaries with the money raised, and levied an income and personal property tax (the Saladin tithe) on everyone *not* embarking on the Second Crusade.

Common Law. After consolidating his holdings, King Henry turned his attention to administration and judicial reform. Here his passion for organization and efficiency resulted in better justice and a wider respect for royal authority. The outcome was a distinctive legal system known as English Common Law. Judges selected the best of local laws and customs and applied them to the whole realm. In time this provided uniform laws for England by which a disputed question of law was decided by legal precedent. This accent on "judge-made" law and trial by jury led to the position that the law was supreme, and even the king could not disregard it.

The King's Justices. Henry II wished to make English justice more uniform and to minimize the overlap and confusion prevailing in various courts. Itinerant judges became trustworthy agents of the Crown as King Henry increased their jurisdiction and introduced courts into every county. The expansion of royal justice made access to the courts easier for the people and at the same time curtailed the power and jurisdiction of the local sheriff or baron. Judges sent on circuit had the sole right to hear murder charges. In the Assize of Northampton (1176) the powers of the royal judges were increased to try all criminals. With the expansion of royal jurisdiction, there arose a broader interpretation of decrees and ordinances (any offense on the "king's highway" was an offense against the Crown). In civil cases the extension of the royal writ increased the business of the royal courts. In Norman times only exceptional suits which involved the King's friends could secure a royal writ which ordered the case to be tried in royal courts instead of local courts. Under Henry II new writs were introduced, and any freeman who had a suit which fit any of these judicial forms could pay a fee for a royal writ and secure trial in a royal court with a better chance of justice being rendered. Royal writs became popular and royal courts expanded rapidly.

The Development of the Jury. Although Henry II did not introduce the jury system, he made it a part of the royal judicial procedure. The jury evolved from the sworn inquests ordered by the Frankish kings whereby a group of men were placed under oath and ordered to provide truthful information. The jury idea arrived in England at the time of the Norman invasion and was expanded under Henry II. At the Assize of Clarendon (1166) King Henry ordered that juries of twelve men in each hundred moot at county court sessions were to denounce criminals in their neighborhood; such groups were called *presentment* or accusing juries (the origin of the grand jury). Trial by jury was also introduced in assizes to decide disputes over ownership of land. In time trial by jury replaced all other types of trial and, by the thirteenth century, was extended to criminal cases through the efforts of the church. The jury was more likely to provide a rational and just decision than trial by ordeal or compurgation, and in later centuries it became an invaluable safeguard of civil liberties.

Property Law. In civil cases King Henry introduced the writ of right which ordered a feudal lord to provide justice for the plaintiff, or the King would step into the case through the sheriff. The writ of *praecipe* ignored the feudal court and ordered the sheriff to command the restoration of land to the plaintiff or have the defendant appear in royal court to explain his failure to comply. Both of these laws were encroachments on the baronial courts.

Church and State. The church's authority had grown greatly in the century preceding Henry II's reign. Powerful popes, the increasing stature of canon law, and a religious revival that resulted in the erection of thousands of churches in eleventh-century Europe had won for the church wider spheres of influence. In England King Stephen had made major concessions to the church to keep its backing. In his efforts to reform the legal system, Henry now ran into conflict with the church over the jurisdictions of secular and ecclesiastical courts.

Constitutions of Clarendon, 1164. The church courts had extended their jurisdiction to include the right to try all cases involving the clergy, whatever their offense. The privilege of "benefit of clergy" was often claimed by anyone who could read or speak Latin, since the penalties of the church courts were extremely lenient. To define the respective powers of church and government, Henry drew up a statement called the Constitutions of Clarendon. It decreed, among its sixteen articles, that accused clergy could continue to be tried in church courts, but, if they were found guilty of criminal offenses, they would be turned over to secular courts for punishment. Inspired by the opposition of Thomas Becket, the newly appointed Archbishop of Canterbury, the bishops were most reluctant to agree to the Constitutions; however, they yielded when it became obvious that Becket's cause was futile.

Thomas Becket. Becket had served as chancellor with such distinction that Henry II nominated him for the vacant archbishopric in 1162. To Henry's angry amazement the investiture turned his former close friend into an adamant champion of the church. Archbishop Becket's stubborn resistance to the Clarendon reforms resulted in his exile. After the pope threatened Henry with excommunication and a papal interdict on England, a reconciliation was arranged between the two antagonists. Again, the unbending archbishop provoked Henry's anger by refusing to absolve the bishops who had participated in the coronation ceremonies of the King's son. This time four overzealous knights, thinking they were doing King Henry a service, took the law into their own hands and murdered Becket on the altar steps of Canterbury. The murder canonized Becket and brought public humiliation to Henry. The King tried to make atonement by visiting Becket's tomb as a penitent and embarking on a crusade to conquer Ireland for the church. Nevertheless, Henry could not pursue his reform of the church courts and was obligated to withdraw some of the terms of the Constitutions. In the long run most of his demands were upheld and the expansion of church courts was halted.

Henry and his Sons. Henry II had far more success ruling his kingdom than his own family. His wife, Eleanor, and their four sons at one time or another all plotted with his enemies to unseat him. This ingratitude and treachery was all the more marked because of Henry's generosity and devotion to his children. Two sons, Henry and Geoffrey, died before their father, but Richard and John continued plotting until King Henry's death. In 1188 Richard and King Philip Augustus of France attacked Henry and forced humiliating terms on him the following year. When Henry heard that his favorite son, John, had also betrayed him, he died, a broken man.

The Angevin Empire. Efforts to hold together Henry II's dominions on both sides of the Channel demanded a skillful and powerful ruler. This Henry was, and his continuous travel permitted him to transplant useful governmental procedure from one region to another. Yet Henry was forced to spend most of his time outside England protecting his domains from rebellion and the schemes of the French King. Under his less skillful successors these landholdings in France became a liability, for they claimed too much attention, depleted the treasury, and provided little revenue in return. King Richard the Lion-Hearted spent most of his reign in France and died besieging a castle. John lost Normandy, Poitou, and Anjou to the King of France. These defeats broke up the Angevin empire although Henry III made feeble efforts to recapture these legacies. In the Treaty of Paris, 1259, Henry III finally renounced his right to Normandy, Anjou, Poitou, Tourraine, and Maine. Not until the Hundred Years' War would English rulers again become so involved in French lands.

Magna Charta

Henry II had provided a strong centralized Government that relied on little more than the feudal contract and the customary laws and practices of the realm to prevent the misuse of royal power. When King John abused his coronation and feudal oaths, the barons' only option was sullen acquiescence or insurrection. Eventually they took up arms and forced John to accept their terms. In the short run the charter was looked upon largely as a feudal document that strengthened the position of the barons and reminded the king that there were certain limitations to his power. In time the charter became enshrined as a symbol of the supremacy of law and the written guarantee of certain legal and political rights.

The Reign of Richard, 1189-99. It was a tribute to the administration which Henry II had set up that England survived intact the reign of King Richard, who, in fact, did little for England. Richard was only in the kingdom for six months of his ten-year reign, and then chiefly to raise money to continue his fighting abroad. A warrior-knight, who became a legendary symbol of romantic chivalry, Richard had no concern for routine administration and farmed out his royal privileges to his brother, Prince John, and the wealthy barons in return for money. Richard's heroic military adventures on the Third Crusade and later in France against Philip Augustus won him glory but consumed his subjects' money. While the King was out of the country, the Government was in the hands of unscrupulous ministers and Prince John, who took advantage of Richard's absence to win power for himself. However, John was thwarted by Richard's supporters (this is the time of the tales of Robin Hood), led by the two justiciars, William Longchamp and Hubert Walter, who were protecting Richard's interests. But the barons were no longer on the defensive as they were in the reign of Henry II, and, emboldened by the lack of royal leadership, they challenged the encroachments of the central government.

Reign of John, 1199-1216. Richard's empty treasury, the restive barons, and a war in France were the legacies John acquired when he won the throne he had so long coveted. Often called England's "worst king," John was a victim of his own character and of circumstances. Although he was courageous and clever, he had the knack of alienating nearly everyone by his cruelty, greed, and utter faithlessness. Above all, he was unsuccessful in every venture he handled, partly because he had the bad luck of being pitted against two of the most powerful figures of the Middle Ages: Philip Augustus of France and Pope Innocent III.

John and the King of France. King John had secured the annulment of his childless marriage and was planning to wed a Portuguese princess, but he fell in love with a fourteen-year old French girl, Isabella of Angoulême, who was betrothed to one of his vassals. Undaunted by the bethrothal he married her only to have Hugh the Brown, the jilted fiancé, appeal to King Philip II for justice. In order to resolve the situation the King of France, as John's suzerain,[2] summoned him to stand trial. When John refused to appear, Philip pronounced the forfeiture of all his French domains. John's reputation was sullied even more by his probable accomplice in the murder of his nephew, Arthur, a rival claimant to the throne. By 1204 John lost all the Plantagenet empire north of the Loire river; only Aquitaine remained unconquered. Repeated defeats had damaged the King's prestige, and to obtain revenue to avenge these losses John extracted money from the barons by old and new taxes, feudal levies, and arbitrary impositions.

John and the Pope. As his next antagonist King John unfortunately challenged the powerful Pope Innocent III. John and the monks of Canterbury had chosen rival candidates as archbishop of Canterbury upon the death of Hubert Walter (1205). Innocent rejected both candidates and picked a third, Stephen Langton. Enraged, John refused to accept Langton and confiscated the revenues of the seat of Canterbury; thereupon, Innocent placed England

---

[2] According to feudal custom, since John held Normandy, Anjou, and Aquitaine as fiefs, he was a vassal of the King of France.

under an interdict (1208) halting all church services. John retaliated by persecuting the clergy and seizing church property; Innocent threatened to depose the King. Although the pope's decrees did not hurt John immediately, they encouraged his enemies, particularly the disaffected barons and Philip II of France. When Philip prepared to invade England with the pope's blessing, John had no recourse but to submit to Innocent (1213). The King accepted Langton as archbishop, restored the confiscated church properties, and relinquished England and Ireland to the pope to receive them back as fiefs of Rome. Saved from invasion and with the pope now on his side, John took the offensive against Philip but figured without the barons.

John and the Barons. In 1214 after his plans to defeat Philip collapsed, King John asked for another scutage from his nobles; however, the barons refused to comply. Instead, they referred to the charter of Henry I as precedent and demanded that John sign a new charter listing his feudal duties and that he abide by them. The barons had felt their position threatened ever since the centralizing trend of Henry II. Confronted with an inept king who had misused royal powers and upset the feudal balance, about half of the barons were prepared, in their own self-interest, to challenge John. Without doubt John had abused his feudal prerogatives (by charging excessive fees for relief, forcing marriage on female wards, imprisoning families of recalcitrant barons) and was quite indifferent to the fact. Archbishop Langton sided with the barons on the conviction that John and the English church were too subservient to the papacy. In the negotiations which followed, Langton served as mediator between the King and his subjects. John delayed and schemed, but could not win over either the barons, the churchmen, or the people of London. On June 15, 1215, at Runnymede he agreed to their demands and signed the Magna Charta.

Magna Charta. The sixty-three clauses of the charter lacked sweeping statements of political doctrine but dealt with feudal grievances and legal protection. Specific abuses in John's use of wardship, relief, and scutage were to end and no extraordinary taxes were to be levied without consent of the Great Council—the germ for later claims of no taxation without representation. Protection from arbitrary arrest was strengthened by clause thirty-nine making it unlawful to arrest a freeman "except by the lawful judgment of his peers or by the law of the land." A committee of twenty-five barons was to make sure the agreement was honored by the King. If he did not, they were entitled to check the King by force of arms. Other clauses dealt with the ancient liberties of London, the rights of merchants, and weights and measures.

Importance of the Charter. The immediate effects of Magna Charta were not too significant. Since its detailed provisions were essentially feudal and addressed to specific problems, the charter soon became dated. Over the years, however, the charter became increasingly meaningful as attested by its confirmation forty times in later reigns. The signing of the charter proved that the King could be brought to terms, and that dissident factions could join together and negotiate peacefully with the King. Later, commoners will use the same method and demand redress of grievances before passing laws desired by the King. Underlying the charter were two principles upon which English constitutionalism grew: the King was not above all law, but was limited by the prescribed laws of his realm, and if the King flaunted the contractual relationships by unilateral action, his subjects reserved the right to force him to observe the laws.

Civil War. Since King John was not impressed by the charter, he immediately repudiated it and, with papal approval, marched against the insurgents in October, 1215. Thereupon the barons of the north offered the Crown to Louis, son of King Philip. While John was attempting to quench this political upheaval, French invasion forces occupied London. Only John's sudden death a year later from over-indulgence in food and drink spared England a full-scale civil war.

Henry III and the Barons

King John's death the year after the signing of the Magna Charta initiated the long reign (1216-1272) of his nine-year old son, Henry III. Henry resembled Edward the Confessor in his piety and simplicity and is consigned, rather appropriately, by the Italian poet, Dante, to the purgatory of children and simpletons. Intimidated by both his French relatives and the Papacy, Henry had the misfortune of being cast as un "un-English" King in an age of rising English patriotism. The outcome was a baronial revolt followed by civil war. In the ensuing experiments in forms of government the parliamentary idea seemed to hold the widest appeal.

Foreign Influence. During King Henry's minority the nobles rallied around the Crown and eventually drove Prince Louis and the French out of England. First William Marshall and later Hubert de Burgh—the last of the great justiciars—served as regents for the young King. When in 1227 Henry came of age and five

years later became sole ruler, he dismissed the masterful de Burgh.
But French advisers soon won the ascendancy, and Henry's reign
became largely a feud between English and non-English factions.
Family Favorites. King Henry alienated many of his subjects
by replacing de Burgh with Peter des Roches of Poitou. The new
justiciar's financial reforms and his dismissal of the sheriffs provoked the English barons. More foreign advisers came in the train
of Henry's charming and clever bride, Eleanor of Provence. She
found posts for eight uncles and many fortune-seeking relations. In
1220 the King's widowed mother remarried and provided Henry
with four half-brothers to keep in royal style.

Papal Power. The Papacy exploited Henry's subserviency to
the point that finally the English clergy united with the barons
against the pope and the King. Financial demands upon the English
church were so exorbitant that one-fifth of its income was ear-
marked for Rome. Next the pope filled vacancies in the English
church with Italian clerics, many of whom never bothered to visit
England, but nevertheless drew good incomes from their posts.

Foreign Affairs. By disregarding the sound advice of the barons
and the Great Council, Henry III was lured into a foolish and
costly foreign policy that won him nothing but heavy debts. He
tried and failed to reconquer the Angevin empire, and the truce
left him only in possession of Gascony (Treaty of Paris, 1259).
Even more expensive was the papal scheme to award the throne of
the Two Sicilies to Henry's second son, Edmund, in return for
substantial military and financial obligations; nothing came of this
far-fetched project but a serious drain on the royal treasury.

Revolt of the Barons. For thirty years the unpopular Henry III
survived the complaints of his subjects. Then in 1258 the barons
moved from idle grumbling to open defiance and brought about a
coup d'état that transferred the powers of the King to a baronial
oligarchy.

Provisions of Oxford, 1258. At Oxford the barons defied the
King's efforts to increase taxes and forced upon him an ordinance
which established a baronial council of fifteen to run the Government in the King's name. Foreign favorites were to be dismissed
and the Great Council—now also called a "parliament"—was to
meet three times a year. These revolutionary proposals limited the
powers of the King but failed to remedy the administrative machinery of the Government. The barons quarreled among themselves,
and a sense of grievance became widespread over the disorder that
prevailed. To win support for their respective positions, the barons
and the King courted the county knights and the town burgesses.

Finally, Henry took advantage of the baronial dissension and appealed to the pope and to Louis IX of France. When both backed Henry, civil war broke out in 1264.

Simon de Montfort. Leading the baronial party was Henry's French brother-in-law, Simon de Montfort, who as Earl of Leicester had championed the Provisions of Oxford with all his energies. He now demonstrated his military abilities and defeated King Henry and his son, Edward, at the battle of Lewes (1264). The next year Montfort summoned to London a parliament that he hoped would replace the monarchy with an enlightened oligarchy. To broaden his support, he included all the elements of future parliaments by requesting two knights from each county and two citizens from each friendly borough to meet with the Lords, thereby making this parliament the most representative body convoked before Edward I's Parliament of 1295. However, Montfort's scheme fell through as the barons became suspicious of each other. In 1265 the royal army, led by Prince Edward who had escaped from imprisonment, defeated the rebellious barons and killed Montfort at the battle of Evesham. The revolutionary idea of abolishing the monarchy had failed, and with Simon de Montfort's demise "vanished the last of the great Frenchmen who helped to fashion England." [3]

Death of Henry III. In 1266 King Henry once again confirmed the Magna Charta and now in his old age gradually turned over control of the Government to his son, Edward, who was wise enough to profit from Montfort's efforts. Some of the more valuable reforms, such as new legal procedures to protect feudal rights, were incorporated into law in the Statute of Marlborough (1267). Five years later the King died while his son was crusading. Henry III had been able to survive the barons' efforts to replace him, but, like his father, he had been forcibly brought to account for his misrule. Most of his heirs and his subjects never quite forgot that fact.

---

[3] André Maurois, *A History of England* (New York: Grove, 1960), p. 137.

Chapter 4 ❧ Medieval Society

During the twelfth and thirteenth centuries the Roman Catholic church acquired its greatest authority and influence. Western Christendom still spoke a common language, Latin, taught a single faith, and brought together rival monarchs for the Crusades to the Holy Land. Only within the religious and cultural bonds of Christendom did Europe find the unity it so conspicuously lacked in political affairs. The Norman Conquest had identified England more directly with medieval European civilization, and the country benefited greatly from the attachment. However, national stirrings made England one of the first countries to show the marks of a separate and unique identity.

The Crusades

In England and in Europe the influence of the Crusades was profound and reflected the magnitude of religious fervor of this period. Although the original goals of converting the Muslim infidels and reconquering the Holy Land failed, several unanticipated results of these religious wars were of real importance.

Appeal of the Crusades. Among the various motives that stirred the Crusaders to action were: (1) the capture of the Holy Land by the Turks and the ensuing mistreatment of Christians on pilgrimages to Jerusalem; (2) the hope of the Papacy to reunite the Eastern church which had separated from the Roman Catholic church in 1054; (3) the influence of powerful preachers, like Peter the Hermit, who could persuade the laity into believing that the Crusades were the will of God; and (4) the promise of material reward and foreign adventure which appealed to less chivalric nobles and knights.

Scope of the Crusades. The Crusades began in 1096 and continued intermittently for two centuries. The First Crusade (1096-99) wrested the Holy Land from the Turks and set up feudal Christian kingdoms; no later Crusade achieved any comparable military success. The Second Crusade (1147-50) failed to recover ground lost to the Muslim reconquest. The Third Crusade (1189-92), led by

Richard I of England, Frederick Barbarossa (the Holy Roman Emperor), and Philip Augustus of France, hoped to retake Jerusalem from Saladin, Sultan of Egypt and Syria. Richard was successful in his siege of Acre, but returned to England when he found his forces insufficient to attack Jerusalem. Numerous other Crusades followed, although not all were fought against the Turks. Some were sidetracked into sacking Constantinople—as the Fourth in 1204—or fighting the Albigenses, the Christian heretics in France. The Knights Templar, one of the new military orders that emerged during the Crusades, laid claim to the Baltic area. Gradually, the Crusades lost their momentum and appeal as the original spirit became vague or expired.

Results of the Crusades. When Acre, the last stronghold of the Christians, fell to the Turks in 1291, the hopes of reuniting Christendom and strengthening Constantinople were abandoned. Despite these failures the results of the Crusades were significant. The very failure of the Crusaders to break the Muslim barrier to overland trade with the East forced Europe to seek new sea routes to the Orient. When these were discovered, England's maritime location would put her in an excellent position for trade. Other indirect results included the increase of royal power in England because of the absence, and frequently the death, of recalcitrant barons; a broadening of English cultural horizons by the fruitful contact with the learning, history, and inventions (gunpowder, paper) of the East; a remarkable growth in towns and commerce which had the effect of increasing the circulation of money and raising prices; and the adoption of new methods of warfare, especially the techniques of fortification and siege that were employed by the Muslims in the Near East. More important, the Crusades contributed a sense of national identity. For many Englishmen the expedition to the Holy Land was their first trip away from their local community; they forgot their parochialism in a foreign land and took pride in being identified as Englishmen.

Monks and Friars

To the medieval world the men who prayed were as indispensable a part of society as those who fought or tilled the soil. The twelfth century became the golden age of the monasteries, to be followed in the next century by the arrival of the mendicant orders.

English Monasticism. The Norman Conquest had produced few changes in monastic life since the French abbotts continued the ways of their English predecessors. Lanfranc (1069-89) and Anselm (1093-1109), the two outstanding monks who became archbishops of Canterbury, had introduced the religious devotion and rigorous standards of Bec Abbey. In twelfth-century England monasticism reached a fullness of manifestation, albeit not of perfection. There were eighty-eight religious houses in 1100; a century later, nearly four hundred. In 1066 one-sixth of the land was owned by monasteries; by the death of King John (1216), between a quarter and a third. As monastic ideals invariably became tarnished by excessive wealth and a laxity of discipline and spiritual devotion, reform movements arose to give new life to the orders. Foremost among the reformers was the Cistercian Order, which reverted to the austere rule of St. Benedict, and which was to make the greatest impact on England. The Cistercian order was founded at Citeaux by Robert of Molesme and Stephen Harding. The latter, an Englishman, wrote the famous Cistercian constitution, *Carta Caritatis* (Rule of Love). Several Englishmen joined the Cistercian order at Clairvaux where Saint Bernard was the first abbot. Early in the twelfth century Cistercian foundations appeared in Surrey and Yorkshire. Insisting on simplicity and asceticism, the monks built in isolated fields, cultivated crops, and reared prize-winning sheep. One purely English order, the Gilbertines, was also important in the thirteenth century; however, their system of double monasteries, houses of nuns and houses of monks within the same enclosure, never achieved the spiritual influence of the major orders.

The Mendicant Orders. In the thirteenth century new religious orders appeared which hoped to avoid the pitfalls of previous monastic communities by serving society in a different capacity. Rather than separate themselves in cloistered abbeys, the *frères* or friars lived in the world to convert sinners and upheld their spiritual values by observance of a common rule and a total rejection of worldly possessions. The Franciscans (founded by Saint Francis in 1210) emphasized a life of service to the poor and sick through good works and charity. The Dominicans (founded in 1216 by Saint Dominic, a Spanish scholar) set out to preach the Gospel and to suppress heresy; but their missionary function never won a respect like that of the Franciscans. The Dominicans reached England in 1221 and the Franciscans in 1224. Both orders gained popularity because of their zealous endeavor, their devotion, and the simplicity of their lives. Two other begging orders, the Augustinians and the Carmelites, followed. Then, like the monks before them, the four orders neglected the rules which had made them great.

Decline of the Religious Orders. The increase in power and possessions which had caused laxity in the monastic orders, also affected the begging friars who grew "too well-fed" and disregarded their vows of poverty and obedience. Contemporaneous critics, Walter Map and Matthew Paris, lamented the greed and immorality found in religious communities. Yet the monasteries continued to run schools, to offer hospitality to travelers, and to administer relief to the sick and poor. Eventually, the schools and hospitals which became dominant in the fields of education and social service were founded outside the pale of the monasteries. As a result, great scholars and church leaders were no longer monks by necessity. Up to the year 1189 all archbishops of Canterbury, except Becket, had been from the regular clergy; after that date only three regulars became archbishops.

Learning and Literature

Long before the intellectual renaissance of the twelfth century—with its establishment of new schools, deeper study of law, logic, and classical literature, and new spirit of inquiry—the English church had promoted education. Until the thirteenth century the church was for all practical purposes the exclusive patron of the liberal arts. Gradually new schools were opened independent of the monasteries, and, instead of scholars moving to monasteries, churchmen now studied at Oxford and Cambridge.

The New Universities.   A direct result of the intellectual revival was the rise of the universities in the twelfth century. These schools consisted of teachers and students with few, if any, buildings. When either the teachers or students organized a guild for the purpose of administering their academic affairs, a university came into existence. These universities were characterized by a cosmopolitan student body, faculties of teachers who had master's degrees, and specialization in one of the higher faculties of law, medicine, or theology. Oxford was "founded" when a quarrel between Henry II and Becket caused English students to leave the University of Paris and form a *studium generale* at Oxford around 1167. In the next century a town-and-gown riot at Oxford contributed to a segment of the academic community migrating to Cambridge. The first Oxford college, Merton, was formally established in 1264, and the first Cambridge college, Peterhouse, twenty years later.

Architecture.   The artistic dimension in medieval England was most beautifully expressed in church architecture. Sixteen of England's present cathedrals (including Canterbury, Lincoln, Durham, Chester, and Gloucester) were originally monastic churches built by men serving both as artists and craftsmen. The architects of Durham Cathedral solved a major problem of medieval architecture—the construction and support of a ribbed vault, oblong in plan, over a central aisle. The French introduced *Norman* architecture, an adaptation of *Romanesque*, with sturdy, massive design, semicircular arches, and flat buttresses. *Gothic* architecture reached England in the reign of Henry II and soon developed distinctive variations: *Early English* (*c.* 1180-1280) with a steeply-pitched roof, lancet windows, and pointed arches; *Decorated Gothic* (*c.* 1280-1380) with broader windows and embellished spires; and the *Perpendicular* (*c.* 1380-1530) with square towers and flatter-pointed arches. New architectural styles were also reflected in castles that incorporated stronger fortifications with round towers and curved walls—an idea brought back by the Crusaders. The manor houses of the country gentry changed little in this period; their central feature remained the great hall.

Writers and Scholars. Western civilization is forever indebted to the monastic scribes who preserved and copied classical manuscripts and who, until the fifteenth century, recorded almost all the chronicles. The abbey of St. Albans was particularly important, for here Roger Wendover and Matthew Paris wrote a detailed account of the period of Henry III in the *Flowers of History*. Other chroniclers who described their times were William of Malmesbury (1125), William of Newbury (1160), and Roger of Havedon (1200). Walter Map (1190) was a satirist. Geoffrey of Monmouth (1150) was a Welsh bishop who sketched the chivalry of the era in his collection of Celtic legends which idealized King Arthur. In the twelfth century Archbishops Lanfranc and Anselm were important scholastics. John of Salisbury, the foremost platonist of the age, wrote a defense of logic and in *Policraticus* described the government, culture, and ethics of the period. Two scholars at Oxford, Robert Grosseteste and Roger Bacon, gained fame in the next century. Grosseteste, first chancellor of Oxford University and later bishop of Lincoln, was a mathematician, physicist, and theologian who often, and rightly, directed charges against the pope and King Henry III. His writings include the *Compendium Scientiarum*. Grosseteste's pupil at Oxford, Friar Bacon, was a brilliant and independent thinker who promoted the inductive and experimental method in the study of science and mathematics. This approach ran counter to the syllogistic method of the scholastics who were attempting to reconcile reason and religious dogma through deductive logic. Bacon's *Opus Majus* was a veritable encyclopedia of knowledge, with treatises on philosophy, physics, mathematics, logic, and grammar. Henry de Bracton (d. 1268) was England's outstanding medieval jurist. His *Laws and Customs of England* is still considered the finest exposition of the laws of England in the Middle Ages.

The Rise of Towns

Feudal law protected the baron and his farm laborers, but the town-dweller also began to insist on his rights. Those who did not fit into the feudal framework formed separate communities and set up their own laws and regulations. These corporations of burgesses, craftsmen, or students played an increasingly important role in the changing economy and society of England.

The Boroughs. During the early Middle Ages town life was replaced by the manor and its closed domestic economy. Then in the eleventh and twelfth centuries town life began to revive as a result of better security and greater self-confidence which, in turn, promoted commerce and industry. After the Norman Conquest law and order accelerated trade in England by providing safe communication within the country. Later, the contacts with the Angevin empire, the immigration of Jews, and the Crusades spurred commercial activities. Although by 1300 towns had doubled in number to two hundred, London with its forty thousand inhabitants remained the only city of any great size.

Political Status. Since the time of William the Conquerer every town was subservient to a local lord and the townspeople were under the jurisdictions of the manor court and the sheriff. Gradually the burgesses bargained for special privileges and bought charters from the King or their landlords. Like the monasteries and colleges, these free towns became independent corporations with the rights to own property, to raise taxes, to hold court, and to elect a mayor and councilors in place of a royal official. They could also deal directly with the King like any important vassal. Since the rising middle class in the boroughs had wealth, one of the quickest ways for a monarch to raise money was to sell borough charters that granted one or more of these rights. The borough citizens determined voting and legal rights and participated in government; whereas in the county only the nobility had influence. The towns, therefore, usually offered increased personal freedom to the citizen and an opportunity to the serf to become legally free if he remained in town for a year and a day.

Merchant Guilds. The first important guild was composed of the leading merchants of the town who regulated trade and protected the vendor and the buyer against excessive competition: this meant selling at a just price to the consumer and protecting the local merchant from outside competition. Guild economic policy opposed an open market and free competition. This policy, in turn, kept the economy from fluctuating by avoiding an artificial rise and fall in prices since both the middlemen and speculators were restricted by guild laws.

Craft Guilds. Townsmen practicing the same craft, such as carpentry, tanning, or goldsmithing, developed craft guilds which regulated admission to the trade and the quality of workmanship. The guild included the master of the trade and his apprentices, who could anticipate becoming master craftsmen by serving the required seven-year apprenticeship. By the fifteenth century the fees for the mastership became so excessive and the masters so exclusive that many expert craftsmen could not set up their own shop; they continued as hired workmen or journeymen for a master and formed a separate guild or "trade union" to protect their interests. Capitalism was beginning to appear.

Consequences of the Rise of Towns. The revival of town life brought about several significant developments. (1) Wealth was no longer only in land; liquid capital was becoming important. (2) Rural peasants found an escape valve in the towns as individual serfs won emancipation. (3) The cities took an active role in Government, and the burgesses represented the urban community in the emerging House of Commons. (4) The townsfolk increasingly sided with the King against their mutual rival—the landed nobles. (5) The urban dwellers became the first to encounter foreign influences: the commercial revolution, the Renaissance, and the Reformation first won support in the towns; however, change came much more slowly in the rural north.

The Medieval Community. Since the medieval world thought in terms of communities rather than of individuals, whatever rights existed were as part of the community. The greatest unifying force was the church. The concept of *Corpus Christianum* made possible the church's dominant role in the shaping of society, and for education, literature, and Government to be so intimately identified with churchmen. Within this ecclesiastical framework more specific communities developed. The feudal arrangement provided laws and privileges for the warrior, landlord, and, indirectly, the serf. When all segments of society could not fit into this military and agricultural structure, clergy and laymen found security in their own associations and insisted on their own rights. Thus when the House of Commons emerged, it did so as a house of communities representing counties, towns, and universities.

Chapter 5 ◈ King and Parliament

The fourteenth and fifteenth centuries were years of transition for England. Both the church and the feudal system were challenged by the ferment of new forces. The fourteenth century, in particular, struggled with the problem of finding a satisfactory substitute for political feudalism, and gradually Parliament slipped into the stream of English life as the institution that could best perform the necessary functions of Government. Not until the seventeenth century would the powers of Parliament again make such gains. Throughout these years a growing sense of nationality and central government—of the King in Parliament—had more lasting effects than the more immediate concerns of the Hundred Years' War in France or civil war at home.

The Three Edwards

In the century following the death of Henry III the judicial system of England became more centralized in organization and more specialized in function; statute law was increased and defined by the King in Parliament; and through conflict and conquest the boundaries of the nation were expanded.

Edward I, 1272-1307. Edward was the first King since the Anglo-Saxon era to be considered primarily English. His personal qualities, coupled with his reputation as a statesman and military leader, made his reign outstanding. Tall (nicknamed "Longshanks") and attractive, King Edward was energetic and resourceful and had learned from his father's turbulent reign that "the King must reign under and through the law." Because of his respect for law and his legal reforms Edward I has been called the English Justinian.

Legal Reforms. Edward I confirmed and codified by legislative enactment much of the legal machinery that Henry II had set up. He did this by statute law—legislation passed by the King in Parliament—and thereby introduced into the English legal system a new type of law which took precedence over all other laws. This flurry of legislative activity was not matched by Parliament until the era of the Great Reform Bill (1830's). Among the new laws were: (1) the Statute of Gloucester, which transferred the jurisdiction over certain cases from baronial to royal courts; (2) the First Statute of Westminster, which set specified limits to feudal aids, marriage fees, and relief; and (3) the Statute of Acton Burnell, which provided for the collection of debts among merchants. In land law the statutes *De Donis Conditionalibus* and *Quia Emptores* reflected the decline of the feudal arrangement and of the private courts and marked the shift in relationship from lord and vassal to landlord and tenant. *De Donis* was a blow to the power of the feudal lord, for no longer could subinfeudation take place freely and by any tenure. Henceforth, the courts were to comply with the wishes of the original grantor (the King) in all matters relating to the descent of land. This meant that the feudal lord did not have full ownership; instead, his estate was *entailed*. *Quia Emptores* ended the benefits of subinfeudation by declaring that the recipient of a land grant would hold it not of the grantor but of the grantor's lord. The legal effect of the statute was to prohibit the creation of new tenures and leave almost all freeholders royal tenants-in-chief.

As baronial jurisdiction declined, royal courts increased and became more specialized in function. Three separate divisions, each stemming from the *curia regis*, were now in operation: the court of the exchequer for tax cases, the court of common pleas for civil cases, and the court of the king's bench for crown pleas or criminal cases. In 1275 for the first time customs duties became part of the regular revenue of the King; "tunnage and poundage" (a two-shilling import duty on each tun of wine and each pound of goods), soon brought in much more than the King's hereditary revenues. However, Edward lost an old source of revenue, but won popular backing, when he expelled all Jews from England in 1290.

Edward and the Church. Edward I was a devout King who remained on friendly terms with the popes yet without imitating his father's subservience to Rome. Since the church was the greatest landholder in the realm and as a perpetual organization never relinquished any of its property to the Crown through escheats, forfeitures, or wardships, Edward attempted to limit further extension of church property by the Statute of Mortmain (1279). This act prohibited laymen from granting land to the church without consent of the grantor's overlord, who was likely to be the King. Edward also demanded a heavy income tax from the clergy to pay for some of the costs of the Crusades. In 1296 Pope Boniface VIII in the bull *clericis laicos* claimed such taxation could only take place with papal consent. Winchelsea, archbishop of Canterbury, directed the clergy to refuse payment. King Edward retaliated by outlawing the clergy and confiscating their possessions. Thereupon, the pope modified his position, and a compromise was arranged whereby "voluntary" gifts were secured from the church.

Military Campaigns. As the first English monarch to envision a union of British peoples, Edward temporarily succeeded in subduing Wales and Scotland, but recurring revolts in these areas so harassed the King that his plans for conquest in France were sharply curtailed. England's foreign policy was essentially dependent on Edward's abilities; a weak successor could not maintain such an aggressive policy.

The Conquest of Wales. Prince Llewelyn led the Welsh in their bid for complete independence from English overlordship. But the two Welsh rebellions (1277, 1282) ended in their defeat by Edward I and the subsequent imposition of English laws and the shire system. The Welsh, unhappy with the changes and their loss of autonomy, revolted in 1287 and again in 1294. With each uprising English repression became so ruthless that, finally, in 1301 the King made his son, Edward, the Prince of Wales and claimed direct control over the restive "marcher lords." Not until 1536 would Wales give up its border lordships and become fully incorporated into the English Government.

The Conquest of Scotland. Edward I had even more trouble imposing his suzerainty over the Scots. He took advantage of a disputed succession to press his claim of feudal overlord and to select John Baliol from thirteen candidates for the throne. When the Scots repudiated the King's demands for money and made an alliance with France, Edward invaded Scotland, deposed King John, and appointed the Earl of Surrey as guardian of the country. The Scots responded by rallying around two national heroes. The first was William Wallace who defeated the Earl of Surrey at Stirling Bridge (1297) and invaded northern England. When King Edward returned from France he crushed the rebellious Scots at Falkirk (1298) and later captured and hung Wallace. The second hero, Robert Bruce, had himself crowned king at Scone but was defeated by the English Army at Methven (1306). In the following year King Edward, now over seventy, again started north but died on the way to the border.

War with France. The Scottish-French alliance of 1295 increased English hostility to the French monarchy since it was apparent that King Philip IV hoped to rescue Aquitaine from English control. When Philip summoned his vassal Edward I to answer for depredations by his Gascon subjects, Edward defied the order just as King John had ignored a similar order from Philip Augustus. Consequently, Philip declared Aquitaine forfeit, and Edward answered by declaring war in 1294; however, he was prevented by the Welsh and Scottish uprisings from any concerted effort. Furthermore, since both Kings were distracted by quarrels with Boniface VIII's sweeping claims for the Papacy and by local rebellions, they agreed to end the war in 1303 and to restore conquered territories. Edward's last years saw peace with France but increasing difficulties at home, because of his inability to control the Scots or to get the men or money from his subjects without making concessions.

Edward II, 1307-27. Once again a strong King was followed by a feeble son as Edward II was to prove himself weak-willed and frivolous. His inability to rule was demonstrated by increasing dependence on favorites, beginning with the Gascon knight, Piers Gaveston. In the Parliaments of 1309-10 the barons, led by Thomas, earl of Lancaster, attempted to reassert their influence. Gaveston was banished, and a council of twenty-one Lords Ordainers was set up to control the appointments of household offices, especially the Treasury and the Wardrobe. In 1312 Edward defied the Lords Ordainers and restored Gaveston to royal favor; the barons retaliated by having Gaveston executed. In 1314 the Scots under the brilliant generalship of Robert Bruce won their independence by crushing the English at Bannockburn. This humiliating defeat forced King Edward to capitulate again to the control of the Earl of Lancaster. Baronial disunity, heavy taxes, and successful raids by the Scots in the north led to civil war in 1322. The rebellion was defeated at Boroughbridge, thus providing a temporary victory for Edward and his new favorite, Hugh Despenser. While Edward's wife, Isabella, was negotiating peace with her brother, the King of France, she became enamored with Roger Mortimer of Wales, and the two began to plot against her husband. In 1326 the Queen and Mortimer landed in England and won an easy triumph over the King. A controlled Parliament in 1327 deposed Edward II in favor of his son, Edward, duke of Aquitaine. Before the end of the year the deposed King was brutally murdered.

Edward III and Scotland. At the beginning of Edward III's reign (1327-77) actual power rested with his mother and her lover, Mortimer. Three years later Edward, now eighteen, halted the greedy guardianship by having Parliament condemn Mortimer to death as a traitor and his mother imprisoned. The young King's charm and chivalry helped to restore authority, and the monarchy won respect for a time. Since Edward never threatened the barons' privileges as his grandfather had done, the magnates followed him in his favorite pastime, fighting. In Scotland King Edward supported Edward Baliol over David Bruce, and at the battle of Halidon Hill (1333) the English revenged their defeat at Bannockburn. England temporarily ruled Scotland until 1341 when David Bruce duplicated his father's feat and drove out the English. By this time Edward was preoccupied with the main objective of his reign—war with France.

Period of Decline. For nearly twenty-five years Edward III carried on intermittent war with France. But the French nibbled away at the English conquests and defeated the English at sea. The barons now began to grumble and made political capital over the jealousy between the King's two sons, Edward the Black Prince and John of Gaunt. By 1370 the King was growing senile and doted on his young mistress, Alice Perrers, who exploited his infatuation. Discontent with the Government and John of Gaunt's political clique came to a head in the "Good Parliament" of 1376, which censured John's conduct of the war, impeached his leading henchmen, and banished Edward's mistress. The Black Prince died later that year, one year before his father, leaving his ten-year old son, Richard, as heir to a shaky throne.

The Rise of Parliament

In the thirteenth and fourteenth centuries a national Parliament evolved out of the King's court and gradually divided into two houses. With the collapse of feudalism as an effective basis of political life, the monarchs, as well as the barons and commoners, found in the institution of Parliament the opportunity to achieve a more mature political community. Parliamentary functions and powers expanded gradually, usually as a response to an immediate need and almost always at the pleasure of the King. The reigns of Henry III and the three Edwards are particularly significant in the development of Parliament. The perennial need of the monarchy for money during the Hundred Years' War became the most effective lever by which Parliament wrung concessions from the King.

Origin. The word "parliament" was a loose term referring to a meeting of the King and certain invited royal officials or influential subjects who gave advice and consent on matters of policy and taxation. Its origin goes back to the Saxon witan and the Norman Great Council, but these appointive councils were limited to the great barons and important churchmen. Under Henry I and Henry II the principle of representation and election was taking shape in the counties through the jury system; whereas King John began the custom of ordering the counties to send representative knights to London to meet with him. Next the King saw an advantage in having knights and burgesses (the commoners) meet with his Parliaments of officials and nobles after the Provisions of Oxford (1258) and Simon de Montfort's Parliament (1265) had suggested the value of such a gathering. Edward I summoned knights and burgesses to thirteen of his thirty-four Parliaments between 1290 and 1310; Edward II, to seventeen of his nineteen Parliaments between 1311 and 1327; and Edward III, to all forty-eight of his Parliaments. Thus an innovation had become a desirable constitutional custom.

Composition of Parliament. The most influential members remained the great lords of the realm, who, in deference to their rank, received individual summonses to Parliament from the King. The Model Parliament of 1295 helped establish the representative principle for the Commons as all forty counties and one hundred and fourteen chartered boroughs were instructed to send two representatives. Eventually, the lesser nobility or knights preferred to join with the town burgesses in Parliament instead of with the lords. By the middle of the fourteenth century these two groups will meet together as the House of Commons. The clergy and the knights met as separate estates in 1295, but thereafter the lower clergy withdrew and voted their own taxes in convocation. The higher clergy united with the lords to form the House of Lords. By contrast, in France the first and second estates of clergy and nobles kept their ranks separate and intact and thereby lessened the significance of the third estate of town representatives.

Parliamentary Functions. Parliament proved to be successful because it met the needs of the various communities within the realm. It became the institution through which the King could inform his subjects of royal policies and financial needs and ascertain national sentiment through the representatives. Loyal subjects could use Parliament to petition the King or to request the removal of unpopular royal officials by impeachment. Parliament also served as the highest court of the land. In the fourteenth and fifteenth centuries Parliament met at least once a year, at which time members exchanged information, lamented their common grievances, and began to share mutual interests. Hence Parliament served to unite the thriving classes of England into a national community—perhaps more than any other institution.

Expansion of Parliamentary Powers. By the end of the thirteenth century Parliament was an established institution, but its powers and functions were still vague until they were sharpened and enlarged during the fourteenth century, at the expense of royal prerogative, largely by parliamentary exploitation of the King's need for revenue. As an example, when Edward I was fighting in France and in desperate financial straits, he was forced to agree to the Confirmation of the Charters (1297) which invoked the Magna Charta and permitted no more levying of direct non-feudal taxes without the consent of Parliament. In 1340 Parliament took advantage of Edward III's need of money to extend its control to indirect taxation. Actually the Hundred Years' War accelerated parliamentary influence since English Kings were habitually in need of money. In 1376 Parliament first used the instrument of impeachment against the King's officials, with the House of Commons presenting the indictment and the House of Lords sitting in judgment. From the right of petition Parliament slowly claimed the right to initiate legislation. The King could still veto those statutes or legislate by royal ordinance independently of Parliament. However, Parliament's influence over finances and legislation had grown strikingly by the end of the fourteenth century.

The Hundred Years' War

For over a century (1337-1453) England fought intermittently on French soil as old rivalries were renewed and new claims asserted. The fighting moved from a feudal and dynastic dispute to a national war. Although the English Kings failed to conquer France, their preoccupation with the war had important side effects in England, such as the rapid increase in the use of the English language, the growth of Parliament, and rising antipapal feeling.

Causes of the War. Actually a series of wars were fought, not just one war, but the term "Hundred Years' War" continues in use. The underlying cause of the war was the heritage of hostility resulting from English possessions in France. These were a constant obstacle to the efforts of the French monarchs to centralize and consolidate their holdings in the fourteenth century. Philip IV had attempted to seize Gascony in 1294, and French interference with the English rule of Gascony continued under his successors. By 1337 Edward III was convinced that only a major war with France could prevent the annexation of Gascony by the French King. Other causes provoking the war included the French alliance with Scotland which increased Edward's difficulties in his war with the Scots, and the piracy which was occurring in the English Channel as "patriotic" privateers preyed on enemy shipping without punishment by either Government. England's economic interdependence with Flanders was also involved. English wool supplied Flemish looms, and this trade was in jeopardy because of the increasing subserviency of the Count of Flanders to the King of France. The clash of economic interests resulted in an alliance between Edward III and the Flemish burghers against Philip VI and the pro-French count. When Edward decided upon war he also resurrected his claim to the French Crown. The powerful Capetian dynasty had died out after Philip the Fair's three sons died without heirs, leaving the line of succession through Philip's daughter, Isabella, mother of Edward III. The French courts, however, had disposed of Edward's claim by invoking an old Salic Law forbidding inheritance through the female line and had declared instead in favor of the nephew of Philip the Fair, Philip VI of Valois.

War: Round One, 1337-60. The conflict between England and France was divided into two phases in each of which the English invaded France and won impressive victories after which the French rallied each time to push back the invaders. Edward III made a minor raid on France in 1339 and in the following year assumed the title of King of France after winning the naval battle of Sluys. In 1346 Edward's major invasion began.

Battle of Crécy, 1346. At Crécy Edward III and the Black Prince met a much larger French army under Philip VI who was confident of victory, but the English annihilated the French cavalry by superior tactics and the innovation of the longbow. The English army then seized the port of Calais after which an eight-year truce halted the war.

Battle of Poitiers. In the summer of 1356 the English army penetrated the heart of France under the leadership of the Black Prince, crushed the French army near Poitiers, and captured King John II and over a thousand knights.

Treaty of Brétigny, 1360. When further expeditions failed, Edward III agreed to the terms of the Treaty of Brétigny and renounced his claim to the French throne. He received Aquitaine, Ponthieu, and Calais and promised the release of King John in return for a ransom of £500,000.

English Decline. The ravages of the Black Death, the Black Prince's misrule in Aquitaine, Edward III's senility, and a new and able French king, Charles V, restored French fortunes in the years following the peace treaty. With better generalship and well-trained troops Charles V won back all but a string of seaports before his death in 1380. In 1396 King Richard II married the child-daughter of Charles VI of France and concluded an uneasy peace that lasted for twenty years.

War: Round Two, 1414-53. When Henry V came to the throne in 1413 conditions in France were again ripe for English intervention. The French King, Charles VI, was insane, and the country was demoralized and sharply divided between rival factions of Burgundians and Orleanists. In 1415 Henry allied with the Burgundians and landed in France with a well-equipped army; his objective was the union of France and England under one crown.

Battle of Agincourt, 1415. On the road to Calais Henry confronted the French army at a woods near Agincourt, and before nightfall the French forces were completely defeated. Two years later Henry returned to France and overran Normandy.

Treaty of Troyes, 1420. With the Burgundians capturing Paris and the one able French leader, Duke John the Fearless, murdered, Henry was in a position to exact his terms. According to the Treaty of Troyes, Henry was to marry Charles VI's daughter, Katherine, and be recognized as heir to, and regent of, the French throne. The territorial clauses were more obscure, but it was clear that Henry would inherit France on the death of Charles VI. This was the highwater mark of English hopes in France. Two years later King Henry, only thirty-five years old, died and left a year-old son, Henry VI, to try and make good his title to France. Charles VI of France died a few months after Henry.

Joan of Arc. At first the English under Henry V's able brother, the Duke of Bedford, made easy headway against the young dauphin who assumed the title of Charles VII at Bourges. By 1429 the English were besieging the weak Charles in his last stronghold, Orléans, and all hope for an independent France appeared doomed. At this juncture a young peasant girl, Joan of Arc, saved France by her vision of divine guidance. Inspired by her leadership the French relieved Orléans and advanced on Paris. Joan was captured by the Burgundians, sold to the English, tried by the French clergy, and burned as a witch. In 1455 the Papacy reversed the decision of the trial and proclaimed her innocence; she was canonized in 1920. The tide now turned as the Burgundians changed sides and in quick succession Paris, Rouen, and Guienne fell to the French. When the war finally ended in 1453 only Calais remained in English hands.

Characteristics of the War. The war reflected the dynastic rivalries and feudal code of the day, but increasingly took on the characteristics of a war between two nations. There were also changes in the type of warfare. The mastery of infantry with longbows over the previously invincible mounted knight revolutionized medieval warfare and hastened the demise of feudalism. A new kind of professional or mercenary army developed with its own national esprit, and with direct taxation (won by Charles VII of France in 1439), to support it.

Results of the War. France won the war even though it lost many famous battles. Nevertheless, England's loss of her French possessions was to her advantage because she was now freed from involvement in wasteful continental rivalries and could turn her attention to problems at home and commercial expansion overseas. During the war years Parliament had exploited the monarchy's constant need for money by bargaining for substantial concessions from the Kings. The merchants increased in prosperity and prestige, usually at the expense of the feudal lords. Finally, the surge of national patriotism resulting from the war made Englishmen eager to limit the influence of a foreign Papacy.

Richard II and Revolution

King Richard's erratic reign (1377-99) spanned a variety of political arrangements that included a factious regency during his youth, a baronial oligarchy, a period of royal tyranny, and a forced abdication. In this seesaw struggle between monarchy and oligarchy the magnates supported Bolingbroke and brought the Angevin line of Kings to an end.

The Regency. The child-king had little chance to mature at court. Dominated and flattered by his ambitious guardians and his beautiful, but flighty, mother, Richard became temperamental with an overwhelming desire to be independent of the magnates who ruled in his name. At the age of fourteen he showed courage and leadership in handling the leaders of the Peasants' Revolt, but he soon gave way to "the art of dissembling" which became a characteristic of his adult life. The great nobles, led by the King's three uncles, took advantage of Richard's youth to conspire against each other in their scramble for powerful positions.

The Lords Appellant. The Duke of Gloucester (an uncle of King Richard) took advantage of England's deteriorating military position in France and Scotland to oppose his nephew. Gloucester's faction became known as the Lords Appellant because they "appealed" or accused Richard's advisers of treason. Soon all power was in the hands of the Lords Appellant, and their "Merciless Parliament" of 1388 banished or condemned to death the King's friends. Five Lords Appellant tried to run the Government but with no more success than earlier efforts at an oligarchy.

Richard as Ruler. In 1389 Richard II surprised the Lords Appellant by asserting his independence and running his own Government. For the next eight years the King ruled in a reasonably "constitutional" manner. In 1390 Parliament tried to curb the private warfare that had disturbed the peace of England every time a lull in the Hundred Years' War brought home mercenary strongmen to fight for a local lord. Richard's statute against "livery and maintenance" of private armies failed to halt the armed ruffians that marched through the countryside. In 1397 the King radically changed his manner of conduct, exhibited the characteristics of a megalomaniac, and made a bid for despotic power. His revenge on the Lords Appellant resulted in the murder of Gloucester, the execution of Arundel, and the banishment of Warwick. He packed Parliament with supporters, passed retroactive anti-treason laws, and began to confiscate estates. When his uncle, John of Gaunt, died in 1399, Richard forbade the rightful heir, Henry of Bolingbroke, from inheriting the estate. This act frightened all propertied classes and at the same time brought forth a leader to rally the opponents of the King.

Revolution and Abdication. Richard II proceeded to Ireland to quell a rebellion. In July, 1399 Henry of Bolingbroke defied his banishment and landed in Yorkshire; within weeks he had won massive support. Richard was captured upon his return, and a partisan Parliament read thirty-three charges against him and forced his abdication. Henry of Bolingbroke claimed the throne by conquest and heredity. Parliament tried to legalize the revolution by statute, but it remained a successful baronial coup and hardly a triumph for constitutionalism, except insofar as it stopped short a move toward royal absolutism. Richard's reign clearly illustrated a basic reason for Parliament's growth: that neither King nor barons were quite strong enough to rule without the other for any length of time; therefore, each element, to protect its own interests, wanted and needed Parliament and the added strength of the third estate.

Fourteenth Century England

The outstanding feature of the century was the manner in which the King, lords, and commons "checked and checkmated" each other and gradually "cooperated and compromised themselves into a state of constitutionalism." [1] But these years also witnessed social, economic, and religious changes. The woolen industry expanded

---

[1] Bryce Lyon, *A Constitutional and Legal History of Medieval England* (New York: Harper & Brothers, 1960), p. 642.

rapidly, the English language soon outranked Latin and French, and antipapal feeling steadily increased.

Trade and Industry. Agricultural prosperity, increasing population, and the growth of woolen exports took place in the first part of the century. Then with the loss of population and the agricultural depression that followed the Black Death, England began to develop a woolen industry, instead of letting foreigners continue to profit by importing English wool, spinning and weaving it, and selling it back as a finished product. The Government intervened in the economy by putting export duties on wool to finance the Hundred Years' War. In 1363 the King granted Calais a monopoly as the sole staple town in the export of wool. The Government also encouraged the cloth industry, since English clothmakers could buy wool more cheaply than foreign competitors, and since cloth had a much wider market than wool. To manufacture cloth the "putting out" system was developed which permitted English capitalists unlimited expansion by separating the functions of production. The merchant could give as many small "contracts" to weavers, dyers, or spinners as he was able to manage. The textile industry became England's first big business.

The Black Death, 1348-49. The bubonic plague, which had swept across Europe from the East, struck England and wiped out close to one-third of the population. It halted the Hundred Years' War for two years and broke up society by the flight of the privileged from the unsanitary towns. While the plague raged, some citizens resorted to looting and licentiousness; others attempted to do penance to placate an angry God, or to find scapegoats for the epidemic. The consequences of the plague were momentous: the great loss of population resulted in a decreased number of servants and increased wages; prices rose and rents fell; farm rentals replaced the feudal system of labor services; and sheep farming increased because it required less manpower. The landlords tried to mitigate these changes by having Parliament pass the Statute of Laborers (1351) which froze both wages and prices; however, the act met with little success.

The Peasants' Revolt, 1381. The profound frustrations brought about by the Black Death, the changing economy, and the dissatisfaction with the Statute of Laborers culminated in a peasants' revolt which began in the two southeastern counties of Essex and Kent. The poll taxes of 1377 and 1380 had touched off a deep sense of economic injustice felt by the peasants against the privileged classes. The insurgents, led by Wat Tyler and Jack Straw, marched on London burning manor rolls and houses of landlords as they went. In London the Government seemed paralyzed while the rioters opened up prisons, burned homes, and murdered the most hated royal officials. At this point the fourteen-year old Richard II bravely met the rioters and pacified them with promises of manorial reform and the abolition of serfdom. When Tyler was unexpectedly slain, Richard halted the wrath of the rebels by claiming that he would be their leader. The rioters went home and smaller revolts elsewhere were subdued. The revolt failed in its objective for the King's promises were never kept and exploitation of peasants continued; yet, attention was focused on the plight of the peasants for the first time.

Religious Discontent. Peasant discontent may also have been inspired, in part, by the growing criticism of the church. The spiritual vigor of the church had declined rapidly in the fourteenth century. The monarchy had virtual control over the appointment of bishops, the clergy all too often preferred business to spiritual interests, and critics condemned the luxurious and immoral practices of many churchmen. It is perhaps indicative of the decline that not one Englishman was canonized in the fourteenth century. Furthermore, the English church suffered when the papal seat was moved by the French to Avignon (1305-78). England, with rising national sentiment, resented such papal subserviency to France, and Parliament proceeded to penalize the pro-French popes by a series of statutes. The Statute of Provisors (1351) made the acceptance of church office without royal consent a criminal offense. The Statute of Praemunire, two years later, penalized efforts to circumvent the jurisdiction of the English courts by appealing to the papal court. In 1366 Parliament repudiated the agreement to pay the annual tribute to the pope that King John had begun.

Wycliffe and the Lollards. John Wycliffe (1328-84) provided the first frontal attack on the political power and material wealth of the church. An Oxford don and a forceful writer he translated the Bible into English, wrote and preached against ecclesiastical ownership of land, and urged the church to find its way back to the Bible as the sole source of authority. He also questioned the doctrine of transubstantiation, but was exempt from punishment because of his popularity and the backing of John of Gaunt. Wycliffe formed a following of "poor priests" (Lollards) who spread his doctrines after his death. Their unconventional and evangelical preaching may have encouraged the Peasants' Revolt in 1381; no matter, it was an opportune moment for the church to suppress the Lollards as heretics. This time no powerful baron protected the priests and the movement was stamped out, but not before Wycliffe's writings had spread to Bohemia where they influenced Jan Hus.

Language and Literature. The anti-French and antipapal feeling aroused by Henry III's favorites in the thirteenth century and the Hundred Years' War in the fourteenth hastened the adoption of the English language. Three years after Crécy, grammar school masters began to construe Latin into English instead of French. In 1362 cases in law courts were pleaded in English, and, in the following year, the chancellor opened Parliament with an address in English. Wycliffe wrote his popular works in English and John Gower (1330-1408?) wrote his later poems in English. The most important poets of the Middle English period were William Langland and Geoffrey Chaucer. Langland's poem, *Piers Plowman* (1362) was composed as a series of allegories attacking in both satirical and didactic fashion the corrupt society of the day. Chaucer (1340?-1400), often called England's first major poet, blended superb literary technique and masterful storytelling. He provided the best account of life as it really was in his *Canterbury Tales*. The conversation of his pilgrims ranged the whole spectrum of medieval life from other-worldliness to the bawdy capers of the knight and the miller. Throughout the tales the sense of religious dissatisfaction and unabashed earthiness foreshadowed the Renaissance and Reformation eras to come.

Chapter 6 ✍ Lancaster and York

At first glance the fifteenth century appears to be little more than a time of violence, conspiracy, and demoralization of society with civil war and political executions almost routine. But the century enveloped more than the breakdown of government: great progress in education took place, foreign trade prospered, Parliament intensified its functions, and medieval society slowly dissolved under the pressures of new conditions.

The Lancaster Kings

Although the Lancasters claimed the throne by heredity, Henry IV did not have the best claim and was actually King by conquest. This usurpation led to a century of disputed successions during which Parliament became the tool of rival factions, and the Lancasters became involved in securing the throne at home and pressing their claim to the throne of France.

Henry IV, 1399-1413. Henry Bolingbroke spent most of his reign defending his title. Astute and experienced in political maneuvering he realized that his sovereignty depended on the allegiance of his subjects; therefore, he handled the church, the nobility, and Parliament with care, using severity only when threatened. In 1401 Parliament granted the church the power to turn heretics (mostly Lollards) over to the state for burning. Although Parliament tried to control Henry and his officials, the King worked prudently with this assembly and was never intimidated by it. When Parliament refused him money, Henry borrowed from the London merchants to pay for his military expenses. In 1403 a serious rebellion took shape when Owen Glendower of Wales aroused Welsh nationalism and allied himself with the Percys of Northumberland in an effort to replace Henry with the Earl of March. Henry intercepted the Percys near Shrewsbury, defeated them, and killed Harry Hotspur, the fiery-tempered son of the Earl of Northumberland. King Henry's eldest son, Henry (Shakespeare's "Prince Hal"), halted the Welsh rebellion. In 1408 royal forces defeated the second Percy rebellion, and Northumberland was killed. Finally, Henry IV was secure in his kingdom but exhausted and ill. Five years later he died.

Henry V, 1413-22. When Henry V ascended the throne, he bent his military and organizing abilities to the conquest of France and gave England ten years of military glory. His victories marked the high tide of English success in the Hundred Years' War. At home he was not seriously threatened by rebellion as was his father, and he seemed to think the Lollards more dangerous than Wales or Scotland. Lollard executions increased, and their new leader, Sir John Oldcastle, was imprisoned and later burned as a heretic in the fires of Smithfield. Henry's meteoric reign ended in 1422 when he contracted dysentery and died in France before he could confirm the terms of the Treaty of Troyes.

Henry VI, 1422-61 *and* 1470-71. Henry VI inherited very little of his father's energy or genius but copied instead the traits of madness of his grandfather, Charles VI of France. During Henry's minority his uncles, the able Duke of Bedford and the not-so-able Duke of Gloucester, conducted the war in France and controlled the Government. After Bedford's death, conditions deteriorated rapidly as the French turned to the offensive and cleared the English from northern France. In addition the frequent changes of command in the English army hastened its demoralization. In 1445 Henry married a fury, Margaret of Anjou, who ruled him and tried to rule the country. Caring only for religion and books, Henry was completely ineffective as King.

Growing Discontent. The humiliation of losing territory in France increased popular dissatisfaction with Henry VI and his administration. This discontent resulted in the murder by royal navy captains of the Duke of Somerset (William de la Pole) who was the favorite of the Queen and the scapegoat for the Government's failures. In 1450 Jack Cade of Kent expressed the restlessness of the gentry and the yeomen by leading a three-county rebellion against the Government. Cade's followers marched into London with little resistance and were offered amnesty by the frightened Government. The rebels asked for better justice, the free election of knights to Parliament, and payment of the King's debts. In time Cade was caught and killed, but other minor uprisings continued. In 1453 when the inept Henry VI went completely mad and at the same time became a father, the stage was set for political factionalism to erupt into warfare.

The Wars of the Roses

Following the end of the Hundred Years' War in France (1453), two rival English Houses with private liveried armies fought each other for the next thirty years in a struggle for the throne. Tradition has labeled the feud the Wars of the Roses, from the white rose emblem of the House of York and the red rose of the House of Lancaster—although, in fact, the Lancastrian emblem was not adopted until the wars were over. These struggles between aristocratic factions decimated the ranks of the nobility but made little impact on the country at large.

Origins of the Wars. The circumstances that led to war did not involve any basic differences in theories of government but centered in the utter failure of Henry VI to provide any kind of strong leadership during his reign. The disappearance of law and order encouraged defiance to the Government. The humiliating defeats in France and the unpopularity of Queen Margaret and of the King's advisers, especially Somerset, made matters worse. The basis for the divided allegiance of the nobility was the dynastic struggle between York and Lancaster. Until 1453 Henry VI was childless, and the best claim to succeed him was made by Richard, duke of York, who had a more direct descent from Edward III than the Lancaster Kings. In 1453 the matter of genealogy was complicated by the birth of a son to Henry and Queen Margaret and by the first of his several periods of insanity. With the King incapacitated the House of Lords appointed York as Lord Protector. The next year the King recovered and the Queen retaliated by ousting York and his friends from office and releasing from prison York's rival, the Duke of Somerset. York resorted to arms and war began.

Course of the War. The battles of this dynastic struggle were brutal and were mostly fought on a small scale by groups of noblemen and their bands of private mercenaries. Except for brief intervals the Yorkists controlled the Government throughout the period with Edward IV, Richard's son, reigning as the first of three Yorkist Kings.

Battle of St. Albans. The fighting began with a Yorkist victory at St. Albans in 1455. Somerset was killed and York became Lord Protector as madness once again disabled King Henry. With his recovery Queen Margaret returned control to the Lancastrians, and in 1459 the leading Yorkists fled into exile to escape parliamentary bills of attainder.

Battle of Towton. In 1460 the Yorkists invaded England from France and Ireland and defeated the royalist forces, but neither the Queen nor the House of Lords would recognize the Duke of York's bid to replace Henry VI as King. Before the end of the year York was killed and Richard Neville, earl of Warwick, was defeated. The Lancastrian interlude was brief as Edward rallied the Yorkists, entered London, and proclaimed himself King. Moving north with his army, Edward IV engaged the Lancastrians at Towton on Palm Sunday, 1461, in what is termed "the bloodiest battle on English soil." Although Henry VI escaped to Scotland and lived another ten years, Towton effectively ended sixty-two years of Lancastrian rule.

Edward IV, 1461-83. The new Yorkist King governed better than the previous Lancastrian and managed this without paying much attention to Parliament. Until the year 1471, King Edward was involved in protecting his throne against the challenges of his friend, Warwick, and his foes, the Lancastrians. By confiscating his enemies' estates and receiving "gifts" from friendly magnates and the merchants of London, King Edward was never in the financial predicament that permitted Parliament to use its most effective weapon of consent to new taxation. In 1475 he invaded France with his brother-in-law, the Duke of Burgandy. Louis XI bought off Edward, and the annual subsidies of £10,000 made life even more comfortable for the King. Edward IV was an astute and brilliant soldier, who preferred indolence, love affairs, and luxury to the arduous task of governing.

Warwick the Kingmaker. The Neville family possessed more land and wealth and hired more soldiers than any other household. With these resources the Earl of Warwick played the role of "kingmaker" throughout the wars. In 1461 he put Edward IV on the throne but turned against him when the King disregarded his efforts to get him a French wife and alliance. In 1469 Warwick changed sides and entered into a conspiracy with the Lancastrian faction, supported by Louis XI of France. Warwick defeated the Yorkist army at Edgcote but, in turn, was forced to flee the country when King Edward's army threatened him. In 1470 Warwick signed a compact with Queen Margaret and the Lancastrians, landed in England and marched on London, where he released Henry VI from prison. The next year Edward IV returned from Burgundy and crushed the Lancastrian army at the Battle of Barnet, during which Warwick was killed. A month later Edward defeated Queen Margaret's army at Tewkesbury; the Queen was captured and her only son was killed. Henry VI died in the Tower, presumably murdered, and the direct Lancastrian line was wiped out.

Richard III. Edward IV died suddenly in 1483 from overindulgence and left two young princes to be protected in their minority by either the Queen Mother, Elizabeth Woodville, or their uncle,

Richard of Gloucester. Richard had served his brother well as an administrator and adviser; however, his overriding ambition and suspicion of the Queen and her relatives caused him to act rapidly and without scruple to win the Crown for himself. In short order, he arrested the supporters of the Queen, intimidated the Great Council into making him Lord Protector, proceeded to imprison the uncrowned Edward V and his brother Richard in the Tower, and had his enemies executed. He falsely claimed that Edward's sons were illegitimate and that he was rightful heir to the throne. On July 6, Richard was crowned King. Shortly thereafter the two princes were murdered in the Tower. The King's fellow conspirator, the Duke of Buckingham, plotted to replace Richard with Henry Tudor, who was remotely connected to the Lancastrian line. When his plans failed, Buckingham was executed and the remaining conspirators fled into exile. In the next two years Richard tried to compensate for his violent seizure of the throne by efforts at good government, but his unpopularity only increased and he soon resorted to repressive measures.

Bosworth Field. As disaffection grew against King Richard, many gentry and clergy joined the Earl of Richmond (Henry Tudor), in France. In August, 1485, with the backing of King Louis XI of France, Henry invaded England. The armies of Henry and Richard met at Bosworth Field where the King showed great personal courage. However, the intervention of Lord Stanley proved decisive, and Richard was killed and his army dispersed and fled. The crown was placed upon the head of the conqueror, the future Henry VII.

End of the Wars. Bosworth Field was the final battle of the Wars of the Roses. The country now yearned for a strong, orderly Government that could bring peace. The wars had exhausted the power of the nobility for they had suffered the greatest casualties and many of their leaders were dead. Parliament, too, went into decline or was used only to sanction the King's actions. At the same time the war brought the King and the townsmen closer together in common opposition to their mutual opponent, the feudal nobility.

Fifteenth Century England

The dynastic and military maneuvers of the fifteenth century overshadow other areas of English life, but in so doing they create a false picture. Political demoralization and decline did not necessarily carry over into all other areas of life. Consequently, the century is more correctly a transitional era as medieval times dissolved into the age of the Renaissance.

The Economy. The export of wool declined during the century, but the manufacture and export of woolen cloth increased and led to a search for new markets and the subsequent growth of the merchant navy. Trading organizations, such as the Merchant Adventurers, began to flourish, and during the reign of Edward IV royal support was given to commerce. There followed a notable rise in the prosperity of city merchants and country gentry which, in turn, augmented their influence. The country gentry were increasingly becoming a *rentier* class, who, instead of farming their lands, rented them out to an emerging yeoman class of small farmers—a class later known as "the backbone" of England. In this century the merchants were also escaping from the inhibiting regulations of the guilds as they looked to the King for support in their attempts at national and international trade.

Education. The fifteenth century saw a significant growth in new colleges and endowments and in the expansion of old schools. About two hundred grammar schools were in existence, including Eton, founded by Henry VI in 1440. Henry also founded King's College, Cambridge, and his wife founded Queens'. Half a dozen other colleges were also established during the century, while in London the famous Inns of Court, established in the thirteenth century, were prestigious centers of legal training.

Literature. The revival of learning came later in England than on the Continent, slowed down, in part, by the confusion and anarchy of the Wars of the Roses. In 1477, under the patronage of Edward IV, William Caxton set up the first printing press in England. In contrast to the secularism of the Italian Renaissance Englishmen in the fifteenth century still read works dealing primarily with moral or semi-religious themes.

Poetry. No author in the fifteenth century approached Chaucer, although several of his disciples tried to imitate him: John Lydgate (*c.* 1420 in *The Story of Thebes* and *The Troy Book,* and Thomas Occleve (*c.* 1411) in the *Dialogue* and *De Regimine Principum.*

Prose. The Paston Letters, the correspondence of three generations of the Paston family of Norfolk, provide some of the most illuminating historical and social documents of the years 1422-1509. In 1469 Sir Thomas Malory wrote *Morte D'Arthur* in which he recaptured the legend of Arthur and the knights of the Round Table. Two important writers in law and political philosophy were

Sir John Fortescue (*c.* 1394–*c.* 1476) and Sir Thomas Littleton (*c.* 1407–81). In his *De Laudibus Legum Angliae* Fortescue showed a mastery of common law, whereas Littleton is distinguished for classic treatises on estates and real property law found in his *Tenures*.

Courts and Parliaments. The spirit of lawlessness and defiance of authority that was characteristic of the century undermined the process of justice: royal judges lost their authority as Kings lost their power; justices of the peace were bribed or intimidated by local lords and their liveried retinues; jurors were bought; and sheriffs frequently were little more than agents of local magnates. The nobles also tried to use the Lancastrian Parliaments as their instrument, but this did not keep the functions of Parliament from becoming more firmly established. Parliament was clearly recognized as the highest court of law in the land. The House of Commons was fully accepted as a separate entity, and in 1429 legislation made the county franchise uniform for electing members to Parliament by limiting the vote to freeholders whose income property was worth a minimum of forty shillings. The Commons continued to exert control over taxation and to present petitions to the King. As the middle class grew in influence, so did the House of Commons.

The King's Council. There were wide variations in membership and power of the King's Council during the century. Under Henry V it was a small group of close friends; under Henry VI it came under the control of the barons chosen by the House of Lords. In the reign of Edward IV the council became largely an administrative body with little influence since real authority resided with the King and certain of his advisers, as the Earl of Warwick. What the century lacked most was "strong governance"; this was to be provided in full measure by the new Tudor dynasty.

History of Scotland 1066-1485

Not until the eighteenth century with the Act of Union (1707) would Scotland become formally united with England. Until then the very location of Scotland made it an important factor in the reign of each English King, either in their efforts to conquer the country or to defend England from Scottish reprisals.

Scottish Government and Society. Although the majority of Scots were Celtic in blood and background, the form of government and manner of speech in Scotland came from Saxon and Norman England rather than from Ireland and Wales. In the Low-

lands (southeast) Norman barons established the feudal arrangement, and Scottish Kings copied English laws. In the north the
Highlanders never accepted this modified "English" society but
rather maintained tribal law and customs until after their final revolt in 1745.

Summary of Scottish History, 1066-1272. Malcolm II who succeeded in unifying Scotland as a kingdom at the beginning of the
eleventh century was followed by Duncan and Macbeth; the latter
was overthrown by Malcolm III in 1057. Malcolm later fought
with William the Conqueror and was forced to do homage to him.
After a period of upheaval David I restored order and lived peacefully with England until 1138 when he was defeated at the Battle of
the Standard. England's suzerainty was recognized in the reign of
Henry II when he claimed and received homage from all Scotland.
Richard I assisted the return of independence to Scotland by his
long absences from England and his annullment of the Treaty of
Falaise for a sum of money. The reigns of Alexander II (1214-49)
and his son Alexander III (1249-86) gave Scotland a lengthy interlude of peace and prosperity.

Baliol, Wallace, and Bruce. Following the death of Alexander
III a disputed succession to the Scottish throne arose. Edward I of
England asserted his claim to the overlordship of Scotland and
awarded the crown to John Baliol.

John Baliol (1292-96). King John grew restive under English
suzerainty because of Edward's constant demand for men and
money for the French wars. In 1295, King John made an alliance
with France, which began three centuries of Franco-Scottish friendship, and renounced his homage to Edward. Edward decisively defeated the Scots at Dunbar (1296), deposed King John, and ruled
Scotland through English commissioners.

William Wallace (1297-1305). After leading a guerrilla campaign, Wallace collected an army and defeated the English at Stirling Bridge in 1297. In the following year the Scots under his
command surrendered to King Edward after the battle of Falkirk.
In 1305 Wallace was captured by the English and hanged as a
traitor.

Robert Bruce (1306-29). A grandson of the claimant against
Baliol, Bruce in 1306 had himself crowned king at Scone, built up
an army, and prepared to meet Edward I; however, the English
King died en route to give battle. By 1314 Bruce had taken all English garrisons in Scotland except Stirling. Edward II finally brought
his army north and met Bruce at Bannockburn in 1314. The battle
became a glorious Scottish victory and made independence pos-

sible. The Treaty of Northampton (1328) confirmed both Bruce's kingship and Scotland's freedom from English overlordship.

Summary of Scottish History, 1329-71. In the fourteenth century the contest for the throne of Scotland was between Edward Baliol, son of John Baliol, and David II, son of Robert Bruce. After an unsuccessful attempt to usurp the crown from King David, Baliol was ousted and fled to England for sanctuary. In 1333 Edward III of England defeated the Scots at Halidon Hill and placed Baliol on the throne; David escaped to France. Baliol was repudiated by the Scots for his homage to King Edward, and intermittent war between England and Scotland took place for the next two decades with France aiding Scotland. In 1346 David invaded England but was captured at Neville's Cross and remained a captive in London. By the Treaty of Berwick (1357) David Bruce was ransomed for 100,000 marks. He reigned until 1371.

The House of Stuart. Toward the end of the fourteenth century and afterward there was a struggle between the Stuarts and their rivals for power. The intrigues and battles that took place resembled those fought south of the border in the Wars of the Roses.

Robert II (1371-90). King Robert, the first of the Stuarts, began his reign by signing a truce with England's John of Gaunt. Then in 1385 Scotland allied with France and Richard II invaded Scotland. Three years later the Scots retaliated by invading England and defeating the Percys at the Battle of Otterburn.

Robert III (1390-1406). Because of his physical disability Robert III was a weak ruler; the real power was administered by the King's brother, the Duke of Albany. The King gave the guardianship of his elder son, David, duke of Rothesay, to Albany, who starved him to death at Falkland. When King Robert died, Albany became a regent of ability.

James I (1406-37). For nearly a decade King Robert's youngest son, James, was held a prisoner by Henry IV. Returning from England in 1424 James promptly introduced English statute law and reformed the judiciary. He also kept the barons in check until he was murdered by Sir Robert Graham in 1437.

James II (1437-60). James was only seven when he inherited the throne so that during his minority Scotland was governed until 1449 by a series of regents. A new civil war between the Stuarts and the Douglases ended in victory for the King. Under James II Scotland again saw security and prosperity as well as some important reforms in land tenure and in the administration of justice. In 1460 James was killed by the accidental explosion of a cannon during the siege of Roxburgh Castle.

James III (1460-88). In 1474 an Anglo-Scottish treaty was concluded that brought peace, after Edward IV had found that his support of the Douglases against the Stuarts was futile. King James patronized the arts, extended his rule over the islands surrounding Scotland, and lived in a luxurious manner. He concluded another truce with Richard III that confirmed his supremacy in Scotland; however, his own nobles rebelled against his increasing powers and murdered him in 1488. His son, James IV, would deal with two of the Tudor Kings of England.

Chapter 7 ❧ The Early Tudors and the Reformation

Henry VII and Henry VIII, each in his own way, reconstructed and strengthened the monarchy as an institution and as the symbol of England's growing national self-consciousness. Strong royal Government provided England with the peace and security that it so obviously lacked through most of the fifteenth century. At the same time the ferment of rising nationalism encouraged an intellectual and religious reawakening that produced a literary renaissance and a religious revolt. The religious issue dominated the reigns of Henry VIII, Edward VI, and Mary.

Henry VII

Henry Tudor faced the enormous problem of restoring order in the country and royal authority, a task made even more difficult by the fact that he, himself, had a very tenuous claim to the throne. In spite of these obstacles King Henry was highly successful in both his domestic and foreign policies and left his son the richest treasury in Europe. Henry probably did "more for Britain in his quiet way than any sovereign since the first Edward." [1]

Consolidation of Power.   With only a remote Lancastrian claim to the throne that he traced through his mother back to John of Gaunt (the younger son of Edward III), Henry VII seemed at first to be only one more temporarily successful dynastic ruler. He immediately moved to strengthen his position by having Parliament confirm his title on the grounds of heredity and conquest. Henry then married Edward IV's oldest surviving daughter, Elizabeth of York, thereby joining the two rival claims of York and Lancaster. His next move was to curb the power of the nobles.

Livery and Maintenance.   Henry's first Parliament revived an earlier statute against livery and maintenance in an effort to eliminate the private armies of the nobles.

Court of Star Chamber.   To enforce the statute Henry's Star Chamber Act (1487) revived the jurisdiction of his Council over all cases of livery and maintenance, bribery, and civil disorder. The

---

[1] Keith Feiling, *History of England* (Macmillan: London, 1959), p. 317.

Court of Star Chamber (so-named because of the starred ceiling of the room where it met), was under Henry's direct influence. The court's officers of state and two Chief Justices operated without juries or common law precedents. Its vigorous prosecution of lawbreakers gradually compelled the nobles to accept royal authority since they could not intimidate or bribe this court as they could a local jury. In King Henry's reign the court was popular with the people for it brought to justice those overlords who disregarded the rights of Englishmen and restored law and order. The unpopularity of the Court of Star Chamber stems from the seventeenth century when its original purposes no longer applied and when the Stuarts used it to oppose Parliament.

Rival Claimants. Domestic and foreign enemies of the King exploited Henry's flimsy title to the Crown by supporting various pretenders to the throne. Lambert Simnel impersonated the Earl of Warwick and won the backing of Yorkist sympathizers and of Margaret, duchess of Burgundy. In 1487 he landed in England with an army of Irishmen and German mercenaries. After the invaders were defeated, Simnel was put to work as a scullion in the royal kitchen. Perkin Warbeck, a Flemish apprentice, claimed that he was Richard, duke of York, the younger son of Edward IV who had been slain in the Tower. By 1493 he had won the support of the Duke of Burgundy and of the Kings of Germany, Scotland, and France. Warbeck's attempted invasion of England in 1495 failed, and Henry's diplomatic successes shortly deprived him of foreign support, except for Scotland. In 1497 a joint invasion by the King of Scotland in the north and Warbeck in Cornwall failed. Warbeck was captured and executed two years later. In each rebellion King Henry remained calm, acted wisely and usually with forbearance to keep his throne by sheer ability rather than by ruthlessness or by general popularity. Although other rebellions appeared, Henry had secured his dynasty and was never seriously threatened after 1497.

Character of the King. Henry VII, unlike his son, never caught the popular imagination. Perhaps his reign appeared dull because his policies were so eminently shrewd and logical that they produced admiration, but hardly enthusiasm. Aloof and colorless, he engendered respect and a sense of confidence, if not of love, in his subjects. By sheer skill and the wisdom to work for limited, rather than grandiose, objectives, he set the monarchy above political faction. The image of King Henry "the miser" is overdrawn; he was personally frugal and meticulous in keeping his financial accounts, because money meant power and freedom from parliamentary grants.

Domestic Affairs. Henry VII was a businesslike King who was convinced that external peace and internal order were dependent upon a prosperous and secure country. His financial policies reflected this conviction.

Taxation. A fundamental weakness of the feudal monarch was his reliance upon vassals for revenue. Beyond these resources the King could only appeal to Parliament. Henry did not want to antagonize his subjects by raising taxes; only five times during his reign did he ask Parliament for direct taxation. To become self-sufficient Henry pared expenditures, personally checked the account books, encouraged foreign commerce in order to increase custom duties, resumed every dormant right of the Crown, levied steep fines in court, and seized the property of attainted enemies. Occasionally he resorted to benevolences or extortion from his rich subjects. In this manner he filled the royal coffers and bequeathed close to £2 million to his son.

Commerce. By treaties and monopolies Henry VII increased the volume of trade and encouraged English shipping. The Navigation Act of 1485 stimulated English shipping, while the *Intercursus Magnus* treaty (1497) with the Netherlands provided for reciprocity of trade. In 1506 the treaty of *Intercursus Malus* gave a monopoly of the English cloth trade in the Low Countries to the Merchant Adventurers. A heavy duty was placed on exported wool to encourage the woolen industry to expand its export of manufactured woolens.

Decline of the Guilds. The craft guilds were already in decline at the beginning of Henry VII's reign. Wealthy masters were becoming so exclusive that journeymen were leaving the towns to avoid the strict regulations of the guilds. Nor did local guilds promote the national interest; rather, they were concerned with a monopoly over local crafts, often at the expense of economic expansion. King Henry accelerated the decline of the guilds by an act in 1504 which forbade any subsequent ordinances of guilds from being binding until approved by certain government officials. Already the craft guilds were being superseded by the domestic system, under which capitalistic merchants became middlemen between the producer and the consumer and supplied the worker in his home with raw materials and bought his finished product. The domestic system developed first in the woolen industry. Although the King was involving the Government by his economic legislation, it was honored only when convenient and no efforts were made at enforcement.

Parliament and Council. Henry VII governed largely through the King's Council which included fewer magnates than previously and more counselors of lower social ranks who were selected for their abilities and loyalty. At the county level Henry upgraded the work and influence of the justices of the peace and won the allegiance of the lesser gentry who held these unpaid posts. The J. P.'s supervised the collection of taxes, held court four times a year, and were the local agents for carrying out the wishes of the central Government. Since the Crown possessed no standing army, royal decrees were effective only to the extent that local agents were able, and willing, to carry them out. Parliament seldom met since Henry only occasionally needed its grants as a regular source of revenue. When it did meet it was usually a willing ally of the Crown, with the Commons effectively managed by Speakers who were royal officials.

Foreign Policy. King Henry's foreign policy centered around the goals of peace and security. He did not want unnecessary wars that could only drain the treasury and jeopardize his throne by possible defeat. Rather he preferred political marriages to military engagements.

Marriage Alliances. Henry VII arranged the marriage of his eldest son, Arthur, to Catherine, daughter of Ferdinand and Isabella of Spain; with Catherine came a handsome dowry. When Arthur died the King had his other son, Henry, betrothed to Catherine to save the dowry and the alliance with Spain. In 1503 he married his daughter Margaret to King James IV of Scotland, thereby preparing the way for the later union of the two kingdoms. His youngest daughter, Mary, was betrothed to Charles of Castile, the grandson of Emperor Maximilian, in return for a large loan and an alliance with Austria.

Continental Policy. Henry VII had little interest in asserting the old Norman-Angevin claims to French holdings or in wasting his resources in one more attempt to recover them. But the English people still considered France its mortal enemy, and Spain made English aid against France a term of the marriage treaty of 1489. Maximilian of Austria also allied with Henry VII against France but deserted him, as did Ferdinand, in 1491. Henry salvaged the situation by appealing to Parliament for money and landing in Calais with a large army. Charles VIII of France had visions of an Italian empire and, therefore, quickly came to terms with Henry to avoid fighting the English as well. The Treaty of Etaples (1492) would provide large annual subsidies to Henry, who preferred tribute instead of a title to Brittany. Henry VII ended up with successful Spanish and Hapsburg alliances and avoided the temptation that befell the other European powers of becoming embroiled in an Italian empire.

Scottish Policy. Not until James IV invaded England in support of the pretender, Warbeck, did Henry VII worry about his northern neighbor. He then responded by threatening Scotland with invasion and giving his support to a rival claimant to the Scottish throne; but Henry, as usual, preferred diplomacy to warfare. The Anglo-Scottish treaty of 1499 promised peace between the two countries and sealed the agreement with a marriage alliance between James IV and Henry's daughter, Margaret.

Irish Policy. Because the Yorkist Irish had supported both pretenders to the English throne, Henry VII sent Sir Edward Poynings to Ireland in 1494 to act as Lord Deputy and to reassert English authority over the island. Poynings failed to control Ulster, but in the Pale (the area around Dublin) he had laws passed which made the Irish Parliament clearly subordinate to the English Crown. Henceforth, no Irish laws could operate without the approval of the Crown, whereas all English laws automatically applied to Ireland. Poynings' Laws were later damned by the Irish, but Henry avoided immediate trouble by restoring the Earl of Kildare, who was acceptable to the Irish, as Lord Deputy.

English Society. The enclosure movement—fencing off former common lands—increased substantially under the Tudors, because landlords saw how much more profitable their common lands could be for sheep-raising. The victims were the peasants who frequently became unemployed vagrants when they were excluded from their share of the meadows and woods. These economic changes reflected the transformation of English social classes as the gentry, yeomen, and merchants (the new men) grew influential at the expense of the old nobility and the peasants. The great baronial families, such as the Percys and the Nevilles, who had been decimated by the Wars of the Roses, were gradually being replaced in English political and social life by the rising country gentlemen or squires. This new landed aristocracy, based more on wealth than on birth, built attractive country houses and became the nucleus of the leisure and governing class in the counties. These amateur administrators took their work seriously and provided the Tudors with local influence that no central bureaucracy of royal officials could have matched.

The Literary Renaissance. Not until the latter part of the fifteenth century did the Renaissance reach England and quicken the torpid intellectual atmosphere of the universities. English scholars who had studied in Italy introduced the curricula of the humanities in English schools. The first generation of these scholars, which included Thomas Linacre (1460?-1524) and William Grocyn

(1446?-1519), made Oxford the center of this literary and educational revival.

The Oxford Humanists. The Christian humanists restored intellectual vigor to the Roman Catholic church by their zealous efforts at ecclesiastical reform through education and classical scholarship. At times they reflected English sentiment by being anti-clerical, but they were by no means anti-religious. John Colet (1467-1519) was a humanist scholar vitally interested in church and educational reform. His discourses on St. Paul's Epistles freed his interpretive theological thinking from medieval scholasticism. He became dean of St. Paul's Cathedral and founded St. Paul's School where he introduced nonclerical education. Thomas More (1478-1535) was a noted administrator who became chancellor under Henry VIII. His *Utopia,* which provided a humanistic parody of the times, idealized human nature in its description of a new society free from feudal conceptions and religious intolerance. Desiderius Erasmus (1466?-1536), a Dutch scholar and colleague at Oxford of More and Colet, was the most celebrated Christian humanist of the early Renaissance. His devastating satire and ridicule of many church practices opened the door for theological criticism of church doctrines.

Henry VIII

Henry VII bequeathed to his son a secure monarchy, a full treasury, and a nation with increased stature in the diplomacy of Europe. Upon this foundation Henry VIII's reign (1509-47) added popular enthusiasm for the Crown and spectacular royal authority, especially observed in his break with Rome and in the confiscation of monastic properties. In this instance royal despotism was successful, because Henry continued to respect traditional forms of English Government and because his policies reflected the feelings of most of his subjects.

Accession of Henry VIII. King Henry came to the throne at the age of seventeen, well-educated, and with a captivating personality. He was a good athlete, knowledgeable in theology, music, and literature, and a born leader; he was also exceedingly vain and ambitious, and his appetites knew no moderation. Ruthless and frivolous on occasion and lacking the restraint of his father, King Henry gained the affection of his subjects in a way Henry VII never could. He won immediate good will by executing Richard Empson and Edmund Dudley, the two ministers who were responsible for Henry VII's legal extortions.

Cardinal Wolsey. At first Henry VIII left most administrative duties in the hands of experienced ministers who had worked for his father, but shortly he delegated almost complete authority to Thomas Wolsey. Wolsey was a self-made man who collected a string of offices in both church and government, including those of Archbishop of York (1514), Cardinal and Lord Chancellor (1515), and Papal Legate (1518). He became Henry's closest adviser, and for fifteen years he managed England, especially in the area of foreign diplomacy. He held his power by hard work and competency and realized that his position rested on royal favor and diplomatic success; therefore, he could afford to be greedy, ruthless, and intolerably arrogant to all but the King.

Foreign Policy. Wolsey organized and directed all but one of Henry VIII's wars. His special forte was diplomacy in which he operated on the balance of power principle—joining with lesser powers against the most powerful. Wolsey's involvement in foreign affairs won England a conspicuous place in the councils of Europe, but only provoked reaction against him at home.

Italian-Spanish Politics. Italy had become the battleground of Europe ever since the French in 1494 had shown how easy it was to plunder the peninsula. The Papacy organized alliances to prevent one-power domination of Italy. The League of Cambrai (1508) reduced the power of Venice, and England joined the pope's Holy League in 1511 to drive the French out of Italy.

The Spanish Alliance. Henry VIII reaffirmed his father's alliance with Spain by marrying his widowed sister-in-law, Catherine, within a month of his accession to the throne. Her father, King Ferdinand, persuaded Henry to join the Holy League. In 1512 an English expedition planned by Ferdinand against the French failed miserably because of inactivity and insubordination. In 1513 Henry redeemed himself by landing in France, defeating the French at the Battle of the Spurs, and capturing Terouenne and Tournai. Ferdinand deserted Henry and made a truce with Louis XII, but this time the English were not left in the lurch as in 1512. Instead, Wolsey arranged a peace with France that gave England a sum of money and fortified the alliance by the marriage of Henry's sister, Mary, to King Louis XII. The success of this diplomatic coup was jeopardized the following year (1515) by the death of Louis XII. Wolsey thereupon tried to build up a coalition against the ambitious new King, Francis I, but did not succeed. In 1518 a treaty of peace was arranged whereby England returned Tournai to France for a handsome profit.

England and the Franco-Spanish Rivalry. The important dynastic struggle in Europe after 1519 was between Francis I of France and Charles V, who was Holy Roman Emperor and King of Spain. In this rivalry, England lined up with Spain even though Henry VIII and Francis I put on a public display of friendship at the Field of the Cloth of Gold (1520). The following year an alliance with Spain committed England to another war against France, but the English campaigns in France (1522-23) were futile and costly. Wolsey alienated Parliament and the citizens of London by his demands for money and his levy of a 20 per cent property tax.

Pro-French Policy. Charles V decisively defeated the French at Pavia (1525), sacked Rome (1527), and made the pope his prisoner. This completely upset the balance of power and forced Wolsey to change sides suddenly and seek a peace with France. In 1526 and again in 1528 England allied with France in an effort to check the emperor; but by this time Wolsey's strategy was no longer effective. The pro-French policy did not sit well with England since the old enmity toward France continued strong; furthermore, the policy was disrupting the cloth-export trade to the Netherlands. More significant was Wolsey's loss of influence with the King; he had failed in his bid to become pope, and Henry was demanding action on his divorce proceedings. In 1529 Francis I and Charles V signed the Treaty of Cambrai without even consulting Wolsey.

Scottish Policy. In 1513 the Scots, under James IV, took advantage of Henry's absence in France and invaded England. However, they were defeated at Flodden Field and King James was killed in battle. James V and his chief adviser, Cardinal David Beaton, were strongly pro-French. Intermittent border skirmishes by both sides continued until the Scots suffered a disgraceful defeat at Solway Moss (1542). The news of the disaster killed James V, and the throne was left to his week-old daughter, Mary Stuart. Henry tried to negotiate a marriage between Mary and his son, Edward, but the Scots turned instead to their old ally, France, and later betrothed Mary to the heir to the French throne.

Wales. In the principality of Wales Henry was quietly successful. For the first time in its history Wales was fully incorporated with England by the Act of Union (1536) which provided for twelve counties and twenty-four representatives to Parliament. A second act in 1543 meshed the legal and administrative procedures of the two regions.

Ireland. The great Anglo-Irish lords, led by the Earls of Ormande and Kildare, were the real powers in the country. The Earl of Kildare revolted in 1533 in protest over the death of his father in the Tower of London and Henry's antipapal policy. However, this revolt was brutally suppressed, and in 1541 Henry assumed the titles of King of Ireland and head of the Irish church. Ireland was temporarily subdued, but the settlement was completely unsatisfactory to the Irish.

The Fall of Wolsey. Cardinal Wolsey had appropriated royal privileges and virtually ruled the country with an autocratic hand without paying much attention to Parliament. Only once between 1515 and 1529 was Parliament summoned. Wolsey's lavish style of living and insufferable arrogance created personal enemies envious of his position and strength. Even though his preoccupation with foreign affairs damaged his reputation in England, he was not threatened as long as he retained the support of King Henry. But royal favor was lost when he was unable to win from the pope an annulment of Henry's marriage. Wolsey was stripped of his offices and arrested in 1529 for high treason. He died enroute to London, and Thomas More took his place as Chancellor.

King and Church: The Breach with Rome

On the Continent, the Protestant revolt was based *primarily* on religious motives; in England the revolt against the Papacy was essentially dynastic and personal, with religious overtones. There was little change in doctrine under Henry VIII; but rather an exertion of his authority over the church in the same manner that he eventually ran the state to keep it in order.

Background Events. (1) The influence of the German and Swiss religious reformers, Luther and Zwingli, had already made some impression on England, and one of their converts, William Tyndale, translated the New Testament into English. However, Henry VIII had no theological argument with the church; he wrote a tract against Luther in 1521 and for his efforts received from Pope Leo X the title of Defender of the Faith—a title still used by the English sovereign today. (2) Religious reformers in England from the days of Wycliffe had urged the church to reform and to curtail its lavish wealth. But for the most part the church had not changed since the thirteenth century. (3) Rising nationalism in England became increasingly hostile to any ultramontane allegiance, and the King and Parliament fed on the strong feelings of anticlericalism to restrict papal powers in England. (4) Deteriorating relations with Spain increased the strain between Henry and his Spanish Queen. (5) The Tudors were dogmatic and were unwilling to be crossed in their plans. The conflict with Rome came to a head with Henry's efforts to win an annullment of his marriage.

Divorce Proceedings. By 1527 King Henry had been married to Catherine of Aragon for eighteen years and only one daughter, Mary, had survived infancy. The fear of the new Tudor dynasty dying out because of the lack of a male heir haunted the proud Henry. Since Henry had obtained a papal dispensation in 1509 to bypass canon law forbidding marriage to a sister-in-law, he now began to develop a conscience over the irregularity of the marriage. His desire to divorce Catherine was heightened by his great passion for the Queen's lady-in-waiting, Anne Boleyn, who would consent to be his wife, but not his mistress.

Appeal to Rome. In 1527 Henry commissioned Wolsey to secure from the pope an annullment of his marriage. However, the pope was virtually a prisoner of Charles V. Furthermore, Charles was the nephew of Catherine and certainly would not appreciate this slight to his aunt. Wolsey worked vigorously for Henry's cause, but the pope used stalling tactics for two years. When no decision had been reached, Henry lost patience with both the pope and with Wolsey; he dismissed Wolsey and took matters into his own hands.

Henry's Maneuvers, 1529-34. When Henry finally broke with Rome, he carried the nation with him. He severed relations step-by-step in the hope that constant pressure on the Papacy would give him his own way short of revolt. Relying on Thomas Cranmer and Thomas Cromwell (later to be Chancellor), he made his divorce case a subject for debate in European universities in 1529 and in 1530 pressured the English clergy into recognizing him as the supreme head of the Church of England "as far as the law of Christ allows." In 1529 Henry had called Parliament into session and for seven years it served as his instrument of anticlerical defiance. By 1533 the pope had made no concessions, and Anne was pregnant. Cranmer was appointed the new Archbishop of Canterbury, and the English ecclesiastical court gave Henry his annullment. Henry married Anne publicly, and in September she gave birth to a daughter, Elizabeth. The King's hopes for a male heir remained unfulfilled.

Act of Supremacy. In 1534 the break with Rome was complete when Parliament by statute declared Henry the supreme head of the Church of England; no change of creed took place.

The Reformation Parliament, 1529-36. Cromwell's most masterful work was in using Parliament (whereas Wolsey had mistrusted it) to achieve royal policy. The Reformation Parliament, managed by the king's officials, but hardly coerced, passed one hundred and thirty-seven statutes, thirty-two of them relating to the church. These included the reduction of pluralities and fees for the clergy, the Act of Annates which halted the payment to Rome of the first year's income from new occupants of benefices, the Act of Appeals which forbade all appeals to the pope, and a Dispensations Act which cut off all payments to Rome, including Peter's Pence. Then in 1534 the Supremacy Act and a new Treason Act made official the independence of the English church and prohibited any other religious allegiance among Englishmen. An Oath of Supremacy was required and executions followed for those who refused, including Henry's Chancellor, Thomas More, and John Fisher, Bishop of Rochester. In the Act of Succession (1534) Parliament secured the Crown for Elizabeth and declared Mary illegitimate. This was altered in an act of 1543 to provide for the succession of Prince Edward, Princess Mary, and Princess Elizabeth, in that order.

The Dissolution of the Monasteries. Henry's Parliament gave him statutes but little money; therefore, Cromwell, the Vicar-General of the Church, sent out commissioners in 1535 to build up a case against the monasteries. Their report emphasized the superstitious practices, excessive wealth (ownership of one-fifth of the land of England), and immoral practices within religious communities. In 1536 Parliament abolished 376 religious houses with an annual income of less than £200 each; during the next four years the larger ones were confiscated on various pretexts, and the confiscation was ratified by statute in 1539. These acts were revolutionary in character as they were neither emergency war measures nor directed against alien houses; rather they were large-scale encroachments on private property by the authority of the King in Parliament, and with no justification in common law.

Political Consequences. Immediately, the removal of the abbots cut in half the number of ecclesiastical lords and changed the complexion of the House of Lords from a predominantly clerical to a predominantly lay group. The combination of conservative Catholic resentment along with the spreading enclosures and increasing taxes resulted in the only serious revolt of Henry's reign, the Pilgrimage of Grace. This revolt rallied those in northern England opposed to, or frustrated by, change. The rebellion, which was firmly squelched by Henry, resulted in the establishment of the Council of the North, as a branch of the Privy Council, to administer the unruly region directly.

Economic Consequences. King Henry became rich temporarily with the income from monastic lands. More important was the sale of two-thirds of the land to his friends, for this gave a large group of influential Englishmen an economic stake in the break with Rome. Many family fortunes and estates date from this period. However, the poor gained nothing; they lost the social services that were offered by religious houses, whereas the new landlords, more interested in profit, accelerated the enclosure of land which, in turn, produced unsettling social consequences for displaced peasants.

Character of the Church. King Henry's quarrel was with the pope, not with Catholic doctrine. He demanded religious conformity from his subjects in the same way that he expected political allegiance. Both Roman Catholics and Anabaptists were burned at the stake for daring to dissent; but they were a small company. Most of the English clergy and laity accepted Henry's version of the church.

Church Practices. English replaced Latin in the church services; in 1535 Coverdale's English translation of the Bible was adopted and placed in the churches for all to read. Relics and shrines were discredited and occasionally destroyed.

Church Doctrine. The Ten Articles of 1536 passed by Convocation reflected some cautious protestantization in declaring the Bible and the creeds the sole authority in matters of faith. However, the King was not in favor of changing the creed, and the Six Articles Act of 1539 reverted to full Catholic doctrine by upholding oral confession, transubstantiation, clerical celibacy, and prayers for the dead.

Last Years of Henry. After Henry had Cromwell executed because of his poor choice in selecting him a new wife, he ceased to employ a chief minister. He relied instead on a Privy Council—an "inner ring" of the Great Council—which included the Duke of Norfolk; Edward Seymour, earl of Hertford; Archbishop Cranmer; and Stephen Gardiner, Bishop of Winchester. Henry's last years were marked with a series of marriages, an inflationary economy, and war with France. Throughout the period Henry's authority over the church and state was supreme, as he made law by proclamation (Statute of Proclamations, 1539) and broadened the scope of treason.

Henry's Six Wives. King Henry tired of his second wife after the birth of a daughter instead of a son, and in 1536 Anne Boleyn was indicted on a charge of adultery and executed. Within a month Henry married Jane Seymour who after giving birth to a son, Edward, died the following year. Chancellor Cromwell next persuaded Henry to contract a marriage with a Lutheran Princess, Anne of Cleves, in order to strengthen the Protestant alliance.

When she arrived Henry was appalled at the sight of the "Flanders mare" and vented his wrath on the chancellor. Cromwell who had been the architect of Henry's Erastian state was executed and Anne divorced. Henry's fifth wife was nineteen-year-old Catherine Howard who lost her head upon conviction of adultery. The King's last marriage in 1543 was to Katherine Parr, who was to outlive Henry as she had her two previous husbands.

Debasement of the Coinage. If enclosures were a major source of discontent, the debasement of the coinage between 1542 and 1547 produced even greater hardships; prices jumped sharply and rents rose to catch up with the price-spiral. Only the King and the cloth-export trade prospered from the debasement. Henry VIII acquired metal extracted from the coinage valued at £227,000. The sale of cloth jumped when the pound sterling dropped in foreign exchange and permitted increased purchases of English exports.

Significance of Henry's Reign. Henry's reign was remarkably sturdy for he controlled events and moulded them to his own and the nation's interests. Selfish, ruthless with individuals, and petulant and degenerate in his old age, King Henry was largely successful in his objectives because he understood the times and his policies reflected the feelings of his subjects; Parliament would not have followed him so readily if it had been otherwise. England prospered under Henry and Parliament became an essential ingredient of the machinery of Government, even if it was used, along with the Henrician Church, as an instrument of royal strategy. The consequences of this "political reformation" were profound, because the assertion of the omnicompetence of the King in Parliament—of "the unlimited sovereignty of statute"—destroyed the medieval concept of Government and society.

Edward VI and the Protestant Reaction

Throughout Edward's brief reign (1547-53) England was again subject to the factionalism of a regency rule. In those years the Henrician Church veered sharply to more Protestant doctrines and practices under the leadership of Edward's three most influential advisers, the Duke of Somerset, the Duke of Northumberland, and Archbishop Cranmer.

The Council of Regency. Edward VI, who was barely ten years old when he became king, was a precocious, serious, but sickly child. His Government was plagued with social and economic problems, war with Scotland, and financial difficulties inherited from his father. Although King Henry had prepared for Edward's minority-rule by setting up a regency council of sixteen with a carefully balanced membership of conservatives and reformers, the reformers were the more powerful and the King's uncle, Edward Seymour, assumed full authority as Lord Protector.

The Protectorship of Somerset (1547-1549). Edward Seymour, duke of Somerset, was ambitious and well-meaning, but unschooled in political maneuvering and administration. He was a moderate reformer in religion and encouraged Protestant doctrines and religious toleration.

Religious Change. Somerset called Parliament in 1547 and had the treason and heresy acts repealed. A committee headed by Archbishop Cranmer reformed the order of public worship by issuing the first Book of Common Prayer (1549) with the approval of Parliament. A mild Act of Uniformity required its use in all public worship. The prayer book combined the majesty and the cadence of former ceremonies with a simplified communion service in the English language. The Six Articles, which were repealed, precipitated an uprising among the country folk of the west who demanded restoration of the old service and the Six Articles. At the same time, the radical Protestants demanded a repudiation of all Catholic customs, and iconoclastic mobs expressed their fanaticism in smashing cathedral windows and destroying religious statuary. Hugh Latimer of Oxford eloquently preached the need for further religious and social change. Somerset finally removed Catholic sympathizers from the Council.

Scotland. Somerset invaded Scotland to hasten the negotiations that Henry VIII had arranged for the marriage of Mary Stuart to Edward VI. Although the Scots were defeated at Pinkie (1547), they were not intimidated and dispatched Mary to France to marry the Dauphin.

France. In 1548 war was renewed with France when the French attacked unsuccessfully the town of Boulogne. However, the peace treaty was a diplomatic setback for Somerset because England returned Boulogne four years earlier than promised in the earlier treaty.

Social Unrest. Religious and economic changes created frustration and uprisings that were gently dealt with by Somerset who sympathized with the poor and attempted a few social reforms. The rapacity of the landlords in forcing enclosures, the inflation from the continued debasement of the coinage, the confiscation of the chantries and the plunder of the churches, and the disendowment of all town guilds, except those in London, increased the miseries of the poor and culminated in Kett's Rebellion near Norwich (1549) which was put down by John Dudley, earl of Warwick.

The Fall of Somerset. The inability of Somerset to ameliorate the economic distress, even after he had Parliament investigate the enclosure problems (the John Hales commission), and the diplomatic setback in France provided grounds for opposition. More important, Somerset antagonized the propertied classes with his ideas on social reform. As a result the Earl of Warwick (now entitled the Duke of Northumberland) ingratiated himself with Edward, built up a party of reaction that included the Roman Catholic faction, and had Somerset ousted in 1549. A few years later Somerset was arrested on a charge of high treason and executed.

The Protectorship of Northumberland (1549-53). Northumberland was an opportunist motivated by an insatiable lust for power. He favored a more radical Protestantism for political purposes and gambled on controlling the succession to the throne.

Religious Developments. Under Northumberland religious changes became more far-reaching: the vacillating and timid, yet scholarly, Cranmer repudiated the doctrine of transubstantiation in the Holy Communion; Lutheran and Calvinistic refugees and professors arrived in numbers from the Continent; clergy were allowed to marry; and the Catholic bishops Bonner and Gardiner were replaced by aggressive reformers, such as John Hooper, Bishop of Gloucester, and Nicholas Ridley, Bishop of London. The Second Act of Uniformity (1552) authorized the second Book of Common Prayer which made Holy Communion essentially an act of remembrance and ended oral confession. The next year the Forty-Two Articles of Faith defined the faith of the Church of England in terms that reflected both Lutheran (justification by faith) and Calvinistic (interpretation of the sacraments) influence.

Succession Schemes. Realizing that King Edward was dying of consumption, Northumberland persuaded him to alter the succession in order to keep Mary Tudor off the throne and prevent her from restoring Catholicism in England. Northumberland's scheme was to marry his son to the attractive Lady Jane Grey, granddaughter of Henry VIII's sister, Mary, and have Edward name her as heir. The dying King agreed and the Privy Council felt it prudent to assent.

Death of Edward. Lady Jane Grey reigned only nine days after the death of Edward. Protestants did not join Lady Jane's cause as Northumberland had anticipated; furthermore, his army deserted him because they feared his designs more than they did the religious identity of Mary. All England flocked to Mary's support when she entered London in triumph to be crowned Queen. Northumberland turned Catholic, but this did not save him from the block. Otherwise Mary was lenient with his supporters.

Mary Tudor and the Catholic Reaction

Mary Tudor, England's first ruling Queen, had experienced an unhappy and fearful childhood in the court of Henry VIII, but through it all she had remained courageous and completely devoted to Catholicism. Her policies were dominated by two overriding convictions—the need to end England's heresy by restoring the Roman Catholic faith, and the value of a close alliance with her mother's native land, Spain.

The Catholic Reformation in Europe. When Mary ascended the throne, Catholic Europe was in the midst of a major reform movement that had the dual purposes of reinvigorating its own beliefs and practices, and winning back some of the ground lost to Protestantism. On both counts the Catholic Reformation was successful through such agencies as the Council of Trent (1545-63), which clarified Catholic doctrine and proscribed heretical works through an *Index of Prohibited Books,* a renewal of the Inquisition to ferret out heretics, and the foundation of new religious orders. The most important of these orders was the Society of Jesus (Jesuits) founded by Ignatius Loyola in 1540; its members gave absolute obedience to the hierarchy of the church and were skilled teachers and missionaries in promoting the Catholic faith. The Catholic emperor who dominated Europe was Charles V, and Mary Tudor was eager to marry his son, Archduke Philip, and thereby bring England into the powerful Catholic empire.

The Return of Catholicism. Queen Mary at first was rather tolerant in her efforts to turn back the clock to pre-Reformation days, but when opposition and revolts hampered her progress she became impatient and intolerant and won the name of "Bloody Mary." She was as obstinate as her father, but without his sensitivity to national sentiment.

Mary's Parliaments. The Queen immediately pressured the three Parliaments of 1553-55 to rescind the religious legislation of Edward's reign, to revive the old heresy laws, and to petition the pope through Cardinal Pole to be received back into the Catholic church. But Parliament balked at her demands to restore confiscated monastic land. By administrative action she forced continental preachers and exiles to leave the country, replaced Protestant bishops with Catholic prelates, and revived Catholic liturgy.

Catholic Marriage. Mary insisted on her marriage to Philip II of

Spain, champion of Catholic orthodoxy, in spite of Lord Chancellor Gardiner's warning and the noisy opposition of her subjects. Parliament reluctantly agreed only after guarantees were given that Philip would not drag England into his continental wars against France, and that he would have no rights in England if Mary died childless. Even so the marriage announcement triggered three rebellions in 1554. The most serious of these was organized in Kent under the leadership of Sir Thomas Wyatt, the son of the poet. His followers were joined by troops who had defected from the Queen. The rebels could have captured Mary if they had not delayed in their attack on London, but by the time they entered London, loyal troops had been assembled and the rebels were defeated. Although Lady Jane Grey was not implicated in the uprising, she and her husband were put to death along with Wyatt.

Persecution of Protestants. By 1555 Queen Mary, sickly and slighted by her husband, tried to speed up the pace of orthodoxy by burning out Protestantism. However, the three hundred burnings at Smithfield, including those of Bishops Hooper, Latimer, Ridley, and Archbishop Cranmer, backfired and evoked sympathy for the persecuted and quickly turned public opinion against Mary and her cause. Ironically, her policy of persecution contributed significantly to the permanence of Protestantism in England.

Foreign Policy. Mary's foreign policy was no more successful than her domestic policy. Declining trade, a recalcitrant Parliament that was opposed to voting taxes for the Queen, and the growing influence of Calvinism in Scotland made her efforts in foreign policy appear fitful. In addition, the quarrel between Pope Paul IV and King Philip, her husband, complicated Mary's religious loyalties. Philip enlisted Mary's aid in 1557 in fighting France for purely Spanish objectives. The English were humiliated by the loss of their last French possession, Calais, in the war.

Death of Mary. The disastrous but brief career of Mary Tudor came to an end with her death in November, 1558. Mary had tried to restore the past but had failed to take into account English nationalism which resented subservience to either Rome or Madrid. The result was that both her life and her reign were barren and tragic.

Chapter 8 ❧ Elizabethan England

After Mary's dismal reign England passed to one of her most glorious ages under Elizabeth I. During her long reign (1558-1603) Queen Elizabeth practiced moderation in an age of religious and political fanaticism in order to provide peace and prosperity for her nation. She also managed to stimulate an esprit and self-confidence in her subjects unmatched in English history. She was not an originator in government; rather she gave free reign to her subjects and allied their individual interests with her state policies. Elizabeth left as her legacy a firmly established Church of England, an influential middle class friendly to the Crown, and a vigorous, increasingly assertive House of Commons. Parliament had little quarrel with the Queen, since no monarch became as popular as Elizabeth or won such loyalty from the people.

The Religious Settlement

The failure of her sister to restore Catholicism in England was not lost on Elizabeth. Besides, she had not forgotten the fact that she was a child of a marriage that the Catholic church refused to recognize. Therefore, it was only logical that Elizabeth should drop the Catholicizing policy of Mary. The outcome was the establishment of a national Church of England that settled for a compromise between Roman Catholicism and Protestantism. Its doctrines were broad enough to satisfy most Englishmen and to spare England the religious wars that wracked France and Germany.

The Elizabethan Compromise. Elizabeth was neither bigoted nor particularly religious, but she could not avoid involvement in the intense religious climate of the times. Her religious settlement restored Protestantism, created a national church and a clergy responsible to the Crown, and produced a church service that was made binding by an act of Parliament. It was, in effect, a lay revolution carried out by the Crown and by the Commons against the will of the bishops.

Parliamentary Religious Acts. Queen Elizabeth's first Parliament in 1559 repealed the heresy acts of Mary's reign and passed the Act of Supremacy, which abolished papal allegiance and recognized Elizabeth as Supreme Governor of the Church of England. Parliament then passed the Act of Uniformity to restore the Second Prayer Book, established the only legal form of public worship, and set up the Court of the High Commission to enforce it. In 1562 Cranmer's Forty-two Articles were modified to Thirty-nine and adopted by convocation; in 1571 they were imposed by Parliament as the doctrine of the Anglican church. The Articles were framed in such a manner that varied interpretations of doctrine could be held, and, with certain revisions, they have remained the basic doctrines of faith of the Anglican church.

Religious Offices. All Government and church officials were required to take an oath of allegiance to the new Queen and governor of the church. Again, as under Henry VIII and Edward VI, these religious changes were passed by Parliament rather than by church convocation. Except for the bishops appointed under Mary, the vast majority of the clergy accepted the religious settlement. These Catholic prelates lost their sees and were replaced by reformed clergy, many of whom were in exile during Mary's reign. The Protestant scholar, Matthew Parker, became Archbishop of Canterbury. If the religious settlement did not evoke much enthusiasm in the country, certainly there was little protest, and it went into effect with little friction or persecution at first.

Later Religious Developments. The Elizabethan settlement, however, did not please Roman Catholics or radical Protestants. Both made efforts to promote their religious viewpoint at the expense of the settlement and brought upon themselves increasing restrictions. The Catholics suffered most because their religious loyalty was also a threat to the Tudor state.

Roman Catholics. The Government's refusal to persecute passive Catholics upset the more militant Catholics who saw their cause withering when their coreligionists found they could live quite comfortably under the Elizabethan settlement. When Pope Pius V excommunicated Elizabeth in 1570 and absolved her subjects from allegiance to her, religious peace disappeared as many English Catholics were forced to choose between their faith and their Queen. During this time two English Catholic seminaries were established on the Continent, and by 1580 over one hundred Catholic priests, under Jesuit leadership, were back in England reawakening Catholic opposition to Elizabeth. Mary, Queen of Scots, was recognized by Rome as the only lawful Catholic candidate for the English throne, and the pope and leading Catholic monarchs on the Continent backed plots on Elizabeth's life. The Government counterattacked by increasing its powers of repression. Fines jumped from one shilling to £20 a month for nonattendance at the Established church. Saying or hearing Mass brought imprisonment, and Catholic priests were charged with treason. After 1581, executions of proselyting Catholics increased. Elizabeth claimed that she punished for political treason, but the cause motivating the Catholic resistance was their faith. Approximately two hundred Catholics were executed during her reign.

The Puritans. While the Catholics were challenging the Anglican settlement from without, members within the Anglican church were also demanding changes. The Puritans wanted to purge all practices that still savored of popery; they favored a more Calvinistic doctrine and wanted a presbyterian, rather than an episcopal, form of church government. The House of Commons became increasingly Puritan in its sympathies and tried to remodel the doctrine and organization of the church with legislation introduced by Walter Strickland, Peter Wentworth, and Thomas Norton. Queen Elizabeth blocked all changes, arguing that religion, like foreign policy and the succession to the throne, was an exclusive preserve of the monarchy and not the business of Parliament. Thwarted in Parliament, the Puritans turned to congregational meetings and pamphlet warfare. Thomas Cartwright, dismissed from Cambridge for his Puritan beliefs, was one of the leading polemicists to argue for a church government on the Geneva model. In the 1580's Puritan preachers began the classical movement in an attempt to reform the church from within by building up a presbyterian organization on the parish level which would lead, hopefully, to a national synod.

The Separatists. The radical Protestants who considered the reform of the Anglican church hopeless formed separate organizations outside of it. They were known usually by the names of their founders—Brownists (Robert Browne), Barrowists (Norman Barrow)—and were predecessors of the Congregationalists. They stressed congregational autonomy and separation of church and state.

Government Response. The Government took repressive measures against Separatist groups because they repudiated the national church, and because the Government considered religious uniformity essential to political unity. The powers of the Court of High Commission were enlarged to permit it to try all cases of nonconformity. Soon Brownists and English Anabaptists were forced to flee the country. In 1583 Elizabeth appointed John Whitgift, the severest critic of the Puritans, Archbishop of Canterbury. Immediately he used his position and the power of the court to penalize opponents without and within the church.

John Knox and the Church of Scotland. The Scottish Church on the eve of the Reformation was both corrupt and wealthy and seemingly ripe for reform. The course of religious change was largely a result of the leadership of John Knox and the political and personal issues created by Mary Stuart. In contrast to England the Reformation in Scotland was promoted by the nobility over the opposition of the Crown.

John Knox (1505-72). Knox was a priest actively interested in the reform of the church and strongly opposed to the French-Catholic regency in Scotland. While in exile on the Continent because of his beliefs, he became a disciple of John Calvin in Geneva. He returned to Scotland in 1558—the same year that the Dauphin of France married Mary Stuart and publicized her right to the English throne. Since the Scots feared absorption into a French-Catholic empire, four Protestant nobles formed a group called the Lords of the Congregation and requested major church reforms from the regent, Mary of Guise (mother of Mary Stuart). When the demands were rejected, Knox rallied the reformers with his evangelistic zeal, and civil war broke out. Only the reluctant intervention by Queen Elizabeth saved the reformers from defeat by the regent's French army.

Treaty of Edinburgh, 1560. The terms of the treaty required the French to withdraw from Scotland and ended three centuries of Franco-Scottish ties. The treaty also contributed to the triumph of Protestantism over Catholicism in Scotland and England. The firm alliance of these two Protestant countries permitted a longer peace between them than heretofore.

The Scottish Parliament. In 1560 the Scottish Parliament broke relations with Rome, banned the Mass, and adopted a Calvinistic profession of faith and a book of discipline prepared by the first General Assembly of the Church of Scotland. When Mary of Guise died that same year, a council of twelve was set up to govern Scotland until Mary Stuart returned from France.

Elizabethan Foreign Policy

For a quarter of a century Elizabeth maintained a clever, yet precarious, neutrality in foreign affairs. The fact that neither France nor Spain subdued the much weaker England was due to the rivalry between these two Catholic countries, and even more to the astute diplomacy of Elizabeth and her brilliant statesmen. With the breathing spell won by this period of nominal peace, England increased national finances, strengthened commercial and maritime power, and developed self-confidence.

Elizabeth and Her Advisers. Undoubtedly, the success of Elizabeth's reign was to a large extent dependent upon her ability to govern and by her selection of wise and loyal advisers. Like Henry VIII, she became an astute political manager.

Character of the Queen. When Elizabeth came to the throne at the age of twenty-five, the country was split by religious faction, trade and finances were in disarray, a worthless war with France still dragged on, and Englishmen were very skeptical about serving another female monarch. However, the Queen soon demonstrated that she possessed the abilities that had been lacking in her half-sister, Mary. Although Elizabeth was vain and iron-willed, she had remarkable political understanding and a personal magnetism that attracted devoted followers. She loved power, but her shrewd mind knew when to concede small points in order to win major ones. Unlike Queen Mary, Elizabeth understood that the strength of the English monarchy, since it lacked a royal army, must be built upon popular consent. Like her father, Elizabeth was well-educated; she loved literature and could speak and write six languages.

The Queen's Advisers. Elizabeth had several shallow court favorites who pleased her vanity, but to hold major offices in the Privy Council she chose experienced and devoted laymen, largely from the gentry class. William Cecil, later Lord Burghley, was Secretary and chief counselor for forty years. His brother-in-law, Sir Nicholas Bacon, was lord chancellor. Robert Dudley, earl of Leicester, was one of the Queen's closest favorites and at one time a probable choice as husband. Sir Francis Walsingham served as ambassador to France and with Cecil organized an effective intelligence service to protect the Queen from foreign attempts on her life.

The Diplomacy of Neutrality. The rivalry between France and Spain was Elizabeth's chief asset in 1558. For the next thirty years she used her shrewdness and her marriageable hand to preserve England from foreign attack and to make the nation prosperous and confident of its abilities.

France. In 1559 the Treaty of Cateau-Cambrésis, which ended the war between France and her enemies, Spain and England, gave Elizabeth the peace that she considered essential to the national welfare. France now became England's most immediate threat when King Francis II openly supported the claim of his wife, Mary

Stuart, to the English throne. However, his sudden death in 1560 left his young widow shorn of French support. The outbreak of the religious wars between Catholics and Huguenots (French Protestants) in 1562 caused Elizabeth to intervene on the side of the Huguenots and to send troops to Le Havre. The war with France was a blunder, and the English garrison in Le Havre surrendered in 1563. Calais was not recovered, and the whole affair was an object lesson to Elizabeth and Cecil. Thereafter, they gave aid secretly to the Huguenots while holding France in line by considering marriage offers from King Charles IV and later from his brothers, the Duke of Anjou, and the Duke of Alençon.

Spain. At first Spain supported Elizabeth and her title to the throne. Despite his hatred of heretics, Philip II was unwilling to have England brought back into the Catholic fold as a province of his enemy, France. He therefore proposed marriage to Elizabeth. Elizabeth was hard put to decline because she could not risk a French-Spanish coalition against her, but neither could she bear Spanish-Catholic domination if she accepted. With typical contrivance she procrastinated so long over Philip's proposal, he finally took a French wife. Gradually, English-Spanish relations worsened as France dropped its designs on England, and as Elizabeth and Philip became the recognized leaders of the Protestant and Catholic camps. By avoiding any deliberate offense against Spain, Elizabeth kept the peace. But she condoned raids on Spanish shipping and colonies by English seamen and gave secret aid to Spain's rebelling subjects in the Netherlands. In turn, Philip aided plots to place Mary Stuart on the English throne.

Ireland. During much of her reign Elizabeth was engaged in suppressing Irish rebellions. A serious revolt occurred in 1598 when Hugh O'Neill, earl of Tyrone, enlisted the aid of Spain and of the pope and crushed the English army at Blackwater before the Spanish forces arrived. Elizabeth's court favorite, the Earl of Essex, landed with reinforcements, but proved to be a worthless field commander. Upon his return to England, Essex was imprisoned and later executed when he entered a conspiracy to overthrow the Government. Lord Mountjoy, who replaced Essex in command, defeated the Irish and the Spaniards, and again, for a time, there was the peace of submission in Ireland.

The Threat of Mary Stuart. Mary Stuart returned to Scotland in 1561 content with neither the Protestant supremacy won the previous year, nor with her position as Queen of Scotland. She spent her days intriguing to become Queen of England as well. The young widow was a fascinating and passionate woman who found the drab Scottish court contrary to her style of living. In 1565 she married her cousin, Lord Darnley, who was a descendant of Henry VII of England. This marriage further strengthened her claim to the English succession. During the next three years Mary succeeded in alienating most of her subjects, both Protestant and Catholic. She quickly lost the support of the Protestant Lords and confided constantly in her private secretary, David Rizzio, who was murdered before her eyes by her jealous husband. After giving birth to a son, Mary fell desperately in love with a Protestant border lord, the Earl of Bothwell, who superintended the murder of Darnley. Upon obtaining a divorce from his wife, Bothwell and Mary were married according to Protestant rites. These events aroused Protestants and Catholics to rebel against the Queen. Mary was imprisoned and forced to abdicate in favor of her son, James VI. In 1568 Mary escaped from prison, tried but failed to regain her throne, and fled to England to ask sanctuary from her cousin, Elizabeth. A Protestant regency succeeded her in Scotland.

For the next nineteen years Mary Stuart served as a magnet for plots against Elizabeth. The royal advisers urged Elizabeth to get rid of Mary, because her very presence was a threat to the Queen's security; but Elizabeth disliked the idea of beheading monarchs and refused to act.

Marriage Diplomacy. Parliament and the people were anxious for Elizabeth to marry in order to preserve the Tudor and Protestant succession. There was no doubt that if the heir presumptive, Mary Stuart, came to the throne, a religious and civil war was almost a certainty. Yet, if the Queen were to marry an English lord, this too would create jealousy. In the first two years of her reign Elizabeth received fifteen foreign proposals of marriage, most of them from Catholic princes; however, she preferred her independence. Certainly, her father's six marriages and Mary Tudor's sorry match had not served as very inspiring examples. Besides, Elizabeth's marriageable state gave her great flexibility in foreign diplomacy and an opportunity to play her hand with almost Machiavellian detachment. She apparently had real affection for only one suitor: Robert Dudley, earl of Leicester.

Plots against Elizabeth. As long as Mary Stuart remained alive and in England, there were repeated conspiracies against the throne of Elizabeth. The plots had as their objectives the full recognition of Mary Stuart as Queen of England and the reestablishment of Catholicism.

Rising of the Northern Earls, 1569. The old nobility of the north were reluctant to submit to the authority of Cecil and other "new men" who were administering the Tudor state. Their plan called for the Duke of Norfolk to wed Mary and reign with her after Elizabeth's death, thereby restoring the power of the old nobility in London. The rebellion, led by Norfolk and the Earls of Westmorland and Northumberland, was easily crushed because English Catholics failed to support it. Northumberland and eight hundred rebel recruits were executed on orders from Elizabeth.

Ridolfi Plot, 1571. Another conspiracy to seize the throne for Mary was concocted by the Italian banker, Ridolfi, with the support of the pope and Philip II. The plotters arranged for the marriage of Mary and the Duke of Norfolk to be the signal for an armed English Catholic revolt and a Spanish invasion. William Cecil caught the plan before it could fully develop, and Norfolk was executed.

Throckmorton Plot, 1583. Francis Throckmorton served as the liaison agent between the Spanish ambassador, Mendoza, the French, and the imprisoned Mary Stuart. Their scheme was to rally English Catholics and overthrow the government of Elizabeth. When apprehended Throckmorton was tortured into a confession and later executed.

Babington Plot, 1586. The plot suggested by Anthony Babington was similar to the others: to murder Elizabeth and put Mary Stuart on the throne. Walsingham allowed secret correspondence between Mary and Babington to continue until he had names and evidence. It was this evidence that finally persuaded Elizabeth to consent to Mary's execution. Babington and his associates were killed, and Mary was found guilty by both Parliament and the law courts. Elizabeth procrastinated until February, 1587, before she finally signed Mary's death warrant.

The War with Spain

The drift of events led England into a war with Spain that Elizabeth and Cecil had struggled to avert for decades. But by 1588 the confrontation was watched with keen interest by all Europe for its outcome would have religious and political consequences affecting the whole Continent. The invincible Armada failed, and Spain's great prestige began to wane; nevertheless, the Armada was the beginning, and not the end, of the war against Spain. In history, the legend of the Armada, like the Magna Charta, became a "heroic apologue of the defense of freedom against tyranny."[1]

---

[1] Garrett Mattingly, *The Armada* (Boston: Houghton Mifflin, 1959), p. 401.

Steps to War. By 1580 only England seemed to stand in the way of Spain's military and political hegemony over Europe. King Philip II persuaded himself that for religious, commercial, political, and personal reasons he had cause to invade England.

Religious Rivalry. Philip was convinced that his divinely inspired mission was to restore religious orthodoxy to Europe. Of the Protestant triumvirate, William of Orange in Holland, Admiral Coligny, leader of the French Huguenots, and Elizabeth, only Elizabeth was left. Coligny was murdered by French Catholics in 1572, and William by an assassin in Spanish pay in 1584. By elimination Elizabeth was the obvious leader of Protestant Europe, and Catholic plots on her life were constantly being projected.

The War in the Netherlands. The Protestant provinces of the Spanish Netherlands were still in open revolt against Spain because of steady English support of the Dutch Sea Beggars. Philip knew that Dutch resistance would be maintained so long as the rebels received aid from England and England controlled the sea route to Antwerp. Elizabeth aided the Dutch rebels because she feared that a Spanish reconquest would end a profitable trade with the Netherlands and would prepare the way for an invasion of England.

Maritime Friction. In 1580 Spain annexed Portugal, and their combined colonial empires gave Philip fabulous overseas wealth. But for over a quarter of a century English sea dogs had been harrying the Atlantic and the Spanish Main, capturing treasure ships, breaking the Spanish monopoly on the slave trade, and suffering few casualties. These adventurers, among whom the most famous were Sir John Hawkins, Sir Francis Drake, Sir Martin Frobisher, and Sir Richard Grenville, were never publicly supported by the Crown; however, Elizabeth backed them privately, knighted them, and took her share of the profits. Goaded to fury, the Spaniards saw no way of assuring control of the seas and stopping this pirateering without defeating England.

Effects of Mary Stuart's Execution. Mary's death forced the issue of succession since she had been the intended instrument of the Catholics for regaining the throne of England from within. While Mary Stuart lived, Philip hesitated to risk Spanish money and blood to win England for her, because she favored France over Spain. Within a week of the news of Mary's execution, Philip moved rapidly with plans for an invasion, even though there was no guarantee that English Catholics would rally to the banner of a hated Spaniard when Spanish troops landed in England.

The Spanish Armada. Philip's plan was to send a great Armada to the Netherlands and ferry the Duke of Parma and the best army in Europe to England, where he hoped that English Catholics would rise in revolt. The whole venture from the beginning was plagued by mishaps. Spain's leading admiral, the Marquis of Santa Cruz, died and was replaced by the old Duke of Medina Sidonia. Sir Francis Drake sailed into Cadiz harbor in 1587 and sank thousands of tons of shipping and stores which delayed the expedition for a year. The army of the Duke of Parma was blockaded by Dutch and English forces and did not rendezvous as planned. Nevertheless, on July 29, 1588, the Armada of one hundred and thirty-one ships was sighted by the English in the Channel.

The Channel Battle. For nine days Admiral Howard's English fleet of smaller and faster ships kept up a running battle but could not break the crescent-shaped formation of the Spaniards. While the Armada anchored for provisions at Calais, the English drove the fleet into confusion with fire ships. On the next day the English cannonade destroyed four Spanish galleons and inflicted heavy damage in the decisive battle fought off Gravelines. Not able to reach Parma, or collect supplies, or retrace its course, the Armada sailed north around the British Isles where fierce storms did even more damage than the English navy. In September the incompetent Medina Sidonia returned to Spain with two-thirds of his fleet—the invasion had failed.

Significance of the Armada. The defeat at sea did not crush Spain or immediately transfer command of the seas from Spain to England. More treasure ships reached Spain in the next fifteen years than in any other similar period. Nevertheless, the defeat of the Armada had important consequences. It saved England from Parma's powerful army and at the same time united English Catholics and Protestants against a common enemy. Equally important, the defeat of the Armada prevented the imposition of both a Catholic and a Spanish hegemony over Europe by force and gave heart to the Dutch rebels to continue their fight for independence. There were also repercussions in the colonial world as the breaking of Spanish sea power opened up new regions in both the Far East and in America. English and Dutch squadrons challenged the fading Portuguese empire in the East, and the French and the English no longer hesitated to settle America. Finally, to Elizabeth and her people the events in the year 1588 reinforced their belief that God and good fortune were on their side, and over the years the legend of victory became an increasingly eulogized example of typical English spirit.

The War Continues. The Armada marked the beginning of a war with Spain that dragged on for the remaining fourteen years of

Elizabeth's reign. The English counterattack on Spain in 1589 under Drake was a fiasco. An invasion force of 150 ships and 1800 men attacked Spain but failed miserably, as disease decimated the land army, and Drake refused to attack Lisbon. English mariners intermittently harassed the Spanish in the Azores, and in 1595 both Drake and Hawkins died in an expedition to the West Indies. Elizabeth became deeply involved in struggles on the Continent by providing English troops to serve regularly in the Netherlands against the Spanish, and in northern France. Between 1589 and 1595, when the assassination of Henry III, the last of the Valois line, made the Protestant Henry of Navarre titular King of France, Elizabeth sent five expeditions to support Henry of Navarre and to block Spain's designs on France. Although Henry became a Catholic in 1593 to win Paris, neither he nor Elizabeth abandoned the Anglo-French alliance until France concluded a peace with Spain in 1598.

In 1596 Howard, Essex, and Sir Walter Raleigh left Cadiz in ruins, and in the following year King Philip retaliated by supporting the Irish rebellion with a second Armada; but it too was dispersed by a gale. The Irish rebellion preoccupied England and cost the English treasury much more than did the repulse of the Armada of 1588. Elizabeth was forced to grant monopolies, increase customs, and sell £876,332 of Crown lands, as well as raise an additional £2 million in taxes to finance the war.

Economic and Colonial Expansion

During the Elizabethan Age prices, trade, and prosperity increased as the commercial revolution and the rise of small industry improved the lot of the merchant, the gentry, and the yeoman. In contrast, the depressed classes often became a floating population of vagabonds and unemployed. The Government recognized the need of dealing with the unemployed poor and introduced economic and industrial legislation in Parliament.

Agriculture. Since the country gentry who administered the laws did not push any enforcement that conflicted with their own interests, the enclosure movement continued in spite of laws passed to restrict it. Wheat raising competed with sheep raising as the rapid growth of towns increased the demand for foodstuffs.

Labor and Welfare Laws. Elizabeth practiced a strict economy by calling in the debased currency early in her reign and replacing it with sound money to restore the country's credit. However, she still had the problem of unemployed poor drifting around the country and supporting any rebellion. Because of this the Government passed more economic legislation—the Parliament of 1563 alone passed fourteen statutes—than in any previous reign.

The Statute of Artificers (or Statute of Apprentices), 1563. The Statute of Artificers transferred the regulation of labor and industry from local to national control in an effort to halt vagrancy by promoting full employment. The act was an attempt to control and recruit labor by enforcing the seven-year apprenticeship in the trades, requiring unskilled labor to work in agriculture in rush seasons if needed, and providing for local justices of the peace to regulate wages and hours.

Poor Laws, 1597, 1601. The plague and the harvest failures of the 1590's caused the Government to nationalize poor relief because municipal relief was too limited and erratic to handle the distress. Here the state took over the earlier role of the church in administering charity, motivated more by fear, than by humanitarianism, of what wandering, hungry people could do. The act made the parish the local unit of administration and leveled stiff penalties for vagrancy. Each parish appointed four overseers who levied rates (compulsory taxes) on property owners in order to build workhouses and provide work and wages for the unemployed. Although considered harsh, the Poor Law became the cornerstone for much later social welfare legislation.

Commerce and Industry. The cloth trade continued as the leading industry. In foreign trade the Merchant Adventurers replaced the Staplers as the most powerful export group after they received a royal charter in 1564. Shipbuilding and coal mining grew rapidly, and new industries, such as salt and alum, became important. The Tudors tightened state controls in order to encourage home industries and to promote a favorable balance of trade. This policy, sometimes termed "mercantilism," was done on a piece-meal basis for specific objectives (as to help fishermen or export traders by legislative acts) and not as part of any doctrinaire view on economics.

Colonies and Chartered Companies. Overseas expansion began much later than that of Portugal or Spain, because those countries had the fleets and power to back up their ventures, whereas England was absorbed in establishing a new dynasty and a new church. John Cabot in 1497, exploring for an English company, discovered Newfoundland and thus provided England with a basis for future claims to North America. John Hawkins broke into the lucrative Spanish monopoly of the slave trade between Africa and the West Indies at the same time the sea dogs were exploring the New World and Sir Francis Drake was making his spectacular voyage around the world (1577-80). Three relatives, Sir Humphrey Gilbert, Sir Walter Raleigh, and Sir Richard Grenville, backed by a royal charter, tried to colonize Newfoundland (1583) and Virginia (1585, 1587), but their efforts were unsuccessful. Martin Frobisher explored northeastern Canada (1576) while searching for a Northwest Passage. With the rise of the merchant navy English foreign commerce expanded through new trading companies chartered by Queen Elizabeth: these included the Muscovy Company (1553), the Levant Company (1592), and the East India Company (1600). The influence of English sea power was just beginning to be felt.

The Machinery of Government

The so-called Tudor despotism of the sixteenth century was actually an authoritarian, yet popular, Government that "provided peace and order without despotism." [2] In the political transformation from a medieval to a national state two important developments took place: the central administration became national and public in scope to replace the medieval practice of the King's Household administering a private estate; and the House of Commons increased in size and significance and became a major instrument of Government.

The Administration. Thomas Cromwell was the chief architect of the administrative reform which transformed a Household administration into a Government regardless of the leadership of the King. Royal administration, both on the local level and in Parliament, relied on the rising gentry class; both worked well together, particularly during the years when the Crown and the gentry had the same aims and felt threatened by either civil war or external invasion.

The Central Government. The center of administrative control from the time of Henry VIII was the Privy Council; it became a formal executive body that took over the functions formerly handled by Household officers. The highest policy decisions, of course, were still made by the monarch. The Council itself was responsible to the sovereign and not to Parliament (in contrast to the present-day Cabinet). An enormous increase in Council business and specialization took place under Henry VIII and Elizabeth with the result that the Household deteriorated into a department of state con-

---

2 G. R. Elton, *The Tudor Revolution in Government* (Cambridge: University Press, 1960), p. 2.

cerned with particular tasks about the sovereign's person. Finances, for example, were under a reformed Exchequer and not under the Treasurer of the Chamber. The Council acquired judicial powers as well as supervisory functions over the Councils of the North and the Marchers (Wales). There was no attempt to find unanimity among the councilors. Rival factions reflecting different viewpoints appealed to Queen Elizabeth. In this way she was informed of possible alternatives in policy, and, at the same time, the Privy Councilors realized that they were not indispensable. When Parliament was in session, councilors drafted Government bills and piloted them through the two Houses as the Ministers do today.

Local Government. The substitution of the parish for the earlier manor or village as a local unit of administration was one of the developments of Elizabeth's reign. The church wardens and the overseers of the poor, supported by the county justices of the peace, administered the Poor Law under the supervision of the Privy Council. On the county level the post of Lord-Lieutenant was created in the 1550's whereby a peer, and frequently a Privy Councilor, served as the formal contact between the central Government and the local administration; he was responsible for the local militia and all emergency measures. However, the justices of the peace were the indispensable officers in local government, and the great increase in their number and the greater diversification of their duties reflected the rising power of the gentry and the efficiency of their work. These unpaid local magistrates presided over local courts, regulated new laws on labor and apprentices, kept the peace, enforced the Poor Laws, and punished vagabonds and absentees from church. Other local officials linking the counties with London were the sheriff, the coroner who investigated sudden deaths and empanelled juries, and the vice-admirals of the coastal counties.

The Courts. The legal profession and legal business expanded greatly in the Tudor period. Also at the same time the authority of statute law was enhanced by the prominence given to it by Henry VIII and the Reformation Parliament. The Inns of Court and the common law resumed their stature under Queen Elizabeth after faltering in the reigns of Henry VIII and Mary. The regular courts consisted of (1) the Petty Sessions, presided over by two or more justices of the peace, which considered minor charges; (2) the Quarter Sessions, meeting four times yearly, which considered more serious county cases; (3) the Assizes where royal judges on circuit presided; and (4) the Common Law Courts at Westminster —King's Bench, Common Pleas, and Exchequer. The prerogative courts of the Crown with no jury were the Chancery, which considered cases of equity and important civil cases; Court of the High Commission, for religious offenses; Court of the North, for northern England; Council of Wales; Court of Castle Chamber, for Ireland; and Court of the Star Chamber.

Parliament. Parliament became increasingly important as an instrument of Government after Henry VIII employed it to complete his break with Rome. Parliamentary proceedings were effectively managed by the Tudors, but only because they were adroit in political maneuvers and because the gentry were co-operative. Thus the Parliaments did not have to be packed to secure a favorable vote. Under Elizabeth Parliament perfected some procedures: three readings for each bill was established; a standing committee for privileges and disputed elections existed after 1588; and the committee system for examining bills was accepted. At the beginning of each session Parliament claimed from the Queen freedom of speech and freedom from arrest.

House of Commons. The Commons gained greatly in power since it represented the growing influence of the middle class—the gentry, the lawyers, and the merchants. The membership of the Commons increased during the sixteenth century from 296 to 462.

House of Lords. The Lords often influenced the selection of members to the House of Commons, but as a class they never exerted the power that they had before the Wars of the Roses. All baronial rebellions against the Tudors failed. The new aristocracy was frequently a creation of the Tudors and, therefore, indebted to them; besides, the removal of the abbots from the Lords and the royal appointment of the remaining bishops gave the monarch direct control of one-third of the Upper House.

The Tudor System. The medieval concept of a king with unlimited authority only in certain recognized spheres was somewhat undermined in practice by the Tudors. However, they were astute enough not to enunciate any doctrine of absolutism for, unlike France, they had no standing army or professional bureaucracy to back such a claim. Instead, Tudor Government relied on the voluntary services of local administrators and on the co-operation of the Crown and loyal subjects. By the end of Elizabeth's reign the House of Commons was becoming vigorous and vocal under such a system and was expanding its privileges.

The Last Years of Elizabeth. By 1590 England felt secure from religious wars and Spanish attack. Therefore, Parliament became restive and grumbled about the cost of the war against Spain and Ireland, censured the Queen for the granting of royal monopolies in

1597, and delayed the passage of bills for as long as four years. Yet direct protest was muted out of respect and affection for the aged Queen; the Commons reserved its opposition for her successor. Elizabeth had refused to name a successor until she reached her deathbed; she then nominated King James VI of Scotland. Her chief adviser, Robert Cecil, son of William Cecil, completed arrangements for a smooth transition of power. In 1603 the dynasty ended with the death of the greatest of the Tudors.

Learning and Literature

The spirit and vitality of the Elizabethan age is perhaps best expressed in its literature. The Renaissance and the Reformation, in different ways, helped mould this literature which assumed a distinctly English character that reflected the new nationalism and revealed a self-questioning and a self-conscious maturity. The awakening was all the more striking because, except for Chaucer, this caliber of writing was previously lacking in English literature. However, no comparable achievement occurred in education.

Tudor Education.   Renaissance scholars turned away from scholasticism and contributed new ideas on learning, especially in the study of Greek classics, whereas the Reformation reduced church influence on education. But the dissolution of the monasteries under Henry VIII and of the chantries under Edward VI closed many elementary schools when the endowments were lost. Not until the end of Elizabeth's reign did the patronage of clergy and nobility restore the grammar schools. In the universities the Renaissance provided some reforms and foundation money, but the Reformation also brought on disputes and division, and only later a greater diversity of knowledge and a freer spirit. Oxford was more affected than Cambridge by the Reformation in its monastic and faculty losses, but continued to be the larger university. Cambridge advanced greatly after the Reformation in size and influence. Elizabeth's inner circle of councilors were all Cambridge men, and the church, from Cranmer to Bancroft, was led by Cambridge scholars. Since Cambridge was more Protestant than Oxford, it stimulated intellectual vigor and controversy as the Puritans grew in power; three of the seven new colleges at Cambridge were established as a direct result of the Puritan impulse. Little change in curriculum took place; theology, logic, and philosophy were still the central studies, although the tutorial system altered teaching methods.

Literature.   The religious and political controversies prior to the middle of the sixteenth century did not encourage scholarship or literary productivity. The real flowering of Renaissance letters with its amazing range of writing occurred during Elizabeth's reign.

Prose. The works of Elizabethan prose writers typically reflect the varied interests of the Renaissance. (1) Roger Ascham, Elizabeth's tutor and secretary, produced an admirable treatise on political education in *The Scholemaster.* It was a plea for the study of classical literature and gentle manners in the public schools. (2) Ralph Holinshed's patriotic *Chronicles* became the source materials for the historical plays of Shakespeare and Marlowe. (3) John Lyly portrayed society in two books on court etiquette and mannerisms, *Euphues* and *Euphues and His England.* His ornate, elaborately-structured prose became a popular vogue. (4) Richard Hakluyt in his *Principal Navigations, Voyages and Discoveries of the English Nation,* John Leland in *The Laborious Journey,* and William Harrison with his *Description of England* stimulated popular interest in geography. and history. (5) The versatile Sir Walter Raleigh, besides being a courtier, financier, explorer, and poet, composed a remarkable *History of the World.* (6) Sir Francis Bacon's *Essays* offered wordly wisdom in an epigrammatic style. His intellectual and philosophical brilliance was observed more sharply in his writings during the reign of James I. (7) Richard Hooker furnished the ablest apologia for the Elizabethan church with his judicious and balanced *Laws of Ecclesiastical Polity.*

Poetry. Before Elizabeth's reign only three Tudor poets claim recognition: John Skelton (1460?-1529) with his satirical *Speke, Parrot* on Cardinal Wolsey, and Thomas Wyatt (1503?-1542) who, along with Henry Howard, the Earl of Surrey (1517?-1542), introduced the sonnet form to England—Wyatt the Italian or Petrarchan form, Surrey the English or Shakespearean. During Elizabeth's reign came the three leading poets of the century, Sir Philip Sidney, Edmund Spenser, and William Shakespeare. Sidney, a gentleman, scholar, courtier, and knight, was the ideal Elizabethan man of letters. His two most admired works are *Astrophel and Stella* (sonnets), and *The Defence of Poesie,* a lofty and imaginative treatise on the art of poetry. Spenser was the poet's poet and his works provided a new stanza of nine lines, a richness of imagery, and a high seriousness that many later poets imitated. His two most noted works are *The Shepherds' Calendar* and *The Faerie Queene.* Shakespeare's non-dramatic poems were written early in his career and consisted of the *Sonnets* and the long narrative poems, *Venus and Adonis* and *Lucrece.*

Drama. No age approaches the Elizabethan in the excellence and variety of drama. Robert Greene, a bohemian university wit and journalist, wrote the farcical *Friar Bacon* and the historical play *James IV.* Christopher Marlowe died in a tavern brawl before he was thirty, but in his short life wrote the first great tragedies in blank verse that included *Tamburlaine, The Jew of Malta,* and *The Tragical History of Doctor Faustus.* Shakespeare climaxed the age with his thirty-four plays which so fully captured the spirit of the Elizabethans and the spirit of man. His plays have continued to be classics because of the universals and the characterizations that underlie them. He attempted all types—comedy, tragedy, and history —and triumphed in each area. Other playwrights of the period were Thomas Sackville (*Gorboduc*), Thomas Kyd (*Spanish Tragedy*), Nicholas Udall (*Ralph Roister Doister*), and Ben Jonson (*Every Man in His Humor*).

The Theater and the Court. At first plays were given in courtyards of inns, then, beginning in 1576, theaters were built in London which soon became the focus of popular entertainment. The Court was the acknowledged center of art and culture, and here the sophisticated, the social climbers, the professional politicians, and the new rich all vied for the honor of Elizabeth's favor.

Chapter 9 ⇜ King Versus Parliament

The first two Stuarts attempted to exert Tudor-like authority in England without the tact of the Tudors and came into conflict with the latent, but growing, power of the gentry. Parliamentary privilege versus royal prerogative became the focal point of the conflict and resulted in the alienation of the House of Commons.

The Religious Question

The growing Puritan influence among the gentry and the freedom from foreign invasion meant that the Elizabethan settlement could no longer remain safe from attack. James I, however, had no intention of sacrificing the episcopal structure. Since the ecclesiastical government was linked so closely to royal authority, King James argued that a retreat in religion was a retreat for royalty. Since neither compromise nor toleration in religion were considered virtues in this age, both the King and the Puritans took unyielding positions.

The Background of James. When Mary Stuart abdicated the throne and fled for safety to England, her only child became King of Scotland before he was a year old. For the next thirty-nine years James survived the plots of kidnappers, a grasping nobility, militant Presbyterian churchmen, and "a thousand intrigues" to prove himself the adept master of an unruly kingdom. He had received a superior education under the tutorship of George Buchanan and was scholarly and intelligent in a pedantic way. The King was a theorist, understanding books far better than he did his subjects—a French contemporary called him the "wisest fool in Christendom." In the Stuart tradition he believed that he was born to rule and wrote a treatise on the divine right of kings to support his argument for absolutism. James loved hunting, riding, and male favorites, and was inclined to be lazy and to conduct government affairs in an erratic manner.

Accession of James. James was overjoyed to become ruler of England and to leave Scotland and its Kirk for a richer and more secure kingdom where he could govern the church as well as the state. To that end he had handled his relations with Elizabeth most properly, even to the point of only mildly protesting to her the execution of his mother. Thus in 1603 when the two kingdoms were joined under one crown, it was the easiest accession of any new English dynasty. Elizabeth's acknowledgment, the support of Robert Cecil and the Privy Council, and the enthusiastic greeting of the people attested to the logic in their choice of the new King. But the Scottish King never fully grasped the differences between the two kingdoms, and his initial popularity soon faded.

Religious Hopes. Puritans and Catholics were optimistic that King James would be more sympathetic to their cause than was Elizabeth. The Puritans hoped that his years as King of Presbyterian Scotland would permit them to bring about reforms in England; the Catholics noted that his mother was Catholic and that James had been tolerant of the Catholic faith in Scotland and seemed friendly toward Spain. James could not please both parties and was rather content with the Elizabethan church.

Hampton Court Conference, 1604. Some eight hundred Puritan preachers presented the Millenary Petition to James in which they requested a simpler ritual than that decreed by Elizabeth, a greater emphasis on preaching, and the abolition of certain ceremonies, such as the cross in baptism. They also requested a new translation of the Bible. James granted the petitioners an audience at Hampton but became enraged by their suggestion to abolish the office of bishop. The conference ended with the Puritans dissatisfied and the King critical of their demands. The King's agreement to authorize a new version of the Bible (the King James Version, 1611) was the only constructive result.

Catholic Plots. When the early friendliness of King James to the Catholics changed to official disfavor, certain Catholics resorted to plots which threatened his life. The "By-Plot" of 1603 hoped to capture James, whereas the Gunpowder Plot of 1605 aimed at blowing up both the King and Parliament. Guy Fawkes was caught with kegs of gunpowder in the cellar of Parliament just before the session opened. This spectacular plot shocked the country and aroused Parliament to enact additional penalties against the Catholics. The Anglican settlement was not to be altered in the reign of James.

James and his Parliaments

Religion and finances became the leading issues generating friction between James and his Parliament. The King never appreciated two important differences between his two kingdoms: the power of the nobility and the weakness of Parliament in Scotland were not duplicated in seventeenth-century England. When Parliament had challenged the Crown in medieval days the powerful barons led the opposition; after 1604 the opposition came from the Commons.

Parliamentary Privileges. In 1604 few established rules existed that clearly indicated the rights and privileges of Parliament. The Commons, however, soon asserted its undefined privileges as inalienable rights and developed a political doctrine to back its position.

The First Parliament, 1604-11. The Goodwin Case which arose out of a disputed election created the first clash between the Crown and Parliament. The Commons argued that it, and not the Court of Chancery, was the judge of its own membership. Finally the King yielded, but with little grace. In 1606 the Exchequer Court found in favor of the King in the Bates Case. The decision recognized the right of the King to levy impositions of duties because there were no limitations on the King's power except his own forbearance. Both merchants and Parliament protested the additional customs. In the session of 1611 James offered to surrender some of his rights, such as wardship, in return for a guaranteed annual income of £200,000. However, the negotiations over this "Great Contract" broke down, whereupon James lectured the members on their failure to respect the prerogatives of the Crown and dismissed them. Parliament then sent an "Apology" to James that was actually a defense of their privileges. Such privileges, said the Apology, were derived from law and tradition, and not from the King.

The Second (or Addled) Parliament, 1614. After three years of trying to govern without parliamentary grants, King James was forced to call Parliament into session. The Commons demanded the redress of grievances before voting any money bills. After a stormy two-month session James dissolved Parliament because it had not passed any acts or granted him any money. For the next seven years James governed without Parliament, and to obtain revenue he exploited every possible resource at his disposal from forced loans to the selling of titles.

The Third Parliament, 1621. The Thirty Years' War caused James to summon this Parliament which promptly retaliated for the dismissal of Chief Justice Coke, the leading opponent of the royal prerogative, in 1616. Resurrecting its old weapon of impeachment, Parliament indicted two courtiers for abusing monopolies and the brilliant Sir Francis Bacon, the King's Chancellor, for receiving bribes. Parliament then examined foreign policy which James, like Elizabeth, considered none of their business. In the second session the King lost his temper over the freedom of speech issue and dissolved Parliament.

The Fourth Parliament, 1624. The King's last Parliament was the most friendly to him because it was anxious to fight Spain and the Catholic League and to assist the German Protestants. James permitted the members to debate foreign affairs, to impeach his financial genius and Treasurer, the Earl of Middlesex, and to invade the royal prerogative by limiting royal control over monopolies. Parliament subsidized an elaborate expedition against Spain. However, James died in 1625 before the fleet set sail.

Parliamentary Theory. The attack of the Commons on royal prerogatives and proclamations was supported by the common law courts which had formerly been allies of the Crown. Led by the tough, irascible Sir Edward Coke, Chief Justice of the Court of the King's Bench, the courts supported the assumption that parliamentary privileges had an ancient, and not necessarily royal, origin, that the King was under law (*rex sub lege*), and that the courts were independent of the Crown. They were not, however, as James proved by removing Chief Justice Coke. Nevertheless, the claims of the judges emboldened Parliament to continue its piecemeal encroachments on royal prerogatives. James was never browbeaten by his Parliaments and only gave in on the matter of royal monopolies because he knew when to compromise. He was wise enough to sense the danger signals and to warn his son, Charles.

Royal Favorites. At first James relied on Elizabeth's chief councilor, Robert Cecil, but gradually royal favorites replaced Cecil (who died in 1612 as Earl of Salisbury) and the Privy Council in influence. The two leading courtiers were Robert Carr, whom James made Earl of Somerset, and George Villiers, who eventually became Duke of Buckingham. The King's dependence on these incompetents aroused the resentment of the Court. With the rise of favorites the Councilors lost their influence on parliamentary legislation since they no longer introduced legislation, as previously in the days of Elizabeth. "By the third decade of the seventeenth century, the commons were in charge of the initiation, formulation, and passage of laws. They were the tail that wagged the dog." [1]

---

[1] George L. Haskins, *The Growth of English Representative Government* (London, 1948), pp. 126-7.

Foreign Affairs

James vigorously pursued a policy of peace even under the most trying conditions and succeeded, except during the first and last years of his reign. The Thirty Years' War caught him in a dilemma: he curried favor with Spain and hoped to marry his son to the Spanish Infanta; at the same time his daughter Elizabeth and her husband, the Elector of the Palatinate, were being harried by a Catholic coalition. England's old enmity toward Spain finally brought war in 1624 and reconciled Parliament to the King.

Scotland and Ireland. King James hoped for the union of England and Scotland, but Parliament was opposed to the idea and even refused free trade and English citizenship to the Scots. Except for removing the danger of border warfare and French influence in Scotland, the two countries remained separate nations with a common King for another century. James tried to pacify the Irish by having his Deputy terminate martial law, dismiss old charges against Irish rebels, and restore certain tribal lands to Irish tenants. However, the attempt to enforce the Anglican supremacy led to new uprisings in northern Ireland. The English Government responded by seizing land in six northern counties and settling Scotch Presbyterians, Welsh, and English in the area known as Ulster. Queen Elizabeth had introduced this Anglo-Protestant colonization and the Stuarts and Cromwell continued the settlement.

Spain. In 1604 James and Robert Cecil ended the war with Spain that had dragged on since the year of the Armada. The peace halted an expensive and fruitless war, but was unpopular in Parliament, particularly among the Puritans and the commercial class. When James pursued a pro-Spanish policy, he was greatly influenced by Buckingham and the Spanish ambassador, Count Gondomar. James had Sir Walter Raleigh executed to placate Spanish demands and attempted to negotiate a marriage between his heir, Charles, and the Spanish Infanta. Buckingham and Charles went to Spain to complete the negotiations but returned in 1623 humiliated and empty-handed—a slight which turned them into angry foes of Spain. Charles and Buckingham and Parliament eventually prevailed on the King to declare war on Spain in 1624. The twenty-year peace was over, and Buckingham dispatched a series of expeditions to the Continent, all of which were frightful failures. The first expedition to free the Palatinate failed because of mismanagement, sickness, and starvation.

The Thirty Years' War. In 1618 bitter religious wars broke out in Germany between the Protestant Union of principalities and the Catholic League. The war began in Bohemia where Protestants deposed their fanatical Catholic King and invited Frederick, the Elector of the Palatinate, to take the throne. The vengeance of the Catholics and the Hapsburgs was swift and cruel. After one winter of rule Frederick and Elizabeth (daughter of James) were ousted, and the Palatinate given to Maximilian of the Catholic League. This development complicated James's Spanish policy because the Spanish Hapsburgs had joined with the German Hapsburgs against Frederick. The flight of his daughter from Catholic forces and the failure of his son's marriage negotiations in Spain reversed James's policy and won him popularity with his subjects. But England had suffered from military stagnation for twenty years and was in no position to take effective action.

American Settlement. The unsuccessful efforts of the Elizabethans to colonize Virginia did not deter Englishmen from trying again a generation later. The London Company succeeded in establishing Jamestown in 1607 as England's first permanent colony. The export of tobacco propped up the colony's meager economy, and in 1619 Virginia set up the first colonial legislature fashioned on the parliamentary model of the mother country. In 1620 a second settlement colony was planted in Massachusetts by Separatists who left the Old World on the "Mayflower" in order to follow freely their religious beliefs in America. Nine years later, under a charter granted by King Charles, the Massachusetts Bay Colony provided a haven for English Puritans to set up their version of a Christian community. This colony prospered and a steady stream of immigrants gave it a population of fourteen thousand by 1640. Bermuda was also settled during the reign of King James and a legislature was introduced in 1624.

Charles I

Parliamentary and Puritan opposition coalesced in King Charles's reign (1625-49) to challenge his high-handed and small-minded manner of ruling. The King's expensive and futile foreign policy only added to his predicament. By ending the wars and governing without Parliament, Charles put off some of his problems, but neither he nor his advisers really understood or cared to grapple with the basic problem that plagued his reign: how to negotiate with a Parliament that refused to accept the traditional royal prerogatives.

Character of Charles. The twenty-five-year-old King was more dignified and attractive than his father, but, like his father, he held exalted notions of kingship and relied on royal favorites. Charles acquired a good reputation as a religious and family man; nevertheless, he was petty and indecisive and conspicuously lacked the art of political managership.

Foreign Affairs. After the pacifist policy of James, Charles and Buckingham promoted within four years six reckless military adventures against the German Catholics, Spain, and France, none of which succeeded. Thereafter, Charles, lacking financial subsidies from Parliament, because essentially a spectator in the political-religious maneuvers of the Thirty Years' War.

Spain. Charles asked his first Parliament (1625) for £40,000 to sustain the war against Spain but refused to discuss his campaign plans with Parliament. When the Commons refused to grant funds, Charles went ahead with his plans. The result was a badly-organized and ill-equipped expedition landing near Cadiz. The demoralized and drunken soldiers failed to take the city, and on the way back to England the fleet was mauled by a storm.

France. Meanwhile England was also drifting into conflict with France. Charles's marriage to Henrietta Maria, sister of Louis XIII, in the first week of his reign purchased a fleeting friendship with France but raised suspicions that the King was susceptible to Catholic influence. When English ships loaned to France were ordered by Cardinal Richelieu against the French Huguenots at La Rochelle, the crews mutinied. Months later war broke out between England and France (1627), and three expeditions were sent to relieve the beleaguered French Protestants at La Rochelle. Buckingham led the second expedition to the Isle of Rhé, where he was repulsed by the French after losing half of his men. In 1630 England made peace with France and Spain, and the nation now became preoccupied with internal controversies.

Charles and Parliament. Since Charles considered such matters as war and peace beyond the pale of parliamentary jurisdiction, he did not justify his requests for money. In turn Parliament, led by such squires as John Eliot, Thomas Wentworth, John Pym, and John Hampden, raised a whole list of grievances and claimed additional powers.

The First Parliament, 1625. Parliamentary opposition to Buckingham and the King's Catholic marriage prevented Charles from receiving more than one-seventh of his financial request, while tonnage and poundage were voted for only a year instead of for life as was customary.

The Second Parliament, 1626. The members of Parliament refused to vote war supplies for the King, and John Eliot's oratory led to impeachment proceedings against the Duke of Buckingham. To save his favorite minister, Charles dissolved Parliament and demanded forced loans from each taxpayer. This aroused opposition, and arrests were made for refusal to pay. Soldiers were quartered in private homes to save expenses. But the King still required additional revenue.

The Third Parliament and the Petition of Right, 1628. Charles was forced to summon a third Parliament to raise more money; however, the leaders of Parliament—Eliot, Coke, Pym, and Wentworth—were determined that no subsidy would be granted until the King redressed their grievances. A Petition of Right was drafted which limited royal prerogative and requested the King to protect ancient liberties. It forbade imprisonment without showing cause, martial law in time of peace, forced loans or taxes without parliamentary consent, and the billeting of soldiers in private homes without consent of the occupants. Charles reluctantly signed the petition in order to have his subsidies approved. The petition, like the Magna Charta of 1215, became, in time, a constitutional landmark in limiting the power of the monarchy, although its immediate effects were slight.

Second Session, 1629. Charles dismissed the first session of Parliament to stave off an attempt to remove Buckingham from office. But during the adjournment Buckingham was assassinated by John Felton, a naval officer, and the nation rejoiced as the King grieved. When Parliament reconvened religious grievances took priority over fiscal matters, and the Commons launched an attack on the High Church policies of the Bishops. When the Speaker attempted to adjourn the fruitless session, members held him in his chair while the Commons hastily passed three resolutions condemning anyone who introduced innovations in religion, or who advised levying tonnage and poundage without parliamentary consent, or who would pay such taxes. When Parliament was finally dissolved, Eliot and eight other members were arrested; three of them were sent to the Tower, and Eliot died there three years later.

Personal Rule, 1629-40. For the next eleven years King Charles ruled without summoning Parliament. To save money he made peace with France and Spain; to raise sufficient money to govern England, royal officials invoked every possible source of revenue short of parliamentary grants.

Revenues. Customs revenues were not sufficient to pay expenses; therefore, the King levied fines on individuals who had violated long dormant forest laws, invented new monopolies and sold patents to companies, and invoked an old statute that required all landholders with an annual income of £40 to be knighted. A large fee was charged if they became knights; a steep fine if they refused. The levy arousing the greatest opposition was the ship money tax which seacoast towns had paid in earlier centuries to provide ships for defense against a threatened invasion. But England was at peace and Charles demanded the tax of inland as well as coastal counties. John Hampden, a wealthy Puritan, refused to pay his tax, arguing that it usurped Parliament's power of the purse. In court the King won the legal verdict, but not the popular one.

Thomas Wentworth. After the assassination of Buckingham (1628) Charles relied largely on two advisers, Thomas Wentworth (later the Earl of Strafford) and Archbishop Laud. Wentworth was a parliamentary leader until he changed sides after the passage of the Petition of Right for personal advantage and because he feared that parliamentary extremism would result in a breakdown of Government. As President of the Council of the North he imposed law and order on the region so effectively that Charles made him Lord Deputy of Ireland in 1633. His Irish policies were thorough, because of the high-handed manner with which he reorganized finances and stimulated trade. His methods kept Ireland temporarily docile, but he alienated both the "old English" Catholic gentry and the "new English" Puritans during his administration.

Charles and the Church. In 1633 William Laud became Archbishop of Canterbury and, as the King's chief adviser, won royal support for religious uniformity in public worship according to High Church (Anglo-Catholic) tradition. Puritans accused him of reverting to Catholicism but Laud, through the Courts of Star Chamber and High Commission, took stern measures against his critics. His measures promoted a Puritan migration to New England and provoked the chain of events that led to civil war in England.

Charles and the Scots. In 1637, when Charles and Laud attempted to force a new prayer book and an Anglican episcopacy on Presbyterian Scotland, the Scots rioted and resisted the innovations. A National Covenant was signed which pledged allegiance to Charles but swore to resist to death all religious changes contrary to their Kirk (Church). Charles determined to invade Scotland but could find neither men nor money to meet the Scottish army that was commanded by Alexander Leslie, and was forced to abandon his campaign. The First Bishops' War (1639) ended in a truce without a battle. Strafford advised the King to call a Parliament and appeal to English patriotism in order to raise money for fighting the

Scots. The Short Parliament of 1640 assembled in an angry mood and refused to vote funds until it had discussed grievances. Within three weeks Charles dissolved Parliament and made desperate appeals for funds and men to fight a Second Bishops' War; however, he met with little success. The Scots invaded England with ease and forced Charles to terms which stipulated that they would stay in English territory and receive £850 daily from the King until a settlement was signed. To pay the bill Charles was forced to summon another Parliament in 1640 which turned out to be a Long Parliament.

Chapter 10 ✍ Civil War and Interregnum

The Long Parliament provided the stage for a confrontation between the King and Parliament, as the House of Commons claimed for itself additional royal prerogatives. The ensuing civil war began largely as a struggle between the King and the parliamentary gentry and ended with the army as victor and Oliver Cromwell as the commanding figure. Cromwell's republican experiments were serious attempts to find a satisfactory, constitutional substitute for the monarchy; however, each alternative failed. He was able to restore England's influence in foreign affairs and to provide the country with order, prosperity, and greater religious toleration. Since military rule was not an acceptable substitute for the monarchy, the Stuart dynasty returned upon Cromwell's death.

Steps to Civil War

The Long Parliament was in general agreement in its efforts to curb the King's powers by legislation, but thereafter Parliamentarians divided as Pym steered the radical wing of the House of Commons toward religious issues and an attempt to control the army. Instead of capitalizing on this division to gain supporters, Charles I, with his genius for miscalculation, forced the issue by sending armed men into the House of Commons, thereby coalescing the opposition against him.

Parliamentary Triumphs. Under Pym's leadership the Long Parliament accomplished a mild constitutional revolution in its first two years. But when revolutionary changes were also demanded in the church and in the control of the militia the positions of the royalists and of the radicals became irreconcilable.

Most of the constructive work of this Parliament was accomplished in its early months and included: (1) the abolition of such prerogative courts as the Star Chamber and the High Commission; (2) no dissolution of Parliament without its own consent; (3) the Triennial Act demanding that Parliament meet at least every three years; and (4) no type of taxation without parliamentary consent.

Execution of Strafford (Wentworth). Parliament attempted to punish Strafford for his supposed influence over the royal policies of the previous decade. When the impeachment proceedings failed to convict, the Commons resorted to a bill of attainder which needed neither legal proof nor a trial, but still required the King's consent. Charles had promised to protect Strafford, but mob and parliamentary pressures intimidated him into signing the death warrant, and in May, 1641, Strafford was executed. Archbishop Laud was also imprisoned and later (1645) executed.

Parliamentary Division. The proposal of the Puritans to abolish bishops (the "Root and Branch" bill) and radically reform the church alienated a considerable number of Parliamentarians who had previously backed political bills. In the summer of 1641 the division was widened by the news of a far-reaching rebellion in Ireland and the massacre of English and Scottish settlers in Ulster. Parliament wished to crush the rebellion by sending over an army, but did not want to place a large force under the control of the King for fear that he might use it to enforce his authority in England. Therefore, the radical members drew up a resolution, the Grand Remonstrance, in which they stated their grievances and demanded parliamentary approval of both the King's advisers and the army officers. After a stormy debate the bill passed the Commons by only eleven votes, which was evidence that the conservative members were opposed to any sweeping changes in the traditional political arrangement.

Attack on the Commons. Instead of waiting and winning over a few more members, Charles committed a political error by marching into the House of Commons with an armed guard to arrest five of its leading members; however, the members had been forewarned and had fled. Soon after this abortive coup, Charles rode north to raise an army and to show by force that he was King. His subjects gradually took sides and prepared for war. In June, 1642, Parliament sent the King an ultimatum (the Nineteen Propositions) requiring that he surrender virtually all his remaining prerogative powers. Such preposterous demands indicated that any hope of compromise was past, and in August civil war began.

Course of the War

At first the Royalists were victorious because of the quality of their cavalry and leadership, yet time favored Parliament because of its superior resources, manpower, and the backing of the navy. By 1646 Parliament was victorious, even though Charles was not willing to recognize this fact. The King's dealings with the Scots brought on a short second Civil War that Cromwell's forces won easily, and that left the army in control of the country. The army promptly purged Parliament of the members it disliked. The resulting Rump Parliament constituted a court to try the King for treason. This illegal court convicted Charles and had him executed. The King was dead; Cromwell and the army were the new rulers.

Royalist Support. Geographically, the King's support centered in the north and in the west. His party included most of the nobility, many of the gentry, Roman Catholics, and the supporters of the established church. Lacking sources of revenue, Charles called upon the loyalty of his peers and gentry to provide him with money and services. And in his two nephews, Prince Rupert and Prince Maurice, Charles found competent military leaders.

Parliamentary Support. Although the lines of demarcation were never sharp between the two sides, Parliament drew its major strength from the south and east of the country. Support also came from the navy, merchants, yeomen farmers, and opponents of High Anglicanism. Parliament had greater resources at its disposal for fighting a war, but the commander-in-chief, the Earl of Essex, lacked generalship and a plan of attack. Not until Thomas Fairfax and Oliver Cromwell took over command could parliamentary leadership rival that of their opponents.

Civil War, 1642-46. The royalist superiority in cavalry gave Charles the edge in the campaigns of the first two years. Parliament then negotiated with Scotland and signed the Solemn League and Covenant (1643) in which it was agreed to establish the Reformed (Presbyterian) church in England in return for the assistance of a Scottish army. At Marston Moor (near York) in 1644 the Parliamentary and Scottish armies won their first important battle, but were unable to follow up their victory. In the next year, with the help of the Self-Denying Ordinance, Parliament reorganized the army, forced the old leadership to resign, and made Sir Thomas Fairfax the new commander. Drawing heavily on Oliver Cromwell's disciplined and dedicated troops, a New Model army was created which decisively defeated the Royalists at the battle of Naseby (1645). Thereafter, the King's position was hopeless and the following year he surrendered to the Scots. By the end of 1646 the first Civil War ended when the Scots agreed to surrender Charles to Parliament and go home.

The Disputed Peace. Parliament had triumphed over the King; however, Parliament did not represent the views of Cromwell's army, and the army was the real power in the land. Factions ap-

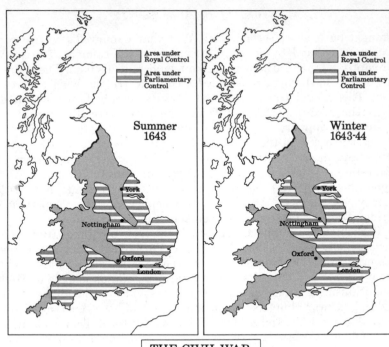

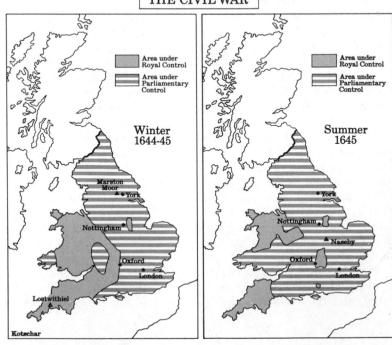

THE CIVIL WAR

peared in Parliament and in the army, as the victors quarreled among themselves and attempted to negotiate separately with the King. Charles responded by trying to play off Parliament, the army, and the Scots against one another. He made conflicting promises to each group so that in the end his scheming made all the parties suspicious of his integrity. No party, at first, had any intention of deposing the King, and the argument revolved around religious controversy. The Presbyterian members of Parliament wanted to impose the National Covenant on England, but the sectarians in Parliament and in the army opposed a Presbyterian establishment. When Parliament ordered the New Model army either to disband without back pay or to go to Ireland under Presbyterian officers, the army threatened mutiny. In the summer of 1647, Oliver Cromwell, who had served as the mediator for the various parties, threw in his lot with the army. Cromwell and his followers proceeded to draft the Heads of the Proposals as a compromise measure to save the nation from both royal absolutism and the democratic republican proposals advocated by the Levelers (the followers of John Lilburne) and other radicals in the army. Cromwell's moderate proposal was ignored by both Parliament and the King. Charles escaped from his army captors to the Isle of Wight where he negotiated with the Scots to invade England and restore him to the throne in return for his support of a Presbyterian church settlement.

The Second Civil War, 1648. The Scottish invasion of 1648 precipitated the second Civil War. General Fairfax crushed Royalist uprisings in the south of England while Cromwell's veterans moved north to rout a superior Scottish-Royalist army near Preston. After Preston the army dominated the situation and vented its wrath on both Parliament and Charles. The soldiers were convinced that Charles was a Man of Blood for breaking his word and reviving the war, and that Parliament was little better because of its efforts to negotiate with such a King even after the second war broke out. In December (1648) Colonel Pride purged Parliament of its Presbyterian supporters. The remaining members—the Rump —took orders from the army.

Regicide. The purged House of Commons, consisting of less than one hundred members, appointed a court of commissioners to try the King as a traitor. Charles never accepted the legality of this tribunal and refused to speak in his own defense. The verdict was never in doubt, for the army had decided upon the execution of the King. In January, 1649, Charles met his death with calmness and dignity.

The Commonwealth and the Protectorate, 1649-60

The execution of the King transformed England into a republic which few Englishmen had foreseen or actually desired. The Government now rested on the power of the army and its rather reluctant hero, Oliver Cromwell. In the ensuing interregnum Cromwell experimented with various alternatives to monarchy, but each attempt foundered over the incompatibility of a constitutional government and the "rule of the saints." Cromwell's leadership saved England from the grim prospects of either anarchy or tyranny, and he achieved prosperity and order in the country and won respect abroad by a vigorous and successful foreign policy but failed to find a satisfactory alternative to monarchy. Cromwell's death brought increasing civilian discontent and the restoration of the Stuarts.

Cromwell and the New Government. The Rump Parliament passed an act which abolished the monarchy and the House of Lords and set up a Council of State of forty-one members to administer the realm. For the next four years this Council served as the nominal executive, but real, if somewhat disguised, power was in the hands of Cromwell. Only Cromwell's statesmanship and self-restraint kept him from abusing his almost unlimited authority, because the constitutional checks demanded by earlier Parliaments of the Stuarts were never applied to him. He was devoutly religious and confident that God was on his side; yet, he was neither intolerant of other faiths nor a "puritan in the narrow sense," for he "liked music and dancing."[1] Led on by the force of circumstances more than by personal ambition, Cromwell successfully met internal and external challenges to the Government.

The Radical Opposition. Cromwell's Government was opposed not only by Royalists but also by radicals within the army. The war had undermined the previous religious and social order, and zealous pamphleteers played upon the feelings of the disenchanted. Some of the Independents in the army were seeking to legalize religious pluralism; others went further in their demands. John Lilburne and his Levelers advocated a democratic republic; whereas Gerrard Winstanley and his fellow Diggers aimed at an agrarian communism that would abolish all manors and landlords. But in politcial and social viewpoints Cromwell and his middle party were not innovators. Thus, when choosing members of the Council of State, they excluded radicals. Both Fairfax and Cromwell acted decisively to smother further revolutionary threats and

---

[1] E. L. Woodward, *History of England* (New York: Harper, 1962), p. 108.

minor mutinies in the army. Lilburne was imprisoned, and a few executions took place. Cromwell turned next to foreign threats.

Foreign Affairs. Cromwell's active foreign policy brought together Ireland, Scotland, and England under a single Government and made England respected in Europe as a powerful naval and commercial power. "Cromwell and Blake, rather than Queen Elizabeth and Drake, really made England mistress of the seas." [2]

Ireland. Royalists and Catholics had joined forces under the Marquis of Ormonde in support of Charles II, son of the executed king, and were attempting to gain control of all of Ireland. In August, 1649, Cromwell and his troops landed in Ireland, relieved Dublin, and within ten months had crushed the rebellion. Cromwell's massacre of the defenders in Drogheda for refusing to surrender was an object lesson to other cities, but was also a blight on his reputation. The land settlement that followed produced additional Irish resentment against Cromwell. About two-thirds of the land south of Ulster was confiscated and given to English Protestants who soon built up extensive estates. For the next two-and-a-half centuries the hostility between the English-Protestant (and often absentee) landlords and the Irish tenants remained unresolved.

Scotland. From Ireland Cromwell returned to England to lead another army (1650) against the Scotch Covenanters who were supporting Charles Stuart's second attempt to gain the throne. Cromwell's efforts for a peaceful negotiation failed, and the superior forces of the Scots hemmed in his army at Dunbar. But his troops won a decisive victory, taking ten thousand prisoners. During the winter Charles was crowned King at Scone and in the spring a new Scottish army moved into England—and into the trap Cromwell had planned. The royal army was surrounded and decimated at Worcester. Charles escaped and fled to the Continent. The battle of Worcester ended the Civil War and united Ireland, Scotland, and England under one Commonwealth Government.

The War with the Dutch, 1652-54. Triumphant over British opposition, Cromwell next faced Holland which was England's chief commercial and naval rival. The Republican navy under Robert Blake had won respect by forcing the rebellious Virginian and West Indian colonies to acknowledge the Commonwealth, and by routing Prince Rupert's fleet. In 1651 Parliament passed the Navigation Act which favored England's commercial class by restricting the maritime trade of the Dutch. The act which reflected

---

[2] Robert Eckles and Richard Hale, *Britain, Her Peoples and the Commonwealth* (New York: McGraw-Hill, 1954), p. 152.

the economic rivalry of the period decreed that trade with England and her colonies could be carried only in English ships or in ships of the producing country, and that all goods from the colonies must be in English ships. Other causes that contributed to the outbreak of hostilities with Holland included: (1) disputes over fishing rights off the coast of England; (2) the harboring of the Royalist supporters of Charles by the Dutch; and (3) the refusal of Dutch ships to dip their flags to English warships in the Channel. Although indecisive sea battles followed, Dutch shipping interests were so badly hurt that peace was made in 1654 on terms favorable to the English. Treaties were also concluded with Sweden, Denmark, and Portugal that benefited English commerce.

Spanish Policy. Cromwell also shared the Elizabethan and Puritan sentiment that Spain was more dangerous to England than France. Admiral Blake's expedition to the Mediterranean (1654-57) was so impressive that England became the dominant naval power in the Mediterranean for the first time. The attack on Spain in the West Indies was only partially successful. Jamaica was taken, but the attempt to seize Santo Domingo failed. The harassment of Spanish possessions led to all-out war with Spain and an alliance between England and France. In the Anglo-French land campaign against Spain in the Spanish Netherlands, the English troops won the Battle of the Dunes and received Dunkirk from Louis XIV for their aid.

Constitutional Experiments. Although successful abroad, Cromwell failed to find a satisfactory constitutional basis for his Government. All efforts foundered over the issue of sovereignty between the rule of the elect—the army leadership—and the elected—the various Parliaments.

The Commonwealth. For four years (1649-53) Cromwell attempted to negotiate the differences between the Rump Parliament and the army since he was the pivotal figure in both. But dissatisfaction with Parliament grew in the army and in the nation. The Rump Parliament was charged with corruption and appeared to be interested primarily in its own tenure of office when it refused to hold a general election. In April, 1653, Cromwell forcibly dissolved the Rump Parliament and replaced it with a nominated "Parliament of Saints." This body was handpicked by Cromwell's council from candidates supplied by the independent churches; Cromwell had no intention of ruling by military authority alone. The Nominated Assembly was zealous but amateurish. When its views on religion became too radical for army leaders, the Assembly was dissolved, and the Commonwealth came to an end.

The Instrument of Government, 1653. The outcome was a new

constitution drawn up by army officers to replace the Common-wealth. The Instrument provided for an executive (Cromwell) who was to be the Lord Protector. A council of state would advise the Protector and share control of the army with him. A one-house Parliament would be elected every three years by an enlarged fran-chise representing England, Scotland, and Ireland. Toleration was granted to all Christians except Anglicans and Roman Catholics. Checks and balances were included to prevent the tyranny of either Protector or Parliament. The first Protectorate Parliament met in 1654 and immediately attempted to amend the Instrument to its advantage. One hundred members were dismissed for refusing to accept Cromwell's four constitutional "fundamentals," but when the remainder continued to wrangle, Cromwell dissolved Parlia-ment in January, 1655.

Military Rule. As a temporary expedient England and Wales were divided into eleven military districts with a major general placed over each. The people disliked the military arrangement, and war with Spain created the need of increased subsidies. There-fore, in 1656 a second Parliament convened which was carefully chosen by the army officers and screened by the council of state. Even this select group asserted its independence from the army and could not be effectively controlled. One of its first acts was to discontinue the rule of the major generals and to propose a new constitution.

Humble Petition and Advice. Leaders in Parliament, wishing to return to a more traditional system of Government, next proposed that Cromwell should become King, that a second chamber, called the "other house," should be filled with the King's appointees, and that the powers of Parliament should be increased. Cromwell de-clined the Crown because acceptance would have violated the whole republican argument. But he accepted the other features of the constitution and the new Parliament met in January, 1658. Almost immediately the House of Commons demanded control over both Cromwell and the Upper House, instead of paying atten-tion to the war with Spain. Once again, Cromwell dissolved Parlia-ment and, before he could assemble another one, he died in 1658.

Fall of the Protectorate. Cromwell's death also doomed the Pro-tectorate, because only the force of Cromwell's personality and the loyalty of the army to its commander-in-chief had held the Gov-ernment together. Oliver's son and successor, Richard, lacked pres-tige and ability to keep the support of the sectarians, the army, and the Puritans. Besides, the nation was weary of Puritan and army control and was ready for the return of the Stuarts. Army commanders, led by Charles Fleetwood and John Lambert, defied Richard and grasped for power, while Royalist and republican uprisings took place. Richard surrendered to the army which promptly replaced the Protectorate Government with the Commonwealth (Rump) Parliament. However, this Parliament got along with the army no better than in earlier years and was dismissed in October. Finally General George Monck, commander of the army in Scotland, marched south to support civilian rule and oppose General Lambert. In London he recalled the Long Parliament of 1640 and had it dissolve itself in favor of a freely-elected Convention Parliament. In 1660 the Convention Parliament recalled Charles II from exile.

Achievements of the Interregnum. The accomplishments of the interregnum were the triumphs of Cromwell since he was the leader largely responsible for preserving order and individual liberty. His foreign policy brought security through strength and his economic policies increased English prosperity. Religious pluralism and free thought were saved from the extremism of sectarians and the uniformity demanded by Anglicans and Presbyterians. The Jews were allowed to return to England after an exile of 350 years; civil marriages were legalized; public schools and universities were reformed.

The Puritan Dilemma. Although Cromwell represented the loftier ideals of Puritanism and frowned upon the "blue laws" that his compatriots favored, he had no doubts about the rightness of the Puritan position. He was convinced that he and his supporters were God's agents sent to save England from the forces of tyranny, whether foreign, Royalist, or religious. This conviction made it impossible to resolve the constitutional conflict in the rivalry between the elect and the elected. Thus the Puritan position created its own dialectic, for although it stressed individualism, it also claimed the guardianship of the saints over the sinners. By 1660 England was weary of this guardianship and anxious for a return to the old ways, perhaps because "the sinners were more numerous than the saints." [3]

---

[3] Woodward, *History of England,* p. 106.

Chapter 11 ◄§ Restoration and Revolution

With the return of Charles II the monarchy, Parliament, and the Anglican supremacy were restored in England, but not simply as a replica of the days of Charles I. Charles II accommodated himself to the changes, but his brother, James II, could not. As a result James lost the throne in the revolution of 1688. The revolutionary settlement transferred ultimate sovereignty from the King to Parliament and replaced a Catholic monarch with the Protestants, William and Mary. The new co-monarchs were rulers, not by divine right or by strict heredity, but by an act of Parliament. King William proceeded to marshal English resources against Louis XIV whom both Charles and James had preferred to serve as clients.

Charles and the Restoration

Charles II learned from the execution of his father some of the risks involved when Parliament and King became hostile rivals. Therefore, the Restoration brought unusual harmony between monarchy and Parliament until Charles's religious and foreign policies produced such opposition that he reigned his last years without Parliament in order to control the succession to the throne.

The Return of Charles. To allay the reservations of Englishmen who had reasons to fear the restoration of the monarchy, Charles issued the Declaration of Breda (Holland) in which he promised: (1) to give the army its arrears in pay before disbanding it; (2) to permit as much religious toleration as Parliament would allow; (3) to grant a general pardon to all political opponents except to those designated by Parliament; and (4) to let Parliament determine the legitimacy of property titles acquired during the interregnum. The Convention Parliament was satisfied with the Declaration, and in May, 1660, Charles returned to London from exile. But the Restoration did not restore all the powers of earlier Kings, for the acts of 1640-41 to which Charles I had given assent (e.g., prerogative courts, unparliamentary taxation, and the arbitrary arrest of members of Parliament without cause) remained illegal. Before its dissolution in 1661 the Convention Parliament, sympathetic to Charles's proclamation of clemency, carried out a moderate policy. Troops were paid and dismissed, except for a standing army of five thousand soldiers, and only thirteen leading officials of the Cromwellian period were put to death.

The New King. Charles II seemed to live only for pleasure and the pursuit of mistresses. He cared little, if at all, about policies except those that were pleasing to his fancy. Yet, when circumstances demanded a display of power, Charles could exert his latent ability and carry on important negotiations successfully. Clever, charming, selfish, and completely cynical, Charles mocked the morals and fears (Catholicism and Louis XIV) of England and held onto his throne and the powers of the monarchy, even though he wasted his authority in the pursuit of Francophile and pro-Catholic policies. When threatened by political opposition, or when the succession to the throne was challenged, the King could control the situation with masterly abilities. Ordinary duties bored him, however, and he preferred to devote himself to more pleasant pastimes; but he was cognizant of his father's fate and was never lazy to the point of letting affairs of state get out of hand.

The Religious Settlement. The parliamentary election of 1661 brought hundreds of enthusiastic Royalists and Anglicans into the House of Commons. The resultant "Cavalier Parliament" proceeded to penalize Puritans and Dissenters, as well as Roman Catholics, by a series of four acts known as the Clarendon Code (1661-65): (1) The Municipal Corporations Act excluded from municipal office all who refused to renounce the Solemn League and Covenant, or to swear not to resist the King. (2) The Act of Uniformity required all clergy to use the revised Book of Common Prayer in their services. When nearly one-fifth of the clergy refused to comply, additional restrictions followed. (3) The Conventicle Act imposed harsh penalties for attending a religious service (conventicle) which did not conform to the Anglican liturgy. (4) The Five Mile Act forbade nonconforming ministers to visit or live within five miles of any organized town where they had previously preached or taught school. These acts clearly restored the Anglican supremacy but at the same time created modern nonconformity in England, because many clergy and laymen no longer found in the Anglican church the religious latitude which had existed in the Elizabethan church. Thousands of Nonconformists in England and Scotland went into hiding or were imprisoned. One Nonconformist, John Bunyan, wrote part of *The Pilgrim's Progress* while imprisoned in Bedford Gaol for dissenting views.

Foreign Affairs. The foreign policy of Charles II was motivated by personal rather than national interests. The independent strength of England under Cromwell soon shifted under Charles to one of subserviency to French interests in return for the secret payment of money to Charles by Louis XIV.

The Marriage of Charles. In 1662 Charles made an unpopular but profitable marriage alliance with Catherine of Braganza, daughter of the King of Portugal. The marriage brought him a rich dowry which included the ports of Tangier in North Africa and Bombay in India; the treaty also aligned England with France against Spain. In the same year Charles sold Dunkirk to France in spite of the opposition of his subjects.

Ireland. Irish Catholics and Royalists had supported Charles during the interregnum and welcomed the Restoration. In return for their loyalty Charles restored to the Irish some of the land that had been confiscated by Cromwell's Government, but this action antagonized his relations with English landlords in Ireland. Moreover, the English Parliament continued its traditional anti-Irish policies by excluding Irish ships from colonial trade and by making illegal the shipment of cattle from Ireland to England.

The Dutch Wars. The continuing commercial rivalry between Holland and England led to the Second Dutch War (1665-67) and the seizure of New Amsterdam in America, which was renamed New York. After the peace treaty Charles asserted a temporary independence from Louis XIV by signing the Triple Alliance (1668) which united England, Holland, and Sweden against the expansionist designs of France. But Louis used bribery to persuade Charles to break this alliance and to attack Holland again. Charles dragged England into the Third Dutch War (1672-74) which Parliament finally halted by refusing to grant additional funds. The strain of naval warfare against England, combined with the land war against France, weakened the resources of the Dutch and contributed to their decline as a major colonial and naval power.

Charles and Louis XIV. Charles II admired the glittering court, the Roman Catholicism, and the unlimited royal power of Louis XIV and instead of opposing France—in line with the balance of power principle—he became an agent in Louis' scheme of expansion. In 1670 Charles secretly signed the Treaty of Dover, whereby he promised to break away from the Triple Alliance, to attack Holland, and to convert to Catholicism as soon as expedient. For this alliance Louis provided Charles with substantial sums of money. Charles kept his promise of declaring war on Holland, but his efforts to relieve the restrictions on English Catholics provoked instead a strong parliamentary protest.

Political Developments. The King and Parliament co-operated on most matters until growing suspicions of Charles's French and Catholic sympathies resulted in legislative efforts to increase restrictions on English Catholics and to prevent James, the Catholic brother of Charles, from succeeding to the throne. To save the Stuart succession, Charles acted forcefully in destroying the political opposition and ruling without Parliament. Louis XIV helped to make this possible by granting additional money to Charles.

Fall of Clarendon. Lord Clarendon made many enemies during his years as chief minister (1661-67). He distrusted the House of Commons, censored the immoral activities of the royal court, and was identified (unfairly) in the minds of Puritans with the harsh Clarendon Code. The unsatisfactory foreign policy, including the King's marriage, the sale of Dunkirk, and the war with Holland, increased his unpopularity. And when the Dutch fleet humiliated the English by sailing up the Thames in 1667 and burning English war ships anchored at Chatham, the King abandoned Clarendon to his enemies. He was dismissed and impeached, then fled to the Continent where he wrote his *History of the Rebellion*.

The Cabal, 1667-73. Instead of replacing Clarendon with another chief minister, Charles decided to direct affairs himself, relying on five unofficial advisers who, for various reasons, favored the efforts of the King to relax the Anglican supremacy. Two were Catholics, Clifford and Arlington; one was a skeptic and Charles's favorite, Buckingham. Ashley Cooper, later Earl of Shaftesbury, was a latitudinarian in religion and an able essayist; and the Earl of Lauderdale was formerly Presbyterian. This cabal of advisers (so-called because their initials spelt "cabal"), broke up in 1673 when opposition to Charles's Declaration of Indulgence for non-Anglicans resulted in the passage of anti-Catholic legislation and bitterness between King and Parliament. Three members left the cabal, and Shaftesbury became the leading critic of the King's policies.

The Rise of Political Parties. The reaction of the fiercely anti-Catholic Parliament to Charles's Declaration of Indulgence was the passage of the Test Act (1673) which required all office holders, civil and military, to take the Anglican sacrament and to deny transubstantiation. By 1674 the friendly Cavalier Parliament had been transformed into a hostile critic of Charles's pro-French, pro-papal policy. The King dropped his scheme for Catholicizing England and tried to court Parliament by making the Earl of Danby his chief minister and the doctrine of royalty and Anglicanism the rallying point for his supporters. The "court party" which emerged under Danby won the epithet Tory [1] from opposing cliques. Rival factions who gravitated toward Shaftesbury and his anti-Tory "country party," were later to be called Whigs.[2] Their supporters came from the city merchants and several powerful aristocratic families who favored further limitations on royal power, toleration for Protestant dissenters, and who were militantly anti-Catholic.

The Popish Plot, 1678. The factions opposed to Charles were aided by the false tales of an unprincipled informer, Titus Oates, who inflamed the populace to hysteria by describing a Jesuit plot to murder Charles, massacre Protestants, and set up, with the help of the French, a Catholic Government under James, duke of York. A shocked and angry Parliament, led by Shaftesbury, impeached and executed several Catholics and began to impeach Danby when the secret dealings of Charles and Danby with Louis XIV were revealed. To save Danby and his own family from attack, Charles dissolved the Cavalier Parliament.

The Parliaments of 1678-81. Charles's second Parliament convened in 1679 with an anti-Catholic Whig majority dedicated to excluding James from succession to the throne. Charles blocked the exclusion bill by dissolving Parliament, but not before it had passed the Habeas Corpus Amendment Act which prevented arbitrary imprisonment and insured a speedy trial. A third Parliament met in 1680 and the House of Commons immediately passed an Exclusion Bill that made Charles's illegitimate son, the Duke of Monmouth, heir to the throne instead of James; but the House of Lords rejected it. A fourth Parliament which was summoned to Oxford in 1681 to avoid the influence of the London mob was dissolved within a week. Charles ruled his remaining years without Parliament.

Personal Rule of Charles II, 1681-85. Once again Charles was receiving subsidies from Louis XIV and no longer needed Parliamentary grants. His last four years were a time of personal and autocratic rule during which he struck hard at the Whig opposition. Shaftesbury fled to the Continent and died in Holland. Other Whig leaders were fraudulently charged with plotting the King's death, and Lords Russell and Sydney were executed. Whig boroughs lost their charters and Tory town governments and sheriffs replaced the influence of such Whig organizations as the Green

---

[1] An appellation for Irish cattle thieves.
[2] The political heirs of the Puritan opposition to Charles I, although the term refers to Scottish robbers who murdered their victims.

Ribbon clubs. When Charles died in 1685, the Whig opposition was scattered, the English monarch was a willing pensionary of France, and the succession had been preserved for the legitimate heir, James.

Restoration Society. Reaction to Puritan morality was observed most transparently in Charles's court where a studied effort was made to imitate the gay and lavish court of Louis XIV. Wit, worldly charm, and love affairs were the stepping-stones of success in any political career. But society at Whitehall never represented England. The nation which was still largely agricultural in its economy and provincial in its outlook was often suspicious of commercial and social life in London. Furthermore, the capital suffered two disasters: the plague of 1665 which took 70,000 lives in London alone; and the Great Fire in 1666 which destroyed over 13,000 buildings and gave the architect, Sir Christopher Wren, a magnificent opportunity to rebuild the city.

The Last Catholic King

James II succeeded to the throne with a minimum of dissension, because the nation expected only a mild Catholic interim until his Protestant daughters came to the throne. James pushed to the extreme his royal prerogative of suspending laws. When his son and heir to the throne was born, who would most assuredly be reared Catholic, leading Englishmen invited William of Orange to lead a revolt against the King. The coup, which turned out to be bloodless and successful, settled the constitutional issue of the century: the sovereignty of Parliament triumphed over the divine right of Kings.

Accession to the Throne. With the Anglican church preaching the Biblical doctrine of non-resistance, the Whig opposition dead or scattered, and the recent civil war still a vivid memory, there was little serious opposition to James's accession as long as the King promised to uphold the established church and to keep his religion private. James was serious-minded, honest, and devoutly Catholic, but he was also arrogant and obstinate and, unlike his brother, insensitive to the political and religious facts of English life. His one overriding goal, like that of Mary Tudor, was to restore Catholicism to England.

Protestant Rebellions. The Duke of Monmouth landed in southern England in a reckless effort to win the throne, but only a few thousand peasants and tradesmen joined his ill-starred venture. Royal troops, under John Churchill, crushed the rebels at Sedgemoor. Monmouth was executed, and the "bloody assizes" under Lord Chief Justice Jeffreys inflicted brutal vengeance on hundreds of Monmouth's followers. In Scotland a Protestant rebellion was led by the Earl of Argyll; however, his little army of Covenanters was dispersed and Argyll was executed.

James and Parliament. With the Whigs in disarray, a cooperative Tory Parliament was elected in 1685 that was willing to grant money to James provided there were no religious changes. However, when James asked for a standing army commanded by Roman Catholic officers, Parliament protested and reduced the King's subsidies. Angered by their criticisms James prorogued Parliament and never called another.

Pro-Catholic Policies. Undeterred by political advisers or the religious sensibilities of his subjects, King James proceeded to restore privileges to Roman Catholics. He encamped an army near London commanded by Catholic officers; appointed an ecclesiastical commission, headed by the notorious Jeffreys, to silence or dismiss Anglican critics like Bishop Compton; appointed Catholics to official positions in universities and in the royal administration; and issued two Declarations of Indulgences (1687-88) which would permit free public worship for Roman Catholics and Protestant Nonconformists. When seven bishops, including the Archbishop of Canterbury, petitioned that the Declaration be withdrawn, James had them arrested on a charge of seditious libel. Their trial became a popular case, and crowds cheered the bishops when the jury acquitted them.

Foreign Policy. King James, like Charles II, aligned his foreign policy with the interest of France which, at this time, was encroaching on neighboring countries. This threat produced a defensive coalition (League of Augsburg) of Protestant and Catholic states which included Holland, Brandenberg, several south German states, and the Hapsburg Emperor. Even Pope Innocent XI did not endorse the Catholicizing policies of Louis XIV and James II. When James persisted in these efforts, William of Orange intervened in English affairs on the grounds that his wife was heir to the throne of England, that he needed English support to fight King Louis, and that according to his agents in England influential Englishmen would back him.

The Glorious Revolution, 1688. With the birth of King James's son in the summer of 1688, the prospects of an interim Catholic monarchy were shattered, since the Crown Prince became heir presumptive in place of his Protestant half-sister, Mary. The prospects of a Catholic dynasty and the exclusion of Mary from the throne dismayed many Englishmen, and in July seven influential Whig and Tory leaders invited William of Orange to lead an English uprising so as to prevent King James from consolidating his movements toward absolutism and Catholicism. Although the English were slow in rallying around William's forces, they did not oppose his advance. Since the revolution was successful, bloodless, and supported by the respectable members of society, the label "Glorious" was soon attached to it.

The Dutch Invasion. William and Mary accepted the invitation and made preparations for the invasion. James became alarmed over the turn of events and began making concessions and promises to the Church of England and to political opponents, but his efforts were too late. On November 5, 1688, William and his army landed at Torbay in southwest England. The involvement of Louis XIV in a war on the Rhine frontier relieved the Dutch from the fear of a French invasion. James's position deteriorated rapidly as soldiers, his commander-in-chief, John Churchill, and his daughter, Anne, defected and turned against him; even Whig and Tory peers began raising forces in their local communities. James began negotiations with William but became frightened when he remembered his father's execution. In December he fled to France, conceding a bloodless victory to William.

Change of Monarchs. A convention Parliament met in January, 1689, to arrange a constitutional settlement (following the precedent of 1660). After searching for a legal loophole that would not force abandonment of the principle of hereditary succession to the throne, the House of Commons finally declared that James had violated the fundamental laws of the land, had fled the country, and had left the throne vacant by his abdication. The Tories claimed that the throne was not vacant but belonged to Mary, because in their eyes James's son was spurious. However, William refused to be a "gentleman-usher" to his wife, so the Crown was offered jointly to William and Mary. Most Tories joined with the Whigs to forfeit the principle of strict succession (and with it the divine right of kings) in favor of a practical and Protestant settlement. Those who refused the settlement and believed that James was still the legal monarch became known as Jacobites.

The Bill of Rights, 1689. Parliament granted the throne to William and Mary on the conditions set forth in the Declaration (later Bill) of Rights. This document cited the failings of James II and, like the Magna Charta and the Petition of Right, was not concerned with political theories but rather with specific restrictions on royal authority: (1) the use of the suspending power or the dispensing power without parliamentary consent was declared illegal; (2) Roman Catholics were prohibited from succeeding to the throne; (3) provisions would be made for frequent sessions of Parliament and freedom of debate; (4) standing armies were prohibited; and (5) the levying of taxes or forced loans without the consent of Parliament was repudiated. The provisions of the settlement made no attempt to revolutionize the political or social structure, because the leaders of the revolution wished to conserve the established order in church and state which they claimed James II had jeopardized. But a fundamental change actually occurred, inasmuch as sovereignty was now transferred from King to Parliament by the Bill of Rights. If Parliament could enthrone monarchs by legislative act, it could also dethrone them. John Locke became the patron saint of the revolution when he justified its legitimacy with his argument for the contract theory of government in *Two Treatises of Government* (1690).

The Dilemma of the Clergy. Under Charles I the clergy and Anglican royalists had few divided loyalties because church and King were on the same side. In 1688 the situation was different. The clergy had a legitimate monarch in James and preached nonresistance to royal authority (divine right of kings). Were the clerics to continue to support the King if he failed to support the established church? When the Convention Parliament forced a decision between elected Kings and hereditary Kings, many clergy had difficulty switching their allegiance and over four hundred clerics refused to take the oath of allegiance to William; they became known as Non-jurors. The majority, however, accepted the *de facto* King as the *de jure* King.

William and Mary

William's first problem was to make good his disputed title of King in the British Isles. Thereafter, he was primarily interested in his lifelong goal of halting the expansionist designs of Louis XIV. Under William and Mary a diplomatic revolution occurred as England reversed its foreign policy from being a satellite of Louis XIV to becoming the leader of the coalition against France.

Revolutionary Settlement. The acceptance of William and Mary as joint monarchs took different patterns in England, Scotland, and Ireland. The Glorious Revolution brought a series of constitutional reforms in England, prosperity to Scotland, but only repression and bitterness in Ireland.

Constitutional Settlement. In England the Bill of Rights which set up the parliamentary conditions by which the monarch must govern was strengthened by several subsequent acts. The Toleration Act (1689), which was supported by William and the Whigs, gave freedom of worship to most Protestant dissenters; Catholics, Unitarians, and Jews were still restricted, and all the civil disabilities of the Clarendon Code and Test Act remained in force. A mutiny among the soldiers led to the Mutiny Act (1689) which allowed the King to raise an army and rule by martial law for a period of six months. To be renewed the Act demanded the annual assent of Parliament. To prevent a repetition of the seventeen-year Cavalier Parliament, the Triennial Act (1694) stipulated a maximum three-year life for any Parliament. The Treasons Act (1696) provided safeguards for accused Englishmen: the accused may see the indictment, be permitted to have counsel, and cannot be convicted without two witnesses to an overt act of treason. The Act of Settlement (1701) concluded the constitutional changes (*see* Domestic Politics, p. 137).

Scottish Settlement. The Church of Scotland and the Lowlanders preferred the Dutch Calvinist William to the pro-Catholic James. Consequently, the Scottish Parliament met in convention, declared that James II had forfeited his crown, and offered it to William and Mary. But the Highlanders, with typical affection for the Stuarts and contempt for the Lowlanders, gathered around Viscount Dundee and defeated William's troops at Killiecrankie (1689). When Dundee was killed in battle, resistance fell apart, and most of the Highland clans took the oath of allegiance to William. By 1692 only the MacDonalds of Glencoe had delayed their submission. William's advisers urged him to extract obedience, and soldiers of the Campbell clan were sent to discipline the clansmen of Glencoe. After being entertained by their unsuspecting hosts for twelve days, the soldiers treacherously slaughtered a large number of MacDonalds in the night. William and Mary made Presbyterianism the established church in Scotland and offered numerous concessions to the Scottish Parliament. But friction with England mounted when the English Parliament excluded Scottish trade from England.

The War in Ireland. With good reason the Irish preferred James II, who favored their religion, to the discrimination that they usually suffered at the hands of their Protestant overlords. Thus the Irish Parliament espoused the cause of James and took advantage of the English revolution to confiscate Protestant lands. In 1689 James arrived to lead the Irish, bringing French troops and money with him. All of Ireland except beleaguered Londonderry and Enniskillen recognized James as King. William and his troops arrived in Ireland in 1690 and on July 12 routed the army of James at the battle of the Boyne River (the "Glorious Twelfth" for Orangemen—members of the Orange Lodge). James fled to the Continent, leaving the Irish Catholics to fight on until their last stronghold, Limerick, capitulated in 1691.

The Irish Settlement. The Treaty of Limerick (1692) offered the Irish generous terms, including retention of the religious privileges given them under Charles II, permission for Irish soldiers to join the French army, and the restoration of estates confiscated since the reign of Charles II. But the Irish Protestants and the English Parliament had no intention of honoring the treaty. Instead, even more oppressive legislation was passed against Ireland. These laws barred Catholics from the Irish Parliament, from teaching in schools, from serving in the army or navy, or from holding any civil office. Protestant heirs received priority of inheritance over Catholic heirs, and inter-faith marriages were penalized. At the insistence of English traders Parliament also passed restrictive acts which effectively destroyed the trade and industry of every Irish staple. Thus the Irish espousal of James resulted in political and religious tyranny followed by poverty.

The War with France. William III added the resources of England and Scotland to his continental coalition against France and halted Louis XIV at the zenith of his power. The ensuing war was the beginning of a series of encounters between England and France which lasted for over a century. This second "Hundred Years' War," unlike the first, was not an effort to seize continental France or the French crown, but was a duel for leadership in commercial, colonial, and sea power.

Causes of the War of the League of Augsburg, 1689-97. The League of Augsburg was formed in 1686 to prevent French conquest of the Spanish Netherlands (modern Belgium). In 1689 William III eagerly attached England to the League to protect the national interests which the Stuart Kings had neglected. France was the most powerful nation on the Continent, and if Louis triumphed in his expansionist schemes, political absolutism and an intolerant Catholicism (as reflected by Louis' revocation of the Edict of Nantes in 1685) would threaten England as well as the Continent. Moreover, France had become England's major opponent in commerce and a colonial rival in India and in North America. Finally, Louis defied and insulted England by refusing to recognize William as King; instead he had kept James at the French court and had provided him with men and money for the invasion of Ireland.

In May, 1689, Parliament declared war, and England returned to the leadership of forces opposed to Catholic absolutism.

Course of the War. The land war was dominated by a series of siege operations in Belgium in which the French won the major battles until William inflicted the first serious check on Louis' army by recapturing Namur. In 1690 the French fleet defeated the combined English-Dutch fleets at Beachy Head, and James and Louis made preparations for an invasion of England. However, the invasion army was kept in port when England and Holland regained control of the Channel in 1692 by routing the French fleet at La Hogue. On the southern front the French army invaded Savoy and made good progress until the English fleet blockaded the French navy and cut off their supplies. Meanwhile, in North America King William's War was being waged between English and French colonies. The French under Count Frontenac with the help of Indian allies made a series of attacks on the New England colonies. Fighting on a small scale also took place in India and Africa.

The Peace of Ryswick, 1697. France was financially exhausted from the heavy expenses of Louis' half-century of intermittent wars, and the coalition had temporarily halted his schemes for expansion. By the treaty of Ryswick France restored all territory conquered since 1678 except Strasbourg; William was recognized as King of England; and the Dutch were allowed stronger fortifications along the French frontier. Although the peace was indecisive, the spread of French power was checked. An important byproduct of the war was the establishment of the Bank of England in 1694 which stabilized England's financial system. To meet the heavy expenses of a world war a permanent national debt was legalized. This meant that the credit of the nation could be used in borrowing, and a portion of the debt payments would be charged to future generations.

Domestic Politics. The aloof and alien William (his wife, Mary, died in 1694) had little popular appeal to Englishmen or political appeal to the Whig and Tory factions, except as the symbol of Protestantism and national independence. For his part, William was irritated by the party bickering which prevented unified support of the war effort.

Whig and Tory Factions. The Whigs hoped that the King would become a party leader and keep the Tories out of office; but William avoided political intrigues. By 1694 Tory opposition to the war was so strong that the Whig faction gained a majority in the Commons and the co-operation of the King. During the interval of peace the Tories returned to power and flouted William by reducing the size of the army and navy. William hoped for a Whig victory in the election of 1701 in order to win support for his plans for a new coalition against Louis XIV; however, the Tories retained control and opposed England's entry in the war.

The Act of Settlement, 1701. The Act of Settlement insured a Protestant succession and reflected the anti-William sentiment of Parliament by placing further restrictions on the monarch. The act provided that the Crown should next descend to Anne and then, if she had no more children, to Princess Sophia of Hanover, granddaughter of the first Stuart King; future English monarchs must join the Church of England and must not leave the country or involve England in war without consent of Parliament; royal officials were excluded from the House of Commons, and, after the Hanoverian succession, no foreigner could hold office or title to land; finally, judges could not be removed from office by the Crown, but only by an act of Parliament.

Renewal of the War with France. The War of the Spanish Succession (1701-13) broke out when King Charles II of Spain died childless and willed his kingdom to a grandson of Louis XIV, despite the Partition Treaties laboriously arranged by William to prevent this threat to the balance of power. King Louis supported the will and antagonized England further by recognizing the son of James II (known as the Old Pretender) as King of England—a violation of the Peace of Ryswick. Once again William fashioned a Grand Alliance of England, Holland, Austria, and several German states against the Bourbon Kingdoms of France and Spain and appointed John Churchill, earl of Marlborough, as commander-in-chief. By December (1701) the House of Commons was in favor of the war, but William died three months later, leaving the administration of the war to Anne and Marlborough.

Chapter 12 ⇜ The Last of the Stuarts

Queen Anne, the last of the Stuarts, succeeded in uniting the two kingdoms of England and Scotland which her great-grandfather, James I, had attempted without success. For all but the final year of Anne's reign England was at war with France and emerged with impressive victories on the Continent and colonial and commercial rewards in the peace treaty. The Queen presided over a kaleidoscopic political alignment that began and ended with a Tory administration, but differed very little in manner of operation, except in the conduct of the war, from the Whigs: the Whigs promoting a pro-war policy until the Bourbon King Philip V of Spain could be dethroned; the Tories supporting the war with reluctance and willing to end it at the first convenient moment.

The War Against France

The War of the Spanish Succession (1702-13) involved England in a world war. In addition to leading the coalition against Louis XIV, England had two armies on the Continent, fleets in the Mediterranean, Atlantic, and North Sea, and confronted the French in North America and in the West Indies. For the first time the armies of Louis XIV were decisively defeated. England's victories brought about a substantial enlargement of her colonial empire as set forth in the Treaty of Utrecht.

Course of the War. The prevalent fear in Europe that Bourbon monarchs on the thrones of France and Spain would facilitate the efforts of Louis XIV to dominate the Continent prompted the formation of the Grand Alliance. John Churchill, serving as commander-in-chief and co-ordinator, succeeded by military genius and diplomatic skill in keeping this Grand Alliance together and achieved its first spectacular victory in 1704. At Blenheim, Churchill, who had joined forces with the equally brilliant commander of the Hapsburg army, Prince Eugene of Savoy, defeated the French and the Bavarians and saved Vienna from a French advance. In the same year an Anglo-Dutch fleet under Sir George Rooke captured Gibraltar, and with it the control of the Mediterranean. In 1706, while Prince Eugene was routing the French from Italy,

Churchill (now the Duke of Marlborough) won a second decisive battle at Ramillies. By 1708 a third victory at Oudenarde forced the French out of the Spanish Netherlands; in the same year the English captured Minorca in the Mediterranean. This time the coalition had achieved its essential goal: the ouster of the French from Italy and the Netherlands. France was exhausted and eager for peace, but several of the allies on the Continent and the Whigs in England insisted on the expulsion of Philip V from Spain. So the war dragged on, becoming more costly in manpower and more controversial in English politics. In 1709 Marlborough won the battle of Malplaquet with such heavy losses that he abandoned plans for the invasion of France.

In Spain the allies took Madrid but could not hold the capital or the country. A treaty with Portugal, however, provided for an Anglo-Portuguese alliance and the exchange of English woolens for Portuguese wines. In 1710 English troops captured Acadia from the French in North America. A year later Marlborough was dismissed, and negotiations for peace began between England and France.

The Politics of the War. At the beginning of the war Marlborough and Sidney Godolphin, the chief ministers to the Queen, had only lukewarm Tory support. The Whigs who favored a vigorous war policy gained the majority in the election of 1705. Marlborough and Godolphin fell into line and for five years worked with the Whig faction now in control of the Commons. When the Whig party refused to treat for peace after English security was achieved, the war-weary electorate voted in a Tory majority in 1710. Tory ministers (Robert Harley and Henry St. John) replaced the Whig junta and pushed for a peace without Spain. Marlborough, the exalted war hero, was discredited by charges of misuse of public funds and went into exile to escape prosecution. Jonathan Swift, who was employed by Harley to justify a separate peace with France, wrote *The Conduct of the Allies* (1711) which helped influence public opinion in favor of the Tory policy. St. John began peace negotiations with France in the Dutch city of Utrecht without the consent of the allies.

The Peace of Utrecht, 1713. The provisions of Utrecht permitted Philip V to keep the Spanish throne, but excluded him from accession to the French throne. Austria acquired Milan, Naples, and the Spanish Netherlands, and England retained Gibraltar, Minorca, Nova Scotia (Acadia), Newfoundland, and title to the Hudson's Bay territory. The English broke the Spanish monopoly trade with her colonies by securing the right to supply slaves to South America (the Asiento Treaty with Philip). The Dutch were allowed to garrison certain border towns. The Peace, which recognized England as a major military and the leading naval power, greatly increased the colonial and commercial empire of Britain at the expense of France and Spain. England's commercial rival Belgium (and particularly the city of Antwerp) was transferred to Austria, a country without a navy. Thus the fear of the Low Countries being ruled by an unfriendly power was removed. However, the Peace embittered several allies of England, because it was made without due consideration of their causes; England's allies, the Catalans, were left to the vengeance of Philip V with no efforts to gain privileges, or even amnesty, for them.

Queen Anne and the Politicians

Anne was devoted to the Anglican church and favored the principles and prejudices of the Tory party. Although the Queen tried to remain above politics, she was forced to include Whigs among her ministers whenever the Whigs controlled Parliament. The Queen's original advisers had great influence over her, but were all dismissed from office before her death.

The Political Triumvirate. In the first half of Anne's reign three persons dominated the Government: Sarah Churchill, duchess of Marlborough, was the Queen's closest confidante; her husband, the Duke, was the Queen's military and political adviser; and Sidney Godolphin, who provided the parliamentary leadership for Marlborough's campaigns, served as Lord Treasurer. Both men were moderate Tories; however, when the High Church Tories attacked Marlborough's conduct of the war and the Nonconformists, Godolphin continued in power only through the backing of Anne at Court and the Whigs in Parliament. After the Whigs increased their numbers in the election of 1705, several ultra-Tory ministers were dismissed by the Queen; nevertheless, the moderate ministers, Godolphin, Marlborough, and Robert Harley were not threatened and remained in office. In 1707 the Duchess of Marlborough was replaced by Abigail Masham, a relative of Harley. The following year the Whig junta increased its majority in the Commons and demanded more ministerial offices; Anne consented under pressure but never forgave the Whigs. Godolphin and Marlborough made a political alliance with the Whig junta, and the war was conducted with vigor. By this time the nation was becoming weary of the war.

Act of Union, 1707. The Godolphin-Marlborough-Harley ministry achieved a major feat with the Act of Union which joined the kingdoms of England and Scotland. The English feared that their security would be menaced if the Scots chose a separate monarch after the death of Queen Anne, which the Parliament of Scotland indicated it would do. The Scots were lured into the union for economic reasons. They were excluded, nonetheless, by English legislation from the rich overseas investments and trade of England, and their own attempt in 1697 to colonize at Darien on the Isthmus of Panama had been an unrelieved disaster for Scottish investors. After a period of name-calling and mutual trade embargoes, commissioners from each kingdom met and negotiated the terms of union: (1) the Scottish Kirk would continue independent of England, as would the court system; (2) Scotland would give up her Parliament and, in place, send forty-five members to the House of Commons and elect sixteen peers to represent the Scottish nobility in the House of Lords; (3) Scotland would agree to the Hanoverian succession; (4) Scotland would receive a large financial grant for assuming her share of the English national debt; and (5) Scotland would receive the same trading rights as England. Although many Scots were unhappy with the prospects of being governed from London, the act brought trade and relative prosperity to Scotland and expanded the potential for political and business leadership in Great Britain.

The New Politicians. The Whigs, already disliked by the Queen, began to lose popular support as the war dragged on. In 1709 the Government impeached Dr. Henry Sacheverell for preaching two sermons in which he criticized Godolphin, the Whig ministry, and the revolution of 1688. The London mobs made Sacheverell a popular hero and attacked Whig homes and Dissenter chapels. The Queen took advantage of this political climate to dismiss Godolphin and other Whig ministers. In the election of 1710 the Tory faction won a majority, and Robert Harley became Lord Treasurer and Henry St. John, his chief colleague. The Tories punished leading Whigs—Robert Walpole was sentenced to the Tower—and negotiated a peace with France. To pursue peace overtures it was necessary to oust Marlborough, the last important leader of the war ministry. In 1711 he was replaced as commander by the Tory Duke of Ormonde. The House of Commons backed Harley in his negotiations with France; however, to win a majority in the House of Lords, Queen Anne was forced to create twelve new peers. The Tory cabinet took advantage of Jonathan Swift's and Daniel Defoe's literary talents to subsidize essays supporting the Government. It was this cabinet that began the practice of coming to a consensus on policy in order to strengthen their case before seeking the Queen's approval. Although Queen Anne favored the Tories and carefully chose her ministers, she realized that a ministry was useless if it could not win votes in Parliament and that changing political alignments in Parliament could not be ignored.

Tory Statutes. With the support of Queen Anne, the Harley-St. John ministry (1710-14) passed a series of acts aimed at punishing the Whigs and the Dissenters. The Occasional Conformity Act put an end to the practice of Dissenter officeholders (mostly Whigs), who complied with the Test Act by taking the Anglican sacrament only once a year. The Property Qualification Act required members of the House of Commons to hold landed property with an annual value of £300 or £600 (depending on the constituency). This act handicapped the Whigs whose wealth was more likely to be in business than in land. The Schism Act was aimed at Dissenter academies; it required all teachers to be licensed by a bishop and to attend the Anglican church.

The Succession Question

As time approached to put into effect the clauses of the Act of Settlement relating to the succession, there was little enthusiasm for the Hanoverian cause. The Whigs favored the Hanoverians for political and religious reasons; however, they were not in control of Parliament. The Tories were divided between allegiance to the Stuarts—the Jacobite faction—and to the church. With his party divided Viscount Bolingbroke (Henry St. John) schemed to become indispensable in determining the succession, but his plans went awry and he was unable to control the situation.

Divided Loyalties. When Anne became ill in 1713, the issue of the succession loomed large. The Tories had tried and failed to get James, the Old Pretender (son of James II), to change his religion. When that hope was rebuffed, they became divided on the succession. Lord Treasurer Harley (now Earl of Oxford) led the moderate Tories who favored the Hanoverian succession. Meanwhile Bolingbroke intrigued with the opportunist Abigail Masham to persuade the Queen to dismiss Oxford on the grounds that he had become apathetic and lazy in office. Finally, on July 27, 1714, Oxford was dismissed as the Queen's chief minister.

The Fall of Bolingbroke. Viscount Bolingbroke, with a mind uncluttered by loyalties to anyone but himself, was one of the most brilliant, witty, and cultured political leaders of Queen Anne's reign. During the two days after he had accomplished the fall of

Oxford, Bolingbroke was the most powerful person in the realm but hesitated to act. His schemes for controlling the succession, whatever they were, collapsed. The Duke of Shrewsbury, a moderate Tory and one of the seven signatories to the petition to William in 1688, took the lead in forestalling Bolingbroke's plans. Supported by the Duke of Somerset and the Duke of Argyll, the Privy Council met on July 30 and rushed through a motion urging the Queen to make Shrewsbury Lord Treasurer, in which capacity he would be responsible for matters relating to the succession. Bolingbroke was not prepared to challenge the Privy Council, and Shrewsbury received the Treasurer's staff from the dying Queen.

The Change of Dynasties. The Tories lost an opportunity to consolidate their position by failing to agree to the succession of the Hanoverians. Instead, they hedged their loyalties so that the early Hanoverians considered the Whigs their friends and the Tories tainted with Jacobitism. Two months before Anne's final illness, Sophia, electress of Hanover, had died and left the succession to her son, George. Upon the death of Anne, Shrewsbury arranged the transition, and in September, 1714, the Elector of Hanover, along with his German advisers, mistresses, and hounds, arrived in England. With the Hanoverian succession Protestantism and a limited monarchy were maintained.

Stuart England

Political participation and social mobility existed to a greater degree in seventeenth-century England than on the Continent, but Englishmen who overcame political and class barriers were the exception, not the rule. The century still belonged to the favored few, not to the common people, because the great majority of Englishmen did not participate in the political events or share in the increasing wealth of the nation. Religious controversy spanned the century, but passions over religious differences were moderated by 1800. The security of the established church and of the country, along with the rationalism of the dawning Enlightenment, muted religious intolerance. Commerce and colonies became increasingly important and prosperous, but their future growth would be contingent on the control of the seas that was won under Queen Anne.

Stuart Literature. Seventeenth-century writing was characterized by a variety of forms and themes, ranging from the majestic sweep of Miltonic blank verse to the shallow, affected drama of the Restoration and the pamphlet literature of Queen Anne's reign.

Poetry. The Anglican clerics, Robert Herrick (1591-1674) and John Donne (1573-1631) are probably the most representative and respected poets of the early seventeenth century. Herrick's lyrical poems, dealing with classical myths of love or pastoral beauty, with occasional touches of fresh irreverence, are unsurpassed in craftsmanship. Donne's earlier works included satires and elegies but his metaphysical poems, such as *Songs and Sonnets,* are imbued with moods of introspection and distinguished by remarkable innovations in stanzaic patterns. His poetry influenced Dryden and a host of later poets. John Milton (1608-74) was the official apologist for the Cromwellian period. Following the Restoration he created three great poems in blank verse, *Paradise Lost, Paradise Regained,* and *Samson Agonistes,* in which his genius blended classical and Biblical themes into epics magnificent in scope and imagery; these heroic, profound, and tragic themes far transcended traditional Puritan theology. Satire and the heroic couplets were the most marked characteristics of poetic efforts in the Restoration period. Samuel Butler (1612-80) ridiculed the Puritans in his *Hudibras;* whereas Andrew Marvell (1621-78) displayed imaginative wit in *To His Coy Mistress* and justly praised the Lord Protector in the *Horatian Ode upon Cromwell's return from Ireland.* The poet laureate of the Restoration was John Dryden (1631-1700) whose versatile endeavors—criticism, poetry, drama, and satire—moved English literature to the threshold of the Augustan Age. His poems included *Absalom and Achitophel, Religio Laici, The Hind and the Panther,* and *Alexander's Feast.* More than anyone else he dominated the last half of the century and dictated its literary taste.

Prose. Essentially, the prose of the seventeenth century is formal, utilitarian, and precise. The *Essays* of Sir Francis Bacon (1561-1626) are polished treatises on civil and ethical matters written in terse, epigrammatic style. John Bunyan's (1628-88) *The Pilgrim's Progress* combines moral instruction with Biblical allegory in a storytelling framework of remarkable invention and technique. The mid-century was dominated by a variety of writers on theology, such as William Chillingworth, Jeremy Taylor, George Herbert, and Richard Baxter, and writers on politics as John Lilburne, William Walwyn, and William Prynee. Isaac Walton (1593-1683) wrote brief biographies of contemporary poets and *The Compleat Angler,* a pleasant, witty treatise on fishing. Samuel Pepys' *Diary* and John Aubrey's *Brief Lives* are invaluable sketches of social history spanning the last half of the seventeenth century. Both were published posthumously.

Drama. The theater had its greatest vogue under James I and

Charles II. Shakespeare, who lived until 1616, had many of his plays performed before King James. Ben Jonson (1572-1637) became the most influential and admired playwright of the early seventeenth century. His vivid characterizations and satirical humor are found in *Volpone, The Alchemist,* and *Bartholomew Fair.* Perfection in dramatic structure and an open interest in the politics of the day were distinguishing features of the plays of Philip Massinger (1583-1640). Puritan disapproval restricted the theater during the interregnum, but with the Restoration theaters were reopened and became popular with Charles II and his court. In reaction to the Puritan spirit, the Comedy of Manners accented lasciviousness and cynical worldliness. Among the playwrights who wrote these mock-heroic and romantic comedies were Dryden, William Wycherley, William Congreve, and John Vanbrugh. By the turn of the century, sentimental, domestic comedy, full of didacticisms and bourgeois respectability, as in Richard Steele's *The Tender Husband* (1705), became the vogue of the "reformed" theater.

History and Philosophy. The writing of history in many cases either shaded into memoirs or into political philosophy. Pre-civil war historians include Sir Walter Raleigh (*The History of the World*), Sir Francis Bacon, Thomas May, and Lord Herbert of Cherbury. Popular post-war works were Lord Clarendon's *History of the Rebellion* and Bishop Burnet's *History of His Own Time.* Political theorists dealt with the issues of ultimate sovereignty, royal prerogative versus common law, and the rights of the state and of the citizenry. King James I justified the prerogative rights of kingship in *The True Law of Free Monarchy.* The philosopher Francis Bacon replaced Aristotelian concepts with an inductive approach to knowledge in *The Advancement of Learning,* and *The New Atlantis.* Sir Edward Coke argued for a "fundamental law" that preceded and was superior to royal law. Sir Thomas Hobbes (1588-1679) was a cynical secularist who argued powerfully for absolute monarchy on the grounds of materialistic self-interest in *Leviathan.* James Harrington's (1611-77) answer to Hobbes was his *Commonwealth of Oceana* (1656) which influenced political thought in the interregnum by an economic interpretation of political power and an argument for a mixed constitution and a "balance of property." In the reign of Charles II, George Savile (1633-95), marquis of Halifax, published anonymously *The Character of a Trimmer*; he was an apologist for the golden mean in politics, which, in his terms, meant a limited monarchy. John Locke (1632-1704) in his epoch-making *Essay Concerning Human Understanding* argued for empiricism—all knowledge comes through experience—and rejected the theory of innate knowledge. In political theory Locke was a utilitarian like Hobbes, but opposed Hobbes's omnipotent state. In the second of his *Two Treatises on Government* Locke supported a government limited to certain areas by a social contract between the governor and the governed. If human government abused the liberty or the property rights of the subjects, the right to cancel the contract and to revolt was permissible. Locke's ideas of individual liberty and freedom from tyranny, religious or political, spread to France and America, and were taken up in the revolutions of the following century.

Scientific Interests. In the Stuart Age, the plea for scientific inquiry, introduced by Bacon in the *New Atlantis* and the *Novum Organum* and coupled with the previous observations of Copernicus and Kepler in astronomy, stimulated pure research in many fields. William Gilbert (1540-1603) offered new ideas in magnetism, and William Harvey (1578-1657) explained the circulation of the blood. With the foundation of the Royal Society (1662), scientists gained additional freedom and respectability. Robert Boyle's law in chemistry replaced outmoded Aristotelian theories; Richard Lauver performed a blood transfusion. But the major scientific event was the publication of Isaac Newton's *Philosophiae Naturalis Principia Mathematica* (1687), a monumental treatise dealing with the motion of celestial bodies according to the law of universal gravitation.

Religious Developments. In no other century were religious and literary issues so interwoven. The controversies and convictions which spanned the civil war and interregnum inspired a variety of religious expressions and freedoms: the Fifth Monarchy men, George Fox and the Quakers, the Brownists and the Congregational church government, and Cromwell's sponsorship of religious toleration. The efforts of Archbishop Laud to enforce religious uniformity aroused Puritan opposition. The Clarendon Code deliberately made the Anglican church more exclusive and forced Nonconformists from its membership. Dissenters influenced English politics in the following century and joined with the rationalists and the utilitarians to make freedom from unfair restrictions, religious or political, a common goal. By the end of the Stuart period the Anglican church was beginning to feel the effects of increasing rationalism and a decline of religious fervor. This development in the church was foreshadowed by the Oxford rationalists, William Chillingworth (1602-44) and John Hales (1584-1656), and the Cambridge Platonists, John Worthington (1618-71) and Ralph Cudworth (1617-88).

Social Developments. Since England's population was still four-fifths rural in the seventeenth century, the relationship of the individual to the land largely determined his social and economic class. The gentry or country squires, who owned large estates, were the most influential class, living in ease in their country manors most of the year but increasingly moving to London for the winter season. Politically, this class supplied the justices of the peace, and under the Stuarts won control of the House of Commons and forced political concessions from the King, such as the Petition of Right, the Triennial Act, and the Bill of Rights. Below the gentry were a diminishing class of yeomen, perhaps numbering 160,000, who were owners of smaller landholdings, but enfranchised and proud of their independence. Tenant farmers were increasing in number, although outnumbered greatly by the rural wage owner who knew the full meaning of poverty and had little opportunity to participate in national affairs except in such episodes as the Leveler movements of the Civil War. The moral tone of Puritanism dominated social customs until the Restoration. The court and the upper classes then repudiated Puritan tradition and took advantage of their new social liberties until a more sober court, prompted by the moralizing essayists of Queen Anne's reign, muted these excesses and encouraged a refinement of social conduct.

Agricultural Improvements. Agriculture continued as the occupation of the great majority of the population, with minor production improvements resulting from the use of fertilizers and the rotation of crops. The enclosure movement continued with less opposition as the need of converting the open-field system into hedged fields became generally recognized; and yet by the end of the century less than half the land was enclosed. Peasants who lost employment because of enclosures found other work in the industries of Bristol, York, Newcastle, and London.

Trade and Commerce. A significant growth in commerce, particularly in foreign trade, characterized the second half of the seventeenth century. Except for the East India and the Hudson's Bay Companies, monopolistic companies were broken by laws favoring competitive enterprise. Foreign commerce was promoted by legislation designed to further imperial trade and guarantee a favorable balance of trade. Commercial legislation, such as the Act of Navigation (1660), was an application of the mercantile theory which assumed that national prosperity was based on a favorable balance of trade and that any expansion of foreign commerce could only be at the expense of commercial rivals (Holland and Spain). Laws promoting exports and restricting imports, the expansion of the merchant navy to move goods, and a stronger navy to protect shipping became accepted features of the mercantile theory. In terms of imperial policy the acts of trade were devised to make the colonies serve as suppliers of raw materials and as markets for manufactured goods; also, the acts attempted to exclude all but English or colonial ships from the carrying trade. The preference given to colonial over foreign goods along with the protection of the royal navy were advantageous to English colonies at first. However, since colonial manufacturing was restricted, the acts would hinder the expansion of the American economy as the colonies developed. In practice, the acts were not a serious deterrent to colonial industry because they were only occasionally enforced; nevertheless, the mercantile policy became a growing source of grievance in the thirteen colonies.

The Growth of Empire. The English colonies exercised far greater independence of action than the colonies of any other European nation in the seventeenth century. In their charters and in their customs the colonies were to be "little Englands"; in the eyes of English lawmakers they were conceived of as "organs for the promotion of English commerce." [1] Economic and religious motives of the seventeenth century were paramount in the establishment of the twelve North American colonies. To most Englishmen, however, the Irish settlement and the colonies in Bermuda and in the West Indies were at least as important as the American colonies. Bermuda received its royal charter in 1615. During the remainder of the century Barbados, Jamaica, and the Bahamas were settled and became prosperous through a lively trade in sugar, molasses, tobacco, and cotton. These colonies, like the American colonies, were administered by an English governor and local assemblies. The East India Company received a new charter as a joint-stock company and, from its centers at Bombay and Madras, competed with the Marathas and the Dutch for trade and spheres of influence. At the same time the Royal Africa Company began a limited period of prosperity following its inception in 1672.

---

[1] Maurice Ashley, *Great Britain to 1688* (Ann Arbor: University of Michigan, 1961), p. 426.

Chapter 13 ✑ Georgian Politics— 1714-1763

The glorious revolution of 1688 had conserved and sanctified, rather than radically altered, the English parliamentary structure. The landed aristocracy dominated politics, and the monarchy remained the constitutional center of government, subject to the practical necessity of finding a ministry that could work with Parliament. Because the Whig politicians believed that the settlement of 1688 could best be protected by supporting the Hanoverian succession, the first two Georges repaid this consideration by choosing parliamentary ministers from among the Whigs. During this period the power of the House of Commons grew as ministries became increasingly dependent upon it for support. Such a development disturbed neither the aristocracy nor the monarchy, because the Commons was not yet a popular body and could be managed by the oligarchy or the Court, either through nomination of candidates in the constituencies or by patronage and influence. No man understood the power of the Crown's extensive patronage or managed the system more deftly than Robert Walpole. For that reason he was "Prime Minister" for two decades. The period, which was relatively peaceful, witnessed the expansion of English influence abroad through colonies, commerce, and seapower.

England at the Accession of George I

In 1714 the majority of Englishmen preferred a Hanoverian succession that would ensure a parliamentary and Protestant supremacy to any of the more controversial alternatives of the day as promoted by the Jacobites. In contrast to the Stuart period during which political and religious controversies divided the nation, the political leaders of the early eighteenth century were satisfied with the settlement of 1688 which had reformed the monarchy even though it had failed to reform Parliament. Abuses in corporate institutions (Parliament, church, municipal government, and universities) continued unchecked as English stability became identified with the status quo and was not to be tampered with. As a result, England's expansion and strength in the eighteenth century came through the abilities and energies of individual men given free rein by the country's liberal laws more than through the reforms or vigor of its institutions.

The New Dynasty. On the death of Queen Anne in August, 1714, George, elector of Brunswick-Lüneburg (commonly called Hanover after its principal city), succeeded to the throne in accordance with the terms of the Act of Settlement. Four months earlier, his mother, Sophia, a granddaughter of James I, had died; hence the throne went to her son who was not so eager about his inheritance as his mother had been. The Hanoverian succession was not the most direct line but was the most Protestant, and English acceptance of the new dynasty meant that there would be little likelihood of a Catholic monarch, French troops, or another civil war. On September 18, George I landed in his adopted realm. Dull, stodgy, and already fifty-four years of age, the new King never learned English and his subjects never learned to love or admire him. If they were attached to him, it was largely because he interfered so little with national institutions and because the return of the Stuarts might jeopardize the Anglican and parliamentary arrangement.

The Structure of Society. In the early eighteenth century, England had a population of about five and one-half million, the vast majority of which was in the rural areas of the south. London grew rapidly, passing the half-million mark, and new towns and industrial villages in the Midlands drained off the rural poor of the south and east. Parliament reflected these changes in its increasing preoccupation with trade, because trade meant wealth and wealth meant power; however, liquid capital had not yet replaced ownership of land as the hallmark of social and political power. Because property was sacrosanct, the laws dealing with crimes against property were numerous and extreme: a child stealing a handkerchief worth a shilling or more was liable for the death penalty.

The Country. At the apex of the social scale were the landed aristocracy, rich in estates and political influence, who lived in magnificence and provided a thin veneer of elegance to society. Their interest in, and profit from, agriculture made them supporters of improved farming methods. Next in rank were the country gentry who exercised local authority, often as justices of the peace. However, because of their more modest means and back-country residence, they seldom influenced national politics and, as a class, were identified with the Tories who resented the Whig oligarchy. As enclosures of common land became widespread, country laborers drifted into towns and became unskilled laborers. Many yeoman farmers who could not compete with the large estate-holders sold their holdings and became tenant farmers.

The Towns. The great merchants had close financial ties with the Government and often bought or married their way into the aristocracy. The smaller merchants and shop owners continued a seventeenth-century tradition of thrift and industry as well as a Puritan attitude toward corruption in high places; many were Dissenters who favored religious toleration at home and an isolationist policy abroad. Craftsmen and artisans worked long hours and made a modest wage so long as trade was good. But the changing economy and spread of a free labor market threatened their position, and two parliamentary acts (1720, 1744) prohibited combination, after unrest in the textile industry had caused workmen to act together to secure their rights. In the coffee houses of London the disaffected expressed their grievances in attacks on Walpole's Government.

The Ruling Class. Dominating the political scene were the great families of England whose ideas of a balanced constitution explained their allegiance to the Hanoverian rather than the Stuart dynasty. From 1707 to 1801—when one hundred Irish seats were added—the membership of the House of Commons remained frozen at 558. Nevertheless, the power of the Lower House grew steadily during the century without any serious efforts by the Lords to halt the trend, because the political and family interests of the two Houses were similar—they represented the same class. By means of political and monetary manipulation the peers could control the selection of candidates in their areas, and in only a minority of constituencies was the outcome of an election ever in doubt. With no uniform franchise (except for the county seats) and no redistribution of seats, the over-represented south produced numerous rotten boroughs in which a handful of voters could easily be managed with bribes or patronage. Pocket boroughs were completely under the control of one individual or family. Thus "the number of votes a peer or squire could secure either by threats, promises, or bribes was the measure of his influence; and a man in eighteenth-century politics was assessed by his influence." [1] With such influence a man could barter for pensions, sinecures, or government appointments. It was not by accident that the position of Prime Minister evolved from the post of First Lord of the Treasury, for patronage secretaries played an essential part in the intimate, yet complex, system of political bargaining that characterized the institutions of the century. With no appointments by examination, political connections and influence were the avenues to success. In this context the borough-mongers and influential families who controlled anywhere from eight to forty-five seats in the

---

[1] J. H. Plumb, *England in the Eighteenth Century* (Baltimore: Penguin, 1950), p. 38.

Commons could translate their local power to parliamentary influence. Increasingly, seats in the House of Commons were being sought as a means of becoming recognized, or of rewarding friends, as training by the eldest son of a peer for his later years in the Upper House, or as a stepping stone to social and political power. The surest way to enter the peerage was by becoming a borough patron who could command votes.

The Cabinet. It was perhaps characteristic of the English that their Cabinet system had no definition in law but was essentially the growth of conventions, which slipped casually into their institutional history under the first two Georges as the most effective arrangement for governing the country, and which served as the link through which the legislature could communicate with, and eventually extend democracy by controlling, the executive. The problem of limiting the King's power and exerting parliamentary sovereignty was solved, not by excluding the King's ministers from the Commons, as the Act of Settlement (1701) specified, but by insisting that the King's advisers sit in Parliament and have parliamentary support. Gradually, the influential members of the Privy Council were called a "conciliabulum" or efficient Cabinet; whereas the term "Prime Minister" came into use initially as a criticism of Robert Walpole for being more prominent in the Cabinet than his colleagues. By the time of Pitt the Younger, the term "Prime Minister" had become generally accepted, and the executive functions of the post increased at the expense of the reigning Sovereign. Although full responsible Government—the Cabinet owing collective responsibility to an elected legislature—did not become a necessity until the nineteenth century when party identity was more clearly defined, Walpole and his successors developed an arrangement whereby the first minister and his Cabinet colleagues could control sufficient support in the Commons (assisted by Government patronage) to make sure of a majority. In practice the Cabinet consisted of a group of politicians, led by one of their number, who could win the support of a majority of those who counted at Court and in Parliament. Thus the Cabinet was not a team but a coalition of individuals who could win first the favor of the King, and then the Commons. Such a Cabinet would stay in power until one of three things happened: the King tired of its members, the members fell out among themselves, or they failed to keep the support of Parliament.

The Whig Supremacy. The Hanoverian monarchs favored the Whigs because the Whigs in turn favored them and were not tainted with Jacobitism as were some of the Tories. Therefore, the

King chose his ministers from the Whig faction, which was controlled by the great landed families and supported by the Nonconformists and the majority of city merchants, particularly in the City of London. The Whigs halted the increasing intolerance of the Harley-Bolingbroke years by repealing the Schism and Occasional Conformity Acts, partly because the Whigs were a minority and needed the support of Dissenters, and also because the Whig leaders were more latitudinarian in their views of the established church. Although the Whigs dominated at Court and at Westminster, they seldom tampered with the local power of the landed gentry who, like Squire Western in *Tom Jones*, were usually Tory, and who exercised influence in the countryside as justices of the peace and as landholders.

Political Developments, 1714-54

After the tempestuous political and religious developments of the Stuart period, the early years of the Hanoverians provided England with domestic peace and governmental stability. During these years the Whigs, although rent into competing factions in Parliament, nevertheless enjoyed the favor of the first two Georges and composed the various ministries. Chief among Whig ministers was Robert Walpole whose long tenure (1721-42) as first minister has never been duplicated. The major threat to the Hanoverian supremacy came from the Jacobites. The two Jacobite uprisings of 1715 and 1745 failed to attract English support for the Stuarts and were easily crushed; each defeat discredited the Tories politically and made them appear synonymous with Jacobitism.

The Hanoverian-Whig Supremacy. The new dynasty was not popular in England. The King's coarse tastes, coldness, and German court were not warmly received. George's inability to speak English and his awareness that he could not rule England in the absolute fashion that he had ruled Hanover made him rely on English ministers and particularly on Whig leaders, because their loyalty to him, unlike that of the Tories, was not in question. In 1714 George appointed a new ministry led by Lord Townshend, and an election early the next year gave the Whigs a majority in the Commons. The Whigs now reciprocated the vindictive partisanship of the Tory years by passing acts of attainder against Bolingbroke and Ormonde and beginning impeachment proceedings against Oxford. When riots and demonstrations flared up in favor of James Edward Stuart, the Old Pretender, the Whigs passed the Riot Act (1715) which empowered a magistrate to order the dispersal within the hour of any assemblage of twelve or more persons who were disturbing the peace. Felony charges could be preferred against those failing to comply.

The Jacobite Rebellion. Stuart supporters who placed their hopes on an uprising joined a band of Highland clansmen under the leadership of the Earl of Mar. A landing was also planned on the south coast of England, but even before the Pretender landed in Scotland, the Jacobites had been twice defeated. The rebellion fizzled because Englishmen were not inclined to risk a civil war to restore a Catholic dynasty that they still mistrusted; also James proved to be an incompetent and dispiriting leader. Furthermore, King Louis XIV died on the eve of the rebellion; his promise of help was not honored by the Duke of Orléans who was regent during the minority of Louis XV.

The Septennial Act. The rebellion further discredited the Tories for their Jacobite leanings and permitted the Whigs to gain a decisive political ascendancy which lasted until 1760. The last Tory was dismissed from the Cabinet, and the Whigs passed the Septennial Act which extended the life of Parliament from three to seven years. The act gave the Whigs four additional years to entrench their political power. The excuse of unsettled conditions permitted the postponement of an election.

The Stanhope Ministry. King George's interest in foreign (Hanoverian) affairs helped make James Stanhope, supported by the Earl of Sunderland, the dominant figure in the remodeled all-Whig ministry. This ministry became divided over Stanhope's adventurous foreign policy; one faction, led by Charles Townshend and his brother-in-law, Robert Walpole, resigned in 1717.

Foreign Alliances. In 1716 George I had completed two alliances of mutual aid with Austria and with France. Stanhope continued this involvement in continental affairs by completing the Quadruple Alliance (1718) which joined England, France, Holland, and Austria against Philip V of Spain, who had designs on Austrian territory and ambitions for the French throne. In 1719 French troops and a British fleet inflicted a double defeat on Spain. Philip abandoned his expansionist plans, dismissed his brilliant minister, Cardinal Alberoni, and negotiated the Treaty of Madrid (1721) which established a defensive alliance with England and France and confirmed earlier political and commercial agreements. Stanhope was just as successful in the Baltic where Charles XII, the powerful King of Sweden, was challenging Hanoverian interests and encouraging opposition to the new dynasty in England. Stanhope sent the English navy to the Baltic, risking war to protect

British interests in northern Europe. The sudden death of Charles made Russia the chief threat in the Baltic. To contain Peter the Great, Stanhope succeeded in allying with Sweden and settling their differences over Hanover by the treaties of Stockholm and Frederiksburg in 1720. Stanhope's foreign policy helped secure the peace of Europe and recognition of the Hanoverian succession.

Domestic Politics. Stanhope was less successful in domestic policies. The Schism Act and the Occasional Conformity Act were repealed, but his efforts to abolish the Corporation and Test Acts were defeated. In 1719 Stanhope introduced his peerage bill which would ensure Whig domination of the Lords by virtually freezing its membership. The political purpose was to keep the Prince of Wales, who bitterly opposed his father, from creating sufficient Tory peers as Queen Anne had done to swamp the Whig majority. Walpole denounced the bill as one making the Lords a private corporation and closing the one avenue to rank and honor open to the country gentry. The opposition and independent members coalesced to defeat the bill which, if nothing else, convinced Stanhope of the wisdom of restoring Walpole and Townshend to the Cabinet.

The South Sea Bubble. In 1711 the South Sea Company was chartered as a joint-stock organization to take advantage of South American trade which opened up through the Asiento clauses of the Treaty of Utrecht. At the time, the Government was trying to liquidate the national debt more quickly by having portions of it absorbed by several great companies, such as the Bank of England and the East India Company. The South Sea Company devised a sinking fund scheme to pay off the entire debt and permitted the Court and members of Parliament to buy a large number of shares. A mania of speculation broke loose as the Government appeared to be backing the company. Stocks soared 1000 per cent, and other promoters took advantage of this bull market to advertise the flimsiest of schemes. The bubble burst in August, 1720, ruining thousands of investors and precipitating a financial and political crisis. The dispossessed clamored for scapegoats, and a parliamentary inquiry revealed gross corruption in high places. Members of the Cabinet were involved and publicly disgraced, and although Stanhope was not implicated, he suffered a stroke defending his innocence in the House of Lords. The King desperately needed a new political manager, one who was not incriminated in the sorry scandal, and one who could restore public confidence and national credit by his financial abilities. Walpole met these requirements and became chancellor of the exchequer. He performed a remarkable job of extricating the Government and the Court from the scandal and in restoring the finances and the confidence of the nation. The South Sea scandal became the turning point of Walpole's career.

"Prime Minister" Walpole, 1721-42. With the death of Sunderland in 1722 the issue of Whig leadership was resolved, and Walpole held onto his newly-won position for twenty-one years. During this time Walpole exerted a primacy among his Cabinet colleagues previously unmatched. Through his loyalty to the Crown, bribery, patronage, enormous energy for work and mastery of detail, he effectively controlled the machinery of government. As Prime Minister he used his uncanny knack for probing the weaknesses of human nature and sensing public opinion to steer England on a course that was wise and profitable, if not always heroic. He was neither an idealist nor a reformer, but his contribution was substantial. Through his policy of peace and prosperity, he left England powerful and its new dynasty secure. A master manager of men, Walpole reflected and played upon the political morality and shifting political alignments of his day.

Rise to Prominence. The son of a Norfolk squire, Sir Robert Walpole left Cambridge when his elder brother died in order to learn the management of a large estate. He became a successful businessman and a typical country squire of his day—coarse in morals and uncouth in manners, a heavy drinker, generous to his friends and indifferent to his opponents. In 1700 he began his political career as a member for a pocket borough belonging to his family. Under Queen Anne, he held several minor offices and built up a reputation in the area of finance. In 1714 Walpole became a Cabinet minister but resigned in 1717. He returned two years later and survived the disintegration of Stanhope's ministry because of his reputation in finance and his timely severance from the South Sea Company.

Minister and King. Under the first two Georges the Cabinet became increasingly independent of the King's domination. Because George I was unable to speak English and was more absorbed in Hanoverian affairs, he rarely attended Cabinet sessions. Under George II this custom hardened into precedent, which meant that as the King's influence in the Cabinet and in parliamentary affairs declined, it became increasingly important to have a Cabinet which could command the support of Parliament. Thus under both Kings Walpole came close to being an indispensable political manager. Throughout his long career, he sat in the Commons and made it the center of Government. Similarly, he made himself the center of the Cabinet either by demanding his colleagues' support of his policies or, on occasion, their resignation. In 1727 George I died and his son came to the throne. George II was dull, pompous, and hostile to the advisers of his father, and, as was expected, the ministers were dismissed, but not for long. Walpole was too valuable a political manager to lose, and returned to office by outbidding his competitors' promise of an increased royal income and through the support of Queen Caroline, the intelligent and politically astute consort, who commanded King George's confidence, if not his fidelity. Thereafter, George II interested himself chiefly in foreign and court affairs, and Walpole consolidated his position through patronage and pensions. Borough patrons and independent members were rewarded with spoils as Walpole and his political colleague, the Duke of Newcastle, manipulated pensions and church and state appointments to sustain parliamentary support.

Economic Policies. Not until Gladstone would another Prime Minister master financial details as completely as Walpole. Convinced that a prosperous country was contingent on peace, Walpole shunned foreign entanglements and gave his attention to a more efficient development of the nation's commerce and industry. He reduced interest on Government borrowing to 4 per cent, relaxed colonial restrictions, simplified the confusing tariff rates, and removed export duties from manufactured articles. His economies kept taxes low, especially the tax on land, which won him the support of landowners at Court and in Parliament. In 1733 Walpole attempted a major reform with an excise bill which would extend the excise system of taxation already highly successful on tea, coffee, and chocolate imports. The bill would apply to tobacco and wine and would free tax collectors from a cumbersome refunding arrangement. Immediately public and political opposition loudly denounced the proposed bill as an increase in bureaucratic power. Finally Walpole yielded to popular and court pressure and withdrew the bill, and then proceeded to punish his supporters who had deserted him on the measure.

Political Warfare. Walpole's notion of good government emphasized peace abroad, prosperity at home, sound finances, and freedom from controversial issues; he did nothing to upset either the Anglican churchman or the local Tory squire. Such policies were difficult to fight at first, especially when prosperity ensued. But gradually the Opposition gained in strength over the years as each colleague Walpole alienated joined their ranks. Bolingbroke, whom Walpole had permitted to return from exile, stood at the center of opposition in the discredited Tory party. Joining the Jacobite opposition were two able, but lazy, Whig leaders, John Carteret and William Pulteney, who were bitter over their exclusion from Walpole's Cabinet. In 1730 Walpole's brother-in-law, Townshend, left the Cabinet after a quarrel and retired. Reaction to the excise bill had increased the ranks of the Opposition; those who changed sides protested Walpole's use of pension and place to keep supporters or were jealous because they were excluded from patronage. Before 1733 there was not a sufficient number of anti-Walpole Whigs to form a Government; after 1733 Chesterfield, Bolton, Cobden and many other Whig peers were eager to provide an alternative ministry. They were joined by a group of young, aspiring Whigs, including William Pitt and George Grenville, who opposed the aging Walpole and his corrupt style of administration. Dubbed the "boy patriots" by the Prime Minister, they claimed to be champions of the people. This heterogeneous "out" group gravitated to the Court of Frederick, prince of Wales, who quarreled publicly with his father and was anxious to assume the throne. The Opposition finally found Walpole vulnerable on foreign policy.

Walpole and Foreign Affairs. The object of Walpole's foreign policy was simple: to keep England out of a continental war because wars were expensive and their outcome uncertain. Through a network of alliances Walpole and Townshend strove to restrict Austria and to keep the Continent from breaking into two armed camps. By the first Treaty of Vienna, Spain and Austria resolved their differences which, in turn, brought on a bellicose attitude in England against Spain. Walpole believed that with the help of France (Treaty of Hanover, 1725) Spain and Austria could be separated; so with indifference to the anti-Spanish sentiment he concluded the Treaty of Seville with Spain in 1729. Two years later, the Second Treaty of Vienna settled the major differences between Hanover and Austria. War was arrested but the alliances depended for their success on a friendly France. In 1733 the French partnership was jeopardized by a Bourbon family compact even though France's involvement in the war over the Polish Succession (1733-35) kept the covenant temporarily dormant. England remained neutral in spite of King George's interest in participating in the war; however, Walpole's peace policy was becoming his *one* vulnerable point, and his opponents quickly capitalized on the anti-Spanish sentiment of the country to condemn his pacific policy as unpatriotic. Hatred of Spain had increased in the thirties as grievances grew out of England's efforts to break the monopoly of Spanish trade in the Americas. British traders evaded the restrictions of the Asiento clause, and smuggling was heavy. In retaliation, Spanish patrols searched ships in Spanish water and, on occasion, maltreated British seamen. Walpole attempted negotiations once more and secured a treaty even though the Opposition and the nation wanted war. When the Cabinet agreed, Walpole yielded to popular pressure and England became involved in the War of Jen-

kins' Ear (1739)[2]. This Anglo-Spanish conflict became the prelude
of the War of the Austrian Succession (1740).

Fall of Walpole. For three years Walpole conducted a war of
which he strongly disapproved. During these years he missed the
assistance at Court of Queen Caroline who had died in 1737, while
in Parliament his supporters gradually deserted him so that the
election of 1741 left him with only a slim majority. His closest
colleagues, including Newcastle, announced their willingness to
work in a new ministry. Under these circumstances Walpole resigned in February, 1742, and accepted a peerage; three years later
he was dead.

War of the Austrian Succession. In 1740 Emperor Charles VI
died, leaving his Hapsburg dominions to his only daughter, Maria
Theresa. Her accession was confirmed by the Pragmatic Sanction
signed by the other leading European States. It was repudiated by
Frederick the Great who came to the Prussian throne in 1740, and
by the Elector of Bavaria; the former wanted Silesia, and the latter
had designs on the Imperial throne. The war, in part, was a struggle
between the Hohenzollern and Hapsburg dynasties for first place
in Germany. It was also a resumption of the struggle between
England and France in which national, commercial, and imperial
considerations were interwoven, because neither nation had achieved
a decisive colonial or commercial supremacy over the other.

The War in Europe. On the Continent, England, Hanover,
Austria, and Holland opposed Prussia, Bavaria, France, and Spain.
England aided the Austrians with money and dispatched an army
to Holland. Frederick invaded and held Silesia and withdrew from
the war when England pressed Austria to recognize his conquest. A
British victory at Dettingen (1743)—where George II was the last
English king to lead an army into battle—was offset by a French
triumph at Fontenoy (1745).

The War Elsewhere. From 1744 to the conclusion of hostilities
Great Britain and France were the chief combatants without either
one winning a decisive engagement. The British were successful in
several naval encounters; the French captured Madras from the
British, and the English took Louisburg (Acadia) from the French.
With commerce suffering and the war drifting on aimlessly, both
sides agreed to peace.

Treaty of Aix-la-Chapelle. In 1748, the Peace of Aachen ended
the War of Austrian Succession. The treaty signed at Aix-la-

---

[2] Named after an English mariner, Robert Jenkins, who claimed that his ship
had been boarded and his ear torn off by the Spaniards. He told his tale and
showed the withered ear to the House of Commons as evidence of Spanish
atrocities. The tale caught the popular imagination.

Chapelle resulted in (1) a restoration of the *status quo ante bellum*, except for Silesia, which Frederick kept; (2) confirmation of the Pragmatic Sanction and the election of Emperor Francis (Maria Theresa's husband); and (3) Spain's agreement to the continuation of British trade with the Americas according to the Treaty of Utrecht. In effect, the treaty became an armed truce, because it left Austria angry over the loss of Silesia, said nothing about the right of search which had led to English-Spanish hostilities, and only offered a breathing spell in the colonial rivalry between England and France until the struggle could be resumed in the Seven Years' War.

Rebellion of 1745. Charles Edward Stuart, the son of the Old Prentender, landed in Scotland to press his father's claim. The Young Pretender commanded an army of loyal Highlanders who seized Edinburgh and defeated the British army at Prestonpans. The energetic and charming Bonnie Prince Charlie moved his Jacobite army as far south as Derby hoping for English support which never materialized. With the help of regiments from the continental wars, the Duke of Cumberland pursued the Scots and finally destroyed their army at Culloden Moor in April, 1746. Charles Edward escaped to the Continent, many of his supporters were executed, and the hereditary jurisdiction of the Highland chiefs was taken away. The "Forty-five" was the last serious effort to overthrow the Hanoverian dynasty and restore the Stuarts.

The Uneasy Peace, 1748-54. The War of the Austrian Succession taught the British, and particularly William Pitt, that a commercial and colonial empire could only be won and held by naval supremacy. Although there was peace in Europe in 1748, the threatening aspects of Anglo-French rivalry in the colonies overshadowed this calm interlude.

Rivalry in India. The truce of 1748 did not extend to India where the rivalry between France and England was shifting from purely commercial competition to a political and military contest. By the eighteenth century the Portuguese and the Dutch were no longer serious competitors. The last of the great Mogul emperors had died in 1707, and, in the scramble for power that ensued among the Indian potentates, conditions were ripe for intrigue. By supporting rival Indian rulers, the French and English expanded their influence beyond their respective "factory" posts. Joseph Dupleix, the energetic French governor of Pondichéry, supported the pro-French candidate to the nabob of the Carnatic who was making a claim of hereditary sovereignty. The British backed Mohammed Ali for the throne of the Carnatic. When war broke out between the French and the British, only the magnificent daring of Robert Clive, a clerk of the East India Company turned military captain, saved the Carnatic and Madras from yielding to the French siege. In 1754 Dupleix was recalled to France, and Clive and the English engaged French interests in the northeast, around Calcutta.

Rivalry in North America. English colonies were strung along the Atlantic seaboard but were not yet interested in a federation (Albany Conference, 1754), which would have utilized their manpower to halt French efforts to link the Mississippi and St. Lawrence territories by controlling the Ohio Valley. The French, who had erected forts in this area, defeated George Washington at Fort Necessity (1754) when the Governor of Virginia sent him to dispute the French title to the territory. The English attempted to punish the French by sending General Braddock and English regiments against Fort Duquesne; however, the French and Indians ambushed the army and killed Braddock. In 1755 the British retaliated by deporting some ten thousand French Acadians [3] from Nova Scotia and scattering them from Maine to Louisiana. Thus war had actually begun in India and America before it was formally declared in Europe.

Diplomatic Revolution. By 1754 the alliances of the War of the Austrian Succession had disintegrated. National self-interest and new jealousies, such as the dislike of the "Three Furies," Czarina Elizabeth, Empress Maria Theresa, and Madame de Pompadour for Frederick the Great, brought about a new diplomatic alignment. When Britain and France declared war in May, 1756, Britain and Prussia were ranged against France, Austria, and Russia.

Domestic Politics. After Walpole's resignation, a "Broad-bottom Administration" led by Lord Wilmington, though dominated by Carteret, brought in some opposition Whigs and a few Tories. Carteret's venturesome conduct of the war and his inability to control the Commons united the Opposition and forced his resignation in 1744. For the next ten years (1744-54), Henry Pelham headed the Cabinet ably assisted in the Lords by his brother, the Duke of Newcastle. The Duke in his painstaking, nervous manner skillfully held together a parliamentary majority for his brother as he had done for Walpole. When George II tried to get rid of Pelham in 1746, the Cabinet resigned in a body, and since no alternative Cabinet could manage Parliament, George was forced to take back the Pelhams on their terms, which included the admission of William Pitt to the ministry. In 1754 Henry Pelham died, and

---

[3] Lamented in Henry Wadsworth Longfellow's poem, *Evangeline: A Tale of Acadie* (1847).

Newcastle took over the leadership of the Cabinet just as England was entering the Seven Years' War.

William Pitt and the Seven Years' War

Although the Seven Years' War broke out over a European question, colonial and commercial rivalry dominated the world-wide areas of conflict. At first the French were successful everywhere, until the tide was turned in favor of the British under the leadership of William Pitt. Convinced of his own and England's destiny, Pitt's genius steered the nation from peril and his war leadership masterminded a string of impressive victories. Pitt led England from defeat and despair to colonial and naval supremacy but could not rescue his own political career, because he lacked the political base to hold onto power when the King and Parliament no longer needed him.

English Defeats.   At the outset, the war was an unrelieved disaster for the English. In India the British garrison at Calcutta fell to the nawab of Bengal, Siraj-ud-daula, and all but 23 of 146 prisoners suffocated or were trampled to death in a small cell, infamously termed the "Black Hole." In North America the brilliant French general, Montcalm, captured Fort Oswego in New York and tightened the encirclement of the English colonies. In the Mediterranean the British lost Minorca when Admiral Byng failed in his mission. The likelihood of a French invasion of England added to the despair when, on the Continent, Hanover fell to French troops. Although the Prussian army won some notable victories in 1756, in the next years Frederick II could only keep at bay the huge armies of his enemies.

Ministerial Crisis.   These misfortunes forced the resignation of the Newcastle ministry in 1756. King George reluctantly accepted a Devonshire-Pitt ministry, even though his old prejudices against Pitt—for his attacks on the King's partiality for Hanover—were as strong as ever. The new ministry labored under a political disadvantage because it could not win a parliamentary majority. When King George dismissed Pitt in 1757, he was immediately faced with a hostile nation demanding the return of the Great Commoner. A political coalition between Newcastle and Pitt was arranged, and, for the next four years, Pitt led the Commons and directed the war, while Newcastle provided the parliamentary majority and raised money to fight a world war.

The Leadership of Pitt.   Unlike Walpole who was a political operator adroit in the handling of men, Pitt worked alone and remained above political faction. He was proud, imperious, and egotistical. His greatness was in his rare ability to translate his own patriotism and vision for England into the nation's belief in their destiny. Such a wide-ranging yet erratic genius, who disregarded normal political conventions to make himself the mouthpiece of English patriotism, did not win lasting political support; nevertheless, he was the right man to lead England in a time of crisis.

Rise to Power. William Pitt, unlike most of his Cabinet colleagues, was not born into a politically and socially established family. The Pitt fortune had been made by William's grandfather, "Diamond Pitt," the governor of Madras. After attending Oxford, Pitt entered Parliament through his grandfather's purchase of the rotten borough of Old Sarum. The young Pitt soon made himself known by his impassioned oratory and attacks on Walpole's Government and the King's Hanoverian interests. In 1746 the Pelhams brought Pitt into the ministry, where he won a popular following and a reputation of incorruptability by refusing to use his position as Paymaster of the Forces to indulge in the usual plundering of public funds. When Newcastle did not give him a major post, Pitt resigned in 1755 and assailed the Government's war policies with telling effect. But a year later Pitt was finally in the position he wanted—minister in charge of the war.

Pitt's War Policies. As war leader, Pitt increased the subsidies to Frederick II and strengthened the Hanoverian army in order to keep France occupied on the Continent while he pursued his primary aim—the crushing of France's navy and trade by the use of superior sea power. The British navy and the army were reorganized, new supplies provided, and young, able commanders, like Wolfe and Howe, were placed in charge of expeditions. A new enthusiasm and energy infected the whole nation.

The Tide of Victory. Almost immediately major English victories occurred on land and sea so that by 1759 Horace Walpole could write, "One is forced to ask every morning what victory there is, for fear of missing one." [4] In North America Louisburg, Frontenac, and Duquesne fell. In 1759 General Wolfe commanded the British expedition against Quebec and defeated the French under Montcalm at the Plains of Abraham, the decisive battle that cost him his life. A year later Montreal and all Canada became British. In Bengal Clive defeated Siraj-ud-daula at Plassey. By 1761 the French fleet was driven away and Pondichéry surrendered, virtually ending the French empire in India. On the seas, the navy captured Guadeloupe in the West Indies and Dakar on the west coast of Africa. In 1759 Admiral Boscawen demolished the Toulon

---

[4] *Letters* (16 volumes; Oxford, 1903-1905) IV, p. 330.

fleet off Lagos, and the French Atlantic fleet was decisively beaten at Quiberon Bay by Admiral Hawke, thereby leaving stranded at Le Havre the French troops who were prepared for an invasion of England. Not since Marlborough's campaigns had the English been so overwhelmingly victorious over the French. Even though Spain joined forces with France in 1761, the English went on to occupy Havana and Manila the following year.

Pitt's Decline. Pitt and his supporters in London believed that trade was wealth (and power) and, therefore, that the war should continue until France was stripped of her commercial empire. However, opposition arguments grew louder after 1760. Some opponents lamented the increasing cost of the war, others were jealous of the prestige and power Pitt had acquired as war minister. Foremost among critics was King George III who disliked his grandfather's ministers, especially one who overshadowed the King in power. Consequently, King George supported the opponents of Pitt. When his colleagues refused to support him in a declaration of war against Spain in 1761, Pitt resigned; Newcastle followed. The Cabinet, headed by Lord Bute, declared war against Spain after it became evident that the secret Bourbon family compact provided for an imminent declaration of war by Spain against Great Britain. In 1762 Havana and Manila were taken from Spain. In the same year Russia withdrew from the war, and King Frederick regained the Prussian territory which Russia and Austria had occupied. Bute quickly began negotiations for peace with France.

Peace of Paris, 1763. The peace settlement left Prussia one of the major powers although Frederick II felt deserted by England in the negotiations. Pitt and London merchants condemned the peace because it wrecked his grand design of destroying the French trading empire. Even so, England retained many of her conquests including: (1) Cape Breton, Canada, and undisputed possession of North America east of the Mississippi; (2) Florida, in exchange for the return of Havana to Spain; (3) all but four of the islands captured from France in the West Indies; (4) the slave port of Senegal in Africa; (5) the recovery of Minorca; and (6) political preponderance in India. The war and the peace settled the Anglo-French rivalry for control of North America, paved the way for English rule in India, bankrupted France and destroyed her navy, and left Britain as the foremost naval and colonial power in the world.

Chapter 14 ⋙ England and the American Revolution

Within twenty years of the Peace of Paris which marked the apex of the First British Empire, Britain was once again in Paris relinquishing the crown jewels of her Empire, the Thirteen Colonies. England blundered into war through failure to remodel her imperial policies to the growing independence of the American colonies. Colonial problems were further complicated by the political sparring which was occurring in England. As the Whig supremacy disintegrated, the Tories regained respectability, and King George III attempted to exercise royal authority in a more vigorous fashion than his two predecessors.

George III and the Politicans

George III had a loftier and a more active conception of kingship than his grandfather; furthermore, the bickerings of the Whig factions seemed sufficient justification for making Cabinet ministers the "King's servants" in fact and for ruling independent of political factions. During the 1760's the young King was able to keep the Cabinets in a state of flux, but his vision of Government was too narrow to offer a more effective system of administration. Certainly, the Whig legend of George III as a domineering tyrant seeking to thwart Parliament by unconstitutional conduct is patently overdrawn. His system of personal Government was unsatisfactory largely because it failed to abolish factions.

The New King. George III was the first of the Hanoverians to be Englishborn. His youth, piety, and seriousness made him popular at first, until other traits of character became evident. He was obstinate and narrow-minded and failed to adapt to changing conditions. He held exalted ideas of the royal prerogative which he was determined to exercise. His stubborn sense of duty and recurrent attacks of mental illness made co-operation between himself and the Cabinet exceedingly difficult, and eventually his popularity faded. One of the first of the dormant royal prerogatives exercised by King George was the power of patronage—a profitable area of political influence previously dispensed by the King's ministers.

George III and the Whigs. By 1760 the Whig rule was disintegrating. This was a development that George III encouraged since he disliked "indispensable" figures among his ministers. From 1760 to 1770 there were seven Prime Ministers and, as a result, an obvious lack of continuity in handling the colonies at a most critical time.

Lord Bute, 1762-63. After the resignation of Pitt in 1761, Lord Bute, the King's mentor, arranged the ouster of Newcastle and became Prime Minister. Bute led the Cabinet until he had pushed the peace treaty through Parliament by exercising the patronage of the Crown to replace Newcastle's appointments. However, Parliament disliked Bute because he was a royal favorite and an outsider, a Scotsman. King George reluctantly accepted his resignation.

George Grenville, 1763-65. George Grenville, Pitt's brother-in-law, obtained a parliamentary majority by allying himself with the Duke of Bedford and his unprincipled parliamentary clique, the Bloomsbury gang. Grenville was an efficient administrator though he was never liked by the King. In 1765 George III dismissed the Cabinet to show his displeasure over the passage of a regency bill.

Rockingham, 1765-66. To rid himself of Grenville, the King turned to the "Old Whig" faction and the Marquess of Rockingham. The new Cabinet repealed Grenville's Stamp Act, but Rockingham could not maintain Whig unity in Parliament, especially after Pitt refused to support the Cabinet. Within a year Rockingham was forced to resign.

Pitt's Coalition Cabinet, 1766-68. Pitt who had accepted a peerage was now known as the Earl of Chatham. His return to the Cabinet was a miserable failure. Suffering with gout and from mental disorders, he was unable to co-ordinate policies or control his colleagues, each of whom went his own way. Pitt, who had been habitually snappish and arrogant, became increasingly uncooperative. Yet nothing except a strong leadership could have held the diversive elements of the non-party Cabinet together. When Pitt failed to recover from a mental breakdown, the Duke of Grafton replaced him as Prime Minister.

The Grafton Government, 1768-70. The Cabinet remained divided under the Duke of Grafton's ineffectual leadership. Colonial policies continued to drift although a new Cabinet post, Secretary of State for the Colonies, was created. By this time, not only the King but also many members of Parliament were restive with the barren Whig ministries.

Lord North, 1770-82. George III finally found a suitable manager of the House of Commons in Lord North. As Prime Minister, North used tact and royal patronage to hold a majority for twelve years, with the support of the Tories and the King's Friends. Through the acquiescent North, George controlled the subservient Cabinet; through patronage he won personal supporters in the Commons (the King's Friends) who looked to him, instead of to Whig ministers, for pensions and jobs.

John Wilkes and Radicalism.   King George resented the popular and literary critics of his peace negotiations (1762-63) with France and singled out John Wilkes, a member of Parliament, to serve as an object lesson. Prime Minister Grenville issued a general warrant for the arrest of everyone connected with the publication of the *North Briton,* issue No. 45, in which Wilkes had sharply assailed the ministerial policy reflected in the King's speech to Parliament. In the ensuing court squabble over the legality of general warrants, Wilkes claimed the privilege of immunity as a member of Parliament and fled to France after his release from prison. However, the House of Commons formally expelled Wilkes for his seditious libel, and the Cabinet outlawed him for refusing to stand trial. Such high-handed action ignited popular indignation in London with the result that the mob and parliamentary opposition united to make a constitutional test case out of the Wilkes affair and to defy the King. The "Wilkes and Liberty" agitation harrassed the Government until 1769, when Wilkes was ejected from the House for the fourth time after his fourth re-election by the independent-minded electorate of Middlesex County. Not until 1774 was he allowed to take his seat. Thus Wilkes, a dissolute drunkard, rather ironically became the hero of the mob and the rallying point for radical agitation which led ultimately to parliamentary reform. English radicalism which stemmed from this episode learned well the techniques of mob psychology and pamphlet warfare. These methods were quickly copied by the American colonists when they, in turn, were coerced by the British Government.

Colonial Policies, 1763-75

With a brooding France and a restless Ireland as neighbors along with radical agitation and Cabinet instability at home, Britain was much too occupied to give serious attention to any new policy for the old and trusted Thirteen Colonies in America. During these years the British Cabinet lacked any imaginative, or even coherent, policy; Cabinet policy seemed to be largely one of doing too little too late. As a result England blundered into a deteriorating relationship with the American colonies which was neither anticipated nor planned in 1763.

Imperial Problems in 1763. The acquisition of huge new territories in the Seven Years' War demanded immediate attention
with regard to boundaries and to relations with the French and
Indian inhabitants. The recent war had also revealed the casual and
inefficient administration of the Empire and the need to co-ordinate
imperial policy. Yet such co-ordination was impossible without a
central authority with power to establish and administer Colonial
policy. With at least six separate central organs, ranging from the
Board of Trade to the Admiralty Courts, responsible for Colonial
administration, it was easy to shift the burden or to handle only
one facet of a problem in the colonies.

Acts of Trade. The mercantilist laws prohibiting trade between
a colony and a foreign territory were never severely enforced by
the British or their customs officials, until the Seven Years' War
revealed how heavy traffic was between the colonies and the
French West Indies. In 1760 when Pitt tried to enforce previous
acts of trade, such as the Molasses Act (1733), Colonial merchants
in New York and Massachusetts stoutly resisted this invasion of
their lucrative, though illicit, trade.

Imperial Defense. The separate colonies were usually unreliable
in supplying either men or supplies when the Empire was at war or
even when a neighboring colony was attacked by Indians. And yet
some type of imperial defense was necessary to control the interior
and to keep peace between the colonists and the Indians, especially
after Pontiac's uprising in 1763. The British determined that a
standing army of ten thousand was necessary, when the end of
French encirclement made the colonists claim they no longer
needed Redcoats for protection.

Colonial Taxation. The expenses of the French and Indian War
and the continued maintenance of troops in America emptied the
British Treasury. Because the colonists derived major benefit from
British protection, they were asked to contribute one-third of the
cost of the standing army, whereas the British taxpayer would pay
two-thirds and the entire cost of naval defense. The type of taxation employed by English ministries to raise these revenues and the
larger issue of their *right* to tax the colonists united the colonists
for the first time in a common protest against the mother country's
parliamentary practices.

Colonial Acts, 1763-74. The thirteen taxation acts passed by
Parliament in eleven years were protested by the Continental Congress in 1774. Apart from trade regulations, Colonial laws had previously originated in the local assemblies. Now Parliament legislated directly for the colonists in an effort to raise revenue, a legal

right which the English Parliament undoubtedly possessed, but which appeared arbitrary to the colonists who had enjoyed practical independence for so long. There was no tyrannical intent in the British policy. Most English statesmen, including such friends of the American colonies as Pitt and Burke, believed that Britain had the right to tax the colonies. The slogan of "no taxation without representation" made little constitutional sense to Englishmen when only one out of ten adult males in England had the vote. Furthermore, the British system of representation was based on interests, not on population; therefore, every Englishman, wherever he resided, was virtually represented in Parliament. The English Government and taxpayers disregarded the intensity of Colonial feeling; the American colonists refused to accept the supremacy of the British Parliament.

Stamp Act, 1765. Grenville renewed the Sugar Act in **1764** while cutting the prohibitive duty by one-half in order to reduce smuggling and raise revenue. The next year Parliament passed his Stamp Act which would raise £100,000 per annum for imperial defense. The tax was in operation in Britain, and although Colonial opinion had been consulted before its passage, the act nevertheless provoked stormy protest in the colonies. A boycott of British goods ensued, and a Stamp Act Congress condemned the levying of an internal tax. The Rockingham Government repealed the Act in **1766** because England could not enforce it and because British merchants protested the loss of trade. The Cabinet accompanied the repeal with a declaratory act asserting the right of Parliament to tax the colonies.

The Townshend Duties. In 1767 Charles Townshend, chancellor of the exchequer, overlooked the colonists' opposition to an internal tax and imposed duties on lead, glass, paint, paper, and tea imported into the colonies. Again the colonists resisted a revenue tax so that in **1770** Lord North's Cabinet repealed all duties except that on tea which was retained as an assertion of parliamentary authority. The Americans refrained from purchasing imported tea, and in **1773** a group in Boston dramatized their feeling against the tax by dumping cargoes of tea into the harbor. This act shifted England's vacillating policy of resoluteness and conciliation to one of coercion.

Coercive Acts. Parliamentary legislation in **1774** closed the port of Boston, strengthened royal authority in the administration of Massachusetts, arranged for the quartering of English troops in America, and stipulated that persons accused of capital offenses could be removed from Massachusetts for trial.

Quebec Act, 1774. The Quebec Act, which was included in the colonists' list of intolerable acts, gave Quebec control over the region of the Great Lakes and offered special recognition to the Roman Catholic church. In reality, it was a wise and liberal decree which Canadians hailed as the "Magna Charta" of their civil liberties, because not only did it allow the French to keep their civil law and their religion, but it also recognized the futility of attempting to Anglicize and assimilate French Canada.

American Unity. A unique result of the friction between the colonies and Britain was the degree of co-operation achieved among the formerly disunited colonies. Committees of correspondence were set up in each colony which permitted an isolated grievance to become a common grievance, and well-organized protest societies, such as the Sons of Liberty, fanned the increasing discontent. The events of 1774 strengthened the influence of a vociferous radical element in the colonies and resulted in a Continental Congress in Philadelphia, which challenged the authority of Parliament and demanded the withdrawal of British troops. In 1775, when the British countered with a search of the Boston countryside, war broke out at Lexington. In the following year, the Continental Congress declared the colonies independent and functioned as the *de facto* Government for most of the war.

British Disunity. If friction with England unified the colonies, it had the opposite effect on English Cabinets. All through this period Cabinet opinion on Colonial policy was confused and divided. Token gestures at Colonial planning were made in 1768 with the creation of the post of Secretary of State for Colonial Affairs; however, the ministers appointed to the post were utterly incompetent. On numerous occasions, the Cabinet split on policy according to the parochial outlook of their personal feelings. Chatham and Burke suggested the possibility of dominion roles for the colonies, but not enough Englishmen had such sufficiently broad vision, and their ideas received no encouragement from the King. Lord North's efforts at conciliation in 1775 were too late. By that time the majority of leaders on both sides of the Atlantic were ready to decide the issue by force of arms.

The American War of Independence, 1775-81

In November, 1774, King George declared that England must either master the colonies or leave them totally to themselves. The English attempted the first alternative, but the outcome of the war forced them to accept the second. The conflict, which began as a civil war within the Empire, with divided opinion on both sides of the Atlantic, changed its complexion after 1778 and became a world war with England fighting alone against an increasing number of European powers. In 1781 the British army surrendered to the French and American forces at Yorktown, and American independence was established.

The Military Ledger. The American colonists declared war on the most formidable naval and industrial power in the world; a nation with a professional army which controlled both flanks of the colonies (Canada and Florida), and which had the support of Indian allies. Furthermore, the Americans had no adequate central Government to co-ordinate activities, lacked money and supplies to sustain a long war, and had only an untrained and unreliable local militia. However, the British were fighting a war three thousand miles away from home under the incompetent leadership of the King's Friends. Often British military orders were obsolete by the time they reached America. Neither side had brilliant military leaders, but George Washington, commander of the Colonial army, understood thoroughly the critical factor that if his army could only endure in the field, time was on their side, and the British would grow weary of trying to subdue such a vast country. Simply defeating the Americans in battle, as they often did, would not enable the British to occupy the interior without vastly larger forces. Unlike previous wars, England had no ally on the Continent, and her isolation encouraged a European coalition against her. "The value of the [French] alliance to the American cause can hardly be overestimated." [1] Throughout the war, the Whigs, under the leadership of the Pitts, Burke, Charles James Fox, Rockingham, and Shelburne, denounced the war as the King's fault. In the colonies only a minority were active "patriots," and perhaps a quarter of the colonists—known as "Loyalists" or "Tories"—supported the British in the war. Thus the initial conflict was essentially a civil war within the Empire rather than a definite clash between Britain and the Thirteen Colonies.

Conduct of the War. In the beginning of hostilities, English opinion was favorable toward the policy of coercion against the ungrateful colonies. King George determined war policy but lacked the ability to plan effective strategy; nor was he aided by his administrators. Lord North was a reluctant and fretful Prime Minister; similarly, Lord Sandwich, in charge of the navy, and Lord

---

[1] John Hicks, *The Federal Union* (Berkeley: Houghton Mifflin, 1952), p. 139.

George Germaine, Secretary of State for the Colonies, sadly lacked talent or the respect of the armed services. A naval blockade would have been the wisest policy to pursue because it would not have embittered the colonists as did the army of occupation; nor would it have required such a large number of troops. But blockades were slow in their effects, whereas a territorial war might produce a decisive battle. Besides, the seemingly insurmountable difficulties of the colonists made it unlikely that they could maintain any concerted opposition: Colonial paper money was worthless; their army was weak; and colonists loyal to the King would probably aid the British in halting the rebellion. A land war was ordered regardless of the problem of logistics in supplying armies in occupied territory.

Course of the War. The British pursued a half-hearted naval war which was inadequate in conception, while they attempted a territorial war in which they overextended themselves. After 1778 the Colonial war became a minor theater when France threatened to invade England.

Campaigns, 1775-78. The colonists forced General Gage and the British army to evacuate Boston in the spring of 1776, though the American effort to conquer Canada that winter was repulsed. The following summer General Howe defeated Washington on Long Island and made New York the principal British base thereafter. Howe failed to pursue the retreating colonials, and Washington's dwindling army rallied during the winter with two victories, Trenton and Princeton. In 1777 British strategy planned to split the colonies by winning control of the Hudson-Champlain route. General Burgoyne and his army moved down from Canada to join Howe's forces moving up the Hudson. Instead, Howe captured Philadelphia and dallied in the city, leaving Burgoyne at the mercy of growing numbers of Colonial forces who forced him to surrender at Saratoga in October. Saratoga became the turning point in the war because it demonstrated to France the prospect of the colonists defeating the British, and because it resulted in foreign alliances which were crucial to American success. The battle also revived American patriotism and turned English opinion against the war effort in the colonies.

World War, 1778-81. The French alliance in February, 1778, furnished the colonists with the essential elements they lacked—sea power, money, munitions, and a professional army. The war took on a different character when the British Isles became vulnerable to attack as well as the widely-scattered British empire. Spain joined France in 1779, and Holland entered the war against England the following year. In 1780 the League of Armed Neutrality (led by Russia and including Sweden, Denmark, and later Holland and Prussia) was organized to resist the British claim of the right of search of neutral vessels on the high seas. For once England failed to enjoy naval superiority. The French had built up a new navy which, when allied with the Spanish, outnumbered the British fleet. The British lost Minorca, most of Florida, two islands in the West Indies, posts on the African coast, and barely withstood a massive siege of Gibraltar. In 1779 the two Bourbon fleets entered the Channel and were prevented only by technical errors from landing forty thousand Frenchmen on England's shores. The threat of invasion kept seventy thousand troops guarding England, leaving few reinforcements for the British army in the colonies. In America, Henry Clinton replaced Howe as commander, and after Saratoga the land war moved to the southern colonies. Clinton and Cornwallis won most of the battles but could not control the interior. In the summer of 1781, Lord Cornwallis moved from the Carolinas to Yorktown, Virginia, where supplies could reach him by sea. This avenue of relief was cut off in September when the French navy under Admiral de Grasse won the crucial battle of Chesapeake Bay and forced Cornwallis to surrender six weeks later to a combined French and American army more than twice the size of the British forces. The surrender virtually assured the independence of the United States.

Politics and the Peace Settlement

Defeat abroad forced the downfall of the personal rule of George III. When the Whigs returned to office, they quarreled with the King and among themselves, thereby blunting the prospects of parliamentary reform which growing discontent within and without Parliament was now demanding. In Paris, Whig negotiators offered generous terms to the Americans in order to restore friendly trade relations between the two countries and to reduce the influence of France on the new nation.

Fall of the King's Friends. The British defeat at Yorktown brought about the disintegration of Lord North's administration. Early in 1782 the Opposition carried a motion to halt the war in America. Lord North recognized that the King's imperial policy had failed and that royal manipulation of Parliament had been repudiated. King George reluctantly accepted North's resignation when he, too, realized that the whole system of Government by which North maintained influence in Parliament was in disrepute. "At the cost of her American colonies Britain regained her traditional political system." [2]

Agitation for Reform. The reform of the corrupt parliamentary system which the Whigs had developed was now demanded by them. In 1776 Wilkes had introduced into the Commons a comprehensive measure for parliamentary reform. In the same year Adam Smith and Jeremy Bentham published theses indicting the economic and institutional premises of English life, whereas the dissenting academies with such teachers as Joseph Priestley and Richard Price led an influential following of Rational Dissenters for reform. In 1780 the Gordon Riots that terrorized London for five days were a surface manifestation of Protestant animosity to the reduction of penal laws against Catholics. The savage rioting mirrored a deep discontent in the working classes and indicated to many members of Parliament the need for constitutional, rather than extreme, action. In public meetings in towns across England petitions for reform were sent to Parliament. The Rockingham Whigs translated this reform agitation into parliamentary legislation in a cautious effort to eliminate royal patronage and influence from Parliament and to make Parliament more representative of the nation. Edmund Burke became the eloquent orator of reform, and in 1780 the Commons passed John Dunning's resolution urging the diminution of the power of the Crown.[3] When the Rockingham Whigs came to power in 1782, they passed two Economical Reform Bills which reorganized the royal Household, limited royal influence by barring Government contractors from sitting in Parliament, and disenfranchised a large number of Government officials. The bill for parliamentary reapportionment failed to win a favorable vote; nevertheless, the influence of the King had been checked, and a movement toward reform was begun.

Whig Factionalism. Complying with George III's request Rockingham formed a Whig Cabinet and persuaded the Chathamite Whigs, now led by the Earl of Shelburne, to join him. But Shelburne soon quarreled openly with Charles James Fox, the leader of the young Whigs, and split the party into two jealous factions—a situation which the King exploited on every occasion. Lord Shelburne was a friend of Adam Smith, Jeremy Bentham, and Benjamin

---

[2] William Willcox, *The Age of Aristocracy, 1688 to 1830* (Boston: D. C. Heath, 1966), p. 116.

[3] John Dunning (Baron Ashburton), was a member of Parliament from 1768-82. He had achieved fame for his defense of the East India Company (1762), and John Wilkes (1763).

Franklin and a brilliant, shrewd critic of England's economic and political institutions; yet because of his aloofness he gave the impression of secretiveness and had few friends. His rival, Charles James Fox, was the most influential and eloquent supporter of political liberty in the House of Commons. Fox's great-hearted and engaging disposition won him a loyal following in spite of his gambling habits and notorious private life. The dispute between these two men concerned their respective authority in controlling peace negotiations in Paris. Fox resigned the day after Rockingham's death and refused to serve under Shelburne. Instead, he disenchanted many of his followers by joining North, whom he had denounced for twelve years, so as to defeat the peace negotiations which Shelburne had completed.

Peace Negotiations. A British naval victory in the West Indies (Battle of the Saints) under Admiral Rodney and the successful defense of Gibraltar against the French-Spanish siege somewhat salvaged Britain's position in the peace negotiations with her European enemies. American independence was ceded at the outset. The British representatives encouraged the American peace commissioners, Benjamin Franklin, John Jay, and John Adams, to disregard the instructions of Congress and negotiate a separate peace with England rather than follow the advice of France as they had been ordered. The French were furious at the generous British terms offered to the Americans; the English were delighted with the discord developing among her opponents.

Treaties of Versailles and Paris, September, 1783. In the Treaty of Versailles with France and Spain, France recovered the islands of St. Pierre and Miquelon off the coast of Newfoundland, won several trading posts in Africa, and regained her trading posts in India. Spain secured Florida and Minorca, in return for the surrender of the Bahamas. By the Treaty of Paris, the United States acquired all territory east of the Mississippi and south of the Great Lakes, fishing rights off Newfoundland, and free navigation on the Mississippi. In return, the American Congress recommended that the States restore confiscated Loyalist property; however, the States failed to do this, and the mistreatment of Loyalists continued. Thousands fled, the majority migrating to Canada.

End of the First British Empire. The loss of the American colonies marked the end of the First British Empire. The loss of most of the English settlements left an Empire which with the exception of Canada was largely tropical. One direct result of the American Revolution was the settlement of Australia to replace Georgia as a penal colony. Another result was Lord North's Renunciation Act of 1778 which set up a policy, learned too late in the Thirteen Colonies, of never again taxing a colony for imperial revenue. The American revolt also reshaped England's attitude toward her colonial Empire; if colonies were like children, then the mission of the motherland was to lead them toward moral and political maturity.

Irish Conditions. The American Revolution had immediate repercussions in Ireland. The Irish were struggling for their rights against the restrictions of Poynings's Law which had for so long prevented a free and equal Irish Parliament. When British troops were withdrawn from Ireland in 1778 to fight in America, regiments of largely Protestant volunteers were raised and encamped outside Dublin, while a Convention under the Earl of Charlemont encouraged the Irish Parliament to pass measures granting legislative independence. When the Rockingham Ministry came to power in 1782, Henry Grattan procured the repeal of Poynings's Law. The following year Fox and North passed the Renunciation Act which made the Irish Legislature and Judiciary independent of the British Parliament; only the Executive remained tied to the English Parliament. Full responsible Government seemed possible had not the French Revolution intervened to frustrate such prospects.

Chapter 15 ✑§ The Era of the French Revolution

The telescoping of an American, French, and a nascent Industrial Revolution into a few decades of time produced complexities and demanded changes in the structure of English society and Government. The landed aristocracy and unrepresentative Parliament could no longer absorb these rapid changes, yet the movement for reform was diverted by a more immediate crisis, the menace of revolutionary France. When France threatened England in her most sensitive area—control of the Low Countries and the Channel by an unfriendly power—England went to war and remained at war for over twenty years. In England the fear of French radicalism turned reform into reaction and turned Pitt from a peace-loving Prime Minister into a war leader, who used sea power to limit Napoleon's grandiose designs and who, with Castlereagh, designed a strategy for a successful peace treaty.

William Pitt the Younger

William Pitt, who knew the art of political management far better than his father, dominated the political scene from 1783 until his death in 1806. Unlike his great political opponent, Charles James Fox, Pitt moved with the times and became the very symbol of England's traditions and virtues during the war with France. Ambitious, astute, often aloof, he understood and used political machinery to win and keep a parliamentary majority, having first assured himself of the Sovereign's goodwill. He also understood the changes occurring in commerce and supported Adam Smith's ideas on free trade. Pitt at the age of twenty-five received the prime ministership, because he was acceptable to George III, and because he had the rare abilities of getting along with the King and winning parliamentary support.

The Problems of 1783. England had been humiliated by defeat in the American War of Independence and in 1783 found herself without European allies. Under the stresses of defeat and incompetence George III's political system had collapsed, and no stable ministry was in the offing as rival political factions wrangled for office.

Economic Dislocation. In 1775 England was already in the midst of fundamental industrial changes which had begun two centuries earlier. Enclosures increased drastically with over three million acres fenced in between 1700 and 1760. By 1790 the country was importing more grain than it exported. In manufactures, the substitution of horsepower for manpower and a series of mechanical inventions moved industry from the home to the factory. These developments introduced a new influential class of industrial capitalists who resented being excluded from political power. Adam Smith's doctrine of unrestricted production, free trade, and freedom from governmental regulations (*Wealth of Nations*, 1776) coincided with the expanding capitalistic economy, but was contrary to the mercantilist theory and the legislation in operation.

The East India Company. The conquests of Clive in the Seven Years' War had altered the East India Company from a trading post to a private imperial empire. The transformation brought on strong criticism from Edmund Burke and the Whigs, because the Company governed Bengal without any legal responsibility for its actions. Impressive fortunes were made by company officials who levied local taxes through Indian puppets. As corruption and lawlessness increased, the House of Commons investigated the company. Lord North modified the exercise of power with the Regulating Act of 1773, which, nevertheless, left the company with its monopoly. Warren Hastings, the first governor under the Regulating Act, saved, and then extended, the company's position in a prolonged war with native potentates who were backed by the French. Hastings won over his enemies in the field, on his council, and in England, but his methods were often arbitrary and his empire building was expensive and involved major administrative expansion. When Hastings was called home to face impeachment proceedings, the testimony against him forced Parliament to recognize that a drastic alteration in the government of India was essential if Britain was intent on remaining there.

The Irish Problem. The Renunciation Act of 1783 had provided the Irish Parliament with legislative independence, but no further attempts were made to eliminate the centuries of discrimination and plunder which the conquering English had inflicted upon the Irish. Henry Grattan in Ireland and Pitt in England realized that basic problems, such as absentee landlordship, religious restrictions, and economic discrimination, needed to be solved or the Irish Parliament would be little more than an agency—which could be bribed—of the English administration.

Political Instability.   The defeat of Shelburne in the Commons introduced the Fox-North Ministry in 1783 which the King regarded as an anathema. He considered North a traitor and Fox, whose debauchery was a bad influence on the Prince of Wales, the most dangerous of the Whig leaders. King George found his opportunity to oust this ministry when Fox introduced a bill which would have reformed the East India Company by transferring its vast patronage to the Government. The King exerted personal influence to block passage of the bill in the House of Lords and used its defeat as the excuse to dismiss the Portland-Fox-North ministry and to invite William Pitt to become Prime Minister.

Prime Minister Pitt.   The young Pitt was masterful in the art of administration and parliamentary maneuvering. Accepting office in 1783 without a majority, he showed the invulnerability of the King's favor by surviving weekly defeats in the Commons at the hands of Fox while whittling away at the Fox-North majority. When the Opposition was reduced to a majority of one, Parliament was dissolved and an election was called.

Election of 1784.   Pitt's remarkable performance in weakening Fox's position in the Commons had won the respect of politicians as well as popular sympathy. Besides using the financial resources of the Treasury to ensure an electoral victory, Pitt was helped in the open constituencies by his alliance with William Wilberforce, and by the voters' dislike of Fox's India Bill. The election gave Pitt a large majority at the expense of his opponents. The new Prime Minister assiduously cultivated the support of the City of London with his policies and with honors and titles; he swamped the Whig rule in the House of Lords by having the King create scores of new peers. This marked the end of Whig supremacy and the beginning of a new political alignment which will become increasingly Tory in principle and in personnel. Although the King preferred Pitt to anybody else, he never controlled him as he had North. Under Pitt the powers of the prime ministership were to be expanded.

Opposition of Fox.   The decimated Whig opposition under Fox's inspired but erratic leadership had difficulty opposing Pitt's successful reform of the national economy and use of patronage. The French Revolution frightened many Whigs, including Edmund Burke, into leaving Fox's liberal camp and joining Pitt. Only in the year 1787-88 was Pitt's supremacy threatened when the temporary insanity of George III made a regency appear necessary. Pitt stalled as long as possible in transferring power to the Prince of

Wales, because he knew that the Prince, as Regent, would immediately call upon Fox to form a ministry. When the King suddenly regained his sanity, the threat was removed.

Pitt's India Act.   After the Lords defeated Fox's East India Bill, Pitt offered an acceptable substitute. In 1784 his India Act established a dual control whereby the Government accepted responsibility for political and civil affairs, while the company retained control of commerce and patronage. A Board of Control, headed by a Secretary of State, assumed responsibility for Indian administration and had the power to remove officials appointed by the company. This system operated until 1858 and, with the governorships of Charles Cornwallis and Richard Wellesley, efficient government came to India, but at the expense of a moral arrogance which increasingly isolated the ruling British from the Indian and his culture.

Financial Reforms.   Pitt reorganized Britain's public finances in his budgets of 1784-1787 because the American War had almost doubled the national debt and jeopardized the credit of the Government. The complicated system of collecting taxes was simplified, and taxes were lowered to provide new revenue and eventually a budgetary surplus. Smuggling decreased because lower tariffs no longer made it highly profitable. Pitt also created a Sinking Fund (1786), the interest of which was to be used to pay off the national debt. Although the scheme produced no financial gain, it did strengthen public confidence. In three years Pitt had stabilized the country for George III as Walpole had done for George I. He encouraged as much free trade as the mercantilist interests in England would permit and in 1786 negotiated a reciprocity treaty with France which permitted the mutual reduction of duties on specified imports.

Further Reform Attempts.   Throughout the 1780's Pitt worked for reform in several areas, pressing his proposals where politically prudent and accepting defeat of other measures with equanimity. Only the fear of France made him quietly drop reform and become a protector of the status quo.

Parliament.   In 1785 Pitt acknowledged his debt to the reformers by introducing a bill for parliamentary redistribution which would have abolished thirty-five rotten boroughs. The bill was defeated, and Pitt did not risk his political majority by pursuing it further; however, he did eliminate numerous pensions and other forms of bribery still prevalent in securing votes. His efforts to repeal the religious disabilities against Catholics and Dissenters were no more successful than his proposals for parliamentary reform.

Slave Trade. The decision handed down in the Somerset case [1] of 1772 freed slaves in England and encouraged reformers in their efforts to ameliorate the horrors of slave trading in the empire. In 1787 Sierra Leone, West Africa, was established as a haven for emancipated slaves. Pitt eloquently, but not forcefully, supported bills for the abolition of the slave trade; however, he met with no success except for one measure to curb the abuses of the Atlantic passage. In the House of Commons William Wilberforce, Pitt's close friend, led the agitation against slave trade. In 1807, the year after Pitt's death, slave trade was abolished by Parliament—the only reform to occur in the war years.

Ireland. Pitt tried to relieve the worst of the commercial disabilities in Ireland by permitting free trade between Ireland and the colonies in return for Irish revenue to support the navy. The Irish Parliament approved, but commercial interests in England spurned Pitt's economic generosity and defeated the measure. The Irish realized that they could only win concessions when England was threatened by foreign invasion.

Colonial Policies. Over forty thousand Loyalists fled the United States to British North America to escape harassment and to continue their loyalty to the Crown. Some ten thousand arrived in Upper Canada (present-day Ontario), and quickly became restive over the political and religious arrangement of the Quebec Act. In 1791 Quebec was divided into Upper and Lower Canada with each province having religious freedom, its own lieutenant governor, a nominated upper house, and a representative assembly. Thus the Loyalists introduced the English system of government to Canada and to the French Canadians. While Canada was being reorganized, Australia was being settled. Captain Cook had charted the land in 1769, and in 1788 the first settlement, largely convicts, founded Sydney. Transportation to Australia was preferable to an English prison, and until the year of the Great Reform Bill (1832), the practice was accepted with little question; afterwards it was condemned on both humanitarian and utilitarian grounds. All told 166,000 penal offenders were transported to Australia.

Foreign Affairs. Pitt had hoped for a period of peace to carry on his administrative reforms, because domestic affairs in the eighties interested him more than foreign affairs. Nevertheless, he proceeded to end England's diplomatic isolation by a Triple Alliance

---

[1] The question of the legality of slavery in Great Britain and Ireland was decided in the case of the Negro Somerset by Lord Mansfield's judgment that "as soon as a slave set his foot on the soil of the British islands he became free."

(1788) with Holland and Prussia which sought to halt the extension of French influence in the Netherlands. Pitt then reversed England's traditional policy of friendship to Russia by using the Triple Alliance to protest Russia's designs in the Near East. He urged Parliament to use force to keep Russia from devouring more Turkish territory, but Parliament refused to back him.

At Nootka Sound off Vancouver Island where a small British settlement was located, the Spanish threatened war in 1790 to make good their claim to the Island by right of discovery. Pitt was prepared to use the navy for defense, but Spain withdrew its claim as no aid from the Bourbon Family Compact would be forthcoming from France because of the incipient revolution. Pitt refused to take action against France or even recognize the strength of the revolutionary movement, until the French advanced into the Low Countries and threatened England in the Channel. As late as 1792, Pitt was predicting fifteen years of peace; however, the next year England was at war.

War with France

Pitt and most Europeans underestimated the strength and efficiency of the French revolutionary movement. When the force of revolutionary nationalism and the appeal of democratic slogans were graphically observed, England and Europe were intent on not only defeating France but the revolution as well. Warfare radically changed as the national spirit of France made the whole nation part of the war effort, with citizen armies routing the professional armies of the old regimes. England relied on her navy and subsidies to continental allies to stave off defeat. Her colonial and industrial resources, sea power, and four coalitions served in the end to checkmate Napoleon. If Waterloo left England the foremost power in the world, it also left her with a host of internal problems which the war had not solved but only set aside.

Revolutionary France. From 1789 to 1791 the National Assembly in France successfully abolished ancient abuses and privileges and expressed their aspirations in the eloquent Declaration of the Rights of Man. The radical changes that were decreed, particularly in the monarchy and in the church, split France into two groups—one accepting, the other rejecting the revolution. The active revolutionists gained the ascendancy, and the ensuing war against Austria and Prussia consolidated their position. Louis XVI tried to flee the country while the demoralized French army, shorn of most of its officers who were loyal to the old regime, retreated before the

Austrian-Prussian armies. The invading forces were halted at Valmy by the French revolutionary army on September 20, 1792. By that time the Jacobin clubs—radical pressure groups led by Georges Jacques Danton and Maximilion Robespierre, who rejected the monarchy in favor of a republic—controlled Paris. However, the "September Massacres" of people suspected of hostility to the revolution mirrored the breakdown of central authority. The National Convention (1792) which replaced the Assembly abolished the monarchy and declared France a republic. The next year Louis XVI was executed, and a Reign of Terror, introduced by the Committee for Public Safety, purged the nation of political opponents. The revolutionary Government also put the national economy on a war footing and began a mass conscription. As the French Republican army began a crusade to liberate the Continent, it spread fear and hatred throughout Europe. Republican France was more expansionistic and successful than the monarchy it had overthrown. It defied treaties, opened up the Schelde to navigation, and annexed Savoy and Belgium.

Reception of the Revolution in England. English public opinion was sympathetic with the French Revolution, likening it to the Glorious Revolution of 1688 and believing that there was no greater compliment to their system of government than imitation of it. Charles James Fox, Charles Grey, and especially William Wordsworth, the Romantic poet, were enthusiastic about the upheaval in France. Stimulated by the revolution, various societies for the reform of Parliament were revived and new ones established, such as the Society of the Friends of the People and the London Corresponding Society—the latter founded in 1792 by Thomas Hardy to promote universal suffrage among working-class people. As the excesses of the revolution dampened this early enthusiasm and as France attempted to stir up revolution beyond her borders, the reformers in Britain became suspect as being only one step away from becoming revolutionaries. This changing mood was witnessed in Burke's pamphlet, *Reflections on the Revolution in France.* His lucid warning that the ideas of the French Revolution, if not checked, would destroy overnight the values and order of western society won an immediate response. Burke's viewpoint appealed to conservatives who were frightened by Thomas Paine's *The Rights of Man,* which advocated the overthrow of monarchial government. Burke and a majority of conservative Whigs joined Pitt, leaving Fox with a small and ineffectual opposition. Pitt, hitherto a reformer, now turned reactionary and repressed all reforms so as to protect security and order.

The First Coalition, 1792-97. The first years of the war were full of mistakes and failures because Pitt, and most of the leaders in Europe, underestimated the strength of a revolutionary France mobilized for total war. When war was declared on February 1, 1793, Pitt at once lined up the First Coalition [2] with the hope of imitating his father's policy of subsidizing continental powers and using sea power to collect France's commercial empire. However, the members of the Coalition were jealous of each other and did little but preserve their respective interests. By 1797 Britain stood alone, her allies beaten by France.

Failure on Land. In 1793 the allied powers were successful when the French suffered defeat in the Netherlands and desertion by her generals; there was also a royalist uprising in France. Pitt agreed to intervention because victory seemed imminent. Henry Dundas, the incompetent secretary of war, sent British troops to various theaters in an attempt to sever French colonies.[3] But under the generalship of Carnot a new French conscript army was organized into a superior fighting force. The allies were severely defeated and British troops were routed from Holland. By 1795 Holland was overrun, and after Prussia and Spain withdrew, only Austria, Russia, and Sardinia remained in the Coalition. Napoleon Bonaparte, the commander of the French armies on the Italian front, demonstrated his military genius with superb tactics against the Austrians and Sardinians. By 1797 only Great Britain faced France.

Failure at Sea. To cover up its obvious inadequacies elsewhere, the British Government emphasized the capture of Cape Town, Ceylon, and certain islands in the Dutch East Indies. A French grain convoy landed at Brest despite British control of the Channel. When the Spanish navy joined the French, a French invasion of Ireland appeared imminent.

Britain in 1797. Britain's fortunes reached their lowest ebb in 1797. Only a violent storm prevented the French army from landing in Ireland. At Spithead and The Nore two naval mutinies over living conditions, food, the system of promotions, and the brutal treatment of sailors lowered English morale but forced redress of grievances. Within the country, the Bank of England suspended cash payments to stop a run on the bank, food became scarce, and Pitt's peace overtures to France were rebuffed. Before the year was out, however, Britain restored her naval supremacy by two major

---

[2] Austria, Prussia, Great Britain, Sardinia, Spain, Portugal, Naples, and the Papal States were eventually all members.
[3] From 1794 to 1796, 40,000 British troops died in the West Indies trying to subdue the French sugar islands.

victories: at Cape St. Vincent the English Mediterranean fleet under the command of Jervis and Nelson routed a Franco-Spanish fleet; at Camperdown the North Sea fleet under Admiral Duncan defeated the Dutch navy.

British Victory and the Second Coalition. Because the two naval disasters had prevented France from invading England, Napoleon led a French army against England's commercial empire in the Mediterranean by invading Egypt in 1798 and marching eastward. Admiral Nelson sighted the French supply ships at anchor in Abukir Bay and in a brilliant maneuver (Battle of the Nile), sank the fleet. At Acre, British sailors checked the French army and forced Napoleon to give up his eastern plan. Abandoning his army, Napoleon slipped back to France where, after being feted as a national hero, he easily unseated the corrupt and incompetent Directory and installed himself as First Consul and virtual dictator. Napoleon's consulate marks the end of the revolutionary decade in France. His immediate plans were to consolidate France's reforms, use the nation as the instrument of his ambition to rule Europe, and eventually become emperor.

To accomplish his aims, Napoleon would have to defeat the Second Coalition [4] which Pitt had arranged after Britain's naval successes in the Mediterranean. While Napoleon was carrying on his campaign in Egypt, the allied forces, rearmed through subsidies obtained by Pitt's new income tax, had recaptured northern Italy. In 1800 Napoleon invaded Italy and quickly crushed the Austrians at Marengo. Another French army under Moreau defeated a second Austrian army at Hohenlinden. The double disaster forced Austria out of the war (Peace of Lunéville, 1801). Russia had already dropped out and turned against England by heading the League of Armed Neutrality of Northern Powers [5] to halt England's search of neutral ships for contraband. Lord Nelson, by a finely-calculated risk, destroyed the powerful Danish fleet at Copenhagen (1801) and sailed into the Baltic to meet the Russians. Meanwhile, Czar Paul had been murdered and the new Czar, Alexander I, wanted peace. The League disintegrated, and the Baltic and the Mediterranean remained open to British ships.

Treaty of Amiens, 1802. The war ended in a stalemate with France supreme on land and England supreme on the seas, and both countries agreeing to peace. The Treaty of Amiens (1) formally recognized the new French Government; (2) required Britain to

---

[4] 1799-1801: Great Britain, Russia, Austria, Turkey, Naples, and Portugal.
[5] Russia, Prussia, Sweden, and Denmark.

withdraw from Malta and restore all conquests except Ceylon and Trinidad; and (3) demanded France to recognize Turkish claims to Egypt and to withdraw from Rome and Naples. The treaty was unduly favorable to France since England gave up far more territory, whereas large areas of Europe remained closed to British commerce. Napoleon regarded the peace as only a breather because his ambitions were not yet satisfied. He acquired Louisiana from Spain, reconquered San Domingo, accelerated his program of naval construction, and by act and utterance seemed to have designs on British possessions. The peace was of short duration.

Domestic Repression. Even before war was declared with France in 1793, the British Government had turned against all political reformers, lumping them in the same bracket as revolutionaries. The repression grew heavier as the war dragged on, and for over a quarter of a century all effective opposition to the Government was considered seditious. In 1792 a proclamation was issued against all seditious writings; the authors of such work would be subject to prosecution. This was followed by an Aliens Act, a Seditious Meetings Act, a Treasonable Practices Act, and the Combination Acts. Their cumulative effect prevented public meetings without the approval of a magistrate, broadened treason to include writing and speaking as well as acting against the Government, and made trade unions illegal. The Habeas Corpus Act was suspended in 1794 and, except for Fox and a dwindling handful of faithful supporters, all opposition to the Government was muzzled.

The French Revolution and Ireland. The French Revolution gave the Irish the opportunity to take advantage of England's extremity, just as the American Revolution had helped their cause a generation earlier. The successful American Revolution, reinforced by the infiltration of radical ideas from France, had encouraged Irish rebellion. Some reforms had recently been granted: Irish Protestants no longer had to submit to the Test Act, and Irish Catholics could lease land for ninety-nine years. However, acts of the Irish Parliament were still subject to veto by the Cabinet at Westminster, and the religious and economic grievances remained. Wolfe Tone, a Belfast lawyer, led the independence movement with his Society of United Irishmen (1791). Another group, called the Defenders, sought to abolish tithes against Catholics and to gain economic concessions by violence if necessary. These groups secured additional reforms, one of which was an extension of the franchise to Irish Catholics (1793). When Tone asked the French for aid, they responded by attempting to send several expeditions. In 1798 a rebellion broke out in Ireland which the English quickly and cruelly suppressed. These developments convinced Pitt that a new arrangement for Ireland was imperative.

Act of Union, 1800. Only by a legislative union, like the agreement between the Scotch and English Parliaments, could the English Cabinet end the independence of the Irish Parliament. However, the Irish Legislature refused to dissolve itself until British gold and peerages were distributed freely and the implicit promise of Catholic emancipation was given. Both Parliaments passed the Act of Union in 1800. Ireland was henceforth represented by thirty-two peers in the House of Lords and one hundred members in the House of Commons. The act also allowed free trade between the two countries, provided for the continuance of the Church of Ireland (Anglican), and abolished the Irish Parliament.

Resignation of Pitt. To make the union effective and pacify Ireland, Pitt proceeded with a bill for Catholic emancipation which George III adamantly refused to consider. Because Pitt could not continue without the King's approval, he resigned early in 1801, and Viscount Addington became Prime Minister. Thus England was deprived of her leading statesman, and Ireland of her promised relief.

Renewal of The War. The British Government knew that the interval of peace was only helping Napoleon prepare for further expansion. Britain, therefore, refused to relinquish control of Malta, according to the terms of the Treaty of Amiens, and declared war in 1803. Napoleon made the invasion of England his objective, and barges were built to ferry the French army encamped at Boulogne. In the fervor and frustration of defending the island Addington proved ineffectual, and the nation demanded the return of Pitt. In 1804 Pitt came back to office, requesting a coalition Cabinet of all political groups. When King George refused, Pitt conducted the war without the services of his most able colleagues. Immediately he strengthened British sea power and resurrected another coalition on the Continent.

Trafalgar, 1805. To safely transport his troops to England, Napoleon had to break British control of the Channel. Consequently, Admiral Villeneuve and the Toulon fleet slipped out of port, lured Nelson's fleet to the West Indies, and hurried back only to find another British fleet under Admiral Calder at the mouth of the Channel. Instead of giving battle, Villeneuve retreated to Cadiz. In October the combined French and Spanish fleets were engaged by Nelson at Cape Trafalgar. Although the English fleet was outnumbered, Nelson's strategy—using a double row of ships to penetrate the enemy line at two places—annihilated the enemy fleets in the last major naval battle fought under sail. Nelson was killed in the engagement, but his victory kept control of the seas for England.

The Third Coalition. Using subsidies and diplomacy, Pitt raised a Third Coalition [6] in 1805 to fight Napoleon on land; however, it was no more a match for Napoleon than the previous Coalitions. Even before Trafalgar, Napoleon had turned eastward and defeated the Austrians at Ulm, and in December, 1805, Austria was forced out of the war at Austerlitz. Prussia entered the war but quickly accepted a humiliating peace after being defeated at Jena in October, 1806. After Russia suffered two defeats, Czar Alexander came to terms with Napoleon at Tilsit (1807). The Russian Emperor allied himself with Napoleon, who was now Emperor of France, and both agreed that Russian influence would be allowed to expand eastward provided that the Czar recognized Napoleon's control of central Europe and supported a boycott on British commerce. After Tilsit Napoleon reached the climax of his power and for the next five years dominated continental Europe. Only England's island location and naval superiority saved her from the invincible French army.

Death of Pitt, 1806. On January 2, 1806, only weeks after the disaster at Austerlitz, Pitt died of overwork at the age of forty-six. His rational approach to problems, his powerful though narrow mind, and his personal character and administrative abilities did much to enhance the prime ministership. Such a statesman could not easily be replaced.

The Continental System. Napoleon devised a method whereby he could crush England without invasion: all Europe was to be closed to English trade. Without sea power Napoleon could not attack England or her colonies, but he hoped to ruin her commerce and break the nation of shopkeepers with an embargo.

War of Decrees and Orders in Council. The Berlin Decree, issued in December, 1806, authorized a blockade of the British Isles, forbade neutrals under French influence to trade with Britain, and declared merchandise exported from British ports lawful prizes. The British Government countered with an order in council forbidding neutrals, under penalty of forfeiting ships and cargoes, to trade with France or her allies or to observe the Berlin Decree. Another order in council (1807) allowed neutral ships to proceed to a French port after securing a license at a British port. In December, 1807, Napoleon answered with the Milan Decree which declared that any ship sailing from England became a lawful prize if it entered a French port.

---

[6] 1805-1806: Great Britain, Russia, Austria, Sweden, and later Prussia.

Problems of Enforcement. If either side had fully enforced the decrees the resulting economic warfare would have destroyed European commerce. However, each side protected its own trade, and Napoleon made no effort to halt exports from the Continent, only imports. Even this was difficult because it demanded a detection system which Napoleon lacked, and a self-sacrifice which satellite nations were not inclined to make. Smuggling developed to unheard-of proportions as resentment arose against the tyranny of the system. Finally, the nationalism which Napoleon had sparked in his conquests backfired and became a weapon the conquered countries used in opposing French imperialism. The Continental System became essentially a paper blockade.

Peninsular Campaigns. To enforce his Continental System, Napoleon attempted to bring Portugal and Spain more completely under his control. After occupying Portugal and deposing the Bourbon King of Spain, Napoleon placed his brother, Joseph, on the throne. This provoked the Spanish popular uprising of 1808 and an invitation to England to intervene. Under Sir John Moore (who was killed in 1809) and Sir Arthur Wellesley (later the Duke of Wellington), the English forces gradually liberated Portugal and co-ordinated their strategy with the guerrilla warfare of the Spanish peasants to restrain the operations of three hundred thousand French troops by hit-and-run tactics. Under Wellesley's superb generalship the British made an orderly retreat when faced with overwhelming odds, attacked the overextended supply lines of the French, and in 1812 took the offensive to drive the Bonaparte Government out of Spain.

Downfall of Napoleon. The uneasy alliance between Napoleon and Alexander I collapsed as each became suspicious of the other's motives. When the Czar violated the Continental System and accepted British goods, Napoleon invaded Russia with over a half million troops. His army captured Moscow in September, 1812, but the Russians refused to surrender. Since winter was fast approaching and the French army was without provisions, Napoleon ordered a retreat that became a nightmarish disaster. The freezing weather, starvation, and the Cossack attacks permitted only a remnant to reach France safely. Meanwhile, England's foreign secretary, Castlereagh, was forging a Fourth Coalition (1812-14). Russia, Prussia,[7] Austria, Great Britain, and many lesser powers combined to take advantage of Napoleon's misfortunes in Spain and

---

[7] Prussia had shaken off her lethargy and humiliation to bring about an intellectual, moral, and military revival between 1808 and 1812.

Russia. At Leipzig in 1813 the allied armies inflicted the first crushing defeat on the army of Napoleon. In the following year they entered Paris, exiled Napoleon (Treaty of Fontainebleau) to the island of Elba in the Mediterranean, and placed Louis XVIII, brother of Louis XVI, on the French throne. The allied powers then gathered at Vienna to negotiate the remaining problems.

Battle of Waterloo. While the victorious delegates were still quarreling over terms, Napoleon escaped from Elba, made a triumphant entry into Paris, and reoccupied the throne. Wellington and Castlereagh organized a Fifth Coalition to confront once again their common enemy in the field. Napoleon's Hundred Days ended with the climactic battle of Waterloo fought near Brussels on June 11, 1815. Wellington and Napoleon dueled for supremacy, but successive charges of French cavalry failed to break the British squares. Before nightfall, Blucher and the Prussian army arrived to reinforce the British and rout the French. Napoleon surrendered to the British and was banished to St. Helena, where he lived out the remaining six years of his life. The diplomats returned to Vienna to complete the peace settlement.

The War of 1812. While the British army was fighting Napoleon, the United States declared war with England for the purpose of annexing Canada and protesting England's violation of the maritime rights of neutrals at sea. The United States gained none of the objectives for which the war was fought. To England the war was only a sideshow, completely overshadowed by the peninsular war in Spain and Napoleon's invasion of Russia.

Steps to War. When the Anglo-French war broke out in 1793, American sentiment favored an alliance with the French, but President Washington immediately declared the neutrality of the United States. American neutral ships did a lively business with both France and England during the war, and American commerce prospered until the Napoleonic decrees and England's orders in council caught the ships in the cross-fire of the belligerents' regulations. Because England's sea power made her able to exercise the right of search more effectively than France, American resentment was directed largely against England. Although Congress declared war on the ostensible grounds of the violation of maritime rights, there were other reasons as well. (1) The sectional ambitions of the South and the West urged expansion into Florida and Canada. These rich lands could easily be annexed, because Spain and England were concentrating all their available forces in the European war; by 1812 only four thousand British troops remained in Canada. (2) The Indian problem was aggravated when Tecumseh, aided by Canadian supplies, established an Indian Confederacy to prevent the encroachment of white settlers. (3) American nationalism was intensified by the War Hawks in Congress who believed that the United States should control the Continent. (4) Anti-English sentiment developed from the aftermath of the American Revolution, Jay's unsatisfactory Treaty of 1794, and the exclusion of American commerce from West Indies trade.

Course of the War. On land the poorly-prepared efforts to conquer Canada failed as the invaders were repulsed in a series of small, but bitter, attacks in which both the British commander, Sir Isaac Brock, and the Indian chief, Tecumseh, were killed. As the war in Europe progressed favorably, England sent troops from Spain to America. In 1814 one army captured Washington and burned it in retaliation for the American burning of York—present-day Toronto. A second army was defeated by Andrew Jackson at New Orleans two weeks after the peace had been made. Admiral Perry's naval victory gained control of Lake Erie, while on the Atlantic American privateers and lone raiders damaged British shipping and pride before the British blockade effectively restrained American commerce.

The Peace. The Treaty of Ghent (December, 1814) provided for a restoration of the territorial *status quo ante bellum*. Nothing was mentioned about the original causes of the war, except that disputes over boundaries and fisheries were to be turned over to the arbitral adjudication of joint commissions. This procedure brought lasting peace between Canada and the United States. Fishing and boundary disputes were peacefully resolved by 1818, and the Rush-Bagot Agreement (1817) brought complete naval disarmament to the Great Lakes. The war put an end to Tecumseh's Indian Confederacy and all efforts of the United States to annex Canada by force. For Canadians the anti-American sentiment engendered by the war became the germ of future Canadian nationalism.

English Politics after 1806. When Pitt died in 1806, George III reluctantly accepted a coalition Cabinet led by Lord Grenville with Fox as foreign secretary. Fox put through the bill for the abolition of slave trade before he died the same year. His Whig colleagues were forced to resign in 1807 because of parliamentary and royal displeasure over their attempt to remove restrictions preventing Catholics from holding military commissions. A Tory Cabinet was assembled under the Duke of Portland. In 1809 Spencer Perceval became Prime Minister and prosecuted the war vigorously until his assassination in 1812. His successor was Lord Liverpool, who because of indolence permitted a variety of inept colleagues to serve under him. The most able and influential member of Liverpool's Cabinet was Lord Castlereagh who did little to oppose the illiberality of his colleagues, but whose sound judgment and successful performance in conducting the peace negotiations won him the respect of Parliament and of Europe. The long tenure of Liverpool's Government was aided by a rivalry among Whig leaders and a liberal-conservative split in their ranks, with the conservative faction supporting the Government in its suppression of reform. Prosecution of critics of the Government continued in the closing years of the war. Sir Francis Burdett, leader of a small group in Parliament who were called "Radicals," and William Cobbett, publisher of *Cobbett's Weekly Register,* were imprisoned for their opinions on reform.

Economic Conditions.   England's industrial revolution gave her an edge over France in the economic competition of the war years. English commerce expanded significantly, but wealth was not evenly distributed. The poor suffered greatly because prices rose faster than wages, food was scarce, and because the Government legislated against labor agitation yet refused to remedy the causes of distress. The wildly fluctuating law of supply and demand caused periodic booms and busts. Thus when manufacturers found a sudden change in demand for products, they were forced to lay off workers. During the depression (1811-13) the misery of the poor produced the Luddite riots during which unemployed workers went through three counties smashing the new machines of the textile industries that had put them out of work. The Government had no answer for the grievances of the poor other than repression.

The Peace Settlement

Five Coalitions had risen against France and finally, after a generation of warfare, Napoleon was defeated and the allied powers gathered to arrange the peace. Coalitions were usually formed in a time of danger against *someone,* not *for something;* but often when the threat was removed, solidarity collapsed and old rivalries returned. The Congress of Vienna was no exception. The final settlement, which came about after months of maneuvering and compromises, did not completely satisfy any of the powers; yet it met the minimum requirements of each for security and preserved the balance of power in Europe until 1871.

Pitt's Proposals.   As early as 1804 Pitt was looking beyond the war to plans for peace which could protect British interests, attract other members of the Coalition, and ensure the peace of Europe.

He corresponded with Alexander I who was contradictory in his goals for Russia and in his own nature. The young Czar could never bring into accord the mystic idealism and the sensuousness in himself or his dreams of being the liberator and the autocrat of Russia. Alexander sent Pitt a policy supporting an international organization to maintain the peace of Europe and proposals for expanding Russia's influence. Pitt tactfully reformulated these propositions to make them still acceptable to Alexander yet palatable to Austria and Prussia. But before this policy could be pursued, Napoleon had to be defeated in the field.

The First Peace of Paris. After Paris capitulated in March, 1814, the victors had to conclude peace with Bourbon France. Since the allies could not agree, they shelved the most controversial matters and concluded a treaty with France which was signed on May 30, 1814. Under the treaty France renounced all claims to Holland, Belgium, Germany, and Malta; French frontiers were set, with a few exceptions, at those which she had held in 1792; and France ceded three colonies to England. The treaty was lenient; there were no indemnities or reparations to embitter defeated France or to jeopardize the position of Louis XVIII. The Czar, by rejecting a proposal on the Polish question, weakened his future prospects and never again attained the dominant position which was his at the time of his triumphal entry into Paris.

Principles and Personnel. Certain professed principles guided the diplomats in their deliberations at Vienna, although national self-interest prevailed during the negotiations in the actual decision-making. The principles were: (1) "legitimacy"—the restoration of disrupted dynasties; (2) encirclement of France with stronger powers; (3) compensation for countries who lost territory in the shuffle; and (4) a balance of power. The Big Four (Great Britain, Russia, Austria, and Prussia), which quickly became the Big Five with the inclusion of France, decided all important matters and left the small powers to participate on committees and to complain about their inferior status. The major delegates were Emperor Alexander I (Russia), Viscount Castlereagh (Great Britain), Prince Metternich (Austria), Prince Hardenberg, chancellor for King Frederick William III of Prussia, and Talleyrand, the opportunist and irrepressible foreign minister of four French regimes.

The Polish Problem. When the delegates gathered at Vienna (September, 1814 to March, 1815), dissension centered on the question of Poland, a country which in 1750 possessed a vast area and a population of over ten million, but which since then had been completely absorbed by Russia, Prussia, and Austria. The Czar saw himself as the liberator of Poland: he would restore an enlarged kingdom of Poland with a liberal Constitution, and yet one totally subservient to Russia. The other powers had no desire to see Russia extend her control to the banks of the Oder River through a satellite. King Frederick William III of Prussia was willing to give up his Polish provinces to Alexander in return for the whole of Saxony. But this would violate the principle of legitimacy by dethroning the King of Saxony and would place Prussia on the doorstep of Austria and France. Talleyrand, with lucid logic, led the opposition to such a scheme. When Prussia blustered and threatened war, a secret alliance among Austria, France, and England called her bluff and then forced Alexander to moderate his demands.

The Vienna Settlement. The final agreement on Poland and Saxony allowed Russia to retain the Polish province of Posen, and Austria to keep the province of Galicia. The remainder of Napoleon's duchy of Warsaw was set up as the kingdom of Poland with a model Constitution, but with an illusory independence since it was placed directly under the suzerainty of the Russian throne. Prussia, in compensation for relinquishing her Polish provinces, received two-fifths of Saxony, Swedish Pomerania, and several Rhenish areas, thus replacing Austria in northern Germany as the First Power. The other provisions included: (1) the return of all British colonial conquests except Ceylon, Cape of Good Hope, Heligoland, Trinidad, Malta, and four of the French colonies—Mauritius, Tobago, St. Lucia, and the Seychelles; (2) the union of Belgium with Holland to deter French expansion in an area vital to British interests; (3) the ceding of Venetia to Austria to compensate for the loss of the Austrian Netherlands; (4) a loose German confederacy of thirty-eight states with a Diet at Frankfurt, and (5) the taking of Norway from Denmark to give to Sweden.

The Second Peace of Paris. Peace negotiations were interrupted by Napoleon's Hundred Days following his escape from Elba. When the conference was resumed, Russia's previous preeminence was reduced, and England's stature was enhanced by Wellington's triumph at Waterloo. Castlereagh and Wellington directed England's policy, and a second peace with France was negotiated. Prussia wanted revenge and reparations. Castlereagh stood for "security but not revenge," and his moderation and consistency in placing the interests and peace of Europe above the acquisition of spoils won the support of the other members. In November, 1815, the Second Peace obliged France to pay an indemnity of seven hundred million francs, to support an allied army of occupation for five years, and to abandon Savoy and a few strips of territory on the Swiss and Belgian frontier. In all essentials, France retained her honor and integrity.

Congress System. At Castlereagh's and Metternich's prompting, England, Russia, Prussia, and Austria formed a Quadruple Alliance in 1815 to maintain the peace settlement and quarantine the revolutionary ideas of France. In 1818 France joined making it a Quintuple Alliance. However, its effectiveness was diminished by the Czar's insistence on a Holy Alliance which Castlereagh dubbed "a piece of sublime mysticism and nonsense." [8] The alliance would join the Kings of Europe in a Christian union of peace, charity, and—in practice—reaction. The Kings of Russia, Prussia, and Austria were members.

Failure of the Congress System. Castlereagh planned to use the alliance to protect the small nations and to keep France from rearming. Metternich, and later Alexander, viewed the two alliances as organs of reaction with the right to intervene in any country to crush national or democratic uprisings. Other rulers of Europe looked upon the Holy Alliance as an arrangement of three Emperors to dominate the Continent, while liberal opinion everywhere condemned the Quadruple Alliance as an effort to protect the status quo in a world demanding change. England's old policy of isolation from the Continent grew popular again, particularly when the Concert of Europe was used as a police organ to defeat internal revolts in Spain and Italy. In 1823 George Canning, Castlereagh's successor, publicly disassociated England from the Congress System.

---

[8] Harold Nicolson, *The Congress of Vienna: A Study in Allied Unity, 1812-1822* (New York: Viking, 1961), p. 250.

Chapter 16 ⁊ Eighteenth Century England

The eighteenth century was predominantly a period of intellectual brilliance, an Age of Reason, a time during which man believed in his ability to use common sense to discover the natural laws which govern society and the arts. This accent on reason permeated the literature of the Augustan Age, the Church of England, the economics of Adam Smith, and Locke's idea of a "balanced constitution." In the first half of the century material interests preoccupied society, public life became increasingly gross, and the church had little spiritual influence. Such calmness and conformity was jolted in the second half of the century by a religious revival, by two revolutions—one in industry and one in France—by the clamor for parliamentary reform and reapportionment, and by the Romanticists who rebelled against the coldness of Augustan literature and believed that human emotions were more important than human reason. All through the century class distinctions separated the comfortable rich from the miserable poor.

Society and Religion

The divisive gulf between the rich and the poor in England created essentially a country with two nations, and with Government, political power, and the comforts of society belonging only to the upper class. The established church, as the handmaiden of the state, did nothing to encourage doubt about the rightness of the social order or to question the morality of the age.

The Condition of England. In eighteenth-century England a man's position was fairly well defined for him by birth, and the distinction of class was the accepted order of things. During this century the national diet was profoundly altered by the introduction of tropical fruits and by the expanding domestic cultivation of the potato, spinach, and the strawberry. The consumption of chocolate, sugar, and tea became a national habit, and coffee houses became lively centers of news, fashion, and politics. The low morals and poor manners of the Hanoverian Court affected the whole of society, at least until the second half of the century when proper manners became the criterion of social refinement. Heavy drinking was common, and the consumption of gin and rum among the lower classes was exorbitant. Gambling became a national pastime. Trevelyan called society in the 1760's "one vast casino." [1] Government lotteries financed the building of Westminster Bridge (1736) and the founding of the British Museum (1755).

The immorality, gambling, and brutality of the period resulted in a ready lawlessness. Mobs gathered at the slightest pretext as a chance for looting and an escape from urban squalor. Public executions were common, serving often as spectacles but not as deterrents to crime. Prison conditions were wretched, and philanthropists worked against the politicians' obsession with the sanctity of property to save children from crime and to ameliorate penal laws and conditions. There were more stable patterns of life in the countryside where tradition and customs changed slowly.

Political Society. The smallness of the voting population meant that the politically-powerful families could control their electorate with considerable ease. It also meant that politics was personal and clannish, because the members within an oligarchy which dominated the town or county knew one another and had common backgrounds and interests. (In 1721 there were only 179 English peers.) The basic unit of Government continued to be the parish in which elected officials, such as the church wardens or the overseers of the poor, were under the supervision of the justice of the peace. The justices and the landed gentry relished the intrigue and electioneering which went on to ensure the control of seats in each constituency. Yet, paradoxically, a growing problem of the unreformed House of Commons was the huge expenditure that was becoming necessary to hold a seat; for a large county election expenses could easily cost a candidate or his patron £100,000.

The Professions. Bishops, university chancellors, admirals, and captains, as well as politicians were usually indebted to Westminster for their appointments. Army commissions were bought and could be cancelled for opposition to the ministry. In the church the bishoprics were political plums which went to assured supporters of the ministry. Independence of political thought could blight a promising career in the church or the army. Beneath the bishoprics was a pyramid of preferments that went to the discreet politician-preacher or to a relative of an influential member of Parliament. Such a system neither won respect for the clergy nor had any particular connection with theological conviction or competence. Other professions also had much patronage; the legal pro-

---

[1] George O. Trevelyan, *Early History of Charles James Fox* (New York: Harper, 1880), p. 77.

fession, except for its highest offices, perhaps having the least of all.

Education. The poor could not afford an education, and the state provided none for them. Primary education for the sons of shopkeepers and artisans expanded in the eighteenth century through the efforts of the charity school movement which provided moral instruction for youth. One result of the increased literacy was the demand for more books and periodicals. However, the universities were dormant in the earlier part of the century, because the prevailing attitude of the gentry was that higher education was useless for the duties and pleasures of the squirearchy. A tutor in the home could teach the fundamentals of reading, writing, and figures. Neither Oxford nor Cambridge had any vitality; the dons were stodgy and pedantic, the students nonchalant and frivolous.

Condition of the Poor. The misery of the poor was taken for granted as part of the divinely-ordained nature of things. The urban laborer was dependent for survival on the whims of the employer or the handouts of his betters or his parish. There was much sentiment for the virtuous poor and their weary lives as compassionately portrayed in Goldsmith's *The Deserted Village.* Individual philanthropists, such as John Howard who helped improve the conditions of prisons, and Thomas Coram who established Foundling Hospitals, did much to relieve distress. It was the poetry of William Blake at the end of the century that aroused the public conscience to a sense of responsibility for social evils. The Government corrected by statute some of the worst social scandals (e.g., the debilitating effects of cheap gin), but there was no significant remedial legislation until the nineteenth century. Gin drinking became a mania since it provided the poor with a temporary escape from their desperate conditions; and yet gin only compounded their problems by ruining their health and increasing crime. Not until the Wesleyan Movement was there any real interest shown in the neglected working class.

Condition of the Church. In 1717 George I prorogued convocation on the advice of the Whigs who wished to reduce the influence of their political opponents, the High Church Tories. This act left the church without a legislative body and made it more than ever an appendage of the state, led by men who won high office by their political connections and who ministered primarily to the governing class. For the vast majority of Englishmen, the church neither ministered to their needs nor won their respect. To the upper class the cold rationalism of the church made no impact on their skepticism or immorality; to the lower class the very fact that the church catered to the well-to-do and copied their way of life served only to deny the poor from the church's ministry.

Deism. The Age of Reason reached into religion in the form of deism—essentially a denial of the supernatural or of special revelation of God to man. Reason was enthroned, enthusiasm and fervor were suspect. This intellectual religion resulted in sermons which were little more than serene and bland discourses on ethics. Spiritual and human needs went untouched as the platitudes failed to help the masses, whereas for the learned deism slipped into either historical or philosophical skepticism.

Wesleyan Movement. When the Anglican church became too moribund to reform itself, the spiritual wasteland of the eighteenth century was restored to life by Methodism. This revival reached people neglected by the established church, transformed thousands of lives, and released an emotional flood which was regarded as indecorous in an Age of Reason. The Methodist movement began in Oxford where John Wesley (1703-91) was preparing for the Anglican ministry and meeting regularly with some friends for Bible study and devotions. The religious devotion of this group was ridiculed by scoffers who labeled the devout members, "Methodists." In the organization were the three future leaders of religious revival: John Wesley, a versatile genius and organizer with a sincere and intense religious nature; his brother Charles, a prolific hymn writer; and George Whitefield, an orator who could move the masses with his preaching.

During his unhappy two-year ministry in Georgia, John Wesley came under the influence of the Moravian Brethren. Back in England his life was suddenly transformed by an assurance of salvation through faith in Christ alone. When Anglican fellow-churchmen refused to let him preach the doctrine of salvation by faith in their pulpits, Wesley and Whitefield preached in the open air to thousands who would never have entered a church. The moral fervor and enthusiasm of these evangelists swept over the land, and hostile mobs turned into responsive crowds. John Wesley never left the Church of England, but when his converts had no place in which to receive further instruction, he built Methodist chapels. Societies were established and co-ordinated under Wesley's organizing skill and singleness of vision into the most effective and dynamic group in England. After Wesley's death the Methodist movement became completely separated from the Anglican church.

Results of the Religious Revival. Because of his political conservatism John Wesley opposed John Wilkes, the American Revolution, and Catholic emancipation. Nevertheless, his contribution was immense. His preaching awakened the Anglican church and revitalized its spiritual life. His stress on the brotherhood of all men and his indictment of social evils produced movements for the abolition of slavery, better working conditions, and prison reform. Some historians argue that the revival saved England from the wave of social and political revolutions that swept Europe. Certainly, Methodism gave meaning and a new self-respect to thousands of the working class who otherwise would have been most ripe for revolution. By the end of the century a renewal of religion had helped change the moral fiber of the nation. Methodist influence, by merging with the Puritan tradition, sharpened the Nonconformist conscience in English society.

The Arts and Sciences

The thought and letters of eighteenth-century England not only mirrored the values of society but also frequently caricatured its standards. The century was rich in intellectual and literary fare and was enhanced by a rational and tolerant spirit which placed increased reliance on observation and on a growing skepticism of traditional attitudes. The "enlightened" man was curious about nature and intensely interested in scientific discoveries.

The Augustan Age. During the first four decades of the century literary men turned to the Augustan Age of Rome for their model. The classics continued to serve as the basis of upper-class education, and the eighteenth-century reader responded to the aristocratic tone, the diction, and the reasoning of Latin authors. The neoclassical writers, therefore, imitated the ancients by writing correct and polished essays on man and by replacing passion and spontaneity with style and dignity. A new and larger reading public was created by the introduction of periodicals. The writers of the period also employed their talents for political pamphleteering or entreated patrons for food and money.

Joseph Addison (1672-1719). Collaborating with Richard Steele on *The Tatler* and *The Spectator,* Addison became a popular and successful essayist who exposed and commented upon all matters of social life in a style that was witty, urbane, and practical. His most famous literary character was the squire, Sir Roger de Coverley.

Daniel Defoe (1659?-1731). Coming from the home of a tradesman, Defoe probably cared little for the classics. He was primarily interested in earning a living and became a political hack until late in life. His novels, written in precise, descriptive prose, tell the story of lower-class existence. *Robinson Crusoe, Moll Flanders,* and *Roxanna* were three of his popular works.

Alexander Pope (1688-1744). Pope's wide-ranging mind and flawless style echoed perfectly the sentiment, "Whatever is, is right," of the Augustan Age. His output covered the fields of literary criticism, social satire, and scholarly editing, but his genius is best displayed in his didactic, subtle poetry. Working within the confining limits of rhymed couplets, his poetry portrayed the aesthetic (*Essay on Criticism*) and intellectual (*Essay on Man*) interests of his age, and includes perhaps the finest mock-heroic attempt (*Rape of the Lock*) in the English language.

Jonathan Swift (1667-1745). Swift's unhappy personal life, in which he hid his virtues and paraded his faults, along with his savage contempt for society, gave him a reputation of being a misanthropist. His original and bold prose scored the follies of man in sinning against the clear light of nature. Swift's devastating satire and irony fill the pages of *Gulliver's Travels* and *A Modest Proposal.*

The Age of Samuel Johnson. In mid-century Samuel Johnson (1709-84) dominated the world of letters, not so much for what he wrote—a *Dictionary* and *Lives of the English Poets*—but for his qualities of character and conversation. These were incomparably described by his constant companion, James Boswell, in his *Life of Samuel Johnson.* Johnson defended the established traditions of church, state, and classical learning, and yet all his contemporaries from Goldsmith to Hume, held him in highest esteem for his independent mind and freedom from cant. Challenging the heavy Augustan standards were the tender, sentimental novels of Laurence Sterne (1713-68), *Tristram Shandy* and *Sentimental Journey,* and Oliver Goldsmith (1728-74), *The Vicar of Wakefield* and *The Deserted Village.* Tears and laughter became respectable and in Goldsmith's satire there was no sting. Poetry again became passionate and personal in William Cowper's (1731-1800) sensitive, religious verses.

The English novel reached perfection in the work of Henry Fielding (1707-54) with the characterization and well-balanced plot of *Tom Jones.* Samuel Richardson (1689-1761) in his novels on middle-class manners, *Pamela,* and *Clarissa,* contributed to the development of the novel form by adding psychological or sentimental detail. The century closed with the forerunners of the Romantic Movement: Thomas Gray, Robert Burns, and William Blake. Gray (1716-71) was a transitional poet, essentially classic in form but novel in his treatment of beauty and sorrow. Burns (1759-96) was an unschooled poet whose songs dealt with such homely and human topics as love, drinking, and married life. His admiration for medieval and rustic society was a departure from Augustan scholarship. The mystical movement of Blake's (1757-1827) thoughts and the elusive symbolism of his painting and poetry seemed, to his contemporaries, little more than the gropings of an undisciplined imagination. Not until the late nineteenth century was his work understood and appreciated. The literary revolt against the classical traditions and aristocratic way of life had begun.

The Theater. In 1698 Jeremy Collier, the essayist and critic, lashed out at the coarseness and frivolity of the Restoration Theater with its Comedy of Manners. Second-rate sentimental comedies, sincere but insipid, played to capacity audiences of the Augustan Age; however, there was relief with the revival of Shakespeare by the actor, David Garrick, John Gay's delightful musical comedy, *Beggar's Opera* (1728), and Henry Fielding's burlesque of dramatic conventions in *Tom Thumb* (1730). Oliver Goldsmith with *She Stoops to Conquer* (1773) and Richard Sheridan in such plays as *The Rivals* (1775) and *The School for Scandal* (1777) revived the theater by using comic wit free from the heavy sentimentality of earlier decades.

Art and Architecture. Eighteenth-century artists painted the fashionable world because society served both as the subjects and the patrons of their work. Sir Joshua Reynolds (1723-92) was the dean of portrait painters and first president of the Royal Academy; his influence was significant on Thomas Gainsborough (1727-88) and George Romney (1734-1802). In contrast to conventional subject matter and style William Hogarth (1697-1764) was a pictorial satirist who painted and engraved the vices of London society. The social caricatures of *Gin Lane* or *Marriage-à-la-Mode* enabled the city to recognize the folly of dissipation.

Classical architecture with its refined sense of proportion exemplified in the work of Sir Christopher Wren remained popular in England. Country and town house architecture revealed several attractive variations of Palladian and Neoclassic design in columns, brickwork, and arches. The leading architects of the century were Sir John Vanbrugh, James Gibbs, William Kent, the Adam brothers, and Sir William Chambers. "Capability" Brown set the style for hedges and gardens and became England's most famous landscape designer. Thomas Chippendale and, later, Thomas Sheraton created delicate, attractive styles in furniture and Josiah Wedgwood captured the world's trade in exquisite china.

Historical Writing. History was popular because it was conceived of as literature and written for a wide audience. The three most influential historians of the century were Hume, Robertson, and Gibbon. David Hume (1711-76), a philosopher-historian, wrote a six-volume *History of England*. William Robertson (1721-93), like Hume, was also a Scotsman, whose writings included histories of Scotland and America and a biography of Charles V. Edward Gibbon (1737-94) with his monumental *Decline and Fall of the Roman Empire* offered a comprehensive and controversial interpretation of the fall of a great classical civilization.

Philosophy: Ideas Concerning a Free Society. In the eighteenth century English philosophers were asking the question: "What are the crucial characteristics of a free society?" Several answers were forthcoming, and these served as the drive shaft stimulating political, social, and economic change as well as the justification or rationalization for perpetuating certain practices. Eighteenth-century thought was greatly influenced by the work of Newton and Locke. John Locke had relied on his contract-natural rights theory to lay the basis for certain fundamental rights (life, liberty, property) of the individual that, in the final analysis, had priority over the claims of the king. If the sovereign overstepped the bounds of his power and became tyrannical, the oath of allegiance should become null and void. Given certain conditions Locke's argument was a justification for rebellion, and Thomas Jefferson largely rephrased Locke's *Second Treatise of Government* to argue the colonial case against George III.

David Hume (1711-76): The Dissolving Question. A skeptical Scotsman, Hume reduced Locke's political problem to a single question: Why is a "contract" which formed a government centuries ago still binding on the present generation? For two reasons only, answered Hume. Because it is to the self-interest of the present generation to have such a government (common good), or because of habitual allegiance (common habit). These two answers became the points of departure for Burke and Bentham.

Edmund Burke (1729-97): The Case for Conservatism. In his two best known works, *On Conciliation with America* and *Reflections on the Revolution in France,* Burke eloquently established a conservative tradition that cautioned against radical change. He approved of the Glorious and the American Revolutions because he claimed they were essentially conservative and were led by responsible citizens who held onto the basic values of the past. In contrast the French revolutionaries repudiated their past and pressed for radical change in the structure of society. Burke expressed no more confidence in the will of the majority than in the absolute will of a king. Instead, he urged slow change—reform through renovation rather than through innovation—and defended the tradition and balance of the British Constitution. To some extent Burke's views ran counter to the ideas of the Enlightenment, because he considered natural man evil rather than good and defended strong checks and balances as necessary to save man from himself. The greatest liability of Burke's viewpoint was its orientation toward a slow-changing argicultural, handicraft society instead of toward the new machine age with its rapid changes.

Adam Smith (1723-90): Free Trade. In his *Enquiry into the Wealth of Nations* (1776) Smith discussed the nation's affluence in terms of individual prosperity and argued that in a free society individuals, inspired by self-interest, will produce a prosperous economy in accord with reason and nature, if not restricted by government regulations. Influenced by the discoveries of the Age of Newton, Smith urged England to apply natural laws to economics: produce what you can most cheaply at home and trade these items freely for other goods, and all will prosper. He was supported by two other classical economists, Thomas Malthus and David Ricardo.

In time the link was drawn between free trade and freedom by Adam Smith's followers. His doctrine proved attractive to the laissez-faire idealists who believed that Government governed best when it governed least, and to the new industrial capitalists who found that the prevailing laws, such as the Apprentice Act, the Corn Laws, and the Navigation Acts, which favored the agricultural and handicraft society were cramping both their expansion and their profits. These manufacturers, therefore, picked up the cry of "free trade" since they had nothing to fear from international competition.

Scientific Discoveries. Edward Jenner (1749-1823), physician and naturalist, made man immune to smallpox with his preparation of a serum from cowpox. The two leading English scientists of the century were Henry Cavendish (1731-1810) and Joseph Priestley (1733-1804). Cavendish discovered that water was composed of oxygen and hydrogen. Priestly was a nonconformist clergyman and experimentalist in many areas—philosophy, history, religion (Unitarian), and science. He built on the work of Stephen Hales and Joseph Black in isolating gases. In 1774 he isolated oxygen and made possible Lavoisier's work in quantitative chemistry. In physics Priestley discovered the Law of Inverse Squares (1766) which formed the bases of the work of the French scientist Coulomb. Fascination with electricity led to numerous experiments with lightning conductors by such amateurs as Benjamin Franklin.

Promotion of Scientific Interest. The hunger for more information and the spread of knowledge was accelerated by the establishment of circulating libraries and philosophic societies; soon every city had both a library and a Literary and Philosophic Society. By 1815 the *Encyclopaedia Britannica* had gone through four editions and new professional journals were appearing. In 1800 the Royal Institution was founded which paralleled the work and interests of the older Royal Society. This scientific interest, however, did not carry over to the application of science to industry. Tradition and superstition retarded the application of practical measures, such as vaccinations or the study in schools of science based upon current investigation. Even the invention of machines was regarded by employer and employee alike as labor and money-saving devices rather than as instruments of industrial growth.

The Economic Revolution

Three interlocking revolutions occurred in the eighteenth century: in agriculture, in industry, and in transportation. These revolutions did not occur suddenly, rather they accelerated and expanded the countless changes which had been going on since the commercial revolution. But the consequences of industrialization for English society, and later, for the world were profound and revolutionary.

Prerequisites for Change. The industrial and agricultural revolutions began first in England because conditions were ripe for change. A half-century of internal peace had encouraged the growth of internal and external trade and this, in turn, promoted increased production. Britain had sufficient capital to pay for expansion and a banking and checking system to facilitate it. More important was the significant growth of population in England after 1740 through improved midwifery, medicine, and foundling hospitals. The expanding population reduced the labor shortage, expanded the home markets, and from 1720 to 1760 helped British exports to double in value. The world wanted English exports, particularly textiles; therefore, inventions to save labor and increase production were urgently needed.

Agricultural Revolution. To secure better farming and increased efficiency, the agrarian changes which had begun slowly in the sixteenth century accelerated rapidly in the eighteenth century.

The new methods of farming brought prosperity and a readiness by landlords to experiment in agricultural production.

Enclosures. The open-field system was destroyed by the wholesale agricultural enclosures of the Georgian period. Between 1761 and 1801 two thousand private acts enclosing three million acres were passed by Parliament. Local landowners petitioned Parliament for such legislation and usually the bill passed, because the wealthy landholding class dominated Parliament and the protests of the poorer villagers went unheeded. Commissioners then carried out the law; land was valued, surveyed, and redistributed among those entitled to receive portions. The enclosures brought many more acres under cultivation, and the new, compact farms permitted each farmer to improve his crops and breed cattle without wasting his efforts as he would have done under the open-field system. Enclosures brought efficiency and wealth to landlords and independent farmers at the expense of the traditional communal life of the village.

Achievements. Wealthy landowners experimented in farming and several had significant success. Jethro Tull (1674-1741) improved seed planting and yield with his inventions of the horse drill which dropped the seeds in rows, instead of the former method of broadcast, and of the horse-hoe for cultivation. After his retirement from politics Charles Townshend (1674-1738) popularized the turnip as winter fodder for livestock. He also experimented with a four-course rotation of crops to eliminate the waste of fallow land. Robert Bakewell (1725-95) turned the attention of farmers to better breeding for an increased supply of meat. The records of London's Smithfield Market show that the average weight of sheep and cattle more than doubled between 1710 and 1795. These farming methods were popularized by Arthur Young in his writings on agricultural economy. In 1793 Young became head of the first semi-public, semi-private Board of Agriculture.

Effects. The diet of Englishmen changed as roast beef and white bread became staples; also the combination of new methods and enclosures helped feed a larger population. However, enclosures had an adverse effect on the lesser tenant who, losing his free fuel and pasturage, could no longer compete and paid the penalty for the changes. The result was the disappearance of the peasant proprietor who sank into proletarian status and became either a rural or urban wage earner.

Industrial Revolution. The changes in industry were even more fundamental. The Industrial Revolution transformed the very nature of society by substituting horsepower for manpower, the factory for the home workshop, and the city for the village. With these changes came greater productivity and wealth for the factory owner and misery for the worker in the factory town, a shift in population to the industrial Midlands, and a challenge by the new industrialists to the political domination of the landed aristocracy.

Inventions. The most remarkable developments of the economic revolution were in technology and in methods of industrial organization. The application of mechanical inventions began in the first half of the century but became extensive only in the latter half as recognizable needs were met by new mechanical improvements. In each case an invention brought about new needs, new problems, and an expansion of the market. A marked advance in one area of manufacturing, such as weaving, produced pressure on the complementary area of spinning to catch up, thereby producing a chain reaction and accelerating the whole pace of technological improvement.

Textiles. Inventions made their first major impact upon the textile industry. The infant cotton industry was aided by the fashion changes in favor of cotton goods and the restrictions on the importation of Indian calico. The increased demand for domestic cottons could not be met by the old domestic system of "putting out" orders to homes on a piecework basis. The outcome was a series of inventions and the transfer of work from the home to the factory, which quickly made England the world leader in the production of cotton goods.

John Kay hastened the weaving process with his flying shuttle (1733), and James Hargreaves' spinning jenny (1767) kept the weavers supplied with more spun yarn. Richard Arkwright's water frame took the weaving industry into factories because the new looms were too large for homes and required water power. These inventions were followed by Samuel Compton's spinning mule (1779) and Edmund Cartwright's power loom (1785) for weaving. By this time the supply of raw cotton could no longer keep up with the demand. This problem was remedied when Eli Whitney, an American, invented the cotton gin (1793) to extract seeds from cotton. The machine made southern United States a land of cotton which soon supplied three-fourths of the total British demand.

Iron, Steel, and Power. Although England had ample iron deposits, the charcoal used in southern England for smelting was becoming scarce, because the groves of oaks providing the charcoal were depleted. After successfully experimenting in smelting with coke made from coal, the Darbys of Coalbrookdale encouraged the iron industry to move north to the coal regions. In 1784 a new type of blast furnace, the "puddling" process, perfected by Henry Cort, made iron tough, malleable, and cheap. New iron machinery, such as rolling mills, made iron available for a wide variety of uses with the result that between the years 1740 and 1840 iron production jumped from 17,350 tons to 1,348,000 tons. Small steel factories were opened at Sheffield and Birmingham, but mass production awaited the invention of Bessemer in the next century.

The problem of removing water from the coal mines led to use of Newcomen's inefficient steam engine in 1705. James Watt improved the steam engine in 1769 and twelve years later he and Matthew Boulton perfected it for use in the iron and coal industries. Because steam replaced water as the principal source of power for industry and transportation, factories could now operate in large cities away from rivers; furthermore, the development of the locomotive and the steamboat was made possible.

The Revolution in Transportation. The industrial revolution called for improved methods for shipping iron and coal. In 1760 travel conditions in England were so wretched that men and goods traveled more slowly than they did in Roman times. The packhorse, slow and expensive, was often the only way goods could be moved, until canals and turnpikes eventually revitalized inland transport. The Duke of Bridgewater had the first canal completed in 1761; immediately the cost of coal was halved in Manchester and new markets were opened. The lesson was quickly learned and by 1815, 2,600 miles of canals crisscrossed England. Ironmasters such as John Wilkinson pressed for major road improvements, and Parliament responded by authorizing Turnpike Trusts to build, maintain, and charge tolls for new roads. Civil engineers, Thomas Telford and John McAdam, provided all-weather roads of crushed rock. Stage coach travel, mail service, a decline in provincialism, and the expansion of industry were some of the advantages to come from rapid and easy transportation.

Results of the Economic Revolution. The enormous increase in industrial output and the cheapness of manufactured goods increased national wealth and gave England a commanding lead in competition for world markets. This wealth was not widely diffused, however, and the factory employee reaped few benefits from these economic changes. Although the picture of the village farmer has too often been romanticized (as in Gray's *Elegy Written in a Country Churchyard*), the social dislocation, slum housing, and exhausting working conditions of the wage earner were neither acknowledged nor ameliorated until the nineteenth century. These hardships were aggravated by twenty years of war with France and muted only by the Methodist religious revival and the development of local authorities to administer basic utilities and social services. The city commissioners believed in efficiency and cleanliness and opened the door for the utilitarian reforms of the nineteenth century. In the eighteenth century, however, the only obvious improvement in the life of the poor was increasing longevity, for the material progress resulting from the industrial revolution was not matched by any significant reforms in political or social institutions.

Chapter 17 ✒ Repression and Reform, 1815-1841

Two decades of war with France had left England with a residue of wartime restrictions and a fear of revolution that made the Tory Government hostile to all demands for reform. Gradually, the aristocracy saw the necessity of change if they were to maintain their position; therefore, a respectable "revolution from above" took place. In contrast to the aristocracy on the Continent, English aristocrats helped introduce parliamentary measures for reform, since a continuing effect of the industrial revolution was the need to broaden the base of political power by enfranchising more social classes. These political changes toward democracy took place gradually without violence because in most cases they made common sense. The most obvious abuse in postwar England was the unreformed Parliament which had failed to keep up with the social and political changes of the eighteenth century. In the wake of the Great Reform Bill (1832) other reforms followed as the public conscience forced changes in English institutional life.

Postwar Problems and Policies

After the war with Napoleon, the people expected some rewards and specific reforms for the sacrifices they had made in that struggle. Instead, the adjustments to a peacetime economy brought depression and unemployment, and the outcome was disenchantment and rioting until the Prime Minister salvaged his unpopular Cabinet by bringing in younger men who quietly began to change the policy of the Government from repression to reform.

The Workers' Grievances. Fundamental in the discontent of the worker was his complaint that the Government persisted in a course of negation and made no attempt to alleviate abuses or to face up to changing conditions.

Causes of the Grievances. As a consequence of the war serious economic problems developed for which no preparations had been made: (1) There was a depression which lasted for five years; the end of the trade monopoly and war shipments to continental allies left England overstocked with goods which impoverished Europe was in no position to buy. (2) Unemployment; the glutted market caused bankruptcy and sharply reduced employment, and the situation was aggravated with the return of 400,000 veterans to the labor force. (3) The Corn Law; following a series of crop failures Parliament revised the corn law in 1815 in order to raise the tariff on imported grain. This act was attractive to the Tory landlord class, but increased the already high cost of bread for the rest of the nation. (4) Taxation; financing the war had raised the national debt to £850,000,000, and although Parliament repealed the income tax in 1816, indirect taxation remained heavy.

Riots and Repression. The spread of economic hardship forced the poor to seek remedies for their grievances by means of demonstrations and mass meetings which frequently led to rioting. This violent agitation resulted in even more repressive legislation.

The Agitators. Following the war the reform movement was re-introduced in typically eighteenth-century style with correspondence societies, working-class clubs, and middle- and upper-class supporters raising the issue; however, when the reformers received little understanding from Parliament, more radical leaders came forward. These radicals were united in the belief that parliamentary reform was the first step in alleviating economic distress. Mass meetings were held by William Cobbett (publisher of *Cobbett's Weekly Register*), Henry Hunt, and John Cartwright, and petitions were presented to Parliament. Soon these protests became blurred in the public mind with the economic unrest of the unemployed and with the physical violence that erupted.

Demonstrations and Riots. From 1812 to 1820 increasingly violent protests occurred as the demonstrators became impatient with their conditions. (1) The Luddite Riots. Unemployed workmen systematically wrecked factory machinery in the industrial towns of northern England. (2) In 1816 the rioting of a huge crowd assembled in Spa Fields near London required police intervention. (3) The March of the Blanketeers (unemployed workers in Manchester) on London was halted under orders from the home secretary. (4) In 1819 a large crowd gathered in St. Peter's Fields, Manchester, to hear Henry Hunt's speech on parliamentary reform. Local magistrates ordered the cavalry to arrest Hunt. The cavalry charged the crowd leaving eleven dead and many more wounded. When the Government publicly commended the magistrates' action, the callous incident was popularly labeled "the Peterloo Massacre." (5) The Cato Street Conspiracy. In 1820 a group of radicals met in Cato Street, London, to plot the assassination of the Cabinet; they were caught red-handed while dining and were eventually tried and executed.

Government Response. The Cabinet looked upon every demonstration as evidence of sedition and passed legislation even more restrictive than existed in wartime. As a consequence of the Spa Fields riot the habeas corpus act was suspended in 1817 and the law restricting public meetings was tightened. The repressive policies of the Government reached a climax after Peterloo with the passage of the Six Acts (1819) which circumscribed the freedom of the press and the right of assembly and strengthened the hand of the magistrates in dealing with disorders.

Accession of George IV, 1820. The unpopular Six Acts and the attempt of the Cabinet to obtain a divorce for George IV on the grounds of his wife's adultery turned the balance of popular opinion against the Government. Although Queen Caroline had exceedingly few virtues, the populace supported her as a woman abused by a man who had even fewer. Only with the death of Caroline in 1821 were the King and the Cabinet relieved of an unpopular position. This royal scandal and the Cato Street conspiracy momentarily diverted the cause of radicalism.

Death of Lord Castlereagh. Castlereagh had served ably as war and foreign minister and as an astute negotiator at the Congress of Vienna. Because he had made no effort to oppose the illiberality of his colleagues in the Cabinet, Castlereagh became indentified with the repressive domestic policies of the Government and was unpopular with the populace. His suicide in 1822 opened the way for the younger Tories, Canning, Peel, and Huskisson, who would moderate the Cabinet's position.

George Canning and Foreign Policy. Canning succeeded Castlereagh as Foreign Secretary and leader of the House of Commons. Continuing his predecessor's policy of nonintervention on the Continent, Canning acquired a liberal reputation (a term brought into currency by the Spanish revolution of 1823), because of his sympathy with reformist groups in other countries and his methods of open diplomacy whereby he took the nation into his confidence—in a reversal of Castlereagh's practice of secret negotiations. By warning the European powers not to interfere with the new South American republics in 1823, he won popular support as well as commercial backing from British merchants eager to break Spain's monopoly on South American trade.

In 1826 Canning ranged himself against the powers of the Quadruple Alliance by ordering British troops to Portugal to prevent an invasion by Spain. In the following year his diplomatic maneuvers helped the Greek insurgents win independence from Turkish despotism. This action gave British foreign policy a reputation in favor of nationalism and liberalism which lasted for decades. Although he won more support from the Whigs than from the conservative wing of his own party, Canning became Prime Minister after Liverpool's resignation in 1827; but within five months he was dead.

Sir Robert Peel, Home Secretary. In domestic affairs Peel supported the "common sense" reforms of the liberal Tories and yet retained the respect of the entire party. His reforms reflected the new humanitarianism that was taking hold of the public conscience and the new industrial leadership of the nation. As home secretary Peel brought about the long needed overhaul of an antiquated and harsh criminal code. He abolished the death penalty for over one hundred offenses, established other punishments on a more rational and humane basis, and organized the nation's first professional police force in London.

William Huskisson and Freer Trade. As president of the Board of Trade, Huskisson worked closely with the chancellor of the exchequer, Frederick Robinson (later Viscount Goderich) in moving away from the traditional policy of agricultural protectionism toward a liberal policy of freer trade. In 1825 the entire tariff was revised and lowered in the manner that Pitt had pioneered in the 1780's. Cognizant of Britain's industrial and commercial supremacy, Huskisson modified the outmoded Navigation Acts, repealed in 1824 the harsh Combination Acts of wartime vintage (aided by the able trade union organizer and political manipulator, Francis Place), and persuaded Canning to introduce a sliding scale of duties on imported grain in place of the old fixed price. (Wellington secured defeat of the bill in the House of Lords, but reintroduced it later, when he became Prime Minister.) Huskisson worked with Canning to exercise diplomatic pressure in bringing about reciprocity treaties with co-operative nations and reprisals for the unco-operative.

Cabinet Changes. All of the administrative reforms mentioned above had occurred under the prime ministership of the benign and amiable Lord Liverpool. When Liverpool resigned because of ill health and Canning died suddenly, Lord Goderich was unable to hold together the coalition with the Whigs that Canning had arranged. Disliked by the King, Goderich was replaced by the Duke of Wellington, the fourth Prime Minister within the year. Wellington was a national hero who at first united both wings of the Tories but soon alienated the Canningites by his opposition to the reform current. Peel was the only reformer to stay in the Cabinet as the ultra-Tories rallied around the Prime Minister's "stand pat" views on the constitution and the church. Nevertheless, Wellington could not stop the current of change and his political leadership, in contrast to his military, consisted largely of a series of retreats. When threatened by riots at home and civil war in Ireland, the Duke gave way and "became despite himself the best ally of liberalism." [1]

Catholic Emancipation. The Protestant Dissenters won their victory in 1828 when a young Whig, Lord John Russell, introduced a bill in the House of Commons to finally remove the political disabilities of the Test and Corporation Acts. Wellington and Peel had agreed to this bill, because annual Indemnity Bills had exempted non-Anglican Protestants. Yet they feared that its passage would only encourage the Catholics to demand emancipation, and their fears proved correct.

William Pitt the Younger had promised Irish Catholics the vote and the right to sit in Parliament at the time of the Act of Union; but George III reneged on his promise to Pitt, and the restrictions against Catholics continued. Led by Daniel O'Connell and his powerful Catholic Association, Irish Catholics were forcing the emancipation issue. Despite the law against Catholics O'Connell was elected to Parliament over a member of Wellington's Cabinet. Fearing civil strife, the Duke beat a strategic retreat and commanded sufficient respect from the King and Peel to win their support on the issue, even though the passage of the bill was against the convictions of all three. The Catholic Emancipation Act was rammed through Parliament in 1829, thereby permitting O'Connell to take his seat in the House of Commons and allowing Catholic peers to resume their vacant seats in the House of Lords. It was perhaps ironical that the bill passed under the aegis of the leading ultra-Tory, rather than under earlier reformers. However, this was the last Tory reform because the High Tories in Wellington's party never forgave him for deserting them and combined in 1830 to bring down his ministry. For that matter, Tory administrative reform had run its course, and, when the even more controversial issue of parliamentary reform came up again, most of the party lined up in opposition to change.

The Great Reform Bill

Once again the radicals and reformers focused their attention on the one area of unanimity among them, the need for parliamentary reform. And again public opinion was ably manipulated by popular

---

[1] André Maurois, *A History of England* (New York: Grove, 1958), p. 426.

leaders, but this time it was strengthened by the demands of the rising industrial class for representation. Sufficient members of the aristocracy sensed the need of aligning the new, wealthy class with them, rather than against them, and took action in time to avoid violence. The bill was a first step and gave encouragement to the nation that more changes would be forthcoming.

The Politics of Reform. The agitation for parliamentary reform was not new; what was new was the action taken by parliamentary leaders to bring it about. By 1830 the reform climate was such that change would come either with or without parliamentary support. The Whig leadership, therefore, introduced the reform bill as a rational measure, rather than a democratic one, to meet the minimum needs of this agitation without destroying the basis of their control in the process.

The Case for Reform. The abuses in the parliamentary system included: (1) The notoriety of rotten boroughs that were available through bribery or influence so that elections, in many cases, became largely a matter of selection. (2) The major shift in population to the north and west of England with no corresponding change in parliamentary representation. Such large centers as Birmingham, Leeds, and Manchester had no representation. (3) A parliamentary system which reflected the traditional influence of the country gentry but not of the burgeoning commercial interests. (4) A House of Commons which neither enjoyed the confidence of the nation nor reflected changes in popular opinion to any great extent. Radicals pointed out that the old system made no pretense of being democratic or of representing individuals instead of interests. In 1830 revolutions wracked the Continent, and "the Last Laborer's Revolt" broke out in southern England. Fears grew that if reform did not come, revolution would.

Defeat of the Tories. The death of George IV required (by law) a general election in July, 1830. The Wellington Government was returned to power; but the voting loyalty of the various Whig and Tory factions was uncertain, and the Whig opposition joined with the new industrial class to reopen the issue of parliamentary reform. Wellington was forced to state his position on current events—the revolution in France, the newly created Belgium and the threat of Metternich to destroy Belgian independence, the Greek question, and the riots in the country. His famous speech at the opening of the new Parliament about the perfection of the British Government caused such violent reaction that he was forced to resign after enough Tories voted against him on a minor bill to show their disapproval of his leadership.

Composition of Lord Grey's Cabinet. The new Whig Cabinet

had a decidedly aristocratic identity with all but two members
either peers or sons of peers. It included several Canningites (Melbourne, Palmerston, and Graham) who combined with such Whig
ministers as Henry Brougham, Lords Russell, Durham, and Althorp
to make electoral reform their prime concern. Led by the elderly,
respected Lord Grey, who had advocated parliamentary reform
since 1795, the Cabinet aimed at retaining the old basis of political
power and representation and remodeling it to eliminate its worse
abuses and give the new industrial centers a political voice.

Passage of the Bill, 1830-32. The new Whig Government drew
up reform proposals that were hardly democratic, but were far-
reaching enough to bring about the strong opposition of the Lords
and the members of boroughs about to be disenfranchised. This
opposition caused the resignation and re-election of Grey's Government before the final passage of the bill.

The Struggle for Passage. The reform bill was introduced by
Lord John Russell in March, 1831, and passed the second reading
by only one vote. Grey, therefore, asked for a dissolution of Parliament in order to take his cause to the country. In the election
campaign the combination of government patronage along with
Whig, Radical, and working class political meetings won the reformers some ninety new seats. The bill now passed the House of
Commons but was thrown out by the House of Lords. When the
King refused to create sufficient peers to pass the bill, Grey resigned. By this time the popular mood of the country showed itself
so angrily that revolution seemed quite possible. Newspapers were
trimmed in black, riots broke out, and bishops were booed for
voting with the lay lords.

When Wellington was asked by the King to form a Government
the Duke found he was without support in either the House of
Commons or in the country. Unable to form a ministry under
Wellington, William IV recalled Grey and promised to create the
necessary number of peers to pass the bill. The threat was as good
as the act, and the King's surrender became the Lords' surrender.
In July, 1832, the reform bill became law.

Major Clauses of the Bill. (1) All boroughs containing less than
two thousand inhabitants were disenfranchised; this eliminated
fifty-six. (2) One member was dropped from each borough containing less than four thousand inhabitants; this eliminated thirty-
two (3) Sixty-five seats were given to new boroughs previously un-
represented. (4) Sixty-five additional seats were given to English
counties; eight to Scotland and five to Ireland. (5) Borough voting
lists were eliminated, and all £10 freeholders were enfranchised. The

county franchise was enlarged to include £10 copyholders and £50 leaseholders. (6) A system of voting registration demanding the compilation of electoral lists was introduced.

Significance of the Reform Bill. The bill met the immediate needs which old abuses and changing times had demanded, and representatives of the new industrial wealth now became associated with the landed aristocracy; but there was no basic shift in power. In the debates neither Whig nor Tory argued for democracy because both parties agreed that any government of the people, or for the people, should still be by the *best* of the people. Thus the right to vote was still limited to the owners or lessees of land, and the working class still had no part in political affairs.

As a result, the radicals were not satisfied since the enfranchisement in England was raised by only some 200,000 voters to one out of every seven adult males. Nor was the composition of Parliament altered radically, for the newly reformed House of Commons of 1833 contained 217 sons of peers. In some ways the most significant consequence of the bill was one wholly unanticipated by the reformers or their opponents. The clause providing for registration of voters caused the creation of local political groups to get the voters registered and get out the vote. From this grew the well-organized and country-wide party organizations.

The First Reform Bill was, therefore, essentially a compromise. Several of the old institutions, such as the monarchy, the House of Lords, and the Cabinet remained unscathed, but the power of popular opinion and political organization made itself felt as never before. The agricultural interests remained, but were now rivaled by the growing industrial interests. However, in one sense it was a revolution, because popular pressure had forced changes in the age-honored principle of parliamentary representation. This was the specter that caused Robert Peel to oppose the bill, saying, "I was unwilling to open the door which I saw no prospect of being able to close." The rest of the century was to prove Peel correct as the parliamentary system was no longer treated as something forever fixed and impervious to change.

Other "Whig" Reforms

The combination of popular agitation, the penny press, reform-minded MPs, and the taste of success which the passage of the Reform Bill had encouraged caused increased demands for parliamentary intervention in other areas of English economic and social life.

Industrial and Social Legislation. Wretched working conditions and squalid housing threatened not only the poor but eventually the industrial system that spawned them. Parliamentary legislation was the state's belated response to social and industrial ills.

Abolition of Slavery, 1833. The issue of slavery dominated all other colonial questions in the first part of the nineteenth century. The act abolishing the slave trade (1807) was found impossible to enforce in international waters, and efforts to reform the institution of slavery were blocked by the West Indian planters. Therefore, humanitarians, led by Wilberforce and Sir Thomas Buxton, campaigned for the abolition of slavery itself and were strongly supported by the Anti-Slavery Society (1823) and the Colonial Office. Gradually, the opposition of the powerful West Indian lobby withered as trade with the West Indies became less important to England and as mass petitions put pressure on Parliament. Lord Stanley, colonial secretary, introduced a bill abolishing slavery throughout the Empire which became operative in 1834. A vested interest was beaten, largely on humanitarian grounds. The slave owners were compensated by a government grant of £20,000,000, and the emancipation was to take place gradually through a system of apprenticeship covering four to six years. The act won great acclaim in England, but led to planter hostility and economic decline in the West Indies and to bitter protests from the Boers in South Africa, culminating in their great trek across the mountains to form two new Boer republics.

The Factory Act, 1833. Because the previous factory acts of 1802 and 1819 lacked provisions for effective enforcement, few factory owners heeded the clauses which attempted to ameliorate the harsh working conditions and long hours of child labor. Three men, in particular, resumed the earlier efforts of Dr. Percival and Robert Owen and pushed through Parliament the first effective factory reform. Michael Sadler, a Tory MP, brought about a Royal Commission in 1831 to investigate working conditions and the treatment of child employees. His graphic and grim report aroused public sympathy for working children. At the same time Richard Oastler, a practical philanthropist, promoted popular support for factory legislation by describing working conditions at mass meetings. Lord Ashley (later the Earl of Shaftesbury), a Tory nobleman and Evangelical religious leader, became known as "the children's friend" for his labors in behalf of factory children. He introduced the bill to correct the abuses in the textile industry and Lord Althorp sponsored its final passage. The act decreed: (1) No employment of children under nine years of age. (2) No child under thirteen was to work more than nine hours per day and each child was to receive two hours of school per day. (3) No child under eighteen was to work more than twelve hours a day (excluding meal breaks). (4) Inspectors were to be appointed by Parliament to enforce these provisions.

The Poor Amendment, 1834. The Elizabethan Poor Law and its accompanying system of parish doles had changed little in two hundred years. But the number of paupers in England had increased to the point that one out of every six inhabitants was on relief. Farmers and manufacturers, knowing that laborers could survive by living off the poor rates, kept wages low. A Royal Commission, headed by Nassau Senior, investigated and recommended procedures to encourage frugality and discourage laziness by providing relief in such a manner that an individual would lose his self-respect by asking for it.

The ensuing amendment to the Poor Law contained the following provisions: (1) All relief was centralized by combining parishes into larger units with three commissioners in London controlling the welfare program. (2) Outdoor relief (assistance to the poor in their own homes) was restricted to the sick, the aged, and children. (3) Able-bodied men who demanded relief were required to live in work houses (denounced as "Poor Law Bastilles" by Thomas Carlyle), where they were separated from their wives, and where food and heat were kept at a minimum.

The Municipal Corporation Act, 1835. The Municipal Corporation Act (along with similar acts for Scotland and Ireland in 1833 and 1840) reorganized urban government according to a uniform plan. Municipal councilors were elected for three years by resident taxpayers. These councilors then elected one-third of their number to serve as aldermen for a six-year term. The council elected the mayor annually, regulated all public utilities, and appointed the salaried officials. The act ended the corrupt and unrepresentative character of municipal government in which a self-perpetuating oligarchy usually chose members of the governing council to serve for life and felt no responsibility to provide such needed services as waterworks, sewers, or police protection for the citizens. The Municipal Corporation Act increased both efficiency and democracy in local government and paved the way for future public health reforms by abolishing the abuses of private monopolies in utilities. Although additional legislation increased the functions and powers of councilors, the act still serves as the basis of English municipal government.

Colonial Policies. Conflicting views on the merit and function of colonies prevented any consistent policy from being applied to all parts of the Empire in the first half of the nineteenth century. Pitt's India Act provided for dual control of British India; England continued to annex territory (Natal) in South Africa; Canada moved toward responsible government; and Australia had a unique situation with her penal settlements. The supporters of free trade and the Manchester School of Political Economy (James Mill, David Ricardo, and Thomas Malthus) argued that free trade had no colonial boundaries, and that the law of supply and demand should work free of government regulations. Therefore, colonies were of little value to England. In contrast, the Radical Imperialists (Gibbon Wakefield, Lord Durham, Charles Buller, and William Molesworth) had an active interest in reviving the Empire by selective emigration from England and by the promotion of local self-government in the colonies of white settlement.

Colonial administration was strengthened by the quality and vigor of leadership found in the colonial office. In 1812 the Earl of Bathurst became Secretary for War and the Colonies and picked Henry Goulburn as undersecretary. These two officials practically created the colonial office; they organized departments, hired specialists, and their active humanitarianism was reflected in colonial policies. Their work was effectively continued in the Colonial Office by Lord Glenelg and James Stephen. Under Bathurst and Stephen the influence of the humanitarian and Evangelical movement produced a colonial policy favoring missionary expansion and racial equality.

Affairs in Canada. Pitt's Canada Act of 1791 had eased the tension between French and English by dividing Canada into two colonies. Yet, friction continued between French and English, and Catholic and Protestant, aggravated by a legislative feud in each province. In Upper Canada the early settlers (the so-called Family Compact) resented the influx of newcomers and tried to keep control of the Assembly in their own hands; in Lower Canada the friction was between the elected Assembly and the upper house, nominated by the governor. The grievances flared into open rebellion in 1837, led by Louis Papineau in Lower Canada and William Lyon Mackenzie in Upper Canada. Although the fighting was insignificant, the rebellion awakened the British Government to the seriousness of the situation and the need to prevent another Colonial revolution from developing. Lord Durham, a liberal Whig Cabinet minister, was sent to investigate and make recommendations.

The Durham Report. Durham sensed two basic problems in Canada: "two races warring in the bosom of a single nation," and representative government without responsibility for its actions leading to irresponsibility. Therefore, his report to Parliament in 1839 recommended: (1) The Union of Upper and Lower Canada so that racial differences would not become indelible in the two provinces, and immigration would eventually provide an English majority. (2) Responsible Government. The governors should choose their ministers from men commanding a majority in the assembly, making the executive responsible to the legislature except for four areas which were reserved for the Imperial Government.

Consequences. The British Government bungled the application of Durham's Report by giving an equal vote to Upper and Lower Canada in the Act of Union of 1840, but, most important, the principle of responsible government was accepted and became a constitutional landmark in the evolution of the British Empire. The principle implied that the bond of empire would be volition, not constraint. The lesson of the American Revolution had been well-learned. In Canada responsible government came in 1848 during the governorship of Lord Elgin, and, in the next decade, was extended to Newfoundland, the five Australian colonies of New South Wales, Victoria, South Australia, Tasmania, and Queensland. Cape Colony in South Africa followed in 1872.

Church Reform

The agitation for reform had a religious as well as a political and social dimension. At the turn of the century religious torpor within the Church of England and mounting protests against religious restrictions on non-Anglicans brought about numerous changes which indicated a significant revival of interest in religion, both without and within the established church.

Religious Emancipation outside the Church of England. The rationalism and latitudinarianism of the eighteenth century combined with the growing political power of the Nonconformists to bring substantial relief from sixteenth- and seventeenth-century religious restrictions. The freedom from disabilities applied to Roman Catholics and to Protestant dissenters.

Roman Catholic Respectability. Catholic Emancipation in 1829 and the conversion to Catholicism of two Anglican leaders of the Oxford Movement (John Henry Newman and Henry Manning) helped restore respectability and a certain popularity to the Catholic church. The improved relations with Rome had been aided by the final demise of Jacobite plots in the eighteenth century and by the new attitude of the Papacy toward the Church of England.

222   *Repression and Reform, 1815-1841*

The Papacy now accepted the existence of the Anglican church and made Catholicism less alien in England by giving English titles to English bishoprics. By mid-century Catholicism was a religious choice and not a political error.

Protestant Dissenters. Following their release from political disabilities in 1827, Nonconformists worked to abolish the remaining restrictions. Several Tithe Acts (1836-60) eased and simplified the collection of the tithe for the support of the established church. The Registration Act of 1837 freed Dissenters from the obligation of being baptized, married, and buried by the Anglican church. In 1829 Dissenters were first admitted to the University of London, although Oxford and Cambridge excluded them until 1861-62. These gains came gradually as a result of a new climate of tolerance within, and political pressure without, Parliament. Nonconformist MPs demanded support of these objectives as conditions for winning their votes. Outside of Parliament such organizations as the Society for the Liberation of Religion from State Patronage and Control brought public pressure to bear on religious inequities.

The influence of Nonconformists went beyond the political. Their evangelical concern for the souls of their fellowmen muted their interest in political revolution and increased their support for foreign missions (as with the London Missionary Society) and the abolition of slavery. At home Nonconformists lent moral and vocal support to rid their communities of corruption and vice and promoted industrial reform and social legislation in Parliament.

Schism in Scotland. Led by the Reverend Thomas Chalmers, the Free Kirk Movement seceded from the Church of Scotland in 1843 when the courts ruled that one man (the patron rather than the congregation) could select the parson. The five hundred secessionist ministers claimed that the state was interfering with the policies and principles of the church.

The Church of Ireland. From 1801 to 1869 the Church of Ireland (canonically, the United Church of England and Ireland) was supported by the tithes of the Catholic South and the largely Presbyterian North—an impossible situation. Both groups opposed the compulsory support of an alien church. This issue was resolved in 1869 with the passage of a bill, sponsored by Gladstone, which disestablished the Church of Ireland and made it a self-governing member of the Canterbury communion.

Reform within the Church of England. The year that the Great Reform Bill was passed Thomas Arnold wrote, "The Church as it now stands no human power can save." Critics attacked the established church for its political subservience, inertia, and sinecures, and reformers talked in favor of disestablishment. Defenders argued that the church was an institution outside the pale of ordinary parliamentary action; their position was strengthened when the Anglican church was aroused by a religious revival of its own.

The Oxford Movement, 1833. The immediate occasion of the Oxford Movement was the suppression of ten Irish bishoprics by Grey's Government, and the fear that the Whigs would now turn their energies from political to religious reform. Anglican clergy could no longer take the church for granted in England simply as the authorized version of Protestantism established by law. To protect the church from the arm of the state, John Keble in his Assize Sermon at Oxford in 1833 called for a spiritual regeneration by reasserting the authority and historical traditions of the church, particularly the authority of Apostolic Succession. Other leading Oxford clergymen, John Henry Newman, Hurrell Froude, and Edward Pusey, joined Keble in a liturgical and theological revival that stressed the writings of medieval churchmen and the early Fathers of the Church. This study inevitably led to a greater admiration for the Roman Catholic church with the result that two leading figures of the movement, John Henry Newman and Henry Manning, joined the Roman Catholic church and eventually became cardinals. This revival was also known as the Tractarian movement because the Oxford preachers advanced their views in a series of tracts.

The results of the Oxford Movement were significant and widespread. Orders of nuns and monks were founded, and the self-government of the Church of England was restored with the revival of the convocations of the provinces of York and Canterbury in 1852. Anglicanism still had its internal divisions commonly known as "High," "Low," and "Broad" Church, but most significantly "men cared about the Church as they had not cared in the latitudinarian eighteenth century." [2] However, by midcentury the real threat to Anglicanism was not in schism, vestment controversy, or disestablishment, but in the onslaught of Biblical criticism and skepticism.

Education: A Neglected Area

Not until 1870 was Parliament able to agree on a national education act. England paid for this failure by having to contend in world competition with the least trained artisans and the most

---

[2] Robert Eckles and Richard Hale, *Britain, Her People and the Commonwealth* (New York: McGraw-Hill, 1954), p. 415.

poorly educated middle class in Europe. The basic causes for the delay were sectarian rivalries and opposition to state subsidies for church schools.

The Voluntary Tradition in Education.   The English system of education had a long tradition of private schools. Some like Winchester, Eton, Harrow, and Rugby had developed excellent reputations and were heavily endowed; they became known as the Public Schools. Throughout the years all kinds of voluntary schools emerged, but by 1830 the educational scene resembled a patchwork quilt, completely without design or administrative pattern, and utterly inadequate for the needs of the times.

Education in 1830.   The Public Schools, Grammar Schools, and Dissenter Academies prepared a small and select number of students for admission to the universities; there was no public system of secondary education. Elementary education was, if anything, even more irregular with the children of the working class completely neglected except for the scattered efforts of philanthropic or religious groups. The latter had most success through the Sunday Schools, begun by Robert Raikes in 1780, in which children were taught reading, writing, and religion on the one day they were not working. In 1797 the Bell and Lancaster system provided the first phase of mass education with the help of monitors. Under this system teachers taught the most able students, who, in turn, repeated the lesson to the rest. Although the program was amazingly successful, it put a premium on memorization and was not designed to go beyond the Three R's.

However, these private efforts were at best inadequate, and no industrial society could long rest on such a substratum of ignorance as dense as the statistics of 1830 indicated. The average term in school was less than two years. In city after city barely half the inhabitants could sign their own name and even less could add sums. It was obvious that public education and some scheme for teacher training was imperative, but beyond this point no agreement could be found for any plan.

State Subsidies and Sectarian Suspicions.   In 1833 the first state grant for education was a modest appropriation of £20,000 to the two largest voluntary associations, the British and Foreign School Society (Dissenters) and the National Society for Promoting the Education of the Poor in the Principles of the Established Church. Six years later the distribution of the parliamentary grant was entrusted to a Committee of Council, but no agreement on curriculum or administration could be found. The Philosophical Radicals had a solution that was practical and logical, but it entirely overlooked the human emotions and values of the age. The more modest plans of Kay-Shuttleworth's Committee of Council collapsed over the issue of religious instruction. "The Dissenters would not stand the parson in a State School. The Establishment would not stand any one else." [3] In 1846 the new system of grants—£1 from the Treasury for every £2 of local funds—again raised the whole issue of state subsidies. This time Thomas Babington Macaulay's eloquent speech in defense of the grants and in support of the Church of England carried the day; thereafter education was acknowledged to be a duty of the state. From this admission the Radical position of universal, compulsory, and largely secular education followed after much argument and church opposition.

Political Leadership and the Monarchy

The Whigs, with a loose and changing coalition of votes, remained in office for most of the decade following the Great Reform Bill, with Melbourne serving as Prime Minister for six of these years. He gave a great deal of time and attention to the tutoring and advising of Queen Victoria, but finally resigned in 1841 when it became apparent that Peel's argument was becoming constitutionally correct. Peel had pointed out that it was "at variance with the principles and the spirit of the constitution for a Ministry to continue in office without the confidence of the House."

The Triumph of Responsible Government. In the years of the Melbourne ministry William IV, Victoria, Peel, Russell, Macaulay, and Melbourne all argued over the question of executive responsibility to the House of Commons. William IV clearly believed he had the right to choose his own ministry; but by 1841 the Crown and Parliament recognized that the executive could not perform its administrative duties without the support of a majority in the House of Commons.

Resignation of Grey. Earl Grey, as Prime Minister, and Althorp, as leader of the House of Commons, had won the respect of most of their Whig colleagues. But following the reform measures of 1832 and 1833 neither man was interested in pursuing the political maneuvering that additional reforms demanded. The Radicals and the Irish, however, were not content to stop. Led by Daniel

---

[3] G. M. Young, *Victorian England: Portrait of an Age* (London: Oxford, 1960), p. 61.

O'Connell and backed by an aroused peasantry and priesthood who opposed the payment of the tithe to the Anglican church, Irish agitation for reduction of the tithe grew stronger, but was opposed by conservative Whigs who would countenance no change in the Irish church. A bill to reduce the tithe split the Cabinet; Lord Stanley (later the Earl of Derby) and James Graham left the Cabinet and joined the Tories. In the ensuing name-calling the elderly Grey resigned in July, 1834, pleased to have fulfilled his youthful pledge of reform and anxious now to be relieved of office.

Melbourne and Peel. The new Prime Minister was Lord Melbourne, an affable and sophisticated former Canningite, whose weak and divided Cabinet held a fragile majority in the House of Commons. William IV dismissed the Whigs and asked Peel to form a Cabinet. After the dissolution of Parliament Peel issued the party's first platform supporting a program of cautious reform. This Tamworth manifesto helped reduce the large Whig-Liberal majority, but not enough to give a Tory victory. Nevertheless, Peel refused to resign and for six weeks tried to govern with minority support before surrendering office to Lord Melbourne.

For the next six years (1835-41) Melbourne in the House of Lords and the quietly persuasive Lord John Russell, leader of the House of Commons, survived threats from both wings (Whig and Radical-Irish) of their supporters. With the help of O'Connell they pushed through a few reforms (Municipal Reform Act, Irish Poor Relief Act) and opened the way for responsible government in the colonies by the acceptance of the Durham Report. During his ministry Melbourne became a political maverick who shifted his political persuasion with the years and who was adept in the art of political maneuvering. He was equally proficient at managing Queen Victoria.

Victoria, Melbourne, and Peel. When William IV died in 1837 with no legitimate heirs, his niece, Victoria, became Queen at the age of eighteen. Since Hanover had a law forbidding a female from ruling, the royal connections with that German state were finally broken. Lord Melbourne, as Prime Minister, now had an opportunity to tutor the young monarch in correct constitutional and court conduct. He was an able teacher, and Victoria accepted the idea of offering only constitutional advice with considerable grace. In 1840 Melbourne helped arrange the marriage of Victoria to Prince Albert of Saxe-Coburg-Gotha. Albert became a knowledgeable and hard-working consort to whom Victoria was deeply devoted, but whom the nation never understood or appreciated during his lifetime.

In the election of 1837, required by the death of William IV, the Tories almost equaled the Whig vote. Two years later Melbourne was defeated over the Jamaica Prisons Bill, and his Cabinet resigned. During his attempts to form a ministry, Peel ordered Queen Victoria to dismiss her Whig Ladies of the Bedchamber because he feared that they might have undue influence on her—as Abigail Masham had had in Queen Anne's Court. This tactless request disturbed the Queen, who was upset over the prospect of losing both Melbourne and her court companions. Instead of complying, Victoria asked Melbourne to remain in office. He accepted and was able to maintain a tenuous majority until 1841. The election of 1841 gave the Tories a clear majority, and the precedent became firmly established that the monarch must choose a first minister who can command a majority in the House of Commons. Peel took office and immediately faced the agitation of the chartists and the Anti-Corn-Law League.

Political Ideas. Motivating the English reformers of the eighteenth and nineteenth century were new ideas on society and its improvements. These ideas by themselves seldom had much impact, and their formulators were invariably ahead of their time. But, in time, many of their proposals slipped into the institutional life of Britain. Often the actual form of the final achievement was quite different from the original plan, or—to put it another way—reformers planned, their plans made a difference, but not always the difference planned. In the early nineteenth century Owen, Bentham, and others added their views to those already spelled out by Locke, Hume, Smith, and Burke on the essentials of a free society.

Robert Owen (1771-1858). Beginning as a penniless shop assistant, Owen combined business ability and humanitarian idealism to become a leading factory owner of his day. He spent his energies and his money in a crusade for improving the working conditions of the factory system. At New Lanark Mills in Scotland he set up a model factory town with schools, good housing, and a co-operative store. He interested members of Parliament in factory acts and helped to pioneer the trade union movement—founding the Builders' Union. His idealistic dreams of reforming society and setting up model communities (New Harmony, Indiana) made him known as a Utopian socialist. Most of his ambitious schemes were failures.

Jeremy Bentham and Utilitarianism (1748-1832). Bentham proved more successful than Owen, perhaps because he was less doctrinaire and, therefore, more appealing to the Englishman's pragmatic mind. Bentham argued with Burke by declaring that respect for tradition dare not excuse the perpetuation of abuses, because a free society must continuously reappraise its institutions in the light of *utility*. Two questions should be leveled at each institution. Utility for what? Promoting happiness. Utility for whom? The greatest number of individuals. Thus each law or custom should be continuously re-examined to see if it provided happiness (according to an arbitrary listing of pleasures and pains) for the many or for the few. Bentham's followers—Edwin Chadwick, Southward Smith, William Cobbett, and Henry Hunt—employed this utilitarian doctrine to prove that the Game Law, parliamentary representation, and factory regulations favored the few and were in need of revision. Perhaps no other single theory was so influential as utilitarianism in bringing about item-by-item reform in the nineteenth century. Benthamites, serving on royal commissions, focused the nation's attention on public abuses, and the result was increasing government intervention and corrective legislation.

Chapter 18 ✌ Peel and Palmerston, 1841-1865

Peel's ministry attempted to identify the Tory party with the economic and political changes wrought by the industrial revolution and the legislation of the thirties. This adjustment to the new middle-class ascendancy meant that both parties eventually accepted the liberal creed of piecemeal reform, free trade, and an industrial, rather than an agrarian, society as the basis of England's prospering economy. However, Peel's decision to repeal the Corn Laws also broke the unity of the Tory party and resulted in a confusion of party loyalties for the next twenty years. In this period of party flux Lord Palmerston, an independent Whig, was virtually the indispensable political figure. His policy of conservatism at home and jingoistic liberalism abroad was popular with the mid-Victorian populace, if not with foreign chanceries. Throughout the Palmerstonian era foreign affairs dominated English politics more than any single domestic issue.

Peel's Policies

Robert Peel's sure administrative grasp provided able leadership for the Tories, and they responded by supporting his financial and factory reforms until political and economic logic convinced the Prime Minister to repeal the Corn Laws. This decision, to become a free trader and to end agricultural protection for Tory landlords, ruined Peel politically, divided his party, and brought forth Benjamin Disraeli as the leader of the country squires.

Peel And The Tory Party. Peel had already reformed criminal law and established the metropolitan police force in his capacity as Home Secretary. In 1841 he became Prime Minister. Although lacking in imaginative ideas or in the ability to anticipate the future, Peel was a skilled administrator and a pragmatist whose integrity and parliamentary performance had won him the admiration of many loyal followers, among them Gladstone. The country squires backed him, often grudgingly, as he met the immediate needs of tariff reform and industrial legislation, until he jeopardized their pocketbooks and their political traditions by supporting the arguments of the Anti-Corn Law League which he was politically obligated to oppose.

Factory Legislation. No provisions had been included in earlier legislation to limit directly the hours of adult workers or to insist on greater safety or better working conditions. Lord Ashley continued to press for such reforms. The investigations of a royal commission revealed some of the frightful conditions in the mines and resulted in Parliament passing the Mines Act in 1842. This act prohibited the employment in mines of boys under ten and of women and girls. The provisions for inspectors of mines were deleted from Ashley's bill by the House of Lords, but were established in another act in 1850. The Factory Act of 1844 restricted the working day of women to twelve hours and for children to six-and-a-half hours. For the first time safety provisions were included to make the fencing of machinery compulsory. Ashley's Factory Act of 1847 reduced the working day for young persons from thirteen to eighteen years old and for women to ten hours. These acts signaled the transition to better treatment of workers after the uncontrolled conditions that existed earlier.

Free Trade. Peel was a businessman who had seen the efficacy of Huskisson's tariff reductions in promoting commercial and industrial expansion and in increasing profits. He immediately began to pursue a similar policy as Prime Minister. To Peel tariff reform was experimental and utilitarian and not part of any doctrinaire position. To others, such as Richard Cobden and John Bright, free trade had become an article of faith which was considered indispensable for a free and competitive society. In the 1840's the propaganda of the Anti-Corn Law League, the depression, and wretched weather conditions combined to convert the public and Peel to free trade.

Tariff and Financial Reforms. In his budget of 1842, Peel succeeded in ending the fiscal confusion which he had inherited from the Whigs. He introduced an income tax of seven pence on the pound sterling on all annual incomes over £150. Never before had such a form of taxation been levied in time of peace; it has never since disappeared from English budgets. Peel then proceeded to reduce the tariff on some 250 articles. When this action increased, rather than diminished, the State revenue, he accelerated further reductions so that by 1846 all duties were removed on exports, almost all raw materials were admitted free, and the tariffs on other imports were slashed. The Bank Charter Act of 1844, which limited the issue of banknotes, stimulated trade and public confidence and reduced inflationary forces.

The Anti-Corn Law League. In 1839 an Anti-Corn Law League was organized in Manchester with the financial backing and political support of the manufacturers. The League wished to rouse public opinion against the corn law which protected agricultural interests by keeping high the price of food and forbidding the import of lower-priced corn. Under the leadership of Richard Cobden and John Bright, two manufacturers of extraordinary energy and oratorical ability, the League sent out persuasive workers who preached the gospel of free trade at mass meetings in the most intensive campaign of popular agitation in the first half of the century. Presented with remarkable lucidity and reams of statistics, free trade became a slogan which promised to guarantee international trade and peace, to lower food prices for the workers and, incidentally, to provide higher profits for the factory owners. Aided by the introduction of the penny post in 1840, the League showered anti-corn law pamphlets (nine million tracts in 1843 alone) on the towns of England, while public meetings focused popular attention on the issue. Cobden and Bright, now members of Parliament, introduced motions in the Commons for free trade, but without success. Not until disastrous weather conditions ruined the harvests was Peel convinced that he must repeal the law which his party insisted that he protect.

Potato Famine in Ireland. The incessant rains in 1845 ruined the wheat crop in England and rotted the potatoes, the peasants' staple, in Ireland. Over one million Irish emigrated as famine stalked the land. After deciding that only an abundance of cheap foreign corn could ease the distress, Peel temporarily suspended the Corn Laws. When his Cabinet divided on the issue, Peel resigned but returned to office after the Whigs under Lord John Russell refused to put together an alternative ministry. Peel was now completely converted to free trade and once convinced, he had the political courage to face the charge of betrayal by his party.

Repeal of the Corn Laws. The protectionist landlords of the Tory party, under the leadership of Lord George Bentinck and Benjamin Disraeli, bitterly assailed Peel for his "treason." Undeterred, Peel introduced his bill in June, 1846, to abolish the Corn Laws over the next three years. The motion passed the House of Commons with the support of the Whigs, Irish, and free traders of the Tory party and passed the House of Lords because of the loyalty of the Duke of Wellington to Peel's Government. But on the night of final passage the vengeful Tories united with the Whigs and Irish to defeat Peel on an Irish coercion bill and to force his resignation. Four years later Peel died.

Significance of Repeal. Politically, the repeal of the Corn Laws ruined Peel and elevated Disraeli to prominence in the Tory party. The ensuing splinter of the Tories into two factions permitted almost two decades of Whig-Liberal rule. Repeal, however, did not produce all the momentous changes predicted. Corn prices remained relatively unchanged until the eighteen seventies when Canadian and American wheat entered England at such low prices that the English farmer could not possibly compete. Nevertheless, repeal was a significant victory for laissez-faire liberalism over protectionism and marked the final triumph of an industrial over an agricultural economy. Free trade shortly became a basic principle of Victorian England. In 1849 the Navigation Acts were abolished. In 1852 Disraeli and the Tory party accepted the inevitability of free trade, and Gladstone, Peel's devoted follower, completed the change to free trade in a series of great budgets. Moreover, the Anti-Corn Law League demonstrated the effectiveness of popular agitation and organized pressure on an increasingly middle-class Government.

The Chartist Movement. The meager political gains from the Great Reform Bill, the collapse of Owen's trade union movement, disillusionment with the Poor Law of 1834, and the hardships of an economic depression produced agitation among the lower-middle and working classes for a voice in Government. In 1838 William Lovett and Francis Place drafted the People's Charter. Its six points called for universal male suffrage, the secret ballot, equal electoral districts, payment of members of Parliament, no property qualifications for members of Parliament, and annual general elections. The Chartists organized large meetings, and at their convention in London in 1839 a monster petition with over a million signatures was prepared and presented to Parliament. With the defeat of the People's Charter the Chartists became divided, and most members refused to use violent methods and drifted into other organizations, such as the Anti-Corn Law League. Led by Feargus O'Connor, the physical-force party of the Chartists engineered riots in 1841, and in the following year various factions combined to present a second petition to the House of Commons which was defeated 287 to 59. Chartism subsided until 1847-48 when economic distress in the country and revolution on the Continent revived the movement. A third monster petition was prepared, and a march on Parliament to accompany the petition was planned. Instead, the petition of two million signatures was carried quietly by cab to Parliament, and shortly afterward the Chartist movement faded into oblivion. Although Chartism was killed by ridicule and reviving prosperity, it drew attention to the political consciousness of the working class and the cause of parliamentary democracy. By 1918 all of the radical proposals of the Chartists, except the annual election of Parliament, were enacted into legislation.

Domestic Politics, 1846-65

The breakup of the Tory party in 1846 resulted in an unstable Liberal hegemony for the next two decades, except for two Derby-Disraeli stopgap ministries which lasted less than three years. Palmerston, Russell, and Gladstone led the loosely-knit Whig-Liberal and Peelite factions during these years. Palmerston was strongly opposed to any significant extension of political or social democracy in England. By mid century, a growing level of material prosperity, along with world leadership in industrial production and foreign trade made Englishmen self-confident and comfortably complacent. The absence of any general European war strengthened this feeling of security and progress.

The Position of England in 1846. Thirty years of peace permitted England to enjoy the benefits of growing national prosperity and prestige abroad. Throughout the nineteenth century the British navy, unchallenged since Trafalgar, provided effective and silent security for Great Britain and her maritime empire. England's parliamentary institutions and the sensitivity of her governing classes to popular pressures gave the nation a unique immunity to the violent revolutions which wracked the Continent in 1848. The middle classes respected the governing institutions which encouraged them to seek wealth through industrial expansion and competition. The laborers, for the most part, accepted the idea that political reforms preceded economic and social improvements; therefore, their agitation was constitutional, urging remedies within the existing framework of things rather than revolution. If the pressures were too great, or if patience was too short, emigration to Canada, Australia, New Zealand, Cape Colony, or Natal served as a safety valve. The annual exodus from Britain for the three years 1847-49 was over a quarter of a million. The population remaining in Britain also increased, doubling between 1801 and 1851. The rapid industrial changes produced social and individual problems which were not solved by a laissez-faire market economy. Yet, in the prosperous period of 1846-65 England lacked the party unity and extra-parliamentary pressures necessary to push through domestic reforms.

Party Alignment. Peel's resignation resulted in the splinter of the Tory party into a protectionist wing dominated by Disraeli and a smaller, but influential, faction loyal to their fallen leader and known as Peelites. Because the factions reciprocated open hostility for each other, the Whigs became the dominant group, even though their supporters were by no means united. The conservative Whigs under Russell and Palmerston, the ex-Tory and Canningite, saw little need for further reform. But the Radicals, led by Cobden and Bright, continued to push for "peace, retrenchment and *reform*." Since party loyalties were loose, members of Parliament frequently changed sides without discredit, and Cabinets usually included more than one faction and changed their personnel frequently to obtain a majority. Furthermore, Cabinets had to straddle issues to hold their divergent factions together, and as a result little controversial legislation passed in these years as compared to the preceding or the succeeding decades.

Russell's First Administration, 1846-52. Lord John Russell, leader of the Whigs in the House of Commons and highly respected for his moral and political integrity, formed the new Government, but with no program and with limited success. Since the Peelites refused to enter and the Radicals were not invited, Russell's Cabinet remained purely Whig in composition. Cabinet policy was constructed to win either Peelite or Radical votes because the Cabinet's continuation in office was dependent upon their support. The immediate problem was Ireland where the potato famine of 1845-46 produced distress and disorders. A Coercion Act passed by Russell's Government and the distribution of free food did not end the disturbances or the feelings of bitterness against the British. Dissatisfied with O'Connell's moderate leadership and influenced by the wave of liberal and nationalistic revolts in Europe in 1848, leaders of a Young Ireland movement plotted an uprising. The rebellion was prevented by the arrest of the leaders, but no solutions were found for Ireland's grievances. Peel and his followers supported the Whig Government in order to save free trade and to repeal the Navigation Acts in 1849. Factory and public health legislation extended the reform measures already argued and accepted a decade earlier.

In 1851 the uninspired Whig Cabinet was defeated on a measure proposing parliamentary reform. When the Tories could not muster sufficient support for their party, Lord Russell returned, hoping for a coalition with the Peelites. This arrangement collapsed when the Peelites opposed Russell's Ecclesiastical Titles Bill forbidding the Roman Catholic hierarchy from assuming English territorial titles for their dioceses. The Cabinet finally fell in 1852 over the ousting of their irrepressible foreign minister, Lord Palmerston, who was the only popular figure in the Cabinet. His style of high-handed and independent diplomacy had long annoyed the Prime Minister and the Queen. When Palmerston approved Louis Napoleon's coup d'état of 1851 in spite of the Cabinet's position of strict neutrality, Russell dismissed him. Palmerston retaliated by helping to defeat the Cabinet before the end of the year.

The First Derby-Disraeli Government, 1852. The earl of Derby (formerly Lord Stanley) became Prime Minister with Disraeli as chancellor of the exchequer and leader of the House of Commons. The rest of the Cabinet consisted of unknown protectionists. By this time Disraeli, with his parliamentary strategy and brilliant oratory, had begun to mold his band of landlords into a compact and disciplined body. Derby held an election on the issue of free trade and discovered that the voters' mandate for free trade left his party in a minority. Disraeli thereupon won the acceptance of his party for the free-trade principle, hoping to win the allegiance of the Peelites. Gladstone rejected the overtures and helped defeat Disraeli's budget, thereby terminating Derby's ten-month ministry.

Aberdeen's Coalition, 1852-55. Lord Aberdeen, a Peelite, brought together a Whig-Peelite coalition of great individual talents which he was unable to manage. Aberdeen opposed Palmerston and Russell in foreign policy, and Palmerston objected to Russell's plan for parliamentary reform. Such dissensions within the Cabinet demanded a strong Prime Minister which the gentle, learned Aberdeen was not. Gladstone, as chancellor of the exchequer, followed in the tradition of Peel. His budgets under Aberdeen and later under Palmerston (1859-65), set up several principles which became the orthodox Liberal theories of national finance: income taxes were to be used for emergencies rather than as a basic source of revenue; taxes were to be reduced by installment; there would be retrenchment in Government expenses; and virtually all duties would be abolished. Lord Aberdeen's leadership was sufficient for peace time, but not for the Crimean War which he opposed and for which the nation's armed forces were sadly unprepared. The resulting military confusion aroused a public outcry against the war cffice and the Government. In January, 1855, Aberdeen resigned.

Prime Minister Palmerston, 1855-58. The stalemate in Crimea made the public clamor for "Pam's" aggressive and patriotic brand of leadership. When Queen Victoria was unable to find an alternative, Palmerston became Prime Minister and infused new vigor into the war effort. The public believed that his leadership helped win the war the next year. By this time the Peelites had left the Cabinet, leaving Palmerston with a precarious Whig majority. In 1857 Palmerston called an election, and the voters demonstrated their confidence in him by giving his supporters a clear majority. But since party lines were still in flux, his majority disappeared the following year when controversy with France developed over the Italian revolutionist, Felice Orsini, who had procured bombs during his stay in England with which to assassinate Emperor Napoleon III. The result was the defeat of Palmerston's Government over his Conspiracy to Murder Bill.

The Second Derby-Disraeli Government, 1858-59. Once again the Peelites refused to unite with the Conservatives, leaving the new ministry with only minority support. A bill proposing parliamentary reform was introduced, and the ministry called an election in 1859 with the hope of having found a popular issue. The Conservatives increased their strength, but not sufficiently to win a majority. Derby's Cabinet thereupon resigned, and Queen Victoria returned the seals of office to Palmerston.

Palmerston's Second Administration, 1859-65. Palmerston's second Cabinet remained in office until his death in 1865. Its comparatively long tenure was due to the continued weakness of the Tories and the fusion, finally, of the Peelites, Whigs, and Radicals into the Liberal party. Palmerston's old Whig and aristocratic convictions tolerated no expansion of political democracy in the country, and the more liberal members, led by Gladstone, had to wait until the Prime Minister's death to introduce further reform legislation. Palmerston and Russell supported the unification of Italy by Cavour and helped to preserve the unity of the United States by an official position of neutrality.

The Age of Machinery. The mid century was a period when England basked in the economic benefits of her claim to the title of "workshop of the world." In the years 1850 to 1870 an industrialized, urbanized, and mechanized Britain increased exports from £71 million to nearly £200 million. Next to agriculture—still the nation's largest single industry—were textiles, employing over one-and-a-half million in 1851 and becoming the most valuable single article of export. Half a million were employed in mines and quarries and over one hundred thousand in the making of machinery. The commercial development of Henry Bessemer's steel process in 1856 enabled Britain to take a commanding lead in iron and steel exports. This rapid development of industry and population meant that the island could supply neither sufficient foodstuff for its cities nor raw materials for its factories. The full impact of this fact, however, was not felt until later decades.

Mid-Victorianism. To many observers the opening of the Crystal Palace—Britain's Great Exhibition—on May 1, 1851, was the high noon of Victorianism, with its firm confidence in the rightness of things English and its faith in the future. The mood created by the nation's wealth, industrial supremacy, and invincible Royal Navy was one of buoyant activism and confidence based upon the unquestioned conviction that the most scientific law of the century was the Law of Progress. No statesman embodied the character and self-assertiveness of the industrial middle class better than Palmerston; perhaps that was why he was so immensely popular. And yet with this self-satisfaction was the acceptance of criticism. With critics like Charles Dickens, Matthew Arnold, and Thomas Carlyle, Englishmen were prodded to improve their social condition.

Material Progress. By any measure Britain's trade and industrial production outranked that of all her competitors. In 1848 Britain produced one-half of the world's pig iron. By 1870 her foreign trade was greater than that of France, Germany, and Italy combined, and four times that of the United States. London, with a population of over three million, became the banker of the world, and sterling, pegged to the gold standard by Peel's Bank Act (1844), became the currency of international banking. Although the burgeoning middle class claimed the largest share of the benefits from this prosperity, the laborers also had better conditions of work than a generation earlier and a higher standard of living. "In 1870 most working-class families were absolutely better off by about ten per cent than they had been in 1850." [1]

Moral Conscience. The typical mid-Victorian was religious as well as materialistic. Christian virtues and the Bible were as important as success in business, and not infrequently linked together. Evangelicalism and the Nonconformist conscience pervaded the entire fabric of life and resulted in the strict observance of Sunday, world-wide missionary work, family devotions, and propriety of dress and manners in public. Coupled with liberal humanitarianism, the public conscience of Englishmen was pricked into improving without violence the condition of the poor, rehabilitating criminals and social miscreants, and extending democratic (and Christian) ideas and institutions to poorer classes.

---

[1] David Thomson, *England in the Nineteenth Century* (Penguin: Baltimore, 1950), p. 144.

Palmerston's Foreign Policy

Lord Palmerston was the third outstanding British foreign minister of the century (following Castlereagh and Canning). For thirty years he personified the attitudes of early Victorian England and acquired a personal ascendancy seldom equaled in English politics. His policy of belligerent partiotism and brinkmanship, backed by the Royal Navy, delighted ordinary Englishmen even as it unsettled his colleagues, the Queen, and foreign rulers. Yet, paradoxically, the fact remains that Palmerston's noisy meddling in European politics and his use of moral sanctions did not involve Britain in any major hostilities, whereas the Crimean war occurred during the ministry of the genteel and peace-loving Aberdeen.

Basic Principles of Nineteenth-Century Foreign Policy. Although Palmerston frequently appeared impulsive and improvised policies on the moment, claiming that England had no eternal or perpetual enemies, certain interests received priority. The more important interests included a balance of power in Europe, keeping the Low Countries free of the control of a great power, maintaining naval supremacy, preserving Turkey against encroachments by Russia, and protecting the sea routes to India. Like Canning, Palmerston also reflected public sentiment. Yet at this time English liberalism, evangelicalism, and humanitarianism favored the support of liberal and nationalist movements abroad and shared a hatred of autocracy. To these sentiments Palmerston gave energetic support.

Great Britain and Belgium. When Palmerston became foreign minister in 1830, he immediately faced the problem of revolution on the Continent, sparked by the Paris uprising in July. The most serious disturbance threatening England's security was the Belgian revolt against the settlement at the Congress of Vienna, which had united the Netherlands and Belgium under the Dutch monarchy. Belgian nationalism never accepted this alien overlordship, and French sympathy was with the Belgian cause. A conference of five powers was called, and Palmerston had the difficult chore of arranging an acceptable settlement. When the Dutch and the Belgians renewed the war and almost drew in other powers, Palmerston, by masterful diplomacy, secured another armistice and forced France and the Netherlands to leave Belgium independent. In 1839 a treaty was signed by the five powers (Britain, France, Austria, Prussia, and Russia) guaranteeing Belgium's independence and perpetual neutrality. Palmerston had kept Belgium free from the control of a major power.

The Near East. In 1832 the army of Mehemet Ali, the able pasha of Egypt, conquered Syria and defeated the army of the Sultan of Turkey. A defensive alliance between the frightened Sultan and Russia led Palmerston to suspect the intentions of Russia in making such a pact. In 1839 a second crisis arose between the Sultan and Mehemet Ali. This time France backed the pasha's claim to Syria and was convinced that Britain and Russia would not co-operate in opposing French interference. But Palmerston's quick work in getting all the major powers, except France, to force Mehemet Ali to relinquish Syria not only kept Turkey from becoming a satellite of Russia, but also kept French influence out of Egypt.

The Far East. Palmerston's Government forced the Chinese to abandon their traditional policy of diplomatic isolation and limited trading privileges for foreigners. Palmerston sent gunboats to China when the Chinese Government refused to receive British officials who were serving as trade envoys for Britain and the East India Company. In 1839 the Chinese Government forced the British commission in Canton to confiscate all opium in the possession of British merchants. This act led to the Opium War in 1840 which the British won with their superior naval and fire power. The Treaty of Nanking (1842) gave diplomatic recognition to Britain, opened five additional ports to trade, required China to pay an indemnity for the confiscated opium, and ceded the island of Hong Kong to Britain.

Peel's Foreign Policy. Only during Peel's five-year ministry (1841-46) did Palmerston relinquish control of foreign affairs for any length of time. The conciliatory Lord Aberdeen directed the foreign office in a much more subdued fashion. Strained relations with the United States were mended by two treaties: the Webster-Ashburton Treaty of 1842 resolved a territorial dispute on the Maine-New Brunswick border; and the Oregon settlement of 1846 averted the possibility of war by extending the forty-ninth parallel to the Pacific as a boundary, but left to Britain all of Vancouver Island.

Palmerston in Controversy, 1846-52. Palmerston's practice of acting independent of the Cabinet or the Monarchy disturbed Prime Minister Russell and angered Queen Victoria. However, Palmerston's prejudices and patriotism, and even his insolent manner in rebuking foreign Governments, won the loyal support of the populace.

Continental Revolts, 1848. Palmerston offered vocal encouragement to the chain of liberal and nationalist uprisings which took place on the Continent and condemned the repressive measures of the old regimes in restoring their authority. This won for him the admiration of British and continental liberals, and made England a haven for political exiles, such as Lajos Kossuth and Guiseppe Mazzini.

Dom Pacifico. In 1850 David Pacifico, a Portuguese Jew who had acquired British citizenship at Gibraltar, sought aid from the foreign office in winning a claim from the Greek Government for damages to his property by a mob in Athens. When diplomatic channels did not bring immediate action, the impatient Palmerston ordered the British fleet to seize Greek ships. Immediately the Greek Government recognized the claim, but such overbearing action brought a censure from the House of Lords and a vote of confidence in the House of Commons. Palmerston won the vote by emotionally arguing that a British subject could count on British protection throughout the world, just as a Roman subject could in the days of the Apostle Paul by claiming *"civis Romanus sum."*

Louis Napoleon. Palmerston unofficially approved Louis Napoleon's overthrow of the French Republic in 1851. Since the Cabinet was taking a position of strict neutrality, Russell used the incident to dismiss his controversial foreign minister in 1852. Without the powerful Palmerston the Cabinet was defeated before the end of the year.

The Crimean War, 1854-56. England blundered into, and through, a war with Russia which only public opinion had wanted. This enthusiasm for the war changed to criticism when the press revealed the bungling of the military commanders and the high mortality rate among the sick and wounded British soldiers. The war forced the abdication of Lord Aberdeen and gave the popular Palmerston his first prime ministership.

Causes. Russia once again became impatient to control the Straits and win access to the Mediterranean. In 1853 Czar Nicholas I renewed the Russian proposal to divide Turkey among Britain, France, and Russia. Britain feared the expansion of Russia southward would lead to Russian designs against the British in India. The precipitating cause of the war was a controversy in Palestine in which priests of the Roman Catholic and the Orthodox churches clashed over control of the Church of the Nativity in Bethlehem. France and Russia immediately claimed the right of protector. The Czar then extended his demands to include the protection of Greek Catholics in Turkey, believing, mistakenly, that the conciliatory Aberdeen would not offer military support to the Sultan. Turkey declared war on Russia, whereupon Russia promptly sank the

Turkish Black Sea fleet. France, England, and Sardinia came to the rescue of Turkey.

Course of the War. After the Russians were driven out of the Turkish provinces, the war revolved around the allied siege of the Russian naval base at Sevastopol. The conspicuous shortcomings of the allied military organization, the breakdown of the commissariat in the bitter cold of the winter, and the lack of medicine and hospital care for the ill were duly reported by the *Times,* causing a public outcry in Britain. When Sevastopol was finally taken (1855), Palmerston wished to continue the war, but Napoleon III had other projects in mind and wanted peace.

The Treaty of Paris, 1856. According to the terms of the treaty, the independence of Turkey was maintained, all Russian and Turkish conquests were restored, the Black Sea and the Dardanelles were closed to warships, the Danube River was placed under the control of an international commission, Serbia gained internal autonomy, and the Sultan promised protection for his Christian subjects. The Congress of Paris also laid down four basic principles concerning the freedom of the seas in time of war. The peace settlement halted the expansion of Russia, but did little more. In England, two important results of the war were the founding of the Red Cross, an outcome of Florence Nightingale's heroic labors in the field hospitals, and the reform of the English army.

The Indian Mutiny, 1857. Disaffected Sepoys—Indian soldiers in British employ—revolted against alien rule and the westernization of their culture. Although the revolt was crushed without too much difficulty, the uprising prepared the way for Indian nationalism, ended Pitt's system of dual control in India, and widened the breach in British-Indian relations.

Background. Between Pitt's India Act (1784) and the zenith of power of the British East India Company under the governor-generalship of Lord Dalhousie (1848-56), British officials had rapidly expanded and consolidated their rule in India. Intervention in native wars and the frequent disorder in Indian states lured empire builders, such as Richard Wellesley, the marquis of Hastings, and Lord Dalhousie, to take over the whole of India and administer it either directly as part of British India, or indirectly, through treaties with native princes. By 1856 the rapidity of westernization through education, industrialization, and attacks on Indian customs made the natives fear that the Hindu culture would be supplanted. Dalhousie's vast annexations and the imposition of the doctrine of lapse (all princely states reverted to England when a prince died without heir) seemed to jeopardize the future of India. Morale in the Bengal army was low because Indian troops were restive over the Foreign Service Act of 1856 which forbade new enlistments unless the soldier would be willing to serve overseas. They were further incensed over the introduction of a new cartridge lubricated with the fat of cows and hogs. The greased cartridge appeared to be a deliberate insult to the Hindu, to whom the cow was sacred, and to the Moslem, who was forbidden to eat pork. In May, 1857, the Bengal army mutinied and marched on Delhi.

Rebellion. The Sepoy mutiny which was largely confined to the upper Ganges Valley was not supported by the native armies of the other regions. At Cawnpore all Europeans were massacred, and only two successive relief columns saved Lucknow. Within a year the revolt was stamped out but its consequences were significant. The political power of the East India Company ended when the India Act of 1858 placed full responsibility for the government of the Indian Empire under a cabinet minister responsible to Parliament. The doctrine of lapse was quietly dropped, and Indians were allowed to compete for the prestigious Indian Civil Service in a belated attempt to remove some of the grievances which had provoked the mutiny. More significant was the change in the British position in India: the mutiny increased the isolation of the colonial ruler from the native, whereas the rebellion made efforts to justify the British presence in India much more difficult. To the Indian people the uprising became a rallying point for later nationalist movements.

Italian Unification. After a second war with China (1857-60) which Parliament thought unjustifiable but which voters applauded, and which won England additional concessions and safeguards in the Far East, Palmerston gained further consensus of support for his adroit handling of diplomatic relations with the Italian states. Here Palmerston, Russell, and Gladstone rallied British opinion in support of Count Cavour's efforts to transform Italy into a united, liberal nation. Emperor Napoleon helped Cavour oust the hated Austrians from northern Italy but withdrew his aid when the separate Italian states began to unite. At this point England stepped in to prevent hostile Austrian or French interference and to permit a plebiscite which resulted in unification. British power was still sufficient for Palmerston to assert moral sanctions without actual military intervention.

The American Civil War. Palmerston and Russell announced no clear-cut public policy, but steered a cautious, neutral course in the controversy over recognition of the Confederate States. The upper classes and the press generally sympathized with the South.

The great cotton factories were hurt by the loss of southern American cotton, but workers accepted the ensuing unemployment in a demonstration of loyalty to the slave-free North. Northern grain helped alleviate the suffering of the unemployed. Nevertheless, two incidents endangered Britain's official neutrality. Sailors from a United States cruiser stopped and boarded a British ship, the "Trent," and arrested two Confederate envoys en route to England. This violation of neutral rights caused the Cabinet to draft a belligerent note which made the North disavow her actions in order to ensure British neutrality. In turn, the North accused the British Government of deliberate negligence in allowing a Confederate raider, the "Alabama," to be launched from a British shipyard to prey on northern shipping. After the war Britain paid substantial damages in compensation. The decisive victories of the Union armies in 1863, coupled with Lincoln's declaration of emancipation, prevented all thought of British intervention in the American Civil War.

Denmark and Prussia. As a final venture in open diplomacy Palmerston supported Denmark in her dispute with autocratic Prussia over the Duchies of Schleswig and Holstein. In the past the threat of British intervention had been sufficient; this time Bismarck forced Palmerston's hand by allying with Austria and invading Denmark in 1864. However, British public opinion would not support involvement on the Continent, and Palmerston had to back down on his promise of aid to Denmark. The Prime Minister died the following year, before the aggrandizement of Prussia completely upset the balance of power. England continued to fear France and Russia far more than an emergent Germany.

End of the Palmerstonian Era. By 1865 Palmerston's influence in the diplomatic world of personal politics and liberal nationalism was already waning and being replaced by the *Realpolitik* of Bismarck. In England reform measures were released which had been impossible while Palmerston was Prime Minister, mainly because of his eighteenth-century Whig ideas on the franchise and on the function of Government. Palmerston was the last of the statesmen-aristocrats to lead England before modern party politics emerged under his successor, Gladstone.

Chapter 19 ✌ Gladstone and Disraeli, 1865-1886

Under the leadership of Gladstone and Disraeli, England moved into a new age of transition and reform. The Victorian Compromise of the Palmerstonian era which was based on the alliance of the aristocracy with the middle class was now adjusted to permit the extension of political democracy. The clashing personalities of Gladstone and Disraeli, statesmen of outstanding, but widely different, abilities, dramatized the political philosophies and social issues of these years. By the time of Gladstone's second administration the overriding issue of the day was the Irish Question.

Gladstone and Reform

Gladstone's political position slowly evolved over the decades from high Toryism to the very embodiment of British Liberalism with its theme of "peace, retrenchment, and reform." His moral earnestness, his faith in the political sense of the common man, and his extraordinary financial talents appealed to the nation and helped complete the metamorphosis of the Whigs into the Liberal party. The legislation of his first ministry brought about institutional reforms long overdue.

Gladstone and Disraeli. Two statesmen, entirely different in background and in style, dominated political affairs for the fifteen years after the death of Palmerston. William E. Gladstone's background was one of wealth, privilege, and upper-class education. After wavering between politics and the Anglican priesthood, Gladstone entered Parliament as a member for the ultra-Tory seat of Oxford and became a follower of Sir Robert Peel. In public life he was determined to put a religious imprint on politics as surely as his personal life expressed a religious conviction. During his half century in the House of Commons, Gladstone became increasingly liberal on religious and political issues. His magnificent oratory, his strong sense of public duty, and his long experience in the Commons made him the conscience of England and leader of the Liberals for nearly thirty years.

In contrast, Benjamin Disraeli rose to the prime ministership despite his Jewish background, his lack of wealth or political connections, and his flamboyant style and dress. A master of sarcasm and debate, Disraeli became the leader of the shattered Tory party after he attacked Peel for abandoning the Corn Law. Once in power he took a vital interest in social legislation and renovated the party's aristocratic traditions to changing times. His pride in England's national institutions and his unabashed imperialism caught the admiration of his colleagues and of Queen Victoria.

The Third Derby-Disraeli Government, 1866-68. Upon the death of Palmerston, Lord Russell became Prime Minister. His Cabinet colleague, Gladstone, introduced a long overdue bill for the moderate extension of the franchise to urban workers. A group of Whigs under Robert Lowe opposed their party's bill and united with the Tories to defeat it. Thereupon, Derby and Disraeli organized a third minority Government. The former apathy about the franchise bill disappeared as trade unions and new organizations of workingmen arranged mass demonstrations and mobs rioted in London. Disraeli persuaded his party to back reform, thereby robbing the Liberals of their program and winning the gratitude of the working classes. Disraeli's bill, as amended by several Liberal members, became even more radical than the Liberals had dared to propose. Gladstone was enraged over Disraeli's tactic, but the bill passed with the assistance of the radical wing of the Liberal party. Lord Derby resigned because of ill health, and for the next eighteen months Liberal votes and popular satisfaction with the reform bill permitted Disraeli to serve as Prime Minister. Subsequently Parliament passed the British North America Act (1867) which created a federal government for Canada. The act marked another peaceful step to colonial self-government and helped to unify the divisive colonies of Canada and protect the new nation from possible American expansion northward.

The Second Reform Bill, 1867. A small redistribution of seats occurred with the Second Reform Bill, but the major change was in the extension of the franchise to every male householder in a borough who paid poor rates. In the counties the franchise was enlarged by reducing from £10 to £5 the annual value of property ownership required for voter qualification. In the towns the low level at which property qualifications were set made male suffrage nearly universal and satisfied most of the groups pressing for reform. The bill nearly doubled the number of voters.

Gladstone's First Administration, 1868-74. Gladstone reunited the dissident wings of the Liberal party by his efforts to redress Irish grievances. Rebellion had broken out in Ireland in a violent attempt to relieve distress and to express bitterness over English rule. The uprising which was planned by the Fenians (a secret organization established in 1858 by Irish Americans) became an abortive effort to win Irish independence. Instead of more coercive acts, Gladstone proposed that the Government pacify the Irish by disestablishing the church in Ireland. Disraeli's opposition cost him his Liberal supporters and he resigned. The election of 1868 endorsed Gladstone and gave the Liberals a majority of over one hundred. Gladstone began the first of his four administrations with an ambitious program of reform.

Disestablishment of the Church in Ireland, 1869. As the first of his remedial measures for Ireland, Gladstone introduced a bill to disestablish and disendow the Anglican church in Ireland. Although a devout Anglican himself, he opposed the injustice of a Catholic populace supporting an alien church attended almost exclusively by their landlords. The bill placed the Anglican church on a voluntary basis and permitted approximately £9 million of its assets to remain within the church; another £7 million was appropriated for charity and education in Ireland.

Irish Land Reform, 1870. A second grievance of long standing was the exploitative custom of landlords leasing land on a year-by-year basis. If peasants improved their tenements, the landlord could either eject the tenent or raise the rent without compensation for improvements. There was no redress in the courts. In spite of landowner opposition, Gladstone pushed through Parliament an Irish Land Act which copied the tenant-custom in Ulster and made illegal the eviction of tenants without compensation for their improvements. The practical results of the bill were disappointing because no provisions were included to prevent unscrupulous landlords from raising rents exorbitantly and ousting tenants for inability to pay. Nevertheless, for the first time the rights of the tenant were recognized by law.

The Education Act, 1870. The great extension of the franchise in 1867 added another argument for establishing a system of public education, since only one-half of the children of elementary school age were in attendance in 1869. The laissez-faire attitude of the Palmerstonian era and the heated controversy over religious instruction in state schools—insisted upon by Anglicans, objected to by Dissenters—had prevented any effective action. W. E. Forster's education bill survived the controversy and passed both Houses. It authorized the local Government, in any locality where existing voluntary schools were inadequate, to permit popularly-elected school boards to establish public schools. These schools were to be maintained by national and local taxes, and by fees which could be remitted in the case of poor children. Attendance between the ages of five and thirteen could be made compulsory by the local school board. State aid to the voluntary schools was increased and religious instruction was left unrestricted. In the new public schools such instruction was to be non-sectarian and non-compulsory and to be scheduled only at the first or the last period of the day. In 1880 attendance at elementary school was made compulsory, and in 1891 all fees were abolished.

Ballot Act, 1872. The aim of the Ballot Act was to establish the Australian (or secret) ballot, recommended thirty years earlier in the People's Charter, in order to protect the newly-enfranchised voter from intimidation at the polls. Especially in Ireland the landlord or shopowner lost his political influence over his workers. The law was a further step toward remedying corrupt political practices.

Judicature Act, 1873. The judicial machinery created in the Middle Ages continued in operation but with increasing confusion and with glaring abuses as three rival courts wrangled over jurisdiction. Simple cases were often involved in legal complexities that delayed justice and raised costs. The Judicature Act co-ordinated this legal machinery into one supreme court of judicature, consisting of a court of appeal and a high court of justice. The latter was divided into (1) the king's bench, (2) the chancery, and (3) the probate, divorce, and admiralty. Certain civil suits could still be appealed to the House of Lords, which continued as the highest court of the land. A system of life peerages was introduced so that lords with legal training could deal with the judicial duties of the House of Lords.

Army Reforms. Secretary of War Edward Cardwell proposed a series of army reforms that were sorely needed, especially after the Crimean War. When the House of Lords prepared to kill sections of the bill, Gladstone put through the measures by royal ordinance instead of by parliamentary statute. The reforms reduced the size of the standing army, organized an effective reserve, provided for short-term enlistments, and abolished the purchase of army commissions. The abolition of the old custom of "purchase" stirred angry protests from the upper classes who provided most of the officers.

Additional Reforms. Gladstone ended the monopoly of the Church of England in higher education by abolishing all religious tests at the universities. In 1870 open competitive exams were inaugurated for positions in the civil service. This reform provided a higher level of competence and more continuity in administration —two significant improvements since the civil service became increasingly important as the State enlarged its influence and activities. In 1871 a Local Government Board was formed to co-ordinate the numerous state supervisory agencies which had been established over several decades. Working conditions were improved by the Factory Act Extension Act (1867) and the Coal Mines Act (1872). A concession to the Dissenters was the Licensing Act of 1872 regulating the supply of alcohol to the public. However, when the act was passed, the brewers and distillers promptly moved over to the Tory camp.

Foreign Policy. Less popular with the voter was the foreign policy of Gladstone. He appeared disinterested in the extension of empire, preferring for England a moral to an imperial prestige. Critics claimed that his financial economies provided budgetary surpluses at the expense of military influence. England remained neutral in the Franco-Prussian War during which Prussia became the most powerful state in Europe. Russia took advantage of the war to denounce the restrictive clauses of the Treaty of Paris. Britain protested but participated with the treaty's signatory powers in a conference which agreed to most of Russia's demands. This decision was regarded by the populace as a British surrender. In dealing with the United States, Gladstone set a wise precedent in submitting the issue of the "Alabama" claims to an international tribunal of arbitration in 1872. The tribunal dismissed the exorbitant, indirect claims but awarded the United States $15,500,000 in gold for direct damages. Once again popular opinion felt that Gladstone was not asserting Britain's position as a great power.

Liberal Defeat. By 1873 the Government's foreign policy was generally condemned as too pacifist for a major power. Furthermore, the Government had carried through so much reform legislation that the electorate seemed satiated. Each bill had alienated certain groups, and members of Parliament resented Gladstone's habit of equating his reforms with moral righteousness. Meanwhile, Disraeli had built up an attractive program and an effective party organization, the National Union, which won the loyalty of many urban workers. In the election of 1874 the Conservatives won a clear majority for the first time since 1841.

Disraeli and the New Toryism

The use of the positive powers of the State to improve the quality of English life was accepted by Disraeli, and as Prime Minister he educated the Conservative party to the social obligations of "Tory democracy." In foreign and imperial policy his ideas were more

dramatic, popular, and also more dangerous than those of Gladstone. He identified the Conservative party with the patriotic imperialism of the day and provided England with a new concept of
empire. Sooner than his contemporaries, Disraeli sensed that the
two most powerful and popular forces of the immediate future
would be social reform and imperialism.

State Intervention. The reforms of Gladstone's ministry laid
the foundation for a novel State in which the old institutions, such
as the House of Lords and the monarchy, were accommodated to
new political and social philosophies. By 1875 the eighteenth-
century liberal philosophy, with its accent on competitive individualism, self-improvement through private initiative, and minimal
government regulation of trade and industry, had given way to a
viewpoint favoring regulative legislation that could improve society where private initiative was inadequate. How to reconcile individualism and collectivism in a free society became a dilemma
which plagued political philosophers and politicians throughout the
late nineteenth and twentieth centuries. John Stuart Mill published
his *Principles* in 1848, and for forty years this treatise served as a
guide to Radicals in their efforts to achieve a more equitable distribution of wealth and the participation of all classes in the benefits
of an industrial society. The failure of laissez-faire to protect society from exploitation and private greed encouraged the casual
growth of municipal ownership—"gas and water socialism." Both
political parties continued to give lip service to their old doctrines,
but each was eager to woo the mass electorate with attractive
programs.

Tory Democracy. Besides guaranteeing the established institutions of England from undue change, Disraeli saw the political
advantage and the human benefits which would accrue from improving the economic and social conditions of the working class.
He convinced his party that the economic and political position of
the upper classes would be jeopardized more by an embittered
working class than by a contented one. An intelligent aristocracy,
argued Disraeli, devotes itself to the social welfare of all classes.
From this time onward Disraeli's emphasis on "Tory democracy"
became an important plank in the Tory political program.

Domestic Legislation. In 1875 a Public Health Act, systematizing sanitary laws, an Artisans' Dwellings Act, permitting municipalities to clear slums and erect new dwellings, and a Rivers Pollu-
tion Act were evidence of Conservative interest in the physical
welfare of the working man. In the same year, the Conservatives
reversed the laws restricting picketing and limiting the bargaining

position of trade unions and passed two measures which made peaceful picketing legal and put employer and employee on the same legal footing. In 1876 trade unions were included within the scope of the Friendly Societies Acts, and collective bargaining was now legally possible. Plimsoll's Merchant Shipping Act (1876) prevented the overloading of merchant vessels and improved the quarters and subsistence of sailors. Two acts halted the historic enclosure of public lands and commons and reversed the process by restoring some lands for use as public parks. In 1878 the Factory and Workshop Act replaced previous legislation on hours and conditions of labor with a completely revised code.

The Changing Economy. Since the international market had become the arbiter of the English economy, England became dependent upon international trade for prosperity. Already, the first signs of future economic trouble were in evidence. Cobden's prophecy of world peace and prosperity through world trade remained a fiction. Instead, Britain was losing her mid-century position of industrial leadership as Germany, France, Italy, and the United States became vigorous competitors and set high tariffs to keep out foreign produce. More conspicuous was the collapse of British agriculture. By 1870 the revolution in transportation brought into Britain cheaper foreign wool and grain than local farmers could offer. Even the perishable market was threatened when commercial refrigeration in the early 1880's permitted Australian, New Zealand, and South American produce to flood England. The shibboleth of free trade halted any effective move to protect agriculture, and a rapid decline set in. During this period, the most successful working-class movement was the growth of the co-operative societies. Founded in 1844 and tracing its ideas to Robert Owen's philosophy of self-help, the movement expanded from retail stores to wholesale trading, and eventually to production and distribution. By 1889 the societies had a membership of 805,000.

Disraeli and Victoria. In 1872 Disraeli made his famous Crystal Palace speech in which he exalted the Crown as the fountain of the new imperialism. Four years later, and over the opposition of his party, he had Parliament confer the title of Empress of India upon Queen Victoria. In turn, the Queen responded to and confided in Disraeli as she had done with no other Prime Minister since Melbourne. Her open dislike for Palmerston and Gladstone was now contrasted to her unconcealed partiality for Disraeli and the Conservatives. She appeared to believe that Disraeli was the only Englishman who had really appreciated Prince Albert, and yet, paradoxically, only Disraeli was able to persuade the Queen to relinquish her seclusion and mourning after Albert's death and return to public life. The harmony of their relationship became an intolerable insult to Disraeli's rival, Gladstone. In 1876 the Queen elevated Disraeli to the peerage as Earl of Beaconsfield, and the Prime Minister left the House of Commons to the uninspired leadership of Sir Stafford Northcote.

Foreign and Imperial Policy. Disraeli, as well as the Queen, was intrigued with the idea of a great eastern empire that would contain further Russian expansion in that area. His policy was vigorous, risky, and generally successful. In contrast to Gladstone, Disraeli actively supported a colonial empire and believed in Britain's imperial destiny.

Suez Canal. In 1875 Disraeli secretly bought for the British Government the 177,000 shares of Suez Canal stock previously owned by the khedive of Egypt. The khedive was chronically bankrupt and had offered his shares for sale in France. To forestall a French monopoly and to give England a voice in the management of the strategic canal route to India, Disraeli borrowed £4 million from the House of Rothschild and beat the French in purchasing the shares. This audacious act delighted the Queen and the nation. The purchase was to lead to British interest in, and eventual occupation of, the Nile Valley.

The Eastern Question. The combination of Turkish mismanagement and persecution of Christian subjects, the Russian support of pan-Slav unrest and interest in annexing the Straits, and the emergent nationalism among the Balkan states which frightened Austria and Turkey led to an international crisis. In 1875 Bosnia and Herzegovina, two Balkan provinces, revolted against Turkey. Russia, Austria and Germany wished to put pressure on Turkey to reform, but Disraeli feared Russian influence in the area more than he resented Turkish misrule. The next year the Bulgarians revolted against the Turks but were crushed after enduring terrible atrocities at the hands of the Sultan's troops. Eventually, the revolt spread, and Serbia and Montenegro joined the Bulgars in fighting their Turkish suzerain. Britain, thereupon, joined the three other great powers in a conference at Constantinople to force reforms on the new Sultan, Abdul Hamid II. The Sultan, who refused all demands, was convinced that Britain feared Russia too much to permit force to be used against him. Russia, therefore, acted alone and invaded the Balkans in 1877. By the following year Russian troops were besieging Constantinople. Disraeli threatened British intervention, but the Turks surrendered, and peace was made at San Stephano. The treaty provided for an enlarged and autonomous

Bulgaria under Russian suzerainty and an independent Serbia, Montenegro, and Roumania. Turkish rule in Europe almost disappeared. The settlement disturbed Disraeli because it gave Russia access to the Mediterranean through a satellite, Bulgaria. Therefore, he held that the treaty was unacceptable and that an international conference must reconsider the entire matter. His ultimatum to Russia was backed up by dispatching the fleet to Constantinople and troops to Malta, and by the vote of war taxes in Parliament. Russia gave way to Disraeli's diplomacy, and a pleased British populace could not help but evoke similar triumphs in foreign affairs under Palmerston.

Congress of Berlin, 1878. Bismarck presided at the conference, but Disraeli was the dominant figure and secured most of his demands. Macedonia was returned to Turkey, and Bulgaria was cut in half, thus keeping Russia away from Constantinople. Bosnia and Herzegovina were placed under Austrian administration. Britain secured the island of Cyprus as a naval base and promised to protect Turkey's Asiatic possessions. Because Disraeli had rebuffed Russia without war and had won a "peace with honour," the settlement was considered a diplomatic triumph. Later events revised this judgment as the suppression of Slav nationalism in the Balkans created incessant friction and precipitated World War I, and as Russia became less a threat in the Near East. Meanwhile, Germany shortly supplanted Britain as the supporter of the Turks.

Imperial Wars. The locale of the next clash between British and Russian spheres of interest was in Afghanistan. Here Britain demanded that the local ruler accept a British envoy to check Russian influence in the country. When the order was refused, a British military expedition was sent to Afghanistan. The Second Afghan War (1878-80) required two British invasions. This open aggression proved unpopular in England.

In 1877 the British annexed the Transvaal, a Boer republic in South Africa, in order to promote federation and avert an impending Zulu war. Although the anarchic and bankrupt conditions in the republic improved, neither federation nor peace followed. Many Englishmen regarded the annexation as undisguised imperialism; furthermore, the annihilation of a British regiment at the outset of the Zulu War in 1879 brought dismay and doubts about Disraeli's imperial policies.

The Election of 1880. In 1876 Gladstone came out of semi-retirement to denounce Disraeli's support of the Turks in spite of their cruel misrule in the Balkans. In the campaign of 1880, Gladstone lumped together all the imperialistic ventures of Disraeli as

examples of the immorality of imperialism. Sweeping through
northern England and Scotland like an itinerant evangelist, he impressed the electors in provincial halls with his lofty principles and
his magnetic oratory. Since the depression and the costly imperial
wars had drained the Treasury, Gladstone did not fail to contrast
this fact with the budgetary surpluses of his last Liberal administration. The election was a clean sweep for the Liberals. Disraeli
retired from politics in poor health and died the next year. Queen
Victoria reluctantly asked Gladstone, who was seventy-one, to become Prime Minister when Lord Hartington, the titular head of
the Liberal party, informed her that a Cabinet could not be formed
without him.

Gladstone and Irish Home Rule

From 1880 to World War I, the Irish question dominated the
English political scene and jeopardized the very foundations of
constitutional parliamentary government. When Gladstone became
convinced that Irish home rule was the only solution, he steadfastly
fought for it, but was unable to carry his entire party with him.
The splintered Liberal party made possible a Conservative ascendancy for the next two decades. In contrast to his effective first
administration, Gladstone's second was bedeviled at every turn by
imperial complications abroad and parliamentary obstruction at
home. Thus very little significant legislation was passed, except for
an Irish land act and a third parliamentary reform bill.

The Rise of the New Imperialism. During the three decades
following 1870, a conscious expansion of empire took place among
European nations, brought on by a new emotional and militant
form of nationalism, and by the ramifications of the industrial revolution. The triumph of nationalism in Germany, Italy, Japan and
the United States was of an explosive and expansive variety, substantially different from the liberal nationalism of the 1840's. Since
physical enlargement was limited in Europe, imperialism took the
form of an expansion overseas, with a scramble for colonies beginning in earnest.

At the same time, imperialism gained momentum by the renewed
interest in colonies as a source of raw materials and as a market for
manufactures. Britain began to be threatened by the industrial and
military rivalry of continental powers. When these powers placed
their flag and protective tariffs over new territories, such militant
and economic nationalism jeopardized Britain's security and her
policy of free trade. By 1880 the revolution in transportation—the

steamship, the railway, the Suez Canal—made imperialism feasible and profitable and opened up new areas of the world to western penetration. It also made practical for the first time the federation of England's self-governing colonies. Joseph Chamberlain became the indefatigable champion of imperial federation after J. R. Seeley's *Expansion of England* (1883), a best seller, put forth the arguments for the founding of the Imperial Federation League in 1884.

The new imperialism caught the popular imagination in England and was reflected not only in the public heroes of the period, but also in the literary output. In the writings of Joseph Conrad, Robert Louis Stevenson, H. Ryder Haggard, and Rudyard Kipling the excitement, pride, and glory of empire were vividly portrayed; the press became sensational and jingoistic, exploiting the popular taste for imperial glory. The admiration given to such heroes as Charles "Chinese" Gordon, Cecil Rhodes, Lord Kitchener, Sir Alfred Milner, Lord Cromer, and Sir Frederick Lugard was in recognition of extraordinary imperial ventures rather than domestic accomplishments. Justifying imperialism on a higher plane was the old humanitarian impulse of a sense of moral mission—Kipling's "white man's burden"—which would bring the benefits of English administration and of Christianity to other people. This conscious effort to equate British self-interest with moral purpose was sincerely accepted by large segments of the English people at the same time that it was condemned by foreign observers as an exercise in hypocrisy.

Gladstone and Imperialism. Gladstone's campaign promises to retreat gracefully from the imperial ventures inaugurated by Disraeli were impossible to fulfill. In the scramble for colonies in the 1880's no major European power could remain unaffected. It is perhaps ironical that the "anti-imperialist" Gladstone was drawn into imperial commitments more extensive than Disraeli had ever entertained. Gladstone, on principle, hesitated to use force on a lesser power and, therefore, usually used force too late and even more fully, because his initial vacillation had frequently increased the disorder. Consequently, the idealism of his policies was blurred by the ineptness of his actions.

South Africa. The Boers in the Transvaal renewed their anti-British sentiments after the Zulu War had relieved them of their fears from that quarter. They confidently expected Gladstone to repudiate the annexation of the Transvaal which he had denounced so fervently when out of power. When, instead, he claimed that British sovereignty was essential to law and order and to the protection of the African, the Boers rebelled in 1880 and defeated a British detachment at Majuba Hill in 1881. Although the British populace demanded retaliation, Gladstone concluded peace negotiations which guaranteed the Transvaal independence subject to British suzerainty. In 1884 the Convention of London deleted the suzerainty clause. The British retreat in the Transvaal was unpopular at home and only encouraged Boer nationalism. The Boers, who already despised the power and the indecisive policies of Britain, were less inclined than ever to come to terms with British colonies in South Africa.

Egypt. In 1876 Britain and France intervened in Egypt to ensure payment of the Egyptian debt when the khedive defaulted on his financial obligations. An ensuing Egyptian uprising against the khedive and the foreign intervention resulted in pillage, anarchy, and the murder of Europeans. A joint French-British fleet was planned, but the French backed out. Gladstone reluctantly permitted British forces to enter alone and put down the rebellion and announced that the occupation was only temporary. Sir Evelyn Baring, the British consul-general, became the real power in Egypt under the nominal sovereignty of the khedive. Baring modernized and reformed the Egyptian Government, while a British army of occupation remained provisionally in the country.

The Sudan. A Muslim fanatic proclaimed himself as the Mahdi, or Messiah, and rallied the Sudanese tribesmen against the chronic misrule of their Egyptian overlords. When an Egyptian army under British generals was overwhelmed trying to subdue the Mahdi in 1883, Baring and Gladstone decided to abandon the Sudan as soon as they had extricated all Egyptian personnel from the country. General Charles Gordon was commissioned to handle the evacuation. Once in Khartoum, he sent out only the women and children and determined to tarry in hopes of controlling the situation; within a month he was cut off. Gladstone's next problem was how to rescue Gordon and the garrison. The Cabinet delayed in committing itself to major intervention but eventually dispatched a relief expedition which arrived two days after Gordon and his force had been slaughtered by the Sudanese. The political repercussions were violent. The Queen and the nation blamed Gladstone for Gordon's death, and the ministry barely survived a vote of censure in the House of Commons.

Colonial Competition. British interest in the interior of Africa had been stimulated by the exciting adventures (1857-73) of Richard Burton, John Speke, Samuel Baker, David Livingstone, and Henry Stanley who were searching for the source of the Nile and exploring the Congo basin. Their arguments in favor of commerce and Christianity, along with the attempt of rival powers to secure colonies, prompted Britain to make territorial claims, usually by granting charters to commercial companies. Gradually Britain extended control over the interior of the Gold Coast colony; in 1850 a British naval squadron captured Lagos, and ten years later it was annexed to the Crown; in 1885 a protectorate over the Niger Delta —the "Oil Rivers"—was proclaimed. In East Africa the sudden interest of Germany in a colonial empire challenged long-time British activity in the area. During the 1880's British North Guinea, North Borneo, and Upper Burma were added to the empire in the east. The ground rules for establishing colonial claims to African territory were laid at the Berlin conference of 1884-85, where fourteen powers gathered to decide the destiny of the Congo (granted to Leopold II of Belgium) and to determine the manner in which Africa could be partitioned among European powers with a minimum of friction. No Africans were invited to the conference.

The Penjdeh Crisis. On taking office, Gladstone ordered the evacuation of British forces from Afghanistan, leaving the country independent. Abd-er-Rahman Kahn, the new Amir, accepted British friendship and money in return for British recognition of his country's independence. In 1885 Russian troops occupied Penjdeh on the Afghanistan border and defeated the Afghans in battle. The way was now open for a Russian advance on India, and the British Cabinet and European powers considered war imminent. The crisis was resolved by Russian acceptance of arbitration, but Afghanistan continued to be one of the areas where Anglo-Russian spheres of interest clashed.

Domestic Politics. The cohesion of Gladstone's first ministry was conspicuously absent in his second. The Whig leaders, Granville and Hartington, were restive over Gladstone's interest in political democracy and in Irish home rule and feared the socialist ideas of such Radicals as Joseph Chamberlain and Charles Dilke. Gladstone, who was half-Tory and half-Radical, had no intense interest in the social legislation of the Radicals or in making the Liberals a labor party. Besides the conflicting ideologies within his Cabinet, Gladstone was plagued by the sustained obstructionism of the Irish Nationalist party and the attacks of the Tory democrats—the Fourth party—led by Lord Randolph Churchill. The Tory democrats made a deliberate effort to clog Liberal legislation and create a progressive image of the Conservatives which would win votes at the next election.

Party Organization. Before 1861 local party supporters had seen to the registration of voters. Then the Liberals set up a national Liberal Registration Association in London under the control of the parliamentary whips. The enlarged electorate after 1867 and the tightening of the election laws demanded major changes in political organization. Constituency associations became part of national organizations, and political clubs were opened for working-men by both parties. Disraeli organized the National Union of Conservatives in 1867 and a Conservative Central Office in 1870. Meanwhile, Joseph Chamberlain, a manufacturer, had established a powerful municipal political machine, the Birmingham Caucus, which selected the candidates, wrote the platform, and won every municipal election in Birmingham. Its success promoted the establishment of the National Liberal Federation in 1877. The Whig wing of the party was opposed to Chamberlain's political machine and the practice of an outside body proposing the policies and platform of members of Parliament. The friction between the leaders of the party and the party headquarters in Birmingham became another problem of Gladstone's second administration.

Gradually, the foundations of the modern party system were being established. Gladstone was the first major political figure to stump the country in a campaign. Elections were being decided more by the appeal of the party leader and his party manifesto than by the qualities of rival candidates in the voters' constituency. This development enhanced the positions and powers of the Prime Minister and of the leader of the Opposition; it also reduced the chances of an Independent, or a critic, winning party backing at election time. With the transition from oligarchy to democracy, the parties became powerful organizations, whereas the independent member of Parliament with a free vote became one of the casualties of the change.

Reform Legislation. Imperial and Irish problems, the divergent views within the Liberal party among Whigs, old Radicals, and the adherents of Chamberlain all combined to hinder the passage of reform legislation. Gladstone made no claim to being a leader in social reform but was interested in political liberalism and in the pacification of Ireland.

The Irish Land Act, 1881. In order to remedy the loopholes of his first land act, Gladstone's second bill guaranteed the "three F's" demanded by Irish tenants: fair rent, fixity of tenure, and free sale of the tenant's rights. A land commission with adjudication rights was appointed. This remedial legislation satisfied the tenants' grievance over high rents, but it arrived too late. By this date nothing short of home rule would satisfy Irish nationalists.

Parliamentary Reform. The third reform bill of 1884 gave virtual household suffrage to the agricultural laborers in the counties. With this act, four out of five adult males became eligible to vote. The act of 1885 redistributed parliamentary seats according to the Chartist proposal of representation in proportion to population. The membership in the House of Commons was increased to 670, and single-member constituencies became the general rule.

Irish Nationalism. Dormant Irish nationalism was revived in the 1870's by Isaac Butt and Charles Parnell. The latter, a Protestant landlord with a violent hatred of the English, became president of the Land League in Ireland in 1879 and succeeded Butt as leader of the Home Rule Association. Parnell determined to get home rule by inciting agrarian outrages and by wresting land from the landlords in Ireland. Correspondingly, the Irish bloc carried on a deliberate policy of obstructionism and filibustering at Westminster in order to make parliamentary procedure impossible so long as Irish independence was denied. The tactics were successful and the Irish question overshadowed all other issues in British politics. Agrarian outrages numbered over 2500 in 1880, peasants boycotted anyone taking a farm from which a tenant had been evicted, and new rules of closure were adopted to permit Parliament to function. Parnell sabotaged Gladstone's Land Act in order to keep up the agitation. Gladstone finally had Parnell arrested and applied coercive acts to Ireland until Parnell agreed to curb the outrages. However, Irish extremists murdered the Irish secretary and under secretary in a Dublin park, and public opinion forced Gladstone to resume coercion and make no more concessions to Parnell. Under these circumstances the Prime Minister privately came to the conviction that only home rule could solve the Irish question.

Fall of Gladstone, 1885. The death of General Gordon and the Penjdeh crisis produced strong popular protests over Liberal foreign policy. In Parliament, the defections among Gladstone's followers over his Irish policy permitted Parnell to ally with the Conservatives and defeat Gladstone's ministry in June, 1885. Lord Salisbury formed a caretaker Government until the act redistributing parliamentary seats could be implemented and an election held. In the interim, Salisbury rewarded Parnell by passing the Ashbourne Act which provided a fund from which Irish peasants could get loans at low interest to buy their land from the landlord.

Election of 1885. Chamberlain's "Unauthorized Program" of social legislation helped the Liberals in the counties, but Parnell's support for the Tories in England increased their borough seats. The election results made Parnell and his eighty-six Irish members

the decisive balance of power. When Gladstone's conversion to
home rule became known, Lord Hartington immediately left the
Liberals and joined the Tories. Salisbury gave up all ideas of concessions to the Irish, and Parnell, of course, threw his support to
the Liberals. Salisbury's Government was defeated in the opening
week of Parliament, and Gladstone began his third administration
with a promise to provide home rule for Ireland.

The First Home Rule Bill, 1886. For sixteen days Gladstone defended his bill which would provide a bicameral Irish legislature
with responsible Government, except for specific reserved areas.
The plan, which was attacked by the Tories, aroused strong protests in the Liberal party from Whigs, old Radicals like John
Bright, and Gladstone's chief colleague, Chamberlain. The latter
left the Cabinet and voted against the bill. Protestant Ulster
(Northern Ireland) promised to fight rather than submit to a Catholic majority in the south. Religious and nationalist emotions in
England were aroused as opponents predicted the dire consequences which would follow Irish independence. In the vote on the
bill, ninety-three Liberals defected to defeat the measure, and Gladstone immediately called an election on the issue.

Split of the Liberal Party. The Whig section, led by Hartington,
had already deserted Gladstone on the issue of home rule, and
Chamberlain, the Radical leader, opposed the purpose of the bill.
In the election of July, 1886, the Radicals refused to back home
rule and, instead, campaigned as a separate Liberal Unionist party.
The coalition of Conservatives and Liberal Unionists won an easy
victory over the Gladstonian Liberals and Irish Nationalists. Gladstone split the Liberal party over Ireland, just as Peel had splintered
the Conservatives forty years earlier over the Corn Laws. Nevertheless, the Irish Question was not solved simply by the electoral defeat
of home rule.

Chapter 20 ✍ Democracy at Home—
Empire Abroad

The transition from the nineteenth century to the twentieth was an unsettling period for Englishmen. The easy supremacy of Pax Britannica no longer guaranteed security against continental militarism. The twentieth century ushered in an era of political deterioration and violence as nineteenth-century liberalism was unable to cope with the revolutionary changes in society. By 1913 the crisis over Irish Home Rule and the reform of the House of Lords had almost reduced Liberal England to ashes.[1] In this era, with its self-conscious restlessness and indirection, the march of social democracy and the extension of empire were the most consistent notes to be found.

Political Realignment

By 1885 the political Radicals were not far from their goal of universal suffrage; the objectives of full democracy and economic collectivism were the logical extension of their utilitarian convictions and won the support of the masses. The county councils, the "People's Budget," and unemployment and old-age legislation marked this political trend. In the process the traditional two-party, two-House arrangement which sheltered multiple-interest groups began to fragment, as the House of Lords became almost solidly Conservative, and as "politics became increasingly identified with economic interests."[2] First the Irish and then the Laborites left the traditional parties to form organizations that would advance their particular interests or class.

Conservative Growth. Reliance on the squirearchy and the clergy had left the Conservative party on the defensive and in the minority until Disraeli expanded the base of this support by his attention to social reform and imperial expansion. In 1886 the Conservatives began two decades of power by keeping their rural constituencies and by gradually winning the allegiance of the bor-

---

[1] George Dangerfield, *The Strange Death of Liberal England, 1910-1914* (New York: Capricorn, 1935), p. viii.
[2] A. F. Havighurst, *Twentieth Century Britain* (Evanston, Illinois: Row, Peterson, 1962), p. 20.

oughs. The urban middle class and the manufacturer joined with the landlord. Two major reasons for this development were the opposition of the middle class to Irish Home Rule, and the dynamic influence of Joseph Chamberlain. First under Lord Randolph Churchill, then under Chamberlain, progressive economic proposals became identified with the Tories rather than with the Liberals. When Chamberlain bolted the Liberal party in 1886, he prodded the Conservative Government with his dynamic program of social reform. Thus Disraeli's emphasis on Tory democracy was revived in the Conservative party by Chamberlain's influence.

Liberal Confusion. Only once after 1886 did the Liberal party again win a majority of seats in England. The party lost control of the urban ridings and remained strong only in the Celtic fringes of Wales, Scotland, and Ireland. The old slogan of "peace, retrenchment, and reform" was no longer suited to an age which wanted more empire and governmental services, not less, and which had already won most of the political objectives that the Liberals favored. The Liberal party was reduced to promoting reforms, such as Welsh Disestablishment or liquor licensing, to hold its Celtic and Noncomformist supporters; but to win urban votes it would have to drop home rule, support imperialism, and lure labor votes by a program of social legislation. The Liberal commitment to home rule, however, pushed aside all consideration for social welfare and lost its most vigorous promoter, Chamberlain. The Liberals were also plagued by the problem of leadership. Gladstone had put such an indelible image on the party that no one of equal stature could be found to replace him; the two most eminent heirs, Charles Dilke and Joseph Chamberlain, were eliminated, one by his divorce, the other by his opposition to home rule. Consequently, the party remained divided and dispirited until 1905.

The Birth of the Labor Party. Trade unionism and non-Marxist socialist societies joined ranks in 1900 to elect labor representatives to Parliament. After receiving full legal rights in 1875, the non-political and conservative Trades Union Congress was at first content to promote industrial legislation through the Liberal party. But the unskilled laborers organized unions and favored strikes and more active political participation. In 1886 a special electoral committee of the Trades Union Congress endorsed and helped eleven working-class members to win parliamentary seats. They sat as Liberals and this "Lib-Lab" alliance continued until 1900. By that date the trade unions had two million members.

Meanwhile, English socialism—insular, non-violent, and evolutionary—had appeared. Except for H. M. Hyndman's Social Democratic Federation, English Socialists were largely non-Marxist intellectuals critical of the existing economic and social structure. The Fabian Society (1883), which attracted such intellectuals as George Bernard Shaw, Graham Wallas, Sidney and Beatrice Webb, and H. G. Wells, promoted gradual social reform through the extensive intervention of the state and were particularly active in the London County Council. Labor churches, preaching social welfare, helped spread Fabian ideas to the workers, as did Keir Hardie, who broke with the Liberals, entered Parliament in 1892 as a labor candidate, and established an Independent Labor party in 1893. The I.L.P. shortly won the approval of the Trades Union Congress for independent political action.

In 1900 a conference of socialist societies, co-operative societies, and trade unions met in London and set up the Labor Representation Committee to establish a distinct Labor group in Parliament. J. Ramsay MacDonald was elected secretary of the committee, and in the general election of that year two seats were won out of fifteen contested. In 1906 the Labor party won fifty-three seats.

The Great Debate. As the virtues of mid-Victorianism were refuted and superseded by a diversity of creeds, latter-day Victorianism probed its conscience and looked for a new set of values. Political and economic freedom were not enough, unless citizens were equipped to improve the quality of life with the new freedom. Should the state preserve freedom of action, or should it improve society directly by collective action? Before the Government could wage war on poverty, unemployment, or on slums, a revolution in finance had to take place. Disappearing with the old individualism was the tendency to fashion legislative programs with the taxpayer in mind. After 1885 the majority of voters favored larger national budgets because the burden of increased taxation would fall on others. By the end of the century the Victorian sense of security and of agreement on the efficacy of representative Government were no longer taken for granted. World problems were more complex than imagined, and the democratic state had bred emotionalism and illiberalism as well as freedom and liberty.

Two Tory Decades

Under two Prime Ministers from the Cecil family, the Marquess of Salisbury and his nephew and successor, Arthur Balfour, the Conservative party, in alliance with the Unionists, governed England from 1886 to 1905, except for one brief Liberal ministry. With the Liberals in disarray, the time was ripe for the Conservatives to extend Disraeli's formula of imperialism and social reforms. Lord Salisbury directed his attention to foreign affairs and permitted Chamberlain to nudge the Tories toward several items of social welfare. Eventually, Chamberlain became too occupied with the Colonial Office to devote much time to domestic reform. The Irish agitation for home rule was contained by the death of Parnell, and by the Government's policy of "killing home rule with kindness." When the Cecils left office after twenty years, neither the Irish question nor England's social problems had been solved. Salisbury's policy of splendid isolation appeared far less appealing after the Boer War emphasized the diplomatic loneliness of such a position.

Lord Salisbury and His Colleagues. Salisbury formed his second administration (1886-92) from Conservatives when the Liberal Unionists declined to join. He appointed his nephew, Arthur Balfour, as Irish Secretary, and under his steady administration Ireland achieved two decades of relative peace and prosperity. Salisbury's chief interest was foreign diplomacy, and he successfully kept England out of war while sanctioning the advance of imperialism. The Prime Minister, although no reactionary, was too aloof from the people to concern himself about social legislation. Lord Randolph Churchill, who became chancellor of the exchequer and leader of the House of Commons, tried to commit his party to a strong labor program by offering to resign if his budget estimates were not accepted. To his surprise he found that he was not indispensible, and the Liberal Unionist, G. C. Goschen, replaced him. The reform measures that were passed, therefore, were largely the effort of Joseph Chamberlain who continued to be as radical a Unionist as he had been a Liberal.

Conservative Administration, 1886-92. Except for occasional disturbances in Ireland, Salisbury's second administration was rather quiet. The Prime Minister was respected for his administrative talents, but he never caught the popular imagination as had Gladstone or Disraeli. To ensure Liberal Unionist support several domestic reform measures favored by Chamberlain were passed. The County Councils Act of 1888 recast the political structure of local government by transferring administrative authority from the justices of the peace to popularly-elected councils. The Technical Education Act of 1889 authorized school boards to offer technical as well as elementary education. Factory employees won additional protection and privileges by the Factory Act of 1890.

Irish Developments. Arthur Balfour, Secretary for Ireland, maintained order through an even-handed enforcement of a permanent coercion act, and at the same time worked vigorously to alleviate the economic and social grievances of the Irish. A series of acts—the Ashbourne Act of 1885, the Balfour Act of 1891, and the Wyndham Act of 1903—partly relieved the squalor of the peasants' living conditions by encouraging them to purchase their farms. The Wyndham Act went so far as to force the landlord to sell. The program was quite successful, and Balfour's efforts were aided by the internal wrangling of the Irish Nationalist party. In 1890 Parnell was named as corespondent in a divorce case. Irish clergy and Nonconformist Liberals alike publicly censured him, and the controversy split his party in two. Parnell died in 1891, but the division between his supporters and his critics continued for a decade until John Redmond reunited the two factions.

Second Home Rule Bill. The election of 1892 left the Conservatives in a minority, and Salisbury's Government met defeat when the Liberals and Irish Nationalists combined to bring down the ministry. Thus at the age of eighty-three Gladstone began his fourth ministry (1892-94). The Liberal platform, known as the Newcastle Program, promised an amazing variety of reform. However, few reform measures were even debated because Gladstone insisted on the priority of a Home Rule Bill. His new bill of 1893 survived all amendments and passed the House of Commons, but was overwhelmingly defeated by the Conservative House of Lords. Rather than force an election on the issue, Gladstone retired the following year, after serving sixty-two years in Parliament. Failing in vision and in hearing, and out of touch with a new Liberal party which wanted bigger military expenditures and more radical social legislation, the Grand Old Man had outlived his age; four years later he died and was accorded a state funeral.

Liberal Leadership. Queen Victoria selected the Earl of Rosebery, a personable, unpredictable aristocrat, to succeed Gladstone as Prime Minister. Although a man of promise, Rosebery's talents were conspicuously hidden in office, and his administration was lacking in achievement. His chief rival was the able Sir William Harcourt, chancellor of the exchequer, whose budgets heavily taxed landed inheritances and anticipated the "socialist" Liberal budgets of the next decade. Two future Prime Ministers also served in Rosebery's Cabinet: Herbert Asquith as home secretary, and Sir Henry Campbell-Bannerman at the war office.

Salisbury's Third Cabinet. The election of 1895 returned 340 Conservatives and 71 Liberal Unionists who now joined forces in a Unionist Cabinet against the outnumbered Liberals (177) and Irish Nationalists (82). Rosebery's aggressive imperial policies had alienated the Liberal rank and file, and Home Rule and liquor licensing had antagonized even more voters. Lord Salisbury claimed the foreign office and was the last peer to hold the office of Prime Minister. Arthur Balfour served as leader of the House of Commons, and Joseph Chamberlain chose the colonial office where his passions for imperial growth and consolidation were soon demonstrated. Chamberlain evoked the latent protectionism of the Tories by his arguments in favor of imperial preference, but he became so engrossed with imperial issues that only one of the Cabinet's projected social reforms was passed—the Workmen's Compensation Act of 1897. This measure made the employer liable for compensation to injured workers according to rates set by the law. Other social schemes were set aside because of the Boer War.

Election of 1900. The Boer War almost ruined the floundering Liberal party which had failed since 1894 to find either an appealing party position or a leader who could update its Gladstonian image. Sir William Harcourt succeeded Rosebery as party leader, but fared no better. Two years later Harcourt was replaced by Sir Henry Campbell-Bannerman, who had served in the Cabinet under Gladstone and whose generous and affable nature seemed to make conciliation possible among the divided Liberals. The outbreak of the Boer War, however, only sharpened the breach. One wing of the party, the Liberal Imperialists led by Asquith, Grey, and Haldane, backed the war without reservation; the other wing under Lloyd-George, Morley, and Reid remained pro-Boer and condemned the imperialist venture. Caught in the cross fire of both wings was Campbell-Bannerman who had misgivings about the war, but who agreed that the war must end in the annexation of the Boer republics. The Unionists exploited this division by holding a general election in 1900.[3] The war was the only real issue, and Unionists equated patriotism with their party by the slogan, "A seat lost to the Government is a seat gained by the Boers." The Unionists won the election but with a reduced majority. More voters were critical of the Government than of the pro-Boer wing of the Opposition.

Death of Victoria. Queen Victoria died in 1901 after the longest reign—sixty-four years—in English history. In her later years, she had regained the esteem of the nation who respected her as the symbol of the nineteenth century and of the British Empire. Her sense of duty, pride in Empire, and conventional morality refur-

---

[3] Commonly termed the Khaki election because the dissolution was an obvious attempt to translate the emotions of wartime patriotism into votes for the party in power.

bished the ideal of monarchy which had been tarnished by the preceding Hanoverian monarchs. She was succeeded by her eldest son, Edward VII, who was nearly sixty. Edward became a much loved and sociable monarch who relished the many public functions demanded of a King. Although he never understood the rapid change which the twentieth century was introducing into English society, his charm and goodwill tours abroad made him the most popular monarch since Charles II.

Economic Conditions. Because of the drop in profits and prices the business world termed the years 1873 to 1898 "the Great Depression"; yet during these years real wages improved 75 per cent. On the other hand, the fifteen years prior to World War I were years of recovery for business with substantial profits and industrial growth, although real wages remained static because of the price rise. In these years of remarkable economic expansion, exports more than doubled, and a very favorable balance of trade permitted an export of capital which was invested in new resources and markets. More than ever Britain's entire economy depended on world trade. However, the advantages of an industrialized society were still very unevenly distributed in Britain. Careful urban studies in 1900 indicated that about 30 per cent of Britain's population lived in a state of chronic poverty. As the problems of slum housing, poverty, health, and equitable distribution of national income were examined free of partisan purpose, an increasing sensitivity to social problems was in evidence as writers and economists sought for the most desirable accommodation between capitalism and socialism. The old complacency was gone; in its place was recognition of the need for social change.

Conservatism in Decline, 1901-06. Following the Boer War a rapid reversal of party fortunes took place as the Liberals dismissed their recent divisions to defend public education and free trade. The Conservatives, sharply divided over postwar policy, faced attacks from Nonconformists, free traders, and critics of the Government's South African policies.

Taff Vale Decision. The House of Lords, in its capacity as the highest court of appeals, decided in favor of the Taff Vale Railway's suit for £32,000 in damages against the Amalgamated Society of Railway Servants. This decision made trade unions financially liable for the actions of its members and drastically handicapped all strike activity. When the Conservatives made no effort to curb by statute the effects of this decision, the trade unions, for the first time, actively supported working-class candidates for Parliament, running under the label of the Labor Representation Committee, which changed its name in 1906 to the Labor party.

Education Act, 1902. In July, 1902 Arthur Balfour succeeded his uncle as Prime Minister. Balfour proved to be an adept parliamentary leader, but was constantly harried by adverse circumstances. His first extensive reform in education replaced 20,000 local school boards by the authority of the local government and made county and borough councils responsible for all types of schools. The state assumed full responsibility for education and brought the voluntary schools under its authority, although religious instruction in schools was retained with optional attendance. The act equalized standards at the local level and permitted a systematic expansion of secondary education. The bill was a political liability, however, because it aroused vigorous opposition from Nonconformists who opposed the intrusion of the state into education and the support of schools where Anglican doctrine would be taught.

The Licensing Act, 1904. The influential temperance movement agitated for a reduction in the number of outlets licensed to sell liquor. Balfour's bill supported local licensing authorities in their refusal to renew the expired licenses of some public houses, but provided compensation from funds distributed by the liquor industry to publicans who lost their licenses. Immediately critics claimed such compensation would endow the liquor trade. The bill passed, but Balfour lost the large temperance vote.

The Tariff Controversy. The shibboleth of "free trade" was challenged by Joseph Chamberlain who embarrassed his Cabinet colleagues by coming out publicly in 1902 for an imperial preference tariff and for import duties on food. A year later he resigned from the Cabinet to stump the country as an advocate of protectionism. By this time the Conservative party was splintered three ways on the tariff issue: the Free Traders, the Tariff Reform League, and halfway between stood the Prime Minister who opposed a food tax and imperial preference, but agreed to a retaliatory tariff to diminish foreign tariffs. By the end of 1903 Balfour had lost both wings of his Cabinet, and only his consummate skill prevented a dissolution. The dissension among the Conservatives handed the Liberal party the one issue, free trade, around which its divided factions could rally.

Chinese Labor. Adding to Balfour's difficulties was the Government's introduction of indentured Chinese labor in South African mines. The mine owners and the Transvaal Government had requested this importation, and the arrival of nearly 50,000 Chinese strengthened the South African economy. Nevertheless, the conditions of their living quarters and the restrictions placed on families coming with the coolies made the policy a political liability. The charge of "Chinese slavery" was made against the Government, and the indentured system became an emotional issue in the election of 1906.

Imperial and Foreign Affairs

In the second half of Queen Victoria's reign British imperialism became a popular movement, and empire builders won a degree of support from home authorities not available to them earlier. These imperialists were men of action who were, of course, often interested in gold and glory, but were also inspired by a sense of duty, often instilled in them in their public-school training, to extend overseas the blessings of English institutions. This ideal was twofold and somewhat paradoxical: to conquer and govern the new empire, and to grant self-government and independence to the old. Nevertheless, this world empire only sharpened the growing hostilities between Britain and militant Germany. German diplomacy failed to realize that such military posturing frightened Britain, France, and Russia into submerging their traditional antipathy to each other to the point of allying themselves against the threat of a powerful Germany.

Self-Government in the Settlement Colonies. Between 1867 and 1907 three of Britain's overseas settlement areas became self-governing nations, bound to Britain only by loyalty, common institutions, and a common allegiance to the throne. The evolution from colony to Commonwealth of Nations was in process. This transition came peacefully with no efforts to halt the process in the white communities because England had profited from experience in the American Revolution.

Canada. In 1867 the British North America Act created a federal union of four provinces. The first of the dominions blended the British cabinet system with a federal-provincial structure necessitated by its large size. Under the vigorous leadership of Prime Minister Sir John A. MacDonald, Canada expanded and consolidated its territories by absorbing the West and Northwest through the purchase of the landholding rights of the Hudson's Bay Company, and by the building of a trans-continental railway—the Canadian Pacific. By 1905 Canada's nine provinces were no longer fearful of annexation by the United States and had become prosperous primary producers. By 1914 only the United States shipped more grain than Canada to Great Britain. Canada's second outstanding Prime Minister, Sir Wilfrid Laurier, grappled with the problem of biculturalism. His political wisdom and statesmanship helped to mute French-English friction. Laurier also led the opposition at colonial conferences to Joseph Chamberlain's attempts to centralize the British Empire, fearing that any steps in that direction would reverse the trend to separate Dominion identities.

Australia. The six separate colonies in Australia had won responsible government between 1852 and 1870. This development was prompted by the discovery of gold in 1851 which multiplied the population and led to a democratization of government. However, federal union was delayed until 1901 because of the rivalries among the colonies. Finally, an Australian Constitution was accepted which provided a federal system that resembled the American prototype except for its cabinet form of government. The practical values of ending separate tariffs and railway gauges, coupled with the fear of Japanese, German, and American expansion in the South Pacific, finally triumphed over separatist loyalties.

New Zealand. Britain annexed New Zealand in 1840, and in 1853 the settlement obtained a large measure of self-government. After two wars with the native Maoris, the white settlers dominated the country. Since New Zealand was small in size, no federal system was necessary, and Dominion status came easily in 1907. By that date planned and systematic immigration and public works had resulted in a society that was responsive to political and social experiments. Under the leadership of Richard Seddon and William Reeves, New Zealand pioneered in social legislation, established manhood suffrage, voting for women, old age pensions, compulsory arbitration in labor disputes, and government ownership of utilities. New Zealand, more than any other Dominion, was dependent upon Great Britain as a market for her meat and dairy produce, and upon the Royal Navy as her first line of defense in the Pacific.

Imperial Federation. Between 1887 and 1922 seven imperial conferences were convened in an effort to promote centralization among the self-governing members of the Empire. Proponents of centralization argued for it on three levels: political (imperial federation), economic (imperial preference), and military (imperial defense). Joseph Chamberlain, colonial secretary (1895-1903), provided the momentum for these conferences, claiming that imperial union made economic and political sense just as federal unions in Canada and Australia were obvious advantages over separate colonies. At these imperial conferences Chamberlain proposed the establishment of a council which could make agreements binding on the member countries, thereby making the self-governing members share in the responsibility and expense of the Empire. His "Weary Titan" speech of 1901 pointed out that the Dominions were enjoying the privileges of naval protection without making any significant contribution to the British navy. Prime Minister Laurier of Canada led the opposition to centralization on the grounds that it was reversing the trend to autonomy, because Britain, by its population, power, and prestige, would inevitably dominate any federation. By 1911 the centralizers had been defeated on every issue.

The Dominions favored reciprocal preferences in trade. Chamberlain left the Cabinet to campaign for imperial free trade, but the British election of 1906 closed the door on this prospect. In 1904 the Committee on Imperial Defense was set up, but the Dominions preferred to build small, separate navies rather than contribute to the Royal Navy. The conference of 1911 sounded the death knell for imperial federation. By this time Australia and New Zealand, anxious for a voice on British policy in the Pacific, favored an Imperial Parliament. But Prime Ministers Laurier and Botha (South Africa) attacked Sir Joseph Ward's (New Zealand) proposal. Prime Minister Asquith ended the discussion by stating flatly that responsibility for foreign policy could not be shared: Britain could not wait for consultation and unanimity before making any diplomatic move.

Popularity of Empire. Popular support for British imperialism was at its patriotic and emotional peak between Queen Victoria's Golden Jubilee and the Boer War. In 1887, and again in 1897 at the Diamond Jubilee of the Queen, the British seized the opportunity to celebrate their successful imperial expansion with magnificent spectacles. Troops and dignitaries from every colony came to London. "Drunk with the sight of power," the populace scarcely heeded the penitential admonition of Rudyard Kipling (poet laureate) whose verse and prose reflected imperialism at its best. The jingoistic and grasping type of imperialism was supported in theory by Social Darwinism, a misapplication of the Darwinian hypothesis to human races, and in print by a yellow press. Alfred Harmsworth (later Lord Northcliffe) reduced the price of his newspaper, the *Daily Mail*, to a halfpenny, which in sensational style glorified imperial heroes and British power. Circulation boomed and other papers copied the format. This type of imperial fever reached a climax in the admiration of the exploits of Lord Kitchener on the Nile and Lord Roberts in South Africa.

Indian Policy. The title of Empress of India that Parliament conferred upon Queen Victoria in 1876 did not shift political control of India to London any more than the India Act of 1858, which placed India directly under parliamentary control. The effective administration and practical government of India depended on the three thousand District Officers and specialists who manned the Indian Civil Service. This efficient and effective bureaucracy was open to Indians, but the nature of the examinations virtually restricted competition to graduates of England's public schools and universities. The successes of the Civil Service were striking: public health, transportation, and the administration of justice were improved, famine decreased, and literacy and population increased. In spite of these benefits, the Indian nationalists desired to be rid of the English. Indian intellectuals, inspired by the western literature of revolt and freedom, stirred the national consciousness and revived native literature and history. The All-India Congress was founded in 1885 to promote Indian self-government. The British made a token response to this growing nationalism by the Council Acts of 1894 which placed a minority of elected Indians on the legislative councils, and by the Morley-Minto reforms of 1909 which introduced elective Indian participation in government and provided an Indian majority in the provincial assemblies. Communal representation—separate electoral roles—was also granted as a concession to Muslims. However, the Hindu-Muslim animosity complicated the introduction of responsible government, because the Muslim minority feared that their rights would be jeopardized by a Hindu government.

During these years British frontier policy for India contained Russian expansion in Afghanistan and checkmated French, German, and Russian ambitions in Persia. After the Penjdah crisis of 1885, the subsequent frontier history was generally peaceful. Lord Curzon's viceroyalty (1899-1906) produced a treaty with Tibet and new Northwest Frontier Provinces as buffers against rival powers. If Curzon's reforming zeal brought about great educational, technical, and economic advances, his unwitting hauteur, nevertheless, alienated him from the Hindus and occasioned his recall in 1905 by the new Liberal Government. He was succeeded by Lord Minto.

Imperialism in China. The ease with which recently industrialized Japan defeated China in the Sino-Japanese war (1895) revealed two things: the rise of an imperial power in the Far East, and the tempting weakness of China. There was an immediate scramble for China's wealth and trade. Russia, France, and Germany forced Japan to restore her conquests on the mainland and claimed economic spheres of influence for themselves. Britain's favorable position in China since 1840 was jeopardized. The partition of China was opposed, but European rivals gave no heed to British protests. When diplomacy failed, Lord Salisbury secured concessions at Weihaiwei and additional territory near Hong Kong. Britain and the United States favored an "open door" policy for China which would give all nations equal rights in economic exploitation, but which would forbid the formal partition of China. As a result, British and American support prevented the political dismembering of China, such as occurred in Africa, but the economy and wealth of China soon became controlled by a consortium of major powers.

African Expansion. The partition of Africa by European powers was completed by 1914. Only France with 4,200,000 square miles exceeded the British holdings of 3,300,000 square miles. Germany followed with 1,100,000 square miles and Belgium with 900,000 square miles.

East Africa. The treaties that Carl Peters and the Society for German Colonization secured from twelve African chiefs reactivated British interest in East Africa which was nominally under the Sultan of Zanzibar. Sir William Mackinnon acquired a charter for the British East Africa Company after an Anglo-German agreement in 1886 recognized German suzerainty in Tanganyika and British influence in Kenya. Meanwhile, a religious war had erupted in Uganda, and Captain Frederick Lugard was sent by the British East Africa Company to restore order; however, he discovered that Peters had already persuaded the king of Buganda to sign a treaty with Germany. In 1890 Lord Salisbury won German recognition of British control over Kenya, Uganda, and the Sudan, and a protectorate over Zanzibar, in return for ceding to Germany the island of Heligoland in the North Sea. In 1895 the British Government purchased Mackinnon's chartered company and began construction of a railroad from the coast through Kenya to Uganda.

West Africa. In 1884 the German annexation of Togoland, Cameroons, and Southwest Africa stirred the British to action. The Royal Niger Company (formerly the United African Company) under Sir George Goldie received a charter in 1886 to administer the Niger delta and the interior. In return, the company would attempt to suppress the slave trade. Sir Frederick Lugard was hired by the company. He made treaties with the natives and subdued the independent north. In 1900 the British Government assumed political administration, and by 1914 northern and southern Nigeria were united under the governorship of Lugard, who became the most successful exponent of indirect rule—Britain claiming paramount power with local government operating through native chiefs.

In 1871 the British purchased Danish and Dutch interests in the Gold Coast, but the small coastal colony was constantly threatened by the fierce Ashanti in the interior. When punitive expeditions and wars did not break Ashanti power, Chamberlain declared a British protectorate over the interior in 1901. The introduction of cocoa soon made the Gold Coast the world's leading producer of cocoa products. Unlike East and South Africa with their temperate climates, there was virtually no white settlement in West Africa.

Sudan. Following Charles Gordon's death the Sudan experienced a decade of frightful anarchy. The disorders were such a constant threat to neighboring Egypt that finally the British determined to restore order. Lord Kitchener led a British army southward and annihilated the Dervishes at the decisive battle of Omdurman in 1898. When Kitchener continued up the Nile to Fashoda, he encountered Captain Marchand and a French expedition which had arrived from the French Congo. This clash of rival imperial ambitions produced a diplomatic crisis and a war spirit in London and Paris. France finally backed down when her one ally, Russia, refused support; she was unwilling to have both Germany and Britain as enemies. Kitchener completed the annexation of the Sudan, and the country was ruled jointly by Britain and Egypt as a condominium.

The Boer War. In the last decades of the nineteenth century relations between Boers and Britons worsened, aggravated by internal circumstances, such as the conflicting personalities of Cecil Rhodes and Paul Kruger and the discovery of gold, and by such external events as German intervention in southern Africa and the popular British sentiment in favor of imperialism. In **1899** the differences led to war.

Background. The discovery of diamonds in 1870 and gold in the Transvaal in 1885 resulted in a great influx of foreigners into South Africa. The Boers feared that their political autonomy and separatist society were jeopardized by this invasion. Under Paul Kruger, president of the Transvaal, the Boers placed disadvantages on the foreigners, excluding them from the franchise, and taxing them heavily. The English immigrants protested and demanded their political rights. Their cause was supported by Cecil Rhodes who, besides making a vast fortune in gold, had organized the greatest of the chartered companies—the British South Africa Company—and had incorporated Rhodesia into the Empire in 1888. The following year Rhodes became Premier of the Cape

Colony and pursued his dream of federating the British and Boer colonies in South Africa and of establishing a Cape to Cairo railway. When the Kruger regime halted these aspirations, Rhodes agreed to a private uprising to bring the Transvaal under British rule. The resulting Jameson Raid of 1895 was a fiasco and only increased the suspicions of the Boers about British intentions. Kaiser Wilhelm II acerbated the friction by publicly supporting Kruger. Between 1895 and 1899 Chamberlain, as colonial secretary, and Lord Alfred Milner, as British High Commissioner, negotiated with Kruger over redress of outlander grievances in the Transvaal; however, Boer nationalism was intransigent, and the negotiations failed. German arms were transported to the Transvaal and the two Boer republics began to mobilize. The British dispatched troops, and in October, 1899, the Boers attacked Natal.

War and Peace. At first mounted Boer commandos swept through Natal and besieged the larger part of the British forces at Ladysmith and at Mafeking and Kimberley to the west of the Orange Free State. An alarmed and humiliated Britain rushed her two most famous generals, Lords Roberts and Kitchener, and the largest British army ever assembled to the relief of the beleaguered cities. Before the end of 1900 the Boer states were invaded and their armies defeated. However, the Boers refused to surrender and for eighteen months mobile commando units waged guerrilla war. By the use of such stringent measures as blockhouses and concentration camps, Boer resistance was gradually overwhelmed, and their Generals Botha and Smuts agreed to negotiations. The terms of the Peace of Vereeniging (1902) were generous. The two Boer republics were added to the Empire but were promised self-government in the near future. The Dutch and English languages were equally recognized in schools and courts, and Britain offered £3 million for economic reconstruction. When the Liberals won the election of 1906, Prime Minister Campbell-Bannerman immediately honored the pledge of self-government to the Transvaal and the Orange Free State. This magnanimity captured the respect and support of Botha and Smuts and permitted Rhodes's dream of a federal union of the four colonies (Cape, Natal, Transvaal, and Orange Free State) to be realized in 1910.

Impact of the War on Britain. Although most of the populace rallied behind the Government and 30,000 troops joined the British army from the Dominions, the Boer War divided the Liberal party and isolated the country diplomatically. The foreign reaction was almost uniformly hostile, and the revelations to Britain that her isolation was anything but splendid (with a powerful Germany rearming) made her eager to find allies.

Relations with the United States. In 1895 President Cleveland threatened force when Britain rejected an American offer to arbitrate a border dispute between Venezuela and British Guiana. Prime Minister Salisbury refused to respond in kind to this martial spirit and consented to arbitration. The outcome was a decision favorable to Britain and, equally important, more friendly relations between Britain and the United States. During the Spanish-

American War only Britain, among the European powers, was sympathetic to the American position. This growing Anglo-American rapport was reflected in the Hay-Pauncefote Treaty (1901) which annulled the previous Clayton-Bulwer Treaty that had guaranteed joint control of any interoceanic canal. The new treaty provided that the United States alone could build and control the new canal. Britain was freely relinquishing her imperial power in the Caribbean to the United States.

From Isolation to Alliance. Moral sanctions and the Royal Navy had permitted the methods of Victorian Liberalism to serve Britain well, until the Franco-Prussian War upset the balance of power on the Continent. Salisbury kept England free of alliances in spite of Germany's adventurous foreign policy. But by 1900 Britain found this position no longer tenable and altered her foreign policy to one of limited commitments. The division of the Great Powers of Europe into two camps, the isolation of Britain during the Boer War, Germany's challenge to British sea power, and the increasing danger to Britain's exposed and scattered colonial and commercial empire made alliances seem worth the risk of continental commitments.

Triple Alliance. In 1882 Bismarck concluded the Triple Alliance (Germany, Austria, and Italy) to strengthen Germany against any effort of France to seek revenge for her humiliating defeat in the Franco-Prussian War. He also arranged an alliance of the three emperors of Germany, Austria, and Russia as protection for Germany's eastern borders. In 1890 the clever and unstable William II let lapse the alliance with Russia, whereupon Russia and France formed an entente out of common fear of Germany; the entente became the Dual Alliance in 1894. Thus the great powers of Europe were again divided into two camps, and Britain found it increasingly difficult to win co-operation from any of their members on foreign or imperial matters.

Anglo-German Relations. Traditional enmity and current imperial rivalries in the Middle East and Africa continued to strain Anglo-Russian and Anglo-French relations and made Germany the logical partner for a British alliance. Under Bismarck relations with England were generally friendly, but deteriorated after his ouster and the Kaiser's abandonment of Bismarck's "limited aims" in Europe. In spite of the provocative and truculent methods of German diplomacy, Britain, through the overtures of Salisbury, Chamberlain, and Lansdowne, made three efforts to conclude a German alliance between 1895 and 1901. The negotiations failed because Germany was convinced that England could not come to terms with France and Russia, and because the German foreign office was both resentful of Great Britain's position and suspicious of her motives in seeking an alliance. In turn, German naval rearmament caused apprehension in Britain, and the Kaiser's provocative interference in the Boer dispute angered the British public. The failure of Germany to join Britain in opposing Russian encroachments in China and Korea drove Britain into a defensive alliance with Japan in 1902, which promised to provide military assistance if either country were attacked by more than one power. This alliance was the first formal step away from isolation.

The Entente Cordiale, 1904. The next step achieved by Prime Minister Balfour was an agreement which settled the outstanding colonial issues dividing France and Britain. The entente was highlighted by French recognition of the British occupation of Egypt in return for British support of French interests in Morocco. Although Anglo-French relations had been cool ever since the Fashoda crisis, these feelings were dwarfed by the need of France for England as an ally, if war broke out between France and Germany, and the desire of England for the friendship of a major European power.

The Triple Entente, 1907. Sir Edward Grey, foreign secretary of the new Liberal Government, concluded an agreement between Russia and Britain. Traditional hostilities between the two nations were reduced after the defeat of Russia by Japan and by the mutual fear of Germany. The Germans were catching up to the British as a result of their crash program of building capital ships, while Russian influence in the Middle East was being threatened by Germany's friendship with Turkey. The entente settled imperial rivalries between the two powers in Persia and along the frontier of India. This agreement between old rivals surprised Germany, and the Kaiser complained about the efforts of Britain, France, and Russia to encircle Germany. Each European camp viewed with increasing suspicion the activities of the other.

The New Liberalism

The years from 1906 to 1914 were a time of anxiety and crisis in England. The rules of political warfare and parliamentary procedure were violated; the duel between the two Houses of Parliament resulted in a drastic reduction of the powers of the Upper House; workers, women, Ulsterites, and army officers disregarded the laws and customs of the land. As a result, the nineteenth-century liberal, with his beliefs in the efficacy of evolutionary reform and the merits of compromise, was replaced by a new generation of voters who felt the urgency of reform and the need to remove the causes of poverty and unemployment. The expansion of political democracy during the nineteenth century produced an electorate that expected increasing economic and social democracy.

Election of 1906. The Liberals won in a landslide, sweeping 377 seats to only 157 for the Conservatives and Liberal Unionists combined. In addition, the 53 members of the new Labor party and the 83 Irish Nationalists would support the Government, rather than the Conservatives, on most measures. The Liberals interpreted their victory as a mandate for social legislation, even if they failed to gauge fully the extent of the unrest among the electorate. The Government was willing to make unenthusiastic concessions to the pressures of the new generation, whereas the Tories attempted to use the Conservative House of Lords to prevent a drift toward socialism.

The Campbell-Bannerman Cabinet. In 1905 Prime Minister Campbell-Bannerman brought together a distinguished Cabinet in which he allocated offices to all factions of the Liberal party without entrenching any. In the ministry were three future Prime Ministers —Herbert Asquith (Exchequer), David Lloyd George (President of the Board of Trade), and Winston Churchill (Undersecretary of the Colonies). The Cabinet also included Sir Edward Grey (Foreign Office), Richard Haldane (War Office), James Bryce (Irish Secretary), John Morley (Secretary for India), Sir Robert Reid (Lord Chancellor), Augustine Birrell (Board of Education) and Herbert Gladstone (Home Office).

The Liberals and the Lords. Unlike the House of Commons, the House of Lords had not been reformed in the nineteenth century. Nor was it a nonpartisan body; since the desertion of the Liberal peers over Gladstone's Irish Home Rule issue, the Upper House had been turned into an overwhelmingly Conservative stronghold. Under the Salisbury-Balfour Government the House of Lords co-operated readily to pass even such partisan issues as the Education Act (1902) which had no electoral mandate. In contrast, the Conservative party now used their great majority in the House of Lords to block measures passed by the House of Commons and to frustrate the Liberal Government. Lloyd George claimed that the House of Lords was no longer a watchdog of the Constitution, it was merely "Mr. Balfour's poodle." [4]

Tory Opposition. Balfour, leader of the Opposition, could not

---

[4] A. F. Havighurst, *Twentieth Century Britain*, p. 97.

block Liberal measures in the House of Commons, but the partisan attitude of the House of Lords was revealed by its rejection of two important measures passed by the Lower House in 1906—an Education bill, and a Plural Voting bill; the latter would limit a man having property qualifications in several ridings to only one vote. In 1908 the peers rejected the Licensing bill which proposed to reduce the number of liquor outlets and to encourage local option in an effort to promote temperance.

Liberal Legislation. Some significant legislation, however, was passed by the Campbell-Bannerman Government. Responsible government was granted in the Transvaal and Orange Free State. A Workmen's Compensation Act (1906) extended the liability of the employer for the payment of compensation to employees injured at work. The Trades Dispute Bill (1906) freed the trade unions from the legal restrictions and liabilities placed upon them in the Taff Vale decision.

Asquith and Social Reform. Campbell-Bannerman resigned in 1908 and was succeeded by Asquith. Prime Minister Asquith was a Nonconformist lawyer, loyal to his colleagues, and noted for his high personal standards and gentlemanly disposition. He was unpretentious and, above all, he was a moderate, believing in the essential rightness of conciliation and compromise. He moved Lloyd George to the exchequer and Churchill to the Board of Trade. These two colleagues, so different in background, helped push social legislation through Parliament. An Old Age Pension Bill (1908) provided for immediate noncontributory pensions for each citizen seventy years of age with an annual income of less than £31. To improve conditions of labor in the sweated industries, a Trade Boards Act of 1909 set up trade councils which fixed by law a minimum living wage and maximum hours of work. In 1911 the National Insurance Act became law and provided for insurance and protection against unemployment, sickness and disability. The Government, employer, and employee all contributed to the scheme which brought fourteen million workers under its provisions.

The People's Budget. The conflict between the Liberal Government and the House of Lords came to a climax with the introduction of the budget by Lloyd George in April, 1909. To pay for naval expansion and the old age pension program, Lloyd George proposed new taxes: a super-tax on annual incomes over £5000, increased death duties, land taxes, and income tax schedules. The tax increase bore most heavily on the wealthy, particularly the great landholders. The House of Commons passed the budget after long and tumultuous debate, but the House of Lords rejected it 350 to 75.

Their repudiation was declared a breach of the Constitution by the House of Commons, because an unwritten but established convention since 1671 denied the House of Lords the right to amend or veto a money bill. The peers replied that the budget was not a legitimate money bill but a scheme to bring about a social revolution.

Reform of the House of Lords. The cry of 1832, "mend it or end it," was now heard as Parliament debated the proper sphere of the Upper House. Checkmated by the House of Lords, the Liberal Government took the issue to the electorate in order to win approval for the budget and for a reduction in the powers of the Lords.

The Election of 1910. Asquith failed to get the mandate that he had anticipated. The election results gave the Liberals 275, Conservatives 273, Irish Nationalists 82, and Labor 40. Asquith's Government was now dependent upon the Irish who held the balance of power. The Irish supported the budget—which was reintroduced and passed in both houses—on the condition that the Upper House would be reformed to prevent the Lords from vetoing Irish Home Rule as they had done previously. Asquith, therefore, introduced resolutions which would permit the House of Lords to delay a money bill for one month and other bills for two years, after which they would become law irrespective of the consent of the peers.

Succession of George V. At this juncture Edward VII died, and a political truce was declared. King George V, conventional in outlook but with a high sense of duty and good judgment, called a conference of the leaders of the two parties to work out a compromise. The five-month conference failed to bring agreement. The Liberal reform bill passed the House of Commons but was rejected by the House of Lords. Therefore, Asquith asked for a dissolution and for the promise of the King to create sufficient peers to pass the Parliament bill if the Liberals were restored to power. The assurance was reluctantly given. The ensuing election (December, 1910), fought on the issue of the House of Lords, gave the Liberals and the Conservatives 272 seats each; once again, Irish and Labor votes returned the Liberal Government to power.

Parliament Act, 1911. Again the Liberal bill passed the House of Commons and went to the House of Lords. Aware of the royal guarantee to create new peers, the Tory leadership advised acceptance of defeat, but a "last ditch" movement among adamant peers almost forced the King to make good his promise. The bill finally passed 131 to 114. The Parliament Act (1) authorized the speaker of the House of Commons to define a money bill; (2) permitted the House of Lords to delay such a bill for only one month if the House of Commons had given its consent; (3) declared all other bills would become law if passed by the House of Commons in three consecutive sessions; and (4) reduced the legal life of Parliament from seven to five years. The act regulated by statute the relationship between the two houses and made it impossible for the peers to challenge again the supremacy of the House of Commons.

Years of Crisis, 1911-14. During these years the traditional values and institutions of England were undermined. The sense of fair play and genius for compromise were buried in the unparliamentary diatribes of His Majesty's Loyal Opposition. There was defiance by Protestant Ireland, the army, the suffragettes, and the workers. Prime Minister Asquith and his Government seemed helpless to halt this breakdown of tradition and order. By 1914 the Liberals had lost the confidence of middle-class Nonconformists, labor, and Ireland—the blocs which had provided the Liberal party with its mandate for social reform in 1906.

The Tory Attack. To repay the Irish Nationalists for their support, Asquith introduced a Home Rule bill. No longer able to rely on the veto of the Upper House to harass the Liberal party, the Tories, with cynical zeal, challenged the Liberals to force Home Rule on Ulster. Andrew Bonar Law, the new leader of the Conservatives, led the attack on Irish Home Rule, effectively assisted by his parliamentary colleagues, Sir Edward Carson and F. E. Smith. Their reckless speeches invited defiance of both law and constitutional process.

Irish Home Rule. The Liberals introduced the third Home Rule bill into the House of Commons in 1912. John Redmond, the Irish Nationalist leader who was fond of Westminster and of England, agreed to a restricted Home Rule measure which would give Ireland autonomy in home affairs, but would reserve certain powers for the British Parliament.

Ulster Reaction. The industrialized and Protestant northeast feared that home rule would reverse their favored position if the rural, Catholic south dominated an Irish Parliament. The Ulster Orangeman clung to his self-conscious separateness and to his hatred of Irish Catholics. Under Carson's provocative leadership, Ulster declared that it would repudiate home rule, regardless of what Parliament might decree. A Volunteer Army was raised in Ulster, and a covenant was signed by half a million pledging to defy home rule at all costs. Southern Ireland insisted that nothing short of a united Ireland would suffice. An Irish Nationalist Volunteer Army, supported by the Gaelic League and the Sinn Fein, was recruited to counter the Ulster Volunteers. The irresponsible talk of the Conservative leadership was matched by the indecision and timidity of Prime Minister Asquith whose leadership was anemic at best. In March, 1914, the Home Rule bill was introduced into the House of Commons for the third and final session. The issue now shifted to the army which was strongly unionist in sentiment. At Curragh British troops refused to obey orders, and their position was supported by Sir Henry Wilson, Director of Military Operations, and by many high-ranking officers. King George intervened in the crisis to bring the party leaders to a conference, but an impasse was reached and reported to the House of Commons on July 24. Only the intervening World War I prevented the domestic crisis from deepening. In September the Home Rule Act became law, but its operation was suspended for the duration of the war.

The Suffragettes. Meanwhile, since no party would support woman suffrage, and since conventional efforts to promote the cause had been unsuccessful, direct action was employed. Mrs. Emmeline Pankhurst, founder of the Women's Social and Political Union (W.S.P.U.), and her daughter, Christabel, led the demonstrations. Their militant tactics included arson, bombings, interruption of public meetings, and hunger strikes when imprisoned. Their sensational exhibitionism, punishment by police officials, and harrassment of parliamentary leaders finally forced Asquith to offer a non-party vote on woman suffrage. However, the Government failed to promote the measure, and no legislation was passed before the war.

Industrial Strife. When the Liberals passed only one significant social measure (the National Insurance Act) after the 1910 election, the workers took direct action to raise their wages and to force the country to hear their demands. Major strikes among dock and railway workers and coal miners (1911-12) forced the Government to intervene and grant the miners' demand for a minimum wage guaranteed by an act of Parliament. The political and class consciousness of the worker was stirred and his dissatisfaction with slow change and negotiations—Asquith's only response—was increasingly in evidence. In 1913 the three big unions of miners, railway men, and transport workers agreed to act together and to make demands of their employers at the same time. Their decision was influenced by the syndicalism popular in continental trade unions and by their dissatisfaction with piecemeal concessions. By the summer of 1914 walkouts in these three industries were imminent, and a general strike, which suggested overtones of a class war, was predicted for autumn.

The Eve of War. The constitutional processes and political institutions of England had been shaken by the actions of those who were impatient with slow change and due process. The Liberal party was unable to absorb this new radicalism and became caught in the crossfire of the Tory Right and the Labor Left. Only the outbreak of war on the Continent halted the deterioration of domestic affairs within England and gave the Liberal party a temporary reprieve.

Chapter 21 ❦ England In the Nineteenth Century

The nineteenth century was England's greatest age in power, material progress, and in political liberalism. Although great diversity characterized the various phases of Victorianism, several generalizations can be made about the century. It was a period free of the wars and revolutions which wracked the Continent. Protected by the Pax Britannica and motivated by its twofold faith in goodness and progress, Britain attained pre-eminence in the world for its stable and constitutional government and for its liberal creed. Until the latter part of the century a certain unity of spirit was recognizable in the nation, brought about by national security, self-confidence, a common moral code based on religious duty, and a belief in the efficacy of utilitarianism and the superiority of British institutions. Real wages increased and the condition of the poor improved substantially. By the turn of the century conditions demanded a new structure of society, and Victorian liberalism gave way to liberal socialism.

The Age of Progress

The almost universal faith in progress, bulwarked by eighteenth-century rationalism and by the persuasiveness of a religion of duty and of political liberalism, was everywhere in evidence, but most of all in England's material prosperity and in the rapid expansion of the economy. In almost every area except architecture, the nineteenth century had geniuses.

Condition of the People. By every statistical index the population of Britain was more numerous, better fed, better housed, more healthy, more literate, and better governed in 1914 as compared to 1815. The rate of material progress which was made possible by British inventions and Britain's headstart in the industrial revolution also helped to liberate the mind from ignorance and old fear. However, modern fears appeared in the guise of mass unemployment and scientific war. As a result of evangelical and utilitarian concern, the public conscience had been awakened, and a growing sense of responsibility for social and economic misery was in evidence. Private charity was increasingly supplemented by massive state assistance, such as the Old Age Pensions Act and the National Insurance Act. Population figures rose from nine million in 1801 to thirty-two million in 1901; the increase due largely to a fall in the death-rate. Real wages in 1900 were almost double the figure for 1850 as the benefits of the industrial revolution were beginning to be more equitably shared.

The Laboring Class. The urban laborers had borne the brunt of the miseries resulting from the dislocations and revolutionary changes of the Industrial Revolution. But in the nineteenth century conditions of the working class improved through such legislative help as factory and public health acts, free elementary education after 1870, old age pensions, more leisure and open spaces, better entertainment, and the growth of trade unions. As the franchise was gradually expanded, workers sensed their political influence and used this power for practical legislative goals. Nevertheless, class differences remained substantial, and in 1900 one-third of the wage earners of Britain still lived in chronic poverty.

Industrial Expansion. The engineering industry and new markets sustained the rapid industrial expansion of the first part of the century. Britain's natural resources, superior industrial organizations, financial stability, and merchant navy prompted an enormous increase in trade. Between 1850 and 1870 exports of coal increased 500 per cent; the exports of iron and steel goods 400 per cent. In 1856 Henry Bessemer's invention which produced steel cheaply in large quantities gave Britain the lead in steel manufacture. This prosperity, in turn, permitted British companies to develop and invest in the economies of other countries. Not until the 1870's was Britain threatened by Germany and the United States as serious competitors. Thereafter, Britain gradually declined from a position of unchallenged industrial leadership.

Transportation. The full effects of the industrial revolution could not be realized until cheaper and more rapid and reliable methods of transportation were available. The revolution in transportation, begun in the eighteenth century, was accelerated in the nineteenth.

Roads. All-weather macadamized roads (1819) and the removal of tolls permitted rapid transportation of commodities and regular wagon and stage coach services between manufacturing centers. Main roads came under the control of the county councils in 1888.

Railways. George Stephenson began the era of the modern railway with the opening of a line between Manchester and Liverpool in 1830 which became an immediate success. Between 1825 and 1837 ninety-three Railway Acts of all kinds were passed by Parliament. By 1848 some five thousand miles of railways were laid;

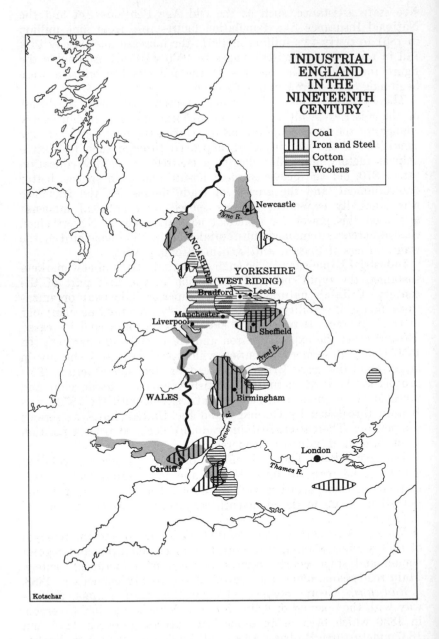

INDUSTRIAL
ENGLAND
IN THE
NINETEENTH
CENTURY

Coal
Iron and Steel
Cotton
Woolens

Newcastle

Tyne R.

LANCASHIRE

YORKSHIRE
(WEST RIDING)

Bradford • • Leeds

Manchester •
Liverpool •
Sheffield

Trent R.

WALES

Birmingham

London

Cardiff

Severn R.

Thames R.

Kotschar

thereafter, consolidation of the rival lines began. Railways, with their cheapness of travel, investment possibilities, and encouragement of heavy industries, helped change the economic structure of the country.

Steamships. Marine freight was another source of wealth because Britain carried nearly two-thirds of her foreign commerce in her own ships. Regular transatlantic steam navigation dates from 1838, but steam tonnage did not catch up with sail until 1883. By that time the problem of the vast space needed for coal storage had been solved by new types of marine engines and the iron hull. The introduction of iron, which the country had in large quantities, made Britain the world's leading shipbuilder. Construction of the Suez Canal (1869) shortened the voyage from England to India and made shipping even more profitable.

Agriculture. The rapid fall of the price of grain after 1815 and the setback suffered by the repeal of the Corn Laws created an agricultural slump. There followed twenty years of prosperity (1853-73) as a result of new tools and machines, better fertilizers, and the opening up of distant markets through railway transportation. However, English farmers could not compete with the cheaper grain from North America or with the meat and dairy products shipped by refrigerated freighter from Australia and New Zealand. Lower food prices benefited the city dweller, but free trade ruined the farmer.

Scientific Achievements. The typical Englishman exulted in the impressive scientific advances of the nineteenth century because they fit in so properly with his idea of progress and material well-being. Charles Darwin's *On The Origin of Species* (1859) revolutionized man's conception of the processes of evolutionary development with its emphasis on "natural selection."

Physics and Chemistry. In 1808 John Dalton introduced a scientific theory concerning atoms which between 1857 and 1879 was elaborated upon by James Clerk Maxwell and J. P. Joule. Clerk Maxwell developed the kinetic theory of gases and established the existence of atoms as real substances. Electromagnetic waves were established theoretically by Michael Faraday, mathematically by Clerk Maxwell; most electric machinery depends upon Faraday's principles. Joule concluded from experiments that heat was a form of energy and recorded the amount of energy necessary to produce a given amount of heat. Lord Kelvin established the principle of degradation of energy, proving that in every transfer of energy some escapes and is therefore less available.

Medicine. James Simpson, a professor of medicine, was the first to use chloroform as an anesthetic. In 1876 Lord Lister established aseptic surgery after his success in the antiseptic treatment of open wounds. Edward Jenner had introduced vaccination against small-pox in the eighteenth century. With the identification of bacilli, vaccines were now developed for other diseases.

Sanitation. Victorian insistence on cleanliness as an outward sign of respectability encouraged both personal hygiene and sanitary regulations for towns and factories. Baths, indoor plumbing, and hot water became available to large numbers. Treitschke declared that "the English think Soap is Civilization." [1] Sewage systems, purified running water, and health legislation were introduced in most municipalities. Disraeli's Factory Act of 1878 included detailed provisions for maintaining cleanliness and proper ventilation in shops and factories.

Geology and Biology. In 1830 Charles Lyell offered a comprehensive explanation of the history of the earth as traced by the record of rocks and fossils. His theory, published in *Principles of Geology,* emphasized the natural and evolutionary development of the earth. In biology Charles Darwin's theory of organic revolution changed a static Newtonian world into a universe of constant change and growth. His advancement of the theory of evolution affected not only the sciences, but many other fields of thought as well. Darwin's hypothesis can be observed in the philosophy of Herbert Spencer, the ethics of Thomas Huxley, the poetry of Tennyson, and in the prose of George Meredith and Matthew Arnold.

Nineteenth-Century Life and Thought

There was no single Victorian theme in literature or in thought because the century encompassed figures as diverse as John Henry Newman and William Morris, or William Wordsworth and John Stuart Mill. However, Victorian life and thought was influenced by the implications of the industrial revolution and the Newtonian and Darwinian conceptions of the universe. Literature, art, religion, and philosophy kept struggling with the questions of mechanism and freedom, empiricism and idealism, creationism and continuity.

Three Phases of Victorianism. Peace, progress, and political liberalism characterized most of the century bounded by the Napoleonic Wars and the First World War. However, the age can be described more accurately in smaller units since Queen Victo-

---

[1] Cited in G. M. Young, *Victorian England: Portrait of an Age* (Oxford: London, 1953), p. 24.

ria's long reign put an illusory uniformity on a period of time in which ideas, manners, and values changed profoundly.

Early Victorianism, 1815-50. Britain accepted the gradual democratization of government and society after the public conscience had been stirred by the ideas of the American and French revolutions and by the convictions of English utilitarians and Evangelicals. National institutions made adjustments to absorb this democratic radicalism and to make England a leader in world opinion at the same time that her industrialization and inventiveness made her preeminent in the production of manufactured goods. By mid-century Britain was near the peak of her power and prestige, confident in the belief that economic prosperity based on free trade and parliamentary institutions could bring happiness and peace.

Mid-Victorianism, 1850-70. This era was the apex of Victorian self-confidence, devotion to duty, and faith in the efficacy of political Liberalism. Generally, English industrial and naval power was used to advance liberalism abroad; in England the accent was on freedom for the individual citizen. Although contemporary critics attacked the easy supremacy and the bourgeois values of the period, the prevailing belief remained firm in the inevitability of progress to solve the nation's problems and to keep England great. To sit in Parliament was the highest ambition of an educated Englishman.

Late Victorianism, 1870-1914. Britain's industrial and commercial supremacy no longer went unchallenged, and militarism and industrial rivalry jeopardized the Pax Britannica. The rest of the world had not been converted to either free trade or to parliamentary democracy. Liberalism, free trade, political compromise, and mid-Victorian moral values were undermined by their failure to guarantee security to the English citizen in a world of aggressive nationalism and impersonal economic forces. In the search for new goals ancient values and institutions were no longer revered or even respected. Novel political, economic, and social forces, such as trade unionism and woman suffrage, demanded recognition.

Victorian Morality. Victorianism was a reaction against the loose morality of the Regency period. Along with the smugness and philistinism which critics such as Matthew Arnold exposed, there were found the characteristic virtues and moral values of a society molded by business interests, Evangelicalism and humanitarianism. Industriousness, self-help, religious duty, Sabbath observance, propriety of moral conduct, liberality of mind, and the stability of family life were the unquestioned standards of the times. Nevertheless, the exceptions to these standards, as seen in the non-conformity of William Thackeray, Oscar Wilde, George Meredith, or Edmund Yates, were so numerous that the stereotype of the age may be more limiting than illuminating, because Victorians were equally engaged in shedding the cant and maudlin sentimentality inherited from the late eighteenth century. The moral fiber and the continuity of national institutions provided the cohesiveness and the astonishing readjustment to change which really marked the century.

Religion. Probably in no other century, except the seventeenth and perhaps the twelfth, did religion, or men such as Gladstone or Charles Kingsley speaking in the name of religion, exercise so much influence. Evangelical convictions, shared by Nonconformists and Anglicans alike, placed high value on Bible reading, upright conduct, moral discipline, and seriousness of purpose. This sense of duty and the satisfaction of such stewardship explains, in part, the Victorian admiration for missionaries, statesmen, and writers, such as Livingstone, Gladstone, and Tennyson. By the latter part of the nineteenth century the catholicity of this religious code disappeared as scientific knowledge increased, Biblical criticism arose, and conventional Christianity was put on the defensive by the attacks of Darwin's followers. Within the church the issue of Fundamentalism versus liberalism was dividing theologians and laymen.

The Universities. Thomas Arnold (1795-1842), headmaster of Rugby, incorporated a sense of service and idealism into the public schools of England by overhauling the curriculum and placing greater emphasis on character training and the obligations of Christian citizenship. The need for reform of institutional life and curricula at the universities was equally evident, but the changes were less striking than those in secondary education. Some internal reforms occurred, and new courses in moral and natural sciences were added before Parliament forced reform in the government of the universities by acts in 1854 and 1856. By 1871 all religious restrictions were abolished. In 1836 the University of London was founded, and in 1848 it granted admission to women students.

Literature. Nineteenth-century literature was remarkable for its diversity of style and content. Wit, drollery, social satire, elegant essays, novels, serious criticism, and tales of adventure appealed strongly to an increasingly literate nation. In no other century did literature have such a popular impact.

Romanticism, 1798-1832. The major Romanticists in this period were the poets William Wordsworth (1770-1850), Samuel Coleridge (1772-1834), Lord Byron (1788-1824), Percy Shelley (1792-1822), John Keats (1795-1821), and the poet-novelist Sir Walter

Scott (1771-1832). In reaction to the neoclassicism of Pope and Johnson with its emphasis on order and classical forms, the Romanticists consciously broke away from these conventions and stressed some or all of the following characteristics: (1) interest in the common man and in simple language, (2) a revival of medievalism, (3) an appreciation of nature, (4) an accent on spontaneity and feeling in the writing of poetry, and (5) faith in the individual which often prompted support of democracy. Byron and Shelley rebelled against the old social order and literary forms and stirred not only a literary revolution with their passionate idealism and novel imagery, but also affected political and social attitudes of the time. Wordsworth and Coleridge were eloquent advocates of liberty and sympathized with the French Revolution. In 1798 they published jointly their *Lyrical Ballads* which introduced simple, rustic themes written in a style of language "really used by men."

Victorian Poetry. Alfred Lord Tennyson (1809-92), sentimental and romantic in inclination, was the most popular of the Victorian poets and became poet laureate in 1850. His *In Memoriam* (1850) is one of the great elegies in English poetry. Robert Browning's (1812-89) poetry was more erudite and original than Tennyson's but was never fully understood by the public and therefore not as popular. Among his finest poems are *The Bishop Orders His Tomb* and *The Ring and the Book*. Elizabeth Barrett Browning's (1806-61) intense feelings and poetical fluency are reflected in her *Sonnets from the Portuguese*. Her *Cry of the Children* gave poetic support to social reform. Dante Gabriel Rossetti (1828-82) and his sister, Christina, were founders, with others, of the Pre-Raphaelite Brotherhood, a group of poets and painters who turned to the themes of the Middle Ages for inspiration. William Morris (1834-96), artist, designer, and poet, revealed his love for the romantic past and for beauty for its own sake in *The Earthly Paradise* and *The Defense of Guenevere and Other Poems*. His socialistic convictions were expressed in *News from Nowhere* and *A Dream of John Ball*. Algernon Swinburne (1837-1909) defied the conventional Victorian mores by writing sensual and pagan lyrics. His metrical skill was not only flawless but also fascinatingly complex in execution.

Victorian Novelists. The novel attained pre-eminence in the nineteenth century. The inimitable Charles Dickens (1812-70) caricatured and sentimentalized Victorian Londoners in such moving stories as *David Copperfield, Oliver Twist,* and *A Tale of Two Cities.* William Thackeray, a contemporary of Dickens, was a master character-painter and satirist of the English upper classes. Avoiding sentimentality, he used subtle wit to expose the sham and hypocrisy of society in such novels as *Vanity Fair, Pendennis,* and *Henry Esmond.* Mary Ann Evans (1819-80), writing under the pseudonym of George Eliot, revealed effective character analysis amidst stern moralizing in *Silas Marner* and *Mill on the Floss.* The Brontë sisters portrayed much of their ill-starred lives in *Agnes Grey* and *Jane Eyre.* Charles Kingsley (1819-75) was a Christian socialist who sympathized with the working men in *Yeast,* attacked evolution in *Water Babies,* and dramatized Elizabethan adventure in *Westward Ho.* Benjamin Disraeli's brilliant and cynical novels *Vivian Gray* and *Coningsby,* examined the different social classes of England. Anthony Trollope (1815-82) modeled his writing after Thackeray and described the respectable people of a cathedral town in *Barchester Towers.* George Meredith (1828-1909) was an intellectual poet and novelist. In novels such as *The Egoist* he is primarily concerned with a psychological study of his characters.

Periodical Literature. Magazines and literary reviews in nineteenth-century England became famous for the high caliber of their editors and contributors, and for the instruction of their reading audience. The *Edinburgh Review,* a Whig quarterly, was founded in 1802. Its rivals were the Tory *Quarterly Review* (1809) and *Blackwood's Edinburgh Magazine* (1817). In 1841 *Punch* began publication as a humorous weekly; its contributors took great delight in lampooning opponents of social reform. The first issue of the *Cornhill Magazine,* edited by William M. Thackeray, appeared in 1860.

Literary Crosscurrents. By the end of the nineteenth century the comfortable supremacy, the unity, and the liberal creed of Victorian England were in retreat. The apprehension and confusion of these years in which social and political forces produced such rapid change were apparent in the literature. A variety of themes and trends resulted which defy classification as writers searched for new values. Influenced by continental writers, the aesthetic school of the 1890's emphasized the symbolic, the sensual, and the worship of ideal beauty. William Butler Yeats (1865-1939) and Oscar Wilde (1854-1900) were the only significant aesthetes. Wilde won fame for his witty comedies, Yeats for his lyrical expressions of Irish nationalism. The novelists of these years were superior to the poets in both the quality and volume of their writing. Samuel Butler's (1835-1902) novel, *The Way of All Flesh,* followed the tradition of the French naturalists, but focused on the author's spiteful comments on Victorian values and against his own family.

Other writers also challenged the art for art's sake school by their accent on rugged action and the romance of adventure. Robert Louis Stevenson (1850-94) became popular with such blood-and-thunder adventure tales as *Treasure Island* and *Kidnapped*. Rudyard Kipling (1865-1936) voiced in verse and prose the imperial glories of the Empire, with special attention to the British "mission" in India. Joseph Conrad (1857-1924) was perhaps the most original of these novelists. The color, rhythm, and psychological probings of his characters are well portrayed in *Lord Jim* and *Heart of Darkness*. Thomas Hardy (1840-1928) wrote beautiful short lyrics and pessimistic novels, such as *Tess of the D'Urbervilles* and *Jude the Obscure*, that were superb in their intimate knowledge of character and of the English countryside. Sir Arthur Conan Doyle (1859-1928) created the brilliant fictional detective hero, Sherlock Holmes. Turn-of-the-century writers and Fabian reformers were H. G. Wells (1848-1946), who wrote about pre-war England with humor and understanding and George Bernard Shaw (1856-1950), Britain's outstanding dramatist of the twentieth century.

Victorian Thought. The industrial revolution wrought such startling changes in the economic, political, and social organization of society that it spawned an intellectual revolution which embraced the world of science. At the same time critics resisted its dehumanizing effects. For many, evolution, material determinism, utilitarianism, and political liberalism were admired as hallmarks of progress. Others feared that individuality of character, beauty, and spiritual values were sacrificed for a bourgeois and mechanistic culture.

Darwin and his School. The publication of *On The Origin of Species* in 1859 which set forth the hypothesis of natural selection not only unsettled many Victorians who believed in the instantaneous creation of the universe, but also upset those who claimed there was some purpose or desirable end in progress. Darwin's evolutionary theory implied only blind, mechanical chance. Undisturbed by the limitations placed by Darwin on his theory, his followers applied the Darwinian hypothesis to society. The philosopher Herbert Spencer (1820-1903) coined the phrase, "survival of the fittest," and applied Darwin's theory of natural selection to social institutions and to the study of humanity; Thomas Huxley (1825-95) popularized Darwin's writings and equated ethics with a scientific understanding of life; and Matthew Arnold (1822-88) applied Darwin's theory of evolution to Christianity.

Critics. For all its buoyant self-confidence Victorian England was saved from complacency by self-criticism. The crass public taste and the worship of material success were indicted by masters of social criticism. Thomas Carlyle (1795-1881) was a Puritan moralist who lashed out at the mechanization and loss of spirituality in Victorian England. *Past and Present* and *The French Revolution* reveal his explosive and eccentric style and his doctrine of hero worship. John Ruskin (1819-1900) aroused public consciousness to the ugliness of the machine age in art and architecture. Ruskin later turned from aesthetics to ethics and economics and wrote on behalf of industrial and social reform. Matthew Arnold who was celebrated as a literary and cultural critic was also a serious Biblical scholar who repudiated literal interpretation of the Bible. His *Culture and Anarchy* was the most devastating critique of the three social classes of mid-Victorianism. John Henry Newman (1801-90), a leader in the Oxford Movement, retained independent views on religion and education even after his conversion to Roman Catholicism. Newman's intellectual achievement and spiritual integrity are compassionately exhibited in the *Apologia pro Vita Sua*. His keen analysis of the value of classical education is presented in the polished prose of *The Idea of a University*.

Historians. Robert Southey (1774-1843), poet laureate and historian, wrote important biographies of Nelson and Wesley. Thomas Carlyle provided fiery and didactic works, such as *Oliver Cromwell's Letters and Speeches, The French Revolution,* and the *History of Frederick the Great.* Whig interpretations of English history, glorifying Parliament, progress, and Protestantism, dominated the nineteenth century especially in the works of Thomas Babington Macaulay (1800-59), George O. Trevelyan (1838-1928), and John Richard Green (1837-83).

Walter Bagehot. In his *English Constitution* (1867) Bagehot discussed the two parts of English Government—the dignified, such as the role of the monarchy, and the efficient. He attempted to show the superior workings of the British cabinet system over the American form of government.

John Stuart Mill and Democratic Liberalism (1807-73). Utilitarianism had served to liberate Englishmen from restrictions and abuses but did not solve economic problems relating to the industrial economy. Personal freedom had failed to bridge the gap between the wealthy employer and the impoverished worker. Classical economists, such as Adam Smith, Thomas Malthus, and David Ricardo, said nothing could be done about it in a free society; the whimsicalness of the law of supply and demand was simply a fact of life. At first Mill accepted their economic doctrines until he viewed the wretched conditions of the factory towns. Then he urged major reforms which included (1) distribution of wealth by means of a progressive income tax, (2) universal education, (3) trade unions to improve the bargaining position of the worker, (4) limitations on inherited wealth through death duties, and (5) community factories to permit workers to share in the profits of their place of employment. Mill saw the same problems as Marx and the Socialists, but supported neither, fearing that Marxian violence and rapid change could introduce greater ills, and that the Socialists' demand for government controls of production would tyrannize a free society. Mill is thus a transitional figure between the eighteenth-century concept of English liberalism, which attempted to free the individual from restrictions, and the twentieth-century concept, which emphasizes a society that provides economic and social security and freedom from exploitation, perhaps at the expense of freedom of action.

Victorian Government

The prestige and influence of nineteenth-century England was derived as much from her political inventiveness as from her industrial supremacy. Without repudiating the traditional forms of institutions, the Victorians adapted their political system to reconcile the demands of a mass electorate with the governing classes within Parliament. Such devices as the party and cabinet systems, civil service examination, and the extension of the franchise permitted democratic change without destroying the continuity of political institutions.

State Intervention. Benthamism with its principle of "the greatest happiness for the greatest number," along with Evangelical and Nonconformist convictions were incorporated into laissez-faire arguments to buttress the opinion that less law would provide more liberty. This doctrine helped abolish political and religious disabilities and the Corn Laws. But its negative interpretation failed to relieve the glaring economic and social inadequacies of industrial England which could not be changed by individual effort. Edwin Chadwick, John Stuart Mill, and the Fabians, transformed Bentham's principle into a positive doctrine which urged massive state intervention to relieve economic misery and to bring about social reform. Government regulations of industry, municipal ownership of utilities, a national education act, and the reorganization of local government were the results.

Institutional Change. Unlike France in the nineteenth century, institutional change in England did not occur through sudden alterations in the form of government, but by modifications and adaptations of the functions and relationships of existing institutions. The political history of one generation became the constitutional practices of the next. Britain remained a constitutional monarchy, but power moved from Parliament to the people.

The Status of the Crown. The monarch remained the most prominent symbol in the political system. Under Queen Victoria the dignified role of the monarchy was enhanced. The Hanoverian rulers who had preceded her were neither loved nor admired by their subjects. Beginning with Queen Victoria, the monarchy was saved by the caliber of the rulers. Admired and, at the end of her reign, venerated, she became the embodiment of the English character and the focal point of the British Empire. The symbolic and emotional significance of the monarchy now outstripped its political functions, although Victoria took an active interest in affairs of state and was outspoken in her opinions on ministerial choices. But the fact remains that after 1839 ministries were formed which the electoral or parliamentary situation demanded despite the Queen's preferences. Her rejection of Peel in favor of Melbourne in 1839 was the last time that the monarch selected a Prime Minister who did not have the support of a parliamentary majority.

The Cabinet. The British cabinet system is essentially the growth of conventions. The transformation of the Cabinet from a group of ministers, responsible to and chosen by the King, to an executive body governing in the King's name and responsible to the majority in the House of Commons, was a gradual process. Whereas the American cabinet system accents the separation of powers, the British arrangement emphasizes the close union of the executive and legislative powers. A cabinet minister *must* be a member of Parliament. Under Queen Victoria cabinet government and homogeneity of cabinet policy became a constitutional convention. Ministers who differed on policy left the Cabinet. As the franchise was expanded and as sovereignty shifted to the people, it became necessary for the Cabinet to become responsible to the House of Commons in order to justify staying in office. In the nineteenth century the Cabinet usually consisted of some sixteen to twenty members.

Parliament. The nineteenth century was the golden age of the private member of Parliament because rigid party discipline had not yet demanded an automatic party vote. Before the century was over Parliament had achieved effective control of the administration and made it responsible to the House of Commons. In turn, the House of Commons became more representative of the people as the removal of religious and property restrictions for membership made it possible for Dissenters, Roman Catholics, Jews, atheists, and the laboring classes to sit in Parliament; women were admitted in 1918. Beginning with Robert Peel and his Tamworth Manifesto, candidates published their views on public questions. This foreshadowed the political platform (the Newcastle Program of 1892) and the practice of "going to the people" to settle a controversial question, as Home Rule for Ireland. Parliamentary procedure became more elaborate as closures on debate were introduced and standing committees established. The Speaker of the House of Commons became nonpartisan. The power and prestige of the Upper House diminished as the political system became democratized, although the membership of the House of Lords more than doubled during the century to over four hundred. The Parliament Act of 1911 formally asserted the secondary role of the House of Lords.

Party Organization. In earlier centuries political parties were often deplored as factions conspiring to divide the nation. During the nineteenth century parties acquired their organizational form, first on a local basis and later nationally. By 1900 parties were not only tolerated but also had become an essential mechanism of the parliamentary system. The growth of party organization was a direct result of the expansion of the electorate. Its purpose was to get out the vote and help get the candidate elected. Parties provided a mandate for some sort of cabinet government and permitted the growth of an "alternative Government." The duty of Her Majesty's Loyal Opposition was to oppose and to keep the Government honest and responsible. Party whips date from 1714 when the office of Patronage Secretary to the Treasury was created. Party organization grew out of the requirements for voter registration in the Great Reform Bill. A political committee, closely associated with the whip, emerged in each party and maintained contacts with local party agents. In 1861 the Liberals set up the first National Liberal Registration Association. In Birmingham Joseph Chamberlain had organized such an effective municipal machine, controlled by a central committee (caucus), that it was expanded to a national party organization in 1877. With its establishment and success the independent candidate and the minor party became victims of the two-party system.

The Civil Service. The vast expansion of the civil service was one index of the increased functions of the state. In 1832 civil servants numbered 21,300. By 1914 some 280,000 were employed. The increasing congestion of parliamentary business and the technical nature of much legislation resulted in much wider discretionary powers (called delegated legislation) being granted to government departments. Patronage was replaced by competitive civil service examinations in 1855 in which the caliber of the candidate's education played an important part. After 1870 all administrative grades were filled by university-level exams.

Local Government. In 1835 municipal councils, elected by rate-payers, were set up in the towns. The Local Government Acts of 1888 and 1894 abolished the numerous appointed and elective local boards and councils in the counties by setting up two new elective units of local government, the County Councils and County Boroughs. These councils managed administrative business and social services formerly handled in an erratic manner by the dozen over-lapping local councils. Social services were improved and expanded under municipal ownership.

Reform of the Judiciary. Complaints over the complicated and competing forms of pleading in various courts led to piecemeal legislation to correct such abuses as the absence of trial by jury in the court of chancery. The whole judicial system, however, was rearranged by the Judicature Acts of 1873 and 1875. A high court of justice took over the jurisdiction of the king's bench, common pleas, and exchequer courts and the probate and divorce divisions. The jurisdiction of the new high court of justice was divided into chancery, king's bench, and probate, admiralty, and divorce. The act also established a court of appeal to hear pleas from these three divisions.

The Waning of Victorian Liberalism. The 1906 election marked the climax of the nineteenth-century reform movement. By that time most of the objectives of earlier Victorian Liberalism were won. England was a parliamentary democracy, and religious and political restrictions on the individual had been removed. Although the moral liberalism of Campbell-Bannerman and John Morley and the social liberalism of the party were still recognizable, the new age checkmated the idealist, reformist, and rational doctrines of the old liberal tradition. Evangelicalism and upper-middle-class rule were being replaced by new moral values and the political force of trade unionism and socialism. The Pax Britannica was jeopardized by mounting international tensions. Victorian Liberalism was simply unable to cope with the ideas and demands of "the New Unionism, the New Hedonism, the New Realism, the New Urbanity, and the New Woman." [2]

---

[2] Alfred E. Havighurst, *Twentieth Century Britain* (Row, Peterson: Evanston, 1962), p. 36.

Chapter 22 ✑ The Great War

The effects of four years of total war beginning with such abruptness and lasting seemingly forever, shattered the lives of a whole generation of Englishmen and produced a greater cleavage between prewar and postwar generations than in any previous conflict. The immediate effect of World War I was disillusionment; it became the explanation for everything that went wrong after the peace. Admittedly, conditions after the war accelerated the tempo of changes already taking place in English life; especially the loss of old beliefs and values, a shift of wealth to new classes, the emancipation of women, the introduction of conscription, and the expansion of state planning and controls under such far-reaching measures as the Defense of the Realm Act. Although these changes were near revolutionary in effect, they suggested no radical break with prewar trends. The war was not a catastrophe for England; in truth, the outbreak of hostilities diverted the disruptive domestic forces that were threatening to engulf Britain in a civil and class war over Ireland and in a general strike. International violence replaced the threat of domestic discord. Out of the war came a new view of the possibilities and powers of the state to bring about victory in war and social change in the postwar years.

The War Years

The German invasion of Belgium unleashed an emotional wave of patriotism that, at least for the first two years, gave England and the Empire almost complete unanimity of purpose in waging war against Germany. No one, however, expected that a general European war could last more than a few months. When the war of attrition dragged on, and the casualties mounted, the cautious Asquith was ousted in favor of the dynamic Lloyd George. He immediately organized a War Cabinet which provided the first highly centralized control of the war effort. The war was finally won in the West, where it began, when the Allies built up a preponderance of power and seized the offensive after American reinforcements arrived.

Background of the War. Between 1870 and 1914 there was an interval of armed peace as national rivalries and a series of diplomatic crises increased tension among European states until the breaking point was reached. Many explanations of the war's origin have been given. No one cause or country was solely responsible, although the fear that Germany was aspiring to a hegemony in Europe provoked Britain's entente with France and Russia as a defensive gesture. Nationalism, sharpened by imperial rivalries and jingoistic propaganda, was probably the most fundamental cause of the war. When war broke out in 1914, the alliance system worked against the localization of the conflict. Prior confrontations included: (1) The First Moroccan Crisis, 1905. German statesmen tested the strength of the recent Anglo-French Entente (1904) by challenging French domination of Morocco. Germany insisted on an international conference (Algeciras, 1906) and suffered a diplomatic defeat as her uncompromising attitude drew Britain, France, and Russia closer together. (2) The Bosnian Crisis. In 1908 Austria annexed Bosnia and Herzegovina in violation of the settlements made at the Congress of Berlin. The Kaiser backed his Austrian ally, and war was only averted when Russia withdrew her backing from the Balkan states. (3) The Second Moroccan Crisis, 1911. Germany sent a gunboat to Agadir to oppose French expansion in Morocco and to win concessions from France. Britain insisted on being consulted and took an active hand in the diplomacy. The crisis was relaxed when France ceded part of the French Congo to Germany in return for German recognition of French interests in Morocco. (4) The Balkan Wars, 1912-13. The Balkan states of Serbia, Bulgaria, Montenegro, and Greece joined to defeat their former overlord, Turkey. At London a peace settlement was reached (1913) when Britain restrained Russian and Serbian demands, and Germany made Austria conciliatory. After a bitter quarrel among the Balkan allies, Greece and Serbia conquered and partitioned Bulgaria. This development weakened Austria's prestige and threatened her polyglot empire. By 1914 the entire Balkan region was simmering over disputed territories and yearning for self-determination.

Declaration of War. The final diplomatic crisis that precipitated the First World War was the assassination of Archduke Francis Ferdinand, heir to the Austrian throne, on June 28, 1914, by Bosnians who were Serbian sympathizers. The Austrian government used this incident as an excuse to end the Serbian menace to its restless empire. With German approval, Austria sent Serbia an ultimatum so calculated as to be impossible to accept. On July 25 Serbia met all but one of the demands. Three days later Austria declared war on Serbia, despite the efforts of Britain's foreign secretary, Sir Edward Grey, to arrange an international conference. This time Russia did not back down but rather began to mobilize on July 30. Since the German war plan counted on a decisive victory in the West before Russia could effectively intervene in the East, Germany demanded Russian demobilization and French neutrality. When the ultimatums were rejected, Germany declared war on Russia August 1 and on France two days later. The Cabinet and public opinion in England were divided over whether to enter the war or to remain neutral until Germany violated a joint treaty obligation to respect the neutrality of Belgium. These events terminated British hesitation since it had long been a cardinal policy in Westminster that no hostile power should dominate the Low Countries. Britain sent an ultimatum to Germany when the latter invaded Belgium on August 4. However, no reply was received, and Britain declared war with Germany.

The War Effort. Both sides expected an old-fashioned, short war like the Franco-Prussian War of 1870 and planned accordingly. Germany pinned everything on the success of her Schlieffen plan—a blueprint which carefully anticipated the swift defeat of France in the west to avoid the traditional fear of a major war on two fronts. The plan failed and trench warfare, with its immobility and attrition, became the occupation of the western front. Thus the decisive factor in the long run was economic or logistic, rather than tactical. At the outbreak of the war, the Central Powers [1] had the superior position for a defensive war, better communications and better equipped armies, and a more centralized command. On the other hand, the Allies had control of the seas and greater reserves of manpower and war materials from overseas areas. These advantages became decisive as the war progressed. Total warfare was introduced as the entire economy, manpower, and willpower of the nation became absorbed in the struggle.

Campaigns in 1914. The prospects of a speedy and conclusive victory in France disappeared as Belgian resistance and the arrival of the British Expeditionary Force assisted the French in stopping the German advance at the first battle of the Marne. The Germans also failed to capture the Channel ports which would have cut Anglo-French communications. By December the battle line consisted of a series of trenches extending from Switzerland to the

---

[1] The coalition of Austria-Hungary, Germany, Bulgaria, and the Ottoman Empire.

coast. On the eastern front large Russian armies moved quickly into East Prussia where they met two disastrous defeats at Tannenburg and the Masurian Lakes. By the end of 1914 the eastern front had become stabilized; the Russians could defeat the Austrians, but the Germans with superior artillery, supplies, and organization systematically pushed back the Russians. Inferior communications, a shortage of munitions, and an utterly incompetent government crippled the Russian war effort. Before the end of the year Turkey joined the Central Powers.

Campaigns in 1915. Heavy casualties occurred on the western front as machine gun placements and barbed wire entanglements made obsolete the persistent infantry charges. By the end of the year Russia had lost Poland as well as a million troops on the eastern front. Bulgaria joined the Central Powers and helped to overwhelm Serbia, whereas Japan entered on the side of the Allies. Italy deserted the Triple Alliance and joined the Entente Powers after being enticed with promises of postwar spoils. To open the Straits and provide vital supplies to Russia, the British began the Gallipoli campaign in February. Blunders in planning and execution forced the British to withdraw in 1916 after heavy casualties. Winston Churchill, sponsor of the plan, became the scapegoat and lost his Admiralty post.

Campaigns in 1916. The Russians recovered from their costly defeats of 1915 and inflicted heavy losses on the Austrians. Roumania joined the Allies but suffered swift defeat by the Central Powers. On the western front the Germans at Verdun-sur-Meuse and the Allies at the Somme failed in their attempts at a major breakthrough. The losses were immense. The Somme offensive alone cost the British 400,000 casualties, the French 200,000, and the Germans 500,000. To rebuild her depleted ranks, Britain adopted compulsory military service for the first time. The only major encounter of the British and German navies occurred at the indecisive battle of Jutland. British losses were heavier, but the German fleet never again ventured out to challenge British control of the seas.

Campaigns in 1917. To end the stalemate and force Britain into a negotiated peace, Germany resorted to unrestricted submarine warfare in the hope of starving the island kingdom into submission. The German government announced that all shipping, enemy or neutral, approaching Great Britain would be sunk on sight. In April alone 875,000 tons of shipping were torpedoed. The ruthlessness of these sinkings helped bring the United States into the war that same month. Offsetting this gain was the military collapse of

Russia and the Bolshevik revolution in November which led to a separate and severe peace treaty dictated by Germany. German armies were now free to concentrate their entire resources on the western front. Here French morale cracked when their offensive collapsed, and the British and Canadians had to hold off the Germans in Flanders. The Allied position worsened when the Italian front was breached and the Italian army was routed at Caporetto. British victories in Mesopotamia and in Palestine, along with the entry of Greece into the war, brought about the defeat of Turkey.

Campaigns in 1918. In March the Germans began their last great offensive on the western front before United States manpower could provide the Allies with the balance of strength. Although the Germans made three successful drives, they could not sustain the attack. With the Allies finally in agreement on a united command under Marshal Foch, and with huge American forces assisting, the counter-offensive broke through the Hindenburg line in August. The four Central Powers were forced out of the war, one by one. On November 11 the German High Command surrendered before Allied armies reached German soil.

Other Fronts. Although the two main theaters were the eastern and western fronts, the war was fought around the world. Except in East Africa, German colonies were easy conquests for Japanese, British, South African, and Australian forces. In the Near East the British, assisted by the fabled exploits of T. E. Lawrence (Lawrence of Arabia), dismantled the Turkish Empire in 1917-18. Aerial warfare played a spectacular but comparatively minor part in the war.

The Home Front. Domestic controversy was sidetracked for the duration of the war as the conflict became a moral crusade that engulfed the emotions and the economy of the entire nation. Parliament dropped all controversial legislation, and opposition to the Government, within or without Parliament, was virtually nonexistent. What little dissent there was, was condemned as unpatriotic. For nine months normal party lines were observed. But when the prospects of a short war disappeared, the Conservatives insisted on sharing in the execution of the war effort. Prime Minister Asquith, pressured by Bonar Law and Lloyd George, brought eight leading Conservatives and one Labor member into a Coalition Cabinet in May, 1915. He muted the criticism of the munitions shortage by moving Lloyd George to the newly-created Ministry of Munitions. However, the Coalition Government of twenty-two members was too unwieldy an instrument with which to execute the quick and critical decisions necessary in a war of such magnitude. Nor was

Asquith, by temperament or experience, able to offer decisive leadership to the Cabinet or rally the country to face the consequences of a long war.

Easter Rebellion, 1916. The militant Sinn Fein extremists in Ireland exploited England's critical condition to stage a general uprising with the assistance of German arms. But the plans for Easter Sunday miscarried as British security blocked the landing of munitions, and Irish public opinion failed to support the Sinn Fein insurgents in Dublin. The rebels surrendered after a week of fierce fighting. Fifteen of their leaders were executed. Asquith shrank back from Lloyd George's imaginative proposal, supported by Unionist leaders, for Home Rule at once for the twenty-six southern counties. English failure to act completed the ruin of the Irish constitutional party. The discredited extremists became martyrs and heroes, and Sinn Fein, instead of dying, replaced the Irish Nationalists as the vital political force in Ireland.

Lloyd George. Asquith had already sacrificed two of his ablest colleagues, Richard Haldane and Winston Churchill, limited the authority of Lord Kitchener, Secretary of War, and agreed to a Coalition Government in order to satisfy his critics. But when the year 1916 brought increasing war weariness, heavy casualties, and no prospects of ending the war of attrition in France, public and press criticism of Asquith's leadership became strong. The nation wanted a man who could offer and demand the supreme effort necessary to win the war. Asquith had hesitated to exploit the emergency powers granted the Government, and his Cabinet was conspicuously lacking in co-ordination. His was the "last experiment in running a great war on the principle of laissez faire." [2] A small war council with full Cabinet power to administer the war effort was demanded by Lloyd George, Bonar Law, and William Maxwell Aitken, the newspaper publisher. Asquith retreated and agreed to the proposal until he realized that in such an arrangement he would be only a figurehead under Lloyd George. In the maneuvering that followed, Asquith resigned and refused to serve in the new coalition. Lloyd George became Prime Minister in December, 1916, backed by the Labor party and Liberal and Tory back-benchers—a revolt of the press and the people against the magnates of both old parties.

The War Cabinet. Lloyd George reorganized the central machinery of Government in order to conduct the war with more vigor and efficiency. A War Cabinet of five members (Lloyd

---

[2] A. J. P. Taylor, *English History, 1914-1945* (Oxford: New York, 1965), p. 34.

George, Bonar Law, Lord Curzon, Lord Milner, and Arthur Henderson) was small enough to meet frequently to exercise supreme command of the war effort. Other ministers were summoned only to discuss questions affecting their departments. This important constitutional change, like the creation of the two wartime Coalition Governments, was accomplished without electoral or parliamentary approval. In 1917 the War Cabinet was expanded on occasion into an Imperial War Cabinet, consisting of the prime ministers of the Dominions, a representative from India, and the colonial secretary, which co-ordinated the resources and fighting forces of the entire Empire.

A Nation at War. Under Lloyd George government control of the economy was greatly accelerated. Permission for this extension was granted by parliamentary action under three Defense of the Realm Acts (DORA). Government agencies managed shipbuilding, food production and distribution, and the supply of wool and cotton. War socialism had already placed munitions, coal, iron, steel, and railroads under state control. Conscription of manpower was necessary in 1916 to fill the ranks decimated by trench warfare. Food rationing began in 1918. The nation became accustomed to extensive state planning and observed the power of the state to bring about rapid social and economic adjustments. However, Englishmen were asking if such controls were effective only in wartime.

Peace and Politics

Lloyd George took advantage of the gratitude of the nation to hold an election in 1918 which perpetuated the Coalition Government into the postwar period. The Coalition candidates swept the election, but at the cost of splitting the Liberal party. The Prime Minister was a leading negotiator at the peace conference which attempted to obtain mutual security and a lasting peace. A compromise, but stern, peace treaty was finally agreed upon which failed to approach the idealism that President Wilson had anticipated in his Fourteen Points. The fundamental problem was that Allied co-operation collapsed at the moment of victory. The alliance against the Central Powers, like all coalitions, was formed *against* some one, not *for* something. With the enemy defeated, old rivalries and national self-interests were reasserted. The peace settlement was further complicated by impulsive promises, such as those made to Italy in the midst of the war, and feelings of vindictiveness toward Germany.

Cost of the War. Over ten million troops were killed and at least twenty million wounded: 760,000 British soldiers died and another 1,700,000 were wounded. Although other major belligerents (except the United States) suffered larger numbers, British losses were highly selective, because many of the casualties (before conscription was introduced) came from the families and public schools that had traditionally provided leadership in public life. The absence of this generation of young men was keenly felt by England twenty years later. Material destruction was slight in comparison to the invaded countries. The greatest loss was in the sinking of 40 per cent of the merchant fleet. More serious was the financial damage. Inter-allied debts were staggering, and New York replaced London as the world's banking center. The war cost Britain £9 billion, most of which was raised by borrowing so that the national debt was fourteen times greater in 1918 than in 1914. In the long run, the chief economic cost of the war was the ruin of foreign trade; Britain never regained the markets lost to Japan and the United States. More intangible, but equally real, was the moral bankruptcy which the war spawned. War psychology and hate propaganda encouraged a spirit of ruthlessness and insensitivity to individuality. After 1916 the savageness and senselessness of the war brought a feeling of disillusionment and futility.

Reforms of 1918. The war hastened the extension of political democracy. Women defense workers made such an important contribution that opposition to woman suffrage disappeared. The Representation of the Peoples Act gave the vote to women over thirty who occupied premises or land with a rental value of £5, or whose husbands did so. The statute also extended the male franchise by abolishing practically all property qualifications. The measure more than doubled the electorate and increased the membership of the House of Commons to 707. An Education Act improved the educational benefits of the working classes by making elementary schooling compulsory between the ages of five and fourteen. Furthermore, child labor was sharply limited; the act halted the large number of children discontinuing school at the age of twelve and becoming unemployed because of lack of skills.

The Coupon Election. With an electorate now swollen by the new franchise and eight years since the last election, Lloyd George had a strong case for a general election. Besides, the Prime Minister was at the peak of his prestige as "the man who won the war." Labor decided to withdraw from the Coalition, and Asquith and his wing of the Liberal party refused to support Lloyd George. The Conservatives and Lloyd George Liberals received a letter of support (the coupon) signed by Lloyd George and Bonar Law. At first, the Coalition candidates campaigned on a note of reconstruction and idealism. But the national temper wanted revenge upon Germany, and by the end of the campaign Lloyd George was appealing to the vindictive mood of the voters. Coalition candidates, largely Conservative, won in a landslide with 478 seats. The Asquith Liberals returned only 28. Labor, with 59 seats became the Opposition. The election introduced twenty-seven years of Conservative hegemony in British life, and postwar politics began in an atmosphere of bitter personal grievances among party leaders.

Peacemaking. By the end of the war the Hapsburg and the Ottoman empires had already disintegrated. The basic problem for the victors was the future of Germany. On this issue the diplomats were often the victims of such circumstances as the demand for a speedy settlement, the French obsession with security against another German invasion, the secret treaties made during the war, and the chauvinism of the victors.

The Fourteen Points. The armistice of November 11 was reached on the basis of President Wilson's Fourteen Points which reflected the ideals of nineteenth-century liberalism in calling for open covenants (treaties), freedom of the seas, removal of tariff barriers, reduction of armaments, and self-determination for subject people. The fourteenth point was the creation of an international organization to keep the peace.

Paris Peace Conference, 1919. Twenty-seven Allied nations sent delegates to the peace conference, but the dominant figures were President Wilson, Georges Clemenceau (Premier of France and chairman of the conference), and Lloyd George. With Italy's Premier Orlando, they formed the Big Four. Lloyd George mediated the differences between Wilson's high idealism and Clemenceau's nationalistic realism. The election victory had added to Lloyd George's prestige, while his mental agility was an advantage in bargaining with Clemenceau and Wilson. He favored reasonable terms of peace with moderate reparations, but popular criticism of his leniency moved him closer to the position of Clemenceau. Early ideals, such as self-determination, were sacrificed to appease the demands of Japan and Italy for territorial gains. Wilson was forced to make concessions but stood firm in his insistence on a League of Nations. The Big Four agreed on German disarmament, but argued bitterly over reparations as the urgency of finishing the draft aggravated the frenzied atmosphere of the conference.

Treaty of Versailles. Germany signed the treaty on June 28, 1919. Article I provided for a League of Nations. Another article placed the guilt for the war on Germany and her allies. Germany ceded Alsace-Lorraine to France; several border provinces to Belgium; portions of East Prussia, including a corridor to the Baltic Sea, to Poland; and Schleswig to Denmark. The Saar was placed under international control for fifteen years, and the Allies were to occupy the Rhineland for the same period. The Rhine's east bank was to be demilitarized. The German standing army was set at 100,000 men, an air force was forbidden, and only a token navy permitted. Furthermore, Germany lost her colonies and had to pay reparations.

Mandates. The German colonies and large portions of the Ottoman Empire were divided among the victors as mandates (trusteeships) under League auspices. Britain received Tanganyika and large parts of the Cameroons and Togoland in Africa. In the Near East Iraq, Palestine, and Transjordan came under British rule. The Union of South Africa received German South-West Africa, and the German Pacific Islands went to New Zealand and Australia.

Reparations. Lloyd George's position shifted during the election campaign to a harsh stand on reparations, contrary to his earlier persuasion, and to the armistice agreement, that reparations should be demanded only for damages to the civilian population. At Versailles he supported the inclusion of war pensions. In 1921 a reparations commission set the final figure at 32 billion dollars, an amount impossible for Germany to pay. Efforts to exact these reparations became one of the most explosive sources of friction among France, Britain, and Germany in the following years.

League of Nations. Wilson preferred an imperfect treaty with the League of Nations to a perfect one without it, because the League was to provide the processes that would promote peace and prevent, or punish, future aggression. He also hoped that this organization could prevent a recurrence of the international anarchy and tensions which had provoked the Great War. The main organs of the League were: (1) an assembly in which each member state had one vote, (2) a council of five permanent members (United States, Britain, France, Italy, Japan) and four elective, (3) a secretariat with limited executive functions, and (4) the World Court of Justice established at The Hague. Lloyd George had no trouble getting the treaty passed by Parliament. Only four members of the House of Commons opposed it. In contrast, the treaty was defeated in the United States Senate. Consequently, the United States retreated into isolationism and never joined the League.

Other Treaties. Within a year of Versailles treaties were also signed with Austria (Saint-Germain), Bulgaria (Neuilly), Hungary (Trianon), and Turkey (Sèvres). The treaty with Austria formally broke up the Hapsburg Empire which had already fragmented into such new states as Yugoslavia and Czechoslovakia on the general formula of self-determination. By 1920 there were eight new sovereign states in Europe.

Appraisal of the Peace. The Treaty of Versailles was soon attacked by John Maynard Keynes, the English economist, and by many other critics as a Carthaginian peace—utterly ruthless. It was true that nationalistic pressures undermined many of Wilson's Fourteen Points; however, to expect a just and moderate peace, given the dislocations and emotions of the time, was impossible. The Treaty of Versailles was less severe than the treaty Germany imposed on Russia after her withdrawal from the war in 1918. In retrospect, the peace turned out to be a half-way measure, neither harsh enough to keep Germany weak, nor moderate enough to conciliate Germany in the postwar years.

Chapter 23 ✌🏷 Britain Between the Wars

After World War I English politics were dominated by economics. Unemployment and a wildly-fluctuating trade cycle forced an agonizing reappraisal of the British economy. One of the casualties was free trade—an article of faith in the prewar Liberal creed. Other casualties of the inter-war years were British naval supremacy, the virtual disappearance of the Liberal party, and the failure of the League of Nations to provide collective security against aggression. For the most part, the two decades preceding World War II were years of disappointment and drift for England, although the rise of the Labor party to power and respectability and the imaginative evolution of the Empire-Commonwealth were significant achievements.

Aftermath of War, 1918-1924

The psychological exhaustion and the disenchantment resulting from World War I produced a desire for a return to normalcy as well as a mood of self-conscious frivolity and cynicism. However, the economic dislocation brought about by unemployment and the loss of foreign markets made reconstruction difficult. When the economy failed to recover satisfactorily, a new political alignment based upon economic class interests began to emerge. The Cabinet under Lloyd George achieved a workable solution to the Irish problem, but could not save itself. The fall of Lloyd George introduced a shifting alignment of minority and coalition Governments which became a political hallmark for the next two decades.

Economic Developments. The rapid demobilization of over four million troops within a year was facilitated by the boom of 1919-20 which absorbed most veterans into the economy. Wartime controls were also rapidly removed in an effort to return to the economic practices of prewar years. Reconstruction proceeded by the system of laissez-faire capitalism which had made England wealthy before the war. Unfortunately, world conditions had changed drastically, and Britain could no longer produce as efficiently as many of her competitors; nor were world markets found to replace those either lost to her competitors or curtailed by the economic nationalism stimulated by the war. Britain failed to live on her own resources and manpower, believing that the previous world-trade system would inevitably right itself. Inflation, strikes, and wage increases marked the boom until it broke suddenly in late 1921. The recession was brought on by the Government's slashing of expenditures, increased taxes, overproduction of primary products, and the fantasy of an insatiable world market. Prices and wages fell. From 1922 to 1929 unemployment jumped to two million and averaged 12 per cent of the labor force—double the prewar figure. The trade unions threatened a general strike in 1920, and the specter of an economic class war loomed near. The Government passed the Emergency Powers Act (1920), restoring its wartime emergency authority to meet the threat. Otherwise the decontrol of industry was accelerated. In 1921 Lloyd George lost working-class support when the striking miners were defeated in their effort to prevent the mineowners from cutting wages. The Government helped the working class by subsidizing the building of more than 200,000 houses and making housing another social service of the Government. The Unemployment Insurance Acts of 1920 and 1922 extended the original insurance scheme of 1911 to the entire working class. This assistance relieved worker discontent by making unemployment bearable—and another obligation of the state. However, no efforts were made to attack the fundamental causes of unemployment and low production.

The Irish Settlement. The Irish problem was the most explosive political issue facing the Coalition. Lloyd George achieved a settlement that kept both Catholic and Protestant Ireland within the Empire and avoided a major civil war in Ireland. However, no Irish solution could placate all parties involved, and the question once again sapped English political stability.

Undeclared War, 1919-20. In the general election of 1918 Sinn Fein members captured 73 of the 105 Irish seats. They refused to go to Westminster; instead, they went to Dublin and declared Ireland independent. An unofficial civil war followed as the Irish Republican Army and a special British occupation army—the Black and Tans—engaged in guerrilla tactics and terrorism.

Partition and Home Rule. World War I had effectively killed the chances of coercing Ulster into a united and independent Ireland, because their generous war services could not be repudiated to appease the rebellious south. Therefore, the fourth Home Rule Bill (1920) provided for the partition of Ireland and two single chamber Parliaments. Each would legislate for its own region except for a few reserved areas which remained under control of the British Parliament. The two Irish Parliaments were to set up a council to administer joint services. Ulster accepted the Government of Ireland Act, but the south ignored it, and fighting continued.

The Irish Free State. George V appealed for a truce, and Lloyd George offered Eamon de Valera dominion status for Ireland. In October, 1921, the Irish delegates, led by Arthur Griffith and Michael Collins, were persuaded to sign an agreement in London which set up the Irish Free State with the right of Ulster to withdraw—a right which it immediately exercised. The moderates among the Irish Republicans accepted independence and dominion status. De Valera led the intransigent faction in repudiating the Treaty ratified by the Irish Dail. In 1922 open warfare began in southern Ireland, this time between the pro-treaty party of Collins, which won the election, and de Valera's extremists. But by December of the same year, the Irish Free State came into existence with William T. Cosgrove as president of the executive council. The Irish settlement was Lloyd George's last great achievement before he was ousted as Prime Minister.

Fall of Lloyd George. The Tory backbenchers, under Stanley Baldwin, President of the Board of Trade, defied the coalition leadership and determined to contest the next election along party lines. They argued that Lloyd George would ruin the Conservative party just as he had divided the Liberals. Bonar Law's support of the backbenchers doomed the Coalition. On October 19, 1922, Lloyd George resigned and Bonar Law became Prime Minister. Contributing to Lloyd George's fall were (1) the Conservatives' suspicions of his dynamic and opportunist leadership and his indifference to party politics; (2) his militant pro-Greek policy in the Chanak crisis which angered many Conservatives and frightened a warweary public; (3) the loss of working-class support in the postwar years; and (4) the political repercussions of the Irish settlement.

Three-Party Politics. No political leader with Lloyd George's capacity or dynamism replaced him, partly because the mood of the populace preferred tranquillity to controversy and crisis. Labor emerged as the dominant party of the left, but the Liberal party refused to disappear. A parliamentary majority became difficult to achieve in the ensuing three-party contests. The Conservative hegemony of these inter-war years was assisted by the division among the Liberals, and by the withdrawal of the large Irish—and usually Liberal-Radical—bloc from Westminster.

Bonar Law's Government, 1922-23. Law formed a Cabinet largely from political unknowns because thirteen Conservative ministers of the Coalition refused to serve under him. He immediately called an election and campaigned on the platform of tranquillity and stability—a platform appropriate for the times and for the Prime Minister's conventional nature. The Conservatives won a clear majority of seats, but only 5½ million out of the 14 million votes cast. Six months later Law left office because of serious illness.

Stanley Baldwin's First Government, 1923-24. King George V chose Stanley Baldwin rather than Lord Curzon (deputy Prime Minister and foreign secretary) to succeed Law largely on the consideration that the Prime Minister should be in the House of Commons. The stolid conservatism and homely virtues of Baldwin appealed to the nation as he eulogized the old virtues of faith, hope, love, and work as the salvation of the country. Within six months he called a surprise election to win a mandate for a protective tariff. The move restored party unity by encouraging Austen Chamberlain, Arthur Balfour, and Lord Birkenhead to rejoin the Conservative party. The election also unified the Asquith and Lloyd George factions on the one issue—free trade—that could bring the Liberals together. The Conservatives lost 90 seats, whereas Labor added 50. The Liberals with 158 seats became the balance of power.

The First Labor Government, 1924. Asquith refused to form a Coalition with the Conservatives, and in January, 1924, Baldwin resigned after losing a vote of confidence in Parliament. J. Ramsay MacDonald became Prime Minister of Britain's first Labor Government. The inexperienced Cabinet showed no more inventiveness than the Conservative Cabinet in dealing with unemployment and other domestic issues. Only the Housing Act (1924), which followed the pattern of the Conservative housing program, was successful. No doctrinaire Socialist program was possible under the circumstances because the Government depended upon Liberal votes for its majority. In foreign affairs MacDonald persuaded France to accept a moderate reparations settlement, but Labor's efforts to restore normal relations with Soviet Russia brought Conservative and mounting Liberal opposition. In October MacDonald's Government fell in the controversy over recognition of Russia forcing MacDonald to call a general election—the third in three years.

Foreign Affairs. After the Paris Peace Conference, Lloyd George took the lead in calling international conferences to promote the economic and financial reconstruction of Europe, but was unable to solve many problems. John Maynard Keynes's indictment of the Treaty of Versailles in his *Economic Consequences of the Peace* (1919) helped Britain to modify its position on German reparations.

But an Anglo-French rift developed when France took a hard line and demanded full measure. In 1923 efforts to exact reparations led to French occupation of the Ruhr and the collapse of German currency. The victimized German middle class considered France and the Treaty the causes of their misfortune. Prime Minister Mac-Donald persuaded the French to accept a plan proposed by Charles Dawes of the United States for stabilizing the German mark and systematizing the payment of reparations. France, with her obsession for security, made bilateral alliances with Belgium, Poland, and Czechoslovakia instead of relying on collective security as England had urged. At the Washington Disarmanent Conference of 1922 Britain abandoned her traditional naval supremacy in order to halt the expensive rivalry with the United States and Japan. A ten-year holiday on new naval construction was adopted, and the ratio of 5:5:3:1.75:1.75 in battleships was established respectively for Britain, the United States, Japan, France, and Italy. However, general disarmament did not follow.

Meanwhile Mustapha Kemal's successful nationalist revolution in Turkey caused the new Turkish government to violate clauses of the Treaty of Sèvres (1920) by routing the Greeks and occupying a neutral zone on the Asiatic side of the Straits. Lloyd George backed the Greeks, but the Conservatives in his Cabinet, along with Italy, France, and the Dominions had no interest in forcing the issue. War was averted, and the Treaty of Lausanne (1923) ended the Chanak crisis but encouraged the Conservatives to unseat Lloyd George.

Postwar Society. A political realignment, intimated in the election of 1906, became a fact after the war. No longer did the political leaders come from the same class or schools or share the same fundamental views of society. Even the term "middle class" had lost its magic. Political identity became increasingly associated with economic interests. The Right was united by opposition to socialism, fear of Soviet Russia, admiration for traditional British institutions and values, and advocacy of protection and limited government regulations. They also favored a political democracy led by the traditional governing class.

The Left drew its mass support from labor and its leadership from the trade unions, socialist societies, and dissident Liberals. They favored nationalization of major industries, opposed the gold standard, supported collective security abroad and friendship with Russia, and the extension of social services. They believed that "one man, one vote" inevitably demanded greater equalization of goods and services.

Thus the immediate postwar years reflected an inevitable reaction against war. The illusions of a better world failed to materialize for the returning soldier. Instead, the old order and the older generation continued to prevail. A lowering of standards occurred at all levels of public life. Indifference to world developments—a psychological isolationism—and the urge for self-indulgence and distraction introduced rapid changes in manners and social customs. The emancipated woman, the flapper, the birth of jazz, the popularity of commercialized sports and movies, and the increase of sexual freedom were indices of this change.[1]

Internal Developments, 1924-1939

The overriding spirit of these fifteen years was one of inertia and drift. Opinions were expressed and consciences prodded, but no positive program, or incisive action, was encouraged by the three Prime Ministers (Baldwin, MacDonald, Chamberlain) of the period. This pointless conservatism, that hesitated to offer a vigorous program of any sort, mirrored a nation seeking stability, normalcy, and peace. Baldwin weathered a general strike but failed to deal with the fundamental economic problems causing it. The economic crisis brought on by a world-wide depression resulted in a National Government. The centripetal pull of the National Government gave it great stability but no concerted program and left only an impotent Opposition that could not provide an alternative Government.

Baldwinism. In 1924 the Conservatives won an easy victory with 411 seats. They benefited from the collapse of the Liberals, who returned only 42 members, and from the Red scare introduced by the "Zinoviev letter" which had the effect of linking the Labor party with Russian Communism. Conciliatory and patient, Baldwin led a united party and a strong Cabinet into a period of prosperous normalcy. In 1925 the postwar economic crisis ended, Germany was stabilized, and British production, profits, and wages began to rise. Winston Churchill, chancellor of the exchequer and now a Tory, returned Britain to the prewar gold standard. This made the pound overvalued and handicapped overseas sales so that by 1929 the annual value of British exports was below the figure for 1925. In 1928 a new Representation of the Peoples Act gave women the vote on equal terms with men. But a conspicuous lack of leadership was evident in fiscal, educational, and unemployment policies.

---

[1] T. S. Eliot's *The Waste Land* (1922) portrayed symbolically the disjointedness of man and his environment during this period.

Social Welfare. The most vigorous action of Baldwin's second Government was in social legislation. Neville Chamberlain, minister of health, pushed through twenty-one bills. With government assistance 400,000 new dwellings had been built by 1929. The Widows, Orphans, and Old Age Pensions Act of 1925 extended the provisions of 1911. Relief benefits were reduced but extended indefinitely to all who were in need. The Local Government Act of 1929 reorganized county councils and reformed the ancient Poor Law structure by transferring the care of the poor to the county.

The General Strike, 1926. The mining industry had been chronically ill since the war, and four Government commissions had studied its problems. Wages in coal mines had lagged far behind the cost of living, yet the Government was preparing to end its subsidy; in addition, the mineowners wanted to slash wages. Neither management nor labor would accept the Simon Report on reorganization of the industry. The Trades Union Congress called a general strike, and for nine days in May some three million union members stopped working. The strike was neither violent nor revolutionary and was soon broken by Baldwin's firm stand, divided union leadership over the purpose of the strike, and the lack of public support. The prestige of Baldwin was at its peak, but he failed to take any constructive action; actually, he did nothing except to restrict the labor movement by the Trade Unions Act of 1927. The act declared all general strikes illegal and prohibited the use of trade union dues for political purposes unless so requested in writing by a member. As a result, union membership dropped almost 50 per cent.

The Second Labor Government, 1929-31. Baldwin fought the election of 1929 on the slogan of "Safety First." The Liberals under Lloyd George offered the most promising platform for increasing production and reducing unemployment. The election gave Labor 289 seats, the Conservatives 260, and the Liberals 58. For the first time, Labor was the leading party, crushing the center Liberals in spite of their spirited campaign. MacDonald began his second minority Government and within five months encountered the Great Depression which had spread from Wall Street across the Atlantic. By 1932 the steep drop in prices reduced purchasing power and increased unemployment in Britain to a peak of over 3 million. Britain was particularly susceptible to economic trends by reason of her reliance on world trade. Although the moderate Labor Government introduced a modest program of public works, the austerely orthodox Philip Snowden at the exchequer discouraged a major attack on unemployment, because current tax revenues could not finance any program of expansion. The Government attempted to mitigate the situation by palliatives, such as separating insurance from the dole and extending the latter, and by passing the Greenwood Housing Act (1930) to subsidize slum clearance. Such meager and traditional legislation was due, in part, to the obvious difficulties of a minority Government confronting a world depression. But it was also due to MacDonald's ineffective leadership which looked for excuses for inaction. Unable to find any unity of purpose among his ministers or to control his own Cabinet, much less the parliamentary Labor party, MacDonald seemed to have lost interest in the Labor program and was on better terms with the Conservatives than with many of his own party. In July, 1931, a parliamentary committee predicted a deficit of £120 million and warned of an approaching financial crisis. The May Report recommended increased taxes and retrenchment in government expenditures, including relief payments. On August 23 MacDonald resigned after the majority of his Cabinet and party opposed the proposed reduction of unemployment relief and pensions.

National Government, 1931-35. MacDonald was persuaded by George V to head a National Coalition Cabinet of four Laborites, four Conservatives, and two Liberals. The Labor party repudiated the new coalition, but the Liberals and Conservatives backed it. The Cabinet cut expenditures and abandoned the gold standard. In the general election of November, the National Government won 554 of the 615 seats. Labor, in opposition, was bitter over the "betrayal" of MacDonald and charged that the crisis had been a bankers' plot to ruin the Labor Government. MacDonald and Baldwin, in their unimaginative and unhurried manner, proposed the orthodox and conservative remedies of protection and frugality to counter the economic slump. The Keynesian theory of massive government interference in the economy to moderate the business cycle was incorporated in the American New Deal, but not in England.

End of Free Trade. The election of 1931 was considered a mandate for protection. The following year a general tariff was established, and at Ottawa an imperial preference and bilateral tariff bargains were negotiated. These changes further split the Liberal and Labor ranks and caused three Cabinet resignations, leaving the National Government overwhelmingly a Conservative Government.

End of Reparations. President Hoover granted a year's moratorium on reparations and war debts before the Lausanne Conference of 1932 virtually cancelled them. The United States, however, still insisted on the payment of war debts, although no reduction in the American tariff was offered to facilitate payment. France quickly ceased payments and Britain paid reduced installments until 1934; thereafter, she ceased payment altogether.

Government by Negation. In 1933 economic recovery began, not from Government action, but from a combination of rising productivity, wages and employment, a housing boom, and favorable terms of trade. By 1935 unemployment fell below two million, yet the recovery was erratic, and the concentration of mass unemployment in depressed areas accented the contrast between poverty and prosperity. The Unemployment Act, which consolidated the insurance and relief system, and the Special Areas Act of 1934, which attempted to move unemployed to more prosperous areas, were mild efforts to relieve unemployment. Nevertheless, the Government made no major effort to intervene in an economy which could not find work for two million of its citizens. A balanced budget, not deficit financing, was the order of the day. In this period economic nationalism and high tariffs had so shrunk international trade that British industry was heavily handicapped. However, little was done to adapt the economy to more domestic trade or to modernize the methods or equipment of the staple industries.

Election of 1935. Because of his health MacDonald resigned in June, 1935, and Baldwin, the real power in the Cabinet, began his third ministry. The November election gave Baldwin's conservative Coalition a vote of confidence with 428 supporters of the National Government successful at the polls. The Labor Opposition jumped from 59 to 154. Clement Atlee became leader of the Labor party after George Lansbury resigned in opposition to a Labor resolution supporting League sanctions against Italy. Atlee's mission was to heal the party which was sharply split over the question of defense. Foreign affairs increasingly occupied the attention of the Government. Ramsay MacDonald remained in the Cabinet under Baldwin until his death in 1937.

Abdication Crisis, 1936. George V, beloved and admired as the ideal constitutional monarch, died early in 1936. He was succeeded by Edward VIII, his eldest son, who was already popular at home and well-known throughout the Empire. For almost a year a self-imposed press censorship prevented the British from knowing of Edward's affection for Wallis Warfield Simpson, a twice-divorced American woman. Baldwin advised the King of the popular disapproval of such a match, whereupon Edward requested a morganatic marriage which would not make his wife the Queen. By this time the news had broken, and a constitutional crisis appeared imminent.

A "King's Friends" party was urged by Churchill and the Rothermere and Beaverbrook presses. But popular opinion, all three political parties, the Church of England, and the Dominion Prime Ministers strongly opposed the marriage. Baldwin handled the situation in a masterful manner in clearing the Abdication Bill by 403 to 5 votes. Edward VIII chose to abdicate rather than abandon the woman he loved. On December 12 his brother, the Duke of York, was proclaimed King George VI. The new monarch gave promise of a return to the esteem and admiration that was his father's, and British and Commonwealth allegiance to the monarchical institution was not jeopardized by the abdication.

Neville Chamberlain. Baldwin retired in 1937 after having presided jointly with MacDonald over British national life for fourteen unheroic years. The resourceful and patient Baldwin had revealed his tactical skill in weathering domestic problems and avoiding strong or controversial action as he had shunned such stronger personalities as Lloyd George and Churchill. He was replaced by Neville Chamberlain, a Conservative who had been in five previous Cabinets and had made his mark, in the tradition of his father, in the field of social legislation. Disraeli, Joseph Chamberlain, Lloyd George, and Neville Chamberlain were the architects of the welfare state that was erected by the Labor Government after the Second World War. Chamberlain had excellent training and ability in domestic affairs; however, he came to power, unfortunately, when foreign affairs were of critical importance. A man of rigid competence and integrity, Chamberlain deceived himself by insisting on handling foreign affairs as if they were commercial problems that could be negotiated by reasonable agreement and by rules of conduct that he considered fair and proper. The consequent disaster of his foreign policy dwarfed his earlier achievements as minister of housing and as chancellor of the exchequer.

Literature. The writings of the inter-war years revealed the disjointed spirit of the times. In the twenties the disillusionment and moral hangover flowing from the Great War was witnessed in the plays of Noel Coward (1899-), the novels of Aldous Huxley (1894-1963), the tragic and allusive poetry of T. S. Eliot (1888-1965), and the stream of consciousness method of James Joyce (1882-1941) and Virginia Woolf (1882-1941). In the thirties escapist fads and cults helped Englishmen get away from the inertia of the Government. Social concern revived, and the condition of England became the theme of such critical authors as J. B. Priestley (1894-) in *English Journey* and George Orwell (1903-1950) in *The Road to Wigan Pier*. The public mood was also reflected in

Coward's play, *Cavalcade* (1931) and Huxley's utopian nightmare novel, *Brave New World* (1932). Since the Right controlled the great newspapers, the Left voiced their opinions in the influential *New Statesman and Nation* and in the economic and political writings of G. D. H. Cole, Harold Laski, and Raymond Postgate.

The Sciences. John Maynard Keynes offered a new and revolutionary economic framework in his *General Theory of Employment, Interest and Money* (1936), but his ideas could not shake the economic orthodoxy of the National Government. In 1919 Sir Ernest Rutherford, director of the Cavendish Laboratory, published an account of his splitting of the nitrogen atom. This led to new fields of discovery in radio-physics and the development of radar in 1935 by Sir Robert Watson-Watt and Sir Henry Tizard. In 1929 Sir Alexander Fleming discovered penicillin. Most pioneer research was conducted at the universities so that during the interwar years Cambridge was recognized as the physics center of the world.

Imperial and Foreign Affairs: Locarno to Munich

Between the wars Britain was eminently more successful in imperial than in foreign affairs. The satisfactory evolution of the self-governing Dominions into the British Commonwealth of Nations was a unique achievement. Only Ireland and India were restless with their ties to Britain. In foreign affairs the quest for security culminated in the Locarno Pact and the Kellogg-Briand Treaty. Thereafter, Japan, Italy, and Germany undertook belligerent foreign policies when they discerned that collective security meant collective fear of strong action. Emboldened by the paralysis of League action and the failure of Britain and France to do anything more than protest, the dictators became aggressive. The thirties were a period of drift and lost opportunities for Britain. The mood of the country and of its leaders was that the risk of war was a greater fear than the growth of tyranny. By 1939 appeasement had produced both tyranny and war in Europe.

Indian Developments. World War I had greatly stimulated Indian nationalism, and in 1917 Britain agreed to the eventual granting of dominion status to India. The Government of India Act (1919) moved in this direction by introducing limited responsible government on the provincial level, and a two-chamber central legislature largely elected, but with real power reserved for the viceroy and his executive council. These concessions were too meager to satisfy Mahatma Gandhi and the Congress Party and prompted him to launch a campaign of nonviolent civil disobedience. During the twenties communal riots, marches, and increasing unrest resulted in a parliamentary commission under Sir John Simon which led to a round table conference in London in 1930-31. The wide differences in the proposals of the Hindus, Muslims, and the Indian princes brought about a constitutional impasse. Gandhi again resumed his civil disobedience campaign and was jailed by the British authorities. The Government of India Act, a British-made constitution, set up a federal system in 1935 with virtually full, responsible government in the provinces, and increased powers for the central legislature. The Conservatives in England felt that the act gave India too much autonomy. The Labor party and Indian leaders denounced it as short of the promised dominion status. World War II intervened before the act was fully implemented.

Dominion Nationalism. The response of the self-governing Dominions in World War I had been the supreme test of Britain's liberal philosophy of empire, and their magnanimous contribution was remarkable. The four Dominions sent one and one-half million men and India an equal number. Imperial unity was so pronounced that the imperial federalists, led by Lionel Curtis and his Round Table, anticipated its postwar extension. In 1917 the Imperial War Conference proposed continuous consultation and concerted action after the war which failed to materialize. The war stimulated Dominion nationalism more than interdependence, and as a result decentralization, rather than centralization, triumphed after the war. The Dominions insisted on signing the peace treaty and joining the League of Nations as individual states, not merely as part of the British Empire delegation. Admiral Jellicoe's postwar tour of the Dominions to raise contributions for the Royal Navy failed to achieve its purpose. The Dominions, except for New Zealand, refused to rally to Britain's cause in the Chanak crisis. Ireland set a precedent by exchanging ambassadors with Washington, and Canada arranged and signed the Halibut Treaty (1923) with the United States. In 1925 a new cabinet office for Dominion affairs separated the Dominions from the dependent empire. By 1926 imperial unity was seen in common institutions and in allegiance to the Crown, but not in common policies or centralized organizations.

Balfour Report, 1926. The Imperial Conference of 1926 attempted to define formally what had already taken place in fact. Lord Balfour presided over the committee that worked out the draft which, for the first time, defined the relations of the Dominions and Britain. The committee wisely refrained from drawing up a constitution or arranging an inflexible relationship that could not continue to evolve. Canada, Australia, New Zealand, South Africa, Newfoundland, and the Irish Free State were all satisfied with the final draft which defined the Dominions as "autonomous communities within the British Empire, equal in status, in no way subordinate one to another . . . united by a common allegiance to the Crown, and freely associated as members of the British Commonwealth of Nations." This acknowledgment of equality of status between the Dominions and Britain was legally confirmed by the Statute of Westminster (1931), which repealed the Colonial Laws Validity Act of 1865 and forbade any act of the British Parliament to apply to a Dominion without the consent of the Dominion. The Balfour Report ranks along with the Durham Report of 1839 as a landmark in the evolution of the British colonies to self-government. Evidently the lesson of the American Revolution had been well learned.

Ireland. In 1923 de Valera, the intransigent republican, dropped his violent opposition to the dominion status of Ireland; instead, he planned to win his objectives from within the Dail. In 1932 he succeeded the moderate Cosgrave as Prime Minister and immediately severed the remaining links with Britain by ignoring the Governor-General, abolishing the oath of allegiance to the Crown, ending appeals to the Judicial Committee of the Privy Council, and starting a tariff war to reduce Ireland's economic dependence upon England. In 1936 the lower chamber abolished the hostile Senate, and the next year de Valera wrote his republican political philosophy into the constitution for the newly-named Eire. Ireland was a reluctant member of the Commonwealth, having come into it against her will after a bitter civil war. De Valera was therefore obsessed with the goal of complete independence. In 1938 England released five naval bases in southern Ireland that had been granted her in the Anglo-Irish Treaty of 1921.

Foreign Affairs, 1924-31. Baldwin's bland insularity did not prevent these years of the inter-war period from being the most promising in foreign affairs. Under two able foreign ministers, Austen Chamberlain and Arthur Henderson, Britain took an active part in improving relations with Germany and France and in supporting collective security through the League of Nations.

High Tide of Security. Before its fall in 1924, the Labor Government had recognized Russia and agreed to the Dawes Plan on German reparations; MacDonald had even helped draft the Geneva Protocol for the pacific settlement of international disputes. Although Parliament never approved the Protocol, the mood of international conciliation it encouraged permitted Austen Chamberlain, the new Tory foreign secretary, to continue MacDonald's efforts of reconciliation among Britain, France, and Germany. This rapprochement produced the Locarno Pacts (1925) whereby the Franco-German frontier was guaranteed by Britain, Italy, France, Germany, and Belgium. There were also provisions for the settlement of disputes by diplomacy, conciliation, or arbitration. The achievement of these treaties permitted Chamberlain to share the Nobel Peace Prize for 1925. The next year Germany entered the League and both European security and economic stability seemed promising. But opportunities were wasted thereafter, not from opposition but from inertia. Lord Cecil finally resigned from Baldwin's Cabinet because of Britain's hesitation to be committed either to international arbitration or to disarmament. Britain signed the Kellogg-Briand Pact (1928) renouncing war, but it was only a platitude and not a plan of action.

Foreign Affairs under Labor, 1929-31. Arthur Henderson and Ramsay MacDonald were more consistent than Baldwin's Government in implementing the principles of arbitration, arms reduction, and security through the League. Diplomatic relations with Russia were restored in spite of the sustained opposition of the Conservatives. At The Hague Henderson presided over the Political Commission which achieved the evacuation of Allied troops from the Rhine, and signed the optional clause of the Statute of the Permanent Court of International Justice which required referral of all international disputes to that court. MacDonald chaired the London naval conference (1930) during which partial success was achieved by Britain, the United States, and Japan in extending the 5: 5: 3 ratio on battleships to other warships as well. France and Italy were less willing to accept naval parity between themselves, whereas Britain agreed to share naval supremacy with the United States.

The Drift to War, 1931-38. Fascists in Italy, Japan, Germany, and Spain were not impressed by collective security based only on paper or moral sanctions. Force and the threat of force met no effective response from the major powers in the League or from the United States, largely because of pacifism in England, fear of the horrors of war, and preoccupation with domestic problems brought on by the depression. The thirties proved that Britain and the Commonwealth would not fight for the enforcement of either League authority or for the sanctity of peace treaties. Hitler and Mussolini interpreted this attitude as a sign of political decadence and military weakness; however, Britain and the Commonwealth would fight when they finally sensed that national survival was at stake.

Japanese Aggression. Collective security collapsed first in Asia when Japanese troops invaded Manchuria in 1931. China appealed to the League of Nations and to the United States, but neither made any response sufficient to deter Japan. A League Commission, under Lord Lytton of Britain, rebuked Japan but hesitated to recommend sanctions. Japan withdrew from the League in 1933 and launched an attack on China proper. In its first major test the League failed to take effective measures to keep the peace; and it was this shortcoming that invited aggression elsewhere.

Failure of General Disarmament. The World Disarmament Conference of sixty nations opened at Geneva in February, 1932. The supporters of collective action anticipated that agreement here would be the capstone to European pacification. Germany demanded equality with other powers and threatened to rearm if other nations did not disarm. France insisted on greater security before she would disarm. In Germany the Nazis and the Nationalists opposed the policy of pacification that Gustav Stresemann had promoted in the twenties. The British delegation, led by John Simon, offered no plan and no leadership in the impasse. British sympathies were with Germany more than with France. In January, 1933, Adolph Hitler came to power. In October he withdrew the German delegates from both the Disarmament Conference and from the League of Nations. The following year the Disarmament Conference was adjourned indefinitely.

German Rearmament. Hitler substituted rearmament for conciliation as a better method to vindicate the "wrongs" of the Versailles Treaty. In 1935 he openly violated the treaty by denouncing its disarmament clauses and by introducing conscription. Although Britain, France, and Italy protested and had the League condemn this action, no further steps were taken to halt German rearmament. The British responded by arranging a naval pact with Germany in June of 1935. This move alienated France and implied British sanction of Germany's rearmament. France bolstered her security with a bilateral defensive pact with Russia.

British Rearmament and Public Opinion. British public opinion opposed rearmament and military action against distant aggression. MacDonald and Baldwin deferred to this viewpoint which was dramatically revealed in the National Peace Ballot of 1934. Over eleven million voters favored international disarmament and collective security through the League. The Labor party, led by George

Lansbury, urged reliance upon collective security while rejecting the armaments to provide it. The Conservatives supported half-hearted independent action outside the League, but their timid action and meager success in increasing armaments neutralized the efficacy of this approach. From 1936 to 1939 Baldwin asked annually for increased armament expenditures.

Mussolini's Aggression. The Italian invasion of Ethiopia in 1935 took place in spite of an appeal from Emperor Haile Selassie for League protection against open aggression. The League invoked mild economic sanctions against Italy but excluded the one essential commodity, oil. Thus the sanctions only angered the Italians without impeding their conquests. In Paris in December Foreign Secretary Samuel Hoare and Pierre Laval drafted a treaty designed to appease Italy and prevent a general European war by offering Bennito Mussolini one-half of Ethiopia. British public opinion loudly denounced this betrayal of the League and of collective security which the National Government had promised to support only a month earlier in the general election. Hoare resigned, and Baldwin appointed Anthony Eden as foreign secretary in an effort to placate public feeling. Mussolini completed the conquest of Ethiopia and contemptuously withdrew from the League in 1937. The Ethiopian crisis divided Europe into two camps and encouraged Mussolini to ally with Hitler in the Rome-Berlin Axis of 1936. Because it had failed to take effective action against aggression, the League, for all practical purposes, became an anachronism after 1936. Furthermore, the Hoare-Laval scheme indicated that the big powers would sacrifice the small powers to avoid a general war. Thereafter, each country looked for new means of protection after the failure of collective security. Belgium became neutral, and Poland exchanged an alliance with France for one with Germany.

Hitler in the Rhineland. While the western powers were preoccupied with Italy's aggression, Hitler took the opportunity to unilaterally break the Versailles and the Locarno Treaties by sending troops into the demilitarized Rhineland. Public and political opinion in Britain would not support sanctions, military or economic, against Germany for militarizing her own territory. France was unwilling to act without British support. The Council of the League denounced Germany's violation of international treaties but recommended no further action. Britain had no desire to risk war to support collective security under the League or to prevent the violation of international treaties.

Spanish Civil War. The division of Europe into a Fascist and non-Fascist camp was sharpened by the civil war in Spain. To prevent the conflict from spreading into a general war, Baldwin's Cabinet, supported by France, took the lead in setting up a committee of non-intervention. Non-intervention aided the Fascist Nationalists because Britain, France and most other states honored the agreement. However, Italy and Germany showed continued contempt for international obligations and liberally aided General Francisco Franco and his troops. Only Russia gave formal assistance to the Loyalists and thereby helped to delay the Fascist victory in Spain until 1939. Churchill lashed out at Baldwin's delays in rearmament, but languor prevailed in the Cabinet. The hope continued that the dictators could be appeased short of war. For the first time significant opposition to the Government's foreign policy was being heard. The ideological implications of the Spanish war split and embittered British politics. Pro-Republicans were charged with Communist sympathies, while the Government was condemned by its critics as a tool of class interests friendly to fascism. Nevertheless, to stop Hitler after 1936 would demand either full rearmament in peacetime or an alliance with Stalin, and neither option was politically palatable; that was the real problem.

Personal Diplomacy. Foreign policy became Neville Chamberlain's personal and primary concern from the day he became Prime Minister in May, 1937. The Foreign Office was bypassed and parliamentary criticism was ignored. Surrounding himself with like-minded advisers, such as Lord Halifax, Nevile Henderson, Samuel Hoare and John Simon, Chamberlain and this inner Cabinet operated on the assumption that Hitler's objectives were limited and his appetite satiable. Thus Chamberlain believed that by reasonable agreement, rather than by force, he could win peace. This industrious, rigid man with confidence in his own abilities and in the purity and rightness of his policies would have provided forceful and efficient domestic leadership in the twenties. But he was tragically miscast for dealing with Hitler who played diplomacy in a manner alien to Chamberlain's rules of conduct. By appeasement Chamberlain probably delayed war for one year. But the delay assisted German rearmament more than Germany's opponents. However, the year permitted Britain to build up an effective air force and to win Commonwealth backing, both of which were lacking in 1938.

German Strategy. Chamberlain's plan was to find satisfactory terms whereby tensions with Germany over Central Europe, armaments, and colonies could be resolved amicably. Interviews with British diplomats convinced Hitler that England would not forcibly oppose his alteration of Europe. Chamberlain knew nothing of

Hitler's meeting with his armed forces in November, 1937, during which he plotted the seizure of Austria and Czechoslovakia.

Italian Negotiations. Chamberlain's policy of appeasement produced an agreement with Italy on April 16, 1938, whereby each country promised not to extend their bases in the eastern Mediterranean. Britain would recommend to the League the recognition of Italian sovereignty over Ethiopia, and Italy would withdraw her troops from Spain. Chamberlain hoped to strengthen his hand in negotiations with Hitler by settling disputes peacefully with Hitler's ally, Mussolini.

Austria. The Nazis had intimidated Austrian leadership since 1934. In March, 1938, Hitler took the country by force. Chancellor Schuschnigg's appeal for help had brought no support from Italy, France, Britain, or Russia. The British Government made only a routine protest of the Nazi coup. Nothing more could be done to prevent Austria's union with Germany after it was an accomplished fact.

Czechoslovakia. Immediately Hitler applied pressure on Czechoslovakia. In September, 1938, Chamberlain met Hitler at Berchtesgaden and agreed to the cession of the Sudeten territory to Germany on the basis of self-determination. A week later at Godesberg Chamberlain was confronted by Hitler's new demands for Sudetenland. When the Godesberg Memorandum was rejected by Britain, France, and Czechoslovakia, Hitler demanded his terms by October 1 or threatened war. A general war now seemed imminent. Hitler suddenly turned conciliatory and promised to make the Sudeten his last territorial claim; he offered to meet with Chamberlain, Mussolini and Edouard Daladier of France.

Munich. During the week of September 22, 1938, Hitler, Chamberlain, Daladier and Mussolini settled the fate of Czechoslovakia without even the presence of Czech representatives. Sudetenland was ceded to Germany, and the integrity of the rest of Czechoslovakia was guaranteed. In France and England there was hysterical relief and praise for the peacemakers. Hitler had privately and publicly stated limits to his policy, and it was now up to him to demonstrate whether he wished to prevent or merely postpone war. In March, 1939, he violated his guarantee and seized the rest of Czechoslovakia. Chamberlain had been deceived; appeasement had failed to halt aggression. British foreign policy now underwent a sudden about face.

Chapter 24 ≤§ The Second World War

After the paralysis and drift of the inter-war years, Britain became galvanized in 1940 to heroic resistance under Winston Churchill's leadership. The war became total, killing as many civilians as soldiers. Once again the war was conducted by a coalition Government whose powers were almost limitless. Far more than in any previous conflict, the Second World War became a struggle for survival, because Hitler's aim was the mastery, not merely a hegemony, of Europe. Air power ended the benefits of insularity and naval supremacy which had protected Britain in previous European conflicts. When Britain refused to yield, Hitler turned elsewhere. His fatal error was overtaxing the German war machine by extending its commitments and bringing against Germany the implacable logic of geography, communications, transportation, and resources. In time a coalition of Allies turned the tide of war as the preponderance of power moved against the Axis powers. The defeat of Germany became almost a Pyrrhic victory for Britain because the peace ended her status as a first-class power.

Mobilization and War

After Munich England reverted to her historic principle of allying with the weak against the strong to prevent one-power domination of the Continent. A crash program of rearmaments and civil defense commenced. Britain promised to protect Poland, but an eastern European security system was ineffective without an alliance with Russia. When Germany and Russia signed a non-aggression pact, Hitler's hand was free to strike against Poland. World War II began on September 1, 1939, when German armies invaded Poland.

Aftermath of Munich. Except for convincing the Dominions and British public opinion that appeasement would not keep the peace and buying time to triple the strength of the Royal Air Force, the balance sheet of Munich was largely negative. A fortified border, thirty-six Czech divisions, the vast Skoda munitions works, and a genuine democratic state were sacrificed. The pact was also a moral and diplomatic loss. The support of Britain for the strongest, instead of the weakest, European power and the failure of France to honor its alliance with Czechoslovakia caused Britain and France to lose prestige and the respect of eastern Europe. Poland became isolated and an easy mark as Hitler's next victim. Russia, in particular, was suspicious of the Munich pact because the decisions at Munich seemed to encourage Hitler to expand eastward. Since Russia could not count on either Britain or France, she was willing to buy her own safety by a non-aggression pact with Germany. Nor did the year of peace salvaged by the Munich conference help increase British war equipment half as much as it aided German military production.

New Alliances. Finally aware of Hitler's treachery, the British anxiously sought security by new military alliances. Guarantees of support were given to Poland, Greece, Roumania, and Turkey, although Britain could not intervene effectively in any of these countries. No eastern European security system was possible without a Russian alliance; however, mutual mistrust between Russia and Britain hindered such an agreement. An Anglo-French mission to Russia made half-hearted efforts at an alliance, but before differences could be reconciled, Russia accepted, on August 23, Germany's proposals of a ten-year Non-Aggression Pact. Stalin gained more by buying time than by an uncertain alliance with Britain and France, and Hitler eliminated the threat of major war on two fronts. In May, 1939, Hitler and Mussolini completed a military alliance in the Pact of Steel.

Mobilization. Chamberlain still had some illusions after Munich about persuading Hitler to keep the peace; therefore, he refused to bring into his Cabinet keen advisers, such as Winston Churchill, who might anger the dictator. Nevertheless, he accepted the inevitability of preparing for the worst. A lavish defense budget for 1939-40 speeded up rearmament. In 1939 approximately eight thousand planes were produced as compared to nearly three thousand in the previous year. The navy was overhauled and was far superior to the German fleet when war broke out. The badly neglected British army of five divisions was to be raised to thirty-five divisions. To obtain such a force conscription was reintroduced. Civil defense preparations under Sir John Anderson provided for air-raid shelters, the evacuation of children from large cities, and emergency fire and transport organizations.

Conquest of Poland. On September 1, 1939, the German invasion of Poland began. Britain and France honored their pledges to Poland and declared war on Germany two days later. The German blitzkrieg (lightning-war) by ground and air forces overwhelmed the smaller, old-fashioned Polish army. On September 17, Russia attacked Poland from the east, and Polish resistance ended on September 29. Neither Britain nor France was able to get troops into Poland. Germany and Russia partitioned Poland according to the terms of a secret protocol signed at the time of the Non-Aggression Pact. Russia occupied Estonia, Latvia, and Lithuania and attacked Finland in November. Finland capitulated in March, 1940, after a stout resistance in the winter war against the Russians. Hitler and others concluded that the Russian army was weak after its poor showing in Finland.

The Phony War. After the fall of Poland there was a six-month lull in land operations. British and French forces took a defensive position behind the elaborately fortified Maginot Line on the border facing the German Siegfried Line. Another long and immobile war like the First World War was anticipated by the French generals. No bombing occurred. Britain began a full-fledged naval blockade of German imports and exports, hoping to strangle Germany's economy and force her to terms. German shipping was swept from the seas and her surface raiders, including the "Graf Spee," were sunk. On April 4 Chamberlain declared that Hitler had "missed the bus" by his inactivity. Five days later the German blitzkrieg in the West was directed against Denmark and Norway.

Chamberlain Resigns. The Prime Minister by temperament and conviction was conspicuously lacking in the qualities needed for war leadership. He made only token efforts to get Labor to join the National Government and seemed undisturbed by the slow transition of the economy to war production. Appeals for a ministry of economic planning were rejected, although ministries for shipping, food, and labor were set up. A War Cabinet of nine, including his former critics, Churchill and Eden, was established. But Chamberlain's optimism during the phony war was misplaced. The failure of British naval and land forces to halt the German conquest of Norway brought angry charges in Parliament against the Prime Minister's conduct of the war from Labor and from his own party. Labor was willing to join a Coalition Government, but not under Chamberlain's leadership. On May 10, 1940, Chamberlain resigned and advised King George to summon Winston Churchill, the only leading Conservative who was not identified in some way with Baldwin-Chamberlain policies. In the crisis of war Churchill was called, whereas he had been shunned as too rash in judgment and too controversial in the prewar years by party leaders. Chamberlain agreed to serve in Churchill's Cabinet, thereby avoiding a party split similar to the one which had occurred in World War I when

Lloyd George succeeded Asquith as Prime Minister. A new Coalition Government of Conservatives, Liberals and Laborites was formed, directed by a small War Cabinet of five (later nine) members.

Total War

With the blitzkrieg in the West the power of the German Wehrmacht dispelled any illusions about the conflict settling down to static trench and economic warfare. The collapse of France left only Britain to face the full force of Nazi power. The ensuing Battle of Britain failed to break British morale or give Germany control of the air. Hitler therefore turned eastward against Russia in June, 1941. By the end of the year the United States and Japan were also major belligerents. Late in 1942 the tide of victory turned as the overextended commitments and theaters of combat placed an impossible burden on Axis power.

No part of British society or of the economy escaped the demands of total war. Old animosities were set aside in a common coalition against Axis powers. Britain and Russia became allies, Labor ministers and the trade unions lent solid support to Churchill, and the emergency powers of the state became virtually unlimited.

The Fall of France. On May 10, 1940, Germany attacked France through Belgium and the Netherlands, thereby outflanking the Maginot Line. The Dutch and Belgian armies capitulated, and by May 23 the Germans had penetrated the line of the dispirited French armies at Sedan and reached the Channel, trapping the British Expeditionary Force and some French units to the north. The surrounded troops turned what could have become a major disaster into the incredible evacuation of Dunkirk. Fighting their way to the beaches, 338,000 soldiers were evacuated to Britain by 887 private and Royal Navy vessels. The army was saved, but all equipment was lost. On June 10, Italy entered the war and attacked France from the south in order to share the spoils. Churchill's offer of union with France was rejected by Premier Pétain. Humiliating armistice terms were accepted by France on June 22, leaving Britain and the Commonwealth, except for neutral Eire, to face Hitler alone.

Battle of Britain. The British turned down Hitler's peace overtures and braced themselves to resist the mightiest military force ever assembled up to that time. Hitler commenced preparations for a sea and airborne assault—Operation Sea-Lion—and invasion barges were assembled in the Channel ports. But first the Nazis had to attain air superiority over England and the Channel. In July the

Battle of Britain began as the German Luftwaffe tried to destroy the Royal Air Force and shatter British morale. For three months up to one thousand bombers came every day, and every night thereafter for six months. The incendiary bombs were aimed at the cities instead of industries. The blitz took a heavy toll in civilian casualties and in property damage, but the will of the British to resist never faltered. Three German planes were shot down for every plane lost by the small but superb Royal Air Force. Instead of winning air superiority, Hitler suffered the loss of more than half of his total first-line air strength. In October Hitler canceled his invasion plans and turned instead toward the Balkans and Russia. British morale was also lifted by the easy victory of General Wavell and his army, even though outnumbered five-to-one, over the Italians in Egypt and Libya.

Battle of the Atlantic. With the entire west coast of Europe in German hands, Hitler now concentrated his submarines and air force against British shipping in the north Atlantic and in the Mediterranean. By June, 1941, over half a million tons a month of British shipping had been sunk—at a rate faster than could be replaced. Yet, as in 1917, food, oil, and other essentials had to reach England or the country would be forced to capitulate. To avoid this peril, President Roosevelt stretched the strict restrictions of the American neutrality legislation of 1935 and provided help to Britain. In September, 1940, the United States gave Britain fifty overage destroyers in return for long-term leases of eight air and naval bases in the western Atlantic. Eventually, the United States took command of Greenland and Iceland and began patrolling the Atlantic shipping lanes. In March, 1941, the Lend-Lease Act authorized Roosevelt to put American resources at the disposal of any country whose defense was deemed vital to the security of the United States. This permitted a steady flow of supplies to Britain and other Allies amounting to $45 billion by July, 1945. The United States Merchant Marine, often protected by escort vessels of the Canadian navy, carried these supplies to Great Britain.

United Nations. Britain finally gained two major allies when Germany invaded Russia and Japan attacked the United States in 1941. Immediately the war was transformed from a European to a global struggle. Although the initial momentum and careful preparations gave Germany and Japan important victories, the entry of Russia and the United States into the war ultimately provided the preponderance of power to bring about Axis defeat. It was the fatal tendency of Germany and Japan to overextend the theaters of war, and in the long run their strategic blunders outweighed their tactical gains. On January 1, 1942, twenty-six nations, henceforth called the United Nations, signed a massive military alliance pledging total co-operation against their common enemy.

Invasion of Russia. In April, 1941, the Germans successfully invaded the Balkan Peninsula and rescued the Italians in Albania from defeat by the Greeks. With the southern flank of the German army protected, Hitler launched his surprise attack on Russia on June 22, 1941, which was aimed at annihilating the Russian armies before winter. Since success depended on immediate and decisive victory, one hundred and fifty German divisions attacked along a 1600-mile front, but were met with unprecedented resistance. By the end of the year, the key objectives of Moscow and Leningrad were still in Russian hands, and the German armies were ill-prepared for the coldest winter in living memory and for the appalling problem of supplying such a distant and extended front. German brutality and contempt for the Russians only stiffened Russian resistance, whereas, at the beginning, many Russian civilians and troops were not too unhappy about the threat to Stalin's regime.

Japanese Aggression. Britain and the Dominions declared war on Japan after the Japanese attack on the United States naval base at Pearl Harbor, December 7, 1941. Britain and the United States were now formal allies. In the next six months Japan rapidly created a new empire in the southeast Pacific and seized the British possessions of Hong Kong, Malaya, Singapore, and Burma, thereby threatening India and sealing off the Burma Road and supplies to China. The Philippines and the Dutch East Indies were also occupied, and the invasion of Australia was expected since the Japanese were already in New Guinea.

The Year of Disasters. Until late 1942 the Allies were on the defensive and suffered successive defeats on every front. The German spring offensive in Russia was carried to Stalingrad, the gateway to the Caucasian oil fields and to control of the Middle East. In North Africa General Rommel and his *Afrika Korps* had repelled the British almost to Cairo. Japan could not be checked in the Pacific. During this time Churchill and Roosevelt agreed to give the war in Europe priority and unify their military and economic operations. Machinery for integrating the war effort was established; in each theater of war one man was given command of the land, sea, and air forces of the United States and the British Commonwealth.[1]

---

[1] The Pacific area was under the command of Admiral Nimitz; the southwest Pacific by General Douglas MacArthur; southeast Asia by Lord Louis Mountbatten; the Middle East by Sir Harold Alexander; and the European Front by General Dwight D. Eisenhower.

The Tide Turns. The summer of 1942 marked the high tide of Axis fortunes in North Africa, Russia, and in the Pacific. Victory in Egypt and at Stalingrad could have linked the two German drives, forced the British out of the Middle East, and brought the German armies to India to join the Japanese advancing from the east. But on all three fronts the Axis thrusts were halted, and successful counter-offensives were undertaken. Thereafter, the United Nations mounted an all-front offensive, and Britain's role in the war, in contrast to the first three years, was overshadowed by the might of Russia and the United States.

North Africa. In October, 1942, the British Eighth Army under General Montgomery won the first decisive battle of the desert war at El Alemein. Rommel's *Afrika Korps* retreated across North Africa. While the retreat was in progress, a great Anglo-American amphibious force landed in northwest Africa and hemmed in the German forces. After heavy resistance in Tunisia the Germans surrendered in May, 1943. More than 250,000 German and Italian troops were captured, including seventeen Axis generals. The "soft underbelly" of Europe—Italy and the Balkans—was now exposed to Allied attack.

The Russian Front. The critical battle of Stalingrad was the turning point of the war in Russia. By January, 1943, the crack German Sixth Army was destroyed, and Stalingrad remained in Russian hands. The Russians began a continuous offensive along the vast front until the last of two hundred German divisions was driven out of Russia in 1944.

The Pacific. British reinforcements to India finally halted and then routed the Japanese in north Burma. The Battle of the Coral Sea on May 7 and the Battle of Midway on June 4-7, 1942, caused heavy damages to the Japanese fleet and frustrated planned attacks on Australia and Hawaii. Later in the summer American and Commonwealth forces landed on Guadalcanal and other Pacific Islands. These operations were limited because Allies were giving priority to the European theater.

Naval and Air Superiority. In 1943 the Allies won the Battle of the Atlantic after suffering over four million gross tons of shipping losses in the preceding year. Unprecedented shipbuilding by the United States allowed new tonnage to exceed losses by late 1943. Radar, depth charges, fast escort vessels, and the use of aircraft cover helped break the U-boat menace. Allied air supremacy was also won in 1943. Day and night British and American bombers reduced many German cities to rubble; however, the massive strategic bombing had little effect on either German morale or production.

Invasion of Italy. Since 1942 Stalin had insisted on a second front in Europe to take German pressure off the Russian front. Unready for a major offensive against Hitler's European fortress, British and American forces instead invaded Sicily in July, 1943, and the Italian mainland two months later. Mussolini resigned and Italy surrendered. Nevertheless, strong German resistance continued, and the Allied advance up the peninsula was slow and arduous. Not until April, 1945, did Allied troops finally reach the Po Valley.

Second Front. On D-Day, June 6, 1944, the long-awaited Allied invasion army, transported from British ports in 4000 ships, landed in force on five Normandy beaches. Within twenty days a million Allied troops were in France. Britain had become an arsenal in the gigantic buildup for Operation Overlord. General Dwight D. Eisenhower was Supreme Allied Commander in western Europe with Air Chief Marshall Sir Arthur Tedder as deputy. The German armies were unable to contain the invaders, and the Allied forces rapidly liberated Paris and western France. On August 15, American and French armies executed an amphibious landing in southern France and pursued the Germans up the Rhone Valley. By the end of 1944 France was almost entirely liberated. A furious German counteroffensive in Belgium—the Battle of the Bulge— only temporarily slowed down the Allied advance. The Germans made their last stand behind the Siegfried Line along the Rhine.

The Final Assault. By January, 1945, Russian troops were deep in eastern Germany; on April 19, they entered Berlin. The western Allied armies crossed the Rhine and reached the industrial Ruhr in April. That same month Russian and American armies met at the Elbe. Germany was split in two, but Hitler insisted on resisting to the last man. During the final year of the war Germany launched its new weapon, the Vengeance Bomb (V-1) against British cities. These pilotless jet planes, or buzzbombs, caused civilian casualties and distress but served no specific military objective. In September the V-2, a rocket-propelled bomb, replaced the V-1 as a more destructive instrument of scientific war.

Victory in Europe. On May 7, 1945, the Germans made an unconditional surrender to General Eisenhower at Reims, and the war in Europe officially ended the following day. Hitler reportedly committed suicide in Berlin while the city was under siege by the Russians, and Mussolini was shot by Italians in Milan.

The War Economy. World War II proved to be a great leveler socially and economically. All classes shared the air raid shelters and suffered the same stringent rationing controls. The tax burden was heaviest on the upper-and-middle-income brackets, the increase in taxes being most obvious on the previously favored middle-income families. Ironically the war alone ended unemployment and sharply raised the wage scales. By 1944 out of every nine members of the total labor force, two were in the armed forces, and three in war production. As in World War I, the powers of the central Government again became virtually limitless, although more tolerance was shown toward individual rights and nonconformity than in the First World War. The Emergency Powers Acts of 1939 and 1940 conferred on the Government wide-ranging control over public safety and the conduct of the war. The concern over excessive power being delegated to ministries resulted in the House of Commons setting up a Scrutiny Committee in 1944 to examine every new order sent out by ministries and to bring any order considered objectionable to the attention of Parliament.

Wartime Conferences. Numerous Allied conferences took place during the war, first to plot the strategy for defeating Hitler, then to arrange a political settlement for the defeated or conquered countries. Agreement on the former came easier than on the latter. As the tide of war turned in favor of the United Nations, national and ideological differences divided the victors. The postwar objectives of Stalin were in direct conflict with the principles of the democracies.

Atlantic Charter, 1941. Churchill and Roosevelt conferred on board the battleship "Prince of Wales" in August, 1941. Although the United States was not a belligerent, the conversations dealt with military strategy and produced a joint statement on war and peace aims. The Atlantic Charter was a declaration of common ideals which echoed Woodrow Wilson's Fourteen Points. The democracies would seek no territorial gains and would support self-determination of nations and the Four Freedoms.[2] On January 1, 1942, representatives of the twenty-six nations endorsed the Atlantic Charter and agreed not to make a separate peace with the enemy.

Casablanca and Quebec, 1943. At the Casablanca Conference in January Churchill accepted Roosevelt's insistence on unconditional surrender as the only basis for peace; however, the Prime Minister and the President could not agree on military strategy. Churchill favored a Mediterranean operation through the Balkans in order to limit Russia's penetration, whereas Roosevelt's military advisers argued for a cross-channel invasion of France. The only agreement reached was on the invasion of Sicily. At the Quebec Conference

---

[2] Defined in a speech to Congress (January, 1941) by President Roosevelt: freedom from fear, freedom from want, freedom of religion, and freedom of speech and expression.

in August Churchill agreed that the second front in France would have priority over an accelerated campaign in the Pacific.

Teheran, 1943. After Churchill and Roosevelt met with Chiang Kai-shek in Cairo in November and agreed to the restoration of Japan's seizures in Asia, the first Big Three meeting took place in Teheran. Stalin strongly supported the American position on a French invasion and repeated his promise that Russia would attack Japan after Germany's defeat.

Yalta, 1945. Stalin was in an excellent bargaining position in February, 1945. Russia already controlled eastern Europe and her armies were approaching Berlin, whereas the Anglo-American armies had not yet crossed the Rhine. Furthermore, western advisers considered Russian assistance essential to the defeat of Japan—a task estimated to last at least eighteen more months after the fall of Germany. The Big Three agreed to divide Germany into occupation zones, to try German war criminals, and to turn over the problem of reparations, so vital to Stalin, to a commission. A decision on the future of Germany was postponed. Concessions in the Far East were guaranteed Stalin in return for declaring war on Japan. The boundaries of Poland were changed. Ukrainian Poland was ceded to Russia, and part of eastern Germany came under Polish control; in turn, Stalin agreed to free elections in independent Poland—a promise he never kept.

Potsdam, 1945. The Grand Alliance visible crumbled at Potsdam. Hitler, the raison d'être of the coalition, was dead. Roosevelt had died in April, and, because of his defeat in the British general election, Churchill had to relinquish his place to Atlee in the middle of the conference. Of the former Big Three only Stalin was left. The conference confirmed the proposals made at Yalta regarding Poland and Germany. A council of foreign ministers was to draft the peace treaties. On other subjects, such as Tito's government in Yugoslavia and recognition of the Balkan governments under Russian control, there was heated controversy. Stalin would not relinquish the control that the Red army had won in central and eastern Europe. After Potsdam Britain had few illusions over Russia's intention to exploit the political vacuum left by the destruction of Germany.

The United Nations Organization. Before the war ended, the Allies took steps to establish a new international organization to replace the discredited League of Nations. In 1943 the United Nations Relief and Rehabilitation Administration (UNRRA) was organized to help victims of Axis aggression. At Dumbarton Oaks (1944) British, American, Russian, and Chinese delegates drafted a charter for the United Nations which was approved at an international conference of more than fifty nations in San Francisco (April-June, 1945). The United Nations consisted of a General Assembly of all member states, and a Security Council of eleven members, with the five major powers—the United States, Russia, Britain, France, and China—having permanent seats. The United States and Russia insisted that the permanent members of the council have veto power over virtually all substantive actions. Russia later used the veto extensively.

Japanese Surrender. The Allied high command gave full attention to Japan following the defeat of Germany. Already the Fourteenth British Army had freed Burma, and American forces had taken Iwo Jima and invaded Okinawa. Vast preparations were under way for the final assault on the Japanese mainland. Instead, the end of the war came suddenly when the United States dropped an atomic bomb on Hiroshima on August 6, 1945, and another on Nagasaki three days later. The awesome destruction produced by these nuclear weapons prodded the Japanese government to accept terms of unconditional surrender on August 14. The formal surrender occurred September 2 on board the battleship "Missouri" in Tokyo Bay. In the interval between the dropping of the two bombs, Russia declared war on Japan in keeping with her promise made at Yalta.

Churchill's War Leadership. In Winston Churchill Britain found the exceptional qualities needed for leadership in war. He became the forceful and eloquent spokesman of English defiance. His indomitable spirit and stirring speeches sustained the firmness of purpose of an island people as they stood alone against Hitler's Third Reich. The Coalition War Cabinet which Churchill had set up was more truly national than any of its predecessors. From Labor he brought in Clement Atlee as deputy Prime Minister and Ernest Bevin as Minister of Labor and National Service. Churchill kept the post of Defense Minister himself and also took over many functions of the Foreign Office, preferring to deal directly with Roosevelt and Stalin. He succeeded in minimizing the friction between politicians and soldiers far better than Asquith or Lloyd George had done in World War I. Churchill asserted British influence and power sufficiently for the term Big Three—Roosevelt, Stalin, and Churchill—to be fully justified during the war years.

Victory in Europe—Socialism in England

Complete military victory came to the United Nations in 1945 as the Axis powers were forced into unconditional surrender. During the war Allied leaders had held a series of conferences to work out military strategy and postwar settlements. The Allies were united in their opposition to Hitler but not by any common postwar goals. In England no one wanted a return of the 1939 social climate with its unemployment and its timid, traditional economic policies. The war had produced a revolution in the thinking of the British people, and they now wished the state would continue to intervene to raise the standard of living. Therefore, the voters gave the Labor party an opportunity to introduce the welfare state. With the war over in Europe, the dismal record of the Conservatives before the war was a deterrent to voting Churchill's party a mandate for dealing with postwar problems.

Social and Economic Planning. Since the war had ended unemployment and provided a sense of collective sacrifice and service, it became evident that this national purpose could be transferred to the goal of a better society by postwar state planning. Before the war was over, social and economic reconstruction became acceptable to the nation, and Keynesian economics had become respectable and orthodox. Numerous reports, such as the Scott Report of 1942, recommended specific courses of state action. A White Paper on Employment Policy (1942) pledged the Government to the subsidizing of full employment. R. A. Butler's Education Act of 1944 raised the school-leaving age to fifteen and made the ministry of education the central authority for education in England and Wales. The Beveridge Report of 1942 attracted an enthusiastic response to its proposals for extending social security to ensure comprehensive protection against poverty, sickness, unemployment, and ignorance, for all individuals "from the cradle to the grave." The report became the charter for the welfare state and provided the principles and the direction for postwar social reform.

Political Revolution. By 1945 the nation was convinced that the systematic planning so vital to military victory could also serve the goals of reconstruction and social justice in peacetime. No one wanted to relapse to prewar conditions. This national mood was decisively revealed in the repudiation of the popular Coalition and in the overwhelming endorsement of the Labor party.

General Election, 1945. Churchill preferred to continue a Coalition Government, but Labor decided to withdraw from the Coalition now that the war was over in Europe. Although Labor gave unstinting support to Churchill's wartime Government, the party had reservations about his unique abilities serving equally well in implementing their postwar reconstruction program. Therefore, Churchill resigned on May 29, but agreed to organize a caretaker Government until an election could be held. The Conservatives were confident that they could "Win with Winnie." Churchill turned his eloquent powers of vituperation against the Labor colleagues of his recent Cabinet and warned the nation that socialism was inseparable from police-state totalitarianism. The populace paid more attention to the Labor manifesto, *Let Us Face the Future,* which offered convincing proposals for housing, full employment, and social security. On these matters the Conservatives spoke only vaguely. Many voters remembered the sorry Conservative record of the thirties, even though Churchill was not identified with the administration of those years. The electorate was more attracted to a program of social reconstruction than to a great war Prime Minister who was now only a party leader seeking a mandate to govern in a postwar era.

Labor Landslide. Only in 1832 and in 1906 had there been a comparable electoral landslide. In the election of July 5, the Labor party took 393 seats to 189 for the Conservatives, and the Liberals won only 11 seats. The magnitude of the change surprised everyone. Clement Atlee, hardworking, conciliatory and modest, was confirmed by his party as their new leader and became Prime Minister on July 26. For the first time the Labor party had a clear-cut majority with a mandate for major change.

Chapter 25 ◄§ Contemporary Britain

World War II reduced Britain to a secondary power. The nation heroically withstood the Nazi onslaught but at such appalling cost that the victory bordered on the Pyrrhic. The emergence of two new super powers, the United States and Russia, meant that, for the first time in five centuries, Western Europe was no longer the axis of political and military power. Britain's ability to accommodate herself to this decline from greatness and transform an empire of 550 million subjects into a self-governing and voluntary Commonwealth of Nations, predominantly non-white, demonstrated the flexibility and the continuity of her institutions. Within Britain rapid social changes occurred in an attempt to equalize the rights and benefits of all citizens regardless of class. Once again the British resolved differences by compromise and accepted electoral decisions, thereby muting the clash of class differences. Consequently, the maturity of Britain's political system withstood the strain of rapid postwar changes, and her decline in strength was not followed by a corresponding decline in influence. Great Britain continues to serve as a broker for the peoples and nations of the Commonwealth and her worldwide commitments and pacts after 1945 have been far more extensive than were any similar obligations undertaken between the two wars. Nevertheless, Britain's first priority by 1970 had clearly shifted to negotiations for entry to the European Community and the security of Western Europe at the expense, if necessary, of her Commonwealth and military interests elsewhere.

The Age of the Common Man

"Imperial greatness was on the way out; the welfare state was on the way in."[1] Since World War II had convinced the British people of the efficacy of planning, the Labor Government promptly attempted to implement a planned economy with a major program of nationalization and extensive social services. During these first years of peace Britain survived the critical economic crisis brought

---

[1] A. J. P. Taylor, *English History, 1914-1945* (New York: Oxford, 1965), p. 600.

on by the war and its aftermath. To restore the economy, rationing and stringent controls were continued for nine years. When the Conservatives returned to power in 1951, further nationalization efforts were halted, but the successful Labor policies of full employment and social services were sustained. Eventually economic conditions improved, and during the fifties Britain experienced a modest prosperity.

Reconstruction. The economic situation in 1945 was desperate for a nation which depended for survival on world trade. To win the war Britain had sacrificed her export market which provided the nation with food and work in time of peace. The invisible income from capital invested abroad and from shipping was lost, one-half of the Merchant Navy had been destroyed, and industrial equipment needed replacement and conversion to peacetime needs. The national debt had tripled to £23 billion, and for the first time reserves in gold and dollars were dangerously low. Bolstering the currency and keeping international payments in balance became the immediate problem. Expanded production to satisfy domestic needs and provide a surplus for exports was essential; but industrial transition took time, planning, and money. The abrupt cessation of Lend Lease by the United States in August, 1945, forced Britain to seek additional loans in order to purchase food and machinery from the United States. In this crisis Britain remained solvent and bought time with a $3.75 billion loan from the United States and a $1.125 billion credit from Canada. From 1948 to 1951 there were over $2 billion in further grants and loans from the United States under the European Recovery (Marshall) Plan.

Controls and Rationing. Wartime restrictions and industrial controls were retained in an effort to discipline the nation to increase exports and prevent an adverse balance of payments. The Labor Government assumed complete control of foreign exchange. Under Hugh Dalton, chancellor of the exchequer, and later (1947) under Sir Stafford Cripps, licenses were required for exports and imports, production controls were decreed for industry, limitations were placed on foreign travel, and exhorbitant taxes were attached to luxury goods in an effort to promote exports. Instead of better times, the deprivations of wartime continued in the postwar years without the incentives of wartime sacrifice. Rationing of meat, sugar, gasoline, tobacco, and clothing remained and was extended in the austerity budget of 1947. Waiting in queues, a scant and monotonous diet, and drab and inadequate housing were the order of the day.

Under Cripps's persuasion compulsory arbitration was required to reduce the loss of production because of strikes, and trade union

leaders reluctantly agreed to a wage freeze in 1949 which deterred
salary boosts until 1951. Late in 1949 the pound was devalued from
$4.05 to $2.80 in an effort to help the balance of payments with the
dollar countries; however, devaluation only increased inflationary
pressures within Britain. Export industries were encouraged but the
controls and steep taxes often inhibited growth. Nevertheless, the
public responded to the spirit of national solidarity and sacrifice
invoked by Prime Minister Atlee, Foreign Secretary Bevin, and
Cripps. The economy slowly improved as exports increased and
employment remained high.

Nationalization. During 1946-47 the Labor Government fulfilled
its campaign promises: the Bank of England, the coal, electrical
power, and gas companies, and internal and external air and transport services came under public ownership by legislative act. The
opposition of the House of Lords to the nationalization of iron and
steel prompted Labor to amend the Parliament Act of 1911, limiting to one year instead of two the power of the Lords to veto
legislation. In 1949 the Iron and Steel Act was passed. Such measures
seemed normal since the nation had grown accustomed to public control of industry and centralized planning during wartime, and considered this program of public ownership and planning for peace a
logical postwar pattern. The sharpest debates in Parliament were
not over the direction of national policy so much as over the undue
and "un-English" haste in putting through such major legislation.
Nationalization, however, proved to be no panacea for the ills of industry. The coal industry remained chronically sick. Employees
experienced little sense of partnership or of ownership in the nation-
alized industries because management remained largely under the
same people. Conditions of employment improved, but the exaggerated hopes of raising production and efficiency through nationalization never materialized.

The Welfare State. More successful and permanent was the
evolution of the welfare state—a postwar trend anticipated by reports and commissions of the National Government during the
war. Fuller social justice and greater security lessened the class
tensions so apparent in the earlier part of the century. "Atlee
achieved in peace what Churchill had magnificently achieved in
war: a spirit of national solidarity and sense of community, able to
transcend the strong fissiparous forces of modern life." [2] Unemployment virtually disappeared. Between 1938 and 1950 public expenditures for social services nearly doubled as the state accepted
responsibility for the economic and physical well-being of its citi-

---

[2] David Thomson, *England in the Twentieth Century* (Baltimore: Penguin,
1965), p. 229.

zens. A shift in the distribution of national income accompanied the taxation policy of the Government. In 1949 only 86 persons in Great Britain had an earned income of over £6000 after taxes. Critics argued that maximum welfare militated against maximum production and greater national income. In the immediate postwar years the state implemented the Education Act of 1944, increased efficiency and acreage in agriculture by expanding wartime controls, and set up authorities to plan new towns.

Social Insurance. The National Insurance Act (1946), by incorporating many of the principles envisaged in the Beveridge report, consolidated previous legislation dealing with unemployment, old age, and sickness and increased benefits and expanded coverage in each category. Every employee from age sixteen to retirement was required to contribute weekly, as was his employer. The Industrial Injuries Insurance Act (1946) replaced employer compensation with a comprehensive contributory scheme in which the Government assumed financial responsibility for all industrial accidents. The National Assistance Act of 1948 ended the long-famous Poor Laws by having the Government assume care of the poor.

The National Health Service. The National Health Service Act of 1946 provided free medical services in an effort to guarantee prescribed standards of health. The need for a more comprehensive health service was agreed upon during the war not only by the three political parties, but also by the British Medical Association and the public. However, doctors were soon antagonized by the details of Aneurin Bevan's bill and by the controversial minister of health himself. After the bill was passed, hospitalization, drugs, medicine, medical services, spectacles and dentures were provided free. Patients chose their own physicians, and doctors were allowed to practice within or without the program. Within five years, 98 per cent of all general practitioners entered the program on either a full-time or part-time basis. Two-thirds of the cost of the program was met by general taxation.

Housing. Aneurin Bevan also undertook a crash program of government-subsidized housing construction. Strong measures were required since five million of England's homes had been damaged or destroyed by bombing raids. The Housing Acts of 1946 and 1949 permitted the construction of 806,000 permanent homes and apartments by 1950 and the repair of an additional 333,000. Priority was given to public, low-cost rental units at the expense of private construction. Comprehensive town planning by county authorities, including the building of entire new towns in less congested areas of the country, was provided by the Town and Country Planning Act of 1947.

The Election of 1950. Labor had abolished the twelve university constituencies and plural voting for businessmen; it had also redistributed and reduced the seats in the House of Commons to 625 under a slogan of "one man, one vote." In the election of February, 1950, the Labor party campaigned on its five-year record and cautiously recommended further nationalization. Since 1945 Lord Woolten had greatly strengthened the Conservative party organization, and this new efficiency was readily apparent. The Conservatives promised to give priority to housing, reduce government controls, halt nationalization, and maintain full employment and postwar social services. The election left Labor with a majority of only six and without a mandate for strong action. Atlee's second term in office was plagued with difficulties, relieved only by an improvement in the foreign exchange in 1950 and the successful Festival of Britain in 1951. The outbreak of the Korean War demanded rearmament expenditures which, in turn, brought about increased taxes and prices. The option of rearmament or expanded social services further split the Labor ranks which were already weakened by the retirement of Sir Stafford Cripps, through illness, and the death of Ernest Bevin. In April, 1951, Aneurin Bevan and Harold Wilson, the leaders of the socialist Left, resigned from the Cabinet in protest over foreign policy. The Prime Minister was ill and other ministers were feeling the strain of Opposition tactics and all-night sittings. The former impetus and unity of the Labor party were conspicuously lacking when Atlee called for a general election in October, 1951.

The Return of Churchill. The Conservatives emerged from the election with 321 seats, Labor with 295, and the Liberals with 6 seats. Winston Churchill, who was now seventy-seven, formed his second Government which included Anthony Eden as foreign secretary and Rab Butler as chancellor of the exchequer. In February, 1952, King George VI died, and his daughter Elizabeth acceded to the throne. The new Conservative Government inherited an acute financial crisis as a result of a large deficit in the balance of payments and a depletion of gold and dollar reserves. Instead of removing controls, austerity measures were continued for another year; thereafter, government controls were gradually relaxed. The general improvement in the world economy reduced the price of raw materials and this, combined with greater freedom from government controls, raised production and the standard of living. A period of moderate prosperity began. The Conservatives extended social services by increasing the family allowance from five shillings to eight shillings for each child, raising unemployment benefits and old age pensions, and building over 300,000 houses a year.

The Interlude of Eden. In April, 1955, Churchill retired and was succeeded by his long-time heir apparent, Anthony Eden. The Churchillian team continued with only a reshuffling of Cabinet posts. Eden called an election in May, 1955, and his slogan of "peace and plenty" appealed to an increasingly affluent society. The election budget of 1955 reduced the income tax rate and ended the purchase tax on textiles. Meanwhile, Labor's intra-party debate continued to divide moderates and left-wingers; their party platform emphasized controls and nationalization—neither of which were attractive to a full-employment and cash-in-hand electorate. The Conservatives raised their parliamentary majority to 60 in the election and embarked on a program to promote partnership in industry and to extend property ownership among the well-to-do working class and the lower middle class—the economic and political center of the electorate. Increasingly, the role of the chancellor of the exchequer, now held by Harold Macmillan, was becoming critical in an effort to cope with the problems of balance of payments, productivity, and inflation. However, these domestic developments under Eden were overshadowed by colonial tensions in Cyprus and Kenya and by the debacle of Anglo-French intervention in the Suez Crisis (1956). In ill health Eden resigned on January 9, 1957, with his party divided over the Suez operation and the public confidence shaken.

New Leadership: Macmillan and Gaitskell. The new Prime Minister, Harold Macmillan, presided over a Conservative comeback and Britain's most prosperous postwar years, instead of over the bankruptcy of his party as had been predicted. His shrewdness, optimism, and genuine concern for the welfare of the people—he was the only leading Tory dissenter to break with the Baldwin-Chamberlain leadership before the war on *both* domestic and foreign policy—restored the confidence of the nation and salvaged Britain's relationship with Washington. Macmillan directed a non-inflationary expansion of a mixed economy with great success in the beginning. His unflappable Edwardian style and astute political touch blended happily with favorable economic conditions in the Western world to provide the British with a real, if temporary, consumer boom. The electorate responded to the Prime Minister's claim that they "never had it so good" by doubling the Conservative majority in Parliament to 100 in the election of October, 1959.

Meanwhile, the Labor party was searching for unity and a new sense of direction after having implemented its earlier goals of social security, full employment, and full legal status for unionism. Some Leftists claimed that doctrinaire socialism and its preoccupation with the material benefits of a welfare state were inadequate.

When Atlee resigned in 1955, Hugh Gaitskell was elected party leader. Gaitskell's moderate position was immediately attacked by the Bevanites who demanded unilateral disarmament and further nationalization. As Gaitskell gradually won party unity, Bevan moderated his position as a member of the shadow cabinet. Bevan's death in 1960 was an acute loss to both the party and Parliament.

Britain in World Affairs: The Decline from Greatness

The decline of Britain as a world power dates from 1918, not 1945. But only after the Second World War did the weakened position of the nation become evident. Until 1961 there was a tendency to maintain the illusion (if not the substance) of former power by overextending military commitments around the world, invoking the majestic prose of Churchill, claiming a special relationship with the United States, and by remaining aloof from European economic and political integration. The most remarkable achievement of these years was the freedom and nationhood Britain granted to over 500 million of her subjects in contrast to the annexation by Russia of over 100 million people into the Communist bloc. Britain found that her role in foreign affairs was severely limited by circumstances resulting from World War II, such as economic bankruptcy and dependence for security upon the United States. Immediate postwar developments were (1) the incompatibility of Russian aims with those of the free world, which Britain realistically accepted as a fact of the Cold War, and (2) Britain's subordinate position to the United States in countering the Communist World.

The Cold War. Foreign Minister Ernest Bevin made sincere efforts to prolong wartime co-operation with Russia, but Russia's blatant manifestations of hostility and expansion in eastern Europe frustrated any such hopes. The utter failure of the Conference of Foreign Ministers (London, 1947) to agree on the future of Germany signaled the onset of the Cold War and a redirection of foreign policy by the West to contain Russian expansion. In March, 1947, Bevin signed a treaty of alliance and assistance with France. Britain was also providing assistance to prevent a Communist takeover of Greece until President Harry Truman intervened with the promise of American aid (the Truman Doctrine) to Greece and Turkey. In March, 1948, Britain declared its involvement in the defense of Europe, along with France, Belgium, Holland and Luxembourg, by signing the Brussels Pact which promised mutual aid to any attacked member.

The four-power rule of Germany collapsed in 1947 and was

followed by a Soviet blockade of Berlin in 1948. Instead of acquiescing to Russian pressure, the United States and Great Britain organized an airlift which supplied the western sector of Berlin with food and necessities during the 323-day blockade. In 1949 Britain took a leading part in forming the North Atlantic Treaty Organization which comprised the signatories of the Brussels Pact, Canada, the United States, Italy, Norway, Denmark, Iceland, and Portugal. Later, West Germany, Greece, and Turkey joined this defensive alliance. Britain was basing her military security on co-operation and alliances with the United States, the Commonwealth, and the countries of western Europe; however, this co-operation with continental Europe did not extend to economic or political union. Britain refused to join the supranational European Coal and Steel Community (the Schumann Plan) established in 1951.

Anglo-American Co-operation. In contrast to the period following World War I, the United States became involved after World War II in aiding free nations against aggression, first in Europe and then around the globe. The European Recovery Program, proposed by George Marshall and approved by Congress, rehabilitated the floundering postwar economies of sixteen countries. In the first year of the program's operation (1948) Britain's economic crisis was eased by $980 million in Marshall aid. President Truman's Point Four Program (1950) was another economic weapon designed to combat Communism by sending capital, technical aid, and equipment to underdeveloped areas of the world. Anglo-American co-operation was especially evident in ending the Berlin blockade and in setting up a Federal German Government at Bonn (1949) to govern the three western zones of occupation. The British Government supported the action of the United States in the Korean War and raised the defense budget over £1 billion to accelerate rearmament. In 1951 Ernest Bevin, the postwar architect of Anglo-American accord, died, but the close Anglo-American relationship continued under Churchill and Eisenhower. The first four-nation (United States, Britain, France, and Russia) summit meeting, proposed by Britain, took place at Geneva in 1955. Not until the presidency of John F. Kennedy was Britain relegated to a conspicuously junior partnership in the Atlantic alliance.

Britain and the United Nations. British statesmen played an active role in the development of the Charter for the United Nations and in the organization's later operations. The Assembly of the United Nations, with 51 states represented, first met in London in January, 1946. The members elected a president and a secretary, barred Fascist Spain from membership, and selected New York as the site of the permanent headquarters. The United Nations, like the League of Nations, was handicapped by lack of co-operation among the great powers. In 1946 Russia used its veto to prevent the creation of a United Nations military force and the international control of atomic energy. The UN Security Council was able to take immediate and strong action against Communist aggression in Korea (1950) only because Russia was boycotting the Council and, therefore, could not veto the proceedings. Britain supported the Indian proposal in the Assembly for a compromise plan in the truce negotiations in Korea.

More successful, although less spectacular, were the specialized agencies affiliated with the United Nations, such as the World Health Organization, the International Monetary Fund, and the United Nations Educational, Scientific and Cultural Organization (UNESCO). These organizations provided food, medical supplies, personnel, and loans to governments in an effort to relieve human misery and hunger and encourage economic growth and stability.

Less Empire and More Commonwealth. The rapid liquidation of the British Empire was another consequence of World War II. The war stimulated nationalist and independence movements in the non-Western world and left the European colonial powers too weak to counter this process successfully. Britain's retreat from empire was achieved, in most cases, with dignity and with a minimum of conflict, so that after becoming independent the former colonies elected to stay in the Commonwealth and continue the parliamentary and legal systems which had been introduced by Britain. The transition to independence was eased by the establishment of dyarchic government whereby power was shared jointly by the colonial governor and a popularly elected cabinet. The flexibility of the Commonwealth was revealed in the decision of the conference of Commonwealth prime ministers in 1949 to accept India's continuing membership even though the country was becoming a republic. The remodeling of the Commonwealth ended the "common allegiance to the Crown" specified in the Balfour Report of 1926. In its place the King was accepted as the symbol of "the free association of its independent member nations and as such the Head of the Commonwealth." Between 1945 and 1970 Commonwealth membership rose from 6 to 28 sovereign states and changed from an all white to a predominantly colored membership.[1]

Palestine. The mandated territory of Palestine was a most complicated imperial problem to resolve. The 100 million Muslims in

---

[1] Commonwealth membership in 1970 consisted of: Australia, Barbados, Botswana, Canada, Ceylon, Cyprus, Fiji, Gambia, Ghana, Great Britain, Guyana, India, Jamaica, Kenya, Lesotho, Malawi, Malaysia, Malta, New Zealand, Nigeria, Pakistan, Sierra Leone, Singapore, Tanzania, Tonga, Trinidad and Tobago, Uganda, and Zambia.

the British Empire insisted that the flow of Jewish immigrants into Palestine be stopped at once. Britain attempted to establish a compromise quota system, but this only brought violent clashes among Zionists, Arabs, and British. In 1947 the British Government announced that it would withdraw from Palestine on May 15, 1948, and the United Nations followed this action by voting to partition Palestine into Jewish and Arab sections. Discord between Arabs and Jews provoked violence throughout the country as Britain tried in vain to maintain order during the last months of its mandate. The four neighboring Arab states refused to accept a sovereign state of Israel in its midst in 1948, but their armies were defeated by Israel and some of their territory was seized. The rest of Palestine was combined with Transjordan to form the new kingdom of Jordan under King Abdullah.

The Middle East. Pan-Arab nationalism was also in opposition to British imperial interests elsewhere in the Arab world. The seven-state Arab League supported the evacuation of British and French troops from Lebanon and Syria in 1946. Rising nationalism caused Egypt to demand a revision of the Anglo-Egyptian Treaty (1936) which would guarantee the withdrawal of British troops from the Suez Canal base and the annexation of the Sudan. In 1952 the corrupt regime of King Farouk was overthrown by a military junta, and Gamel Abdel Nasser, one of the leaders, became premier in 1954 and president two years later. Under Nasser's leadership a seven-year Anglo-Egyptian treaty was signed in Cairo which planned for the final evacuation by 1956 of the British from the Suez Canal. The following year saw the creation of the Middle East Treaty Organization, a Cold War alliance against Russia, whose membership included Britain, Pakistan, Turkey, Iran, and Iraq. With the signing of the Baghdad Pact tensions were eased between Britain and Iran over the attempted nationalization of the lucrative Iranian oil fields.

Southeast Asia. In 1942 Sir Stafford Cripps was sent to India to obtain support of the National Congress party for Britain's war effort, in return for which he proposed a plan for self-government in India after the war. The British Labor party, after the election of 1945, honored its promise of independence for India; but the complex negotiations for withdrawal were bedeviled by the bitter communal dissensions between Hindu and Muslim and the adamant demands of the Muslim leader, Mohammed Ali Jinnah, for a separate state. Lord Louis Mountbatten, the new and able viceroy, succeeded in persuading Gandhi, Nehru, and Jinnah to work out a mutually satisfactory transfer of power. The deadlock was broken by the British, Hindus, and Muslims finally accepting partition as the only way to preserve peace. On August 15, 1947, the Dominions of India and Pakistan came into existence. Nevertheless, large-scale violence marked the division of the country, and more than one million people were killed in the turmoil generated by communal and religious differences, among them Gandhi, who was assassinated in 1948. In the same year Ceylon gained its independence and elected to remain in the Commonwealth, while Burma became independent but chose to leave the Commonwealth. Conferences in London set up a new Federation of Malaya in 1957 (now expanded into Malaysia), after large British forces had finally crushed Communist guerrilla activities in the countryside. As the Cold War intensified in Asia, the United States and Britian attempted to check Communist expansion by the Southeast Asia Treaty Organization (SEATO) of 1954, whose membership included the United States, Britain, Pakistan, Australia, New Zealand, France, Thailand, and the Philippines.

Cyprus.   Bitter Greek-Turkish differences complicated independence for Cyprus. The Greek majority insisted on union with Greece; the Turks favored partition. After a period of terrorism by Greek Cypriots a settlement was agreed upon in 1960 by representatives of Britain, Greece, and Turkey, making the island an independent republic within the Commonwealth with a Greek Cypriot president, Archbishop Makarios, and a Turkish Cypriot vice president. But violence and communal suspicions continued, and United Nation troops were required to intervene in 1964 to restore peace.

Central African Federation.   In 1953 the Central African Federation was formed by the union of Southern Rhodesia and the two protectorates of Nyasaland and Northern Rhodesia. The Federation was an experiment in multi-racial partnership, but was established too late and offered too limited a franchise to the 8½ million Negroes (vis-à-vis 300,000 whites) to have any hope of success. In 1963 the ten-year experiment under federal Prime Minister Roy Welensky collapsed when Britain reluctantly gave Northern Rhodesia the right to secede from the Federation. The next year Northern Rhodesia became the Republic of Zambia, and Nyasaland took the name of Malawi. Both countries became sovereign members of the Commonwealth. The ruling white minority in Southern Rhodesia was determined that no African majority would replace their privileged position. Britain, in turn, refused to grant their request for independence until a constitution was provided that would guarantee the gradual enfranchisement of the whole populace. The white supremist Rhodesian Front Government under Ian Smith defied Britain by proclaiming a unilateral declaration of independence in

1965. The British Government promptly declared the action illegal and arranged for an economic boycott of Rhodesia through the United Nations, but neither the boycott nor the constitutional proposals offered Smith by Prime Minister Wilson in 1968 changed the position of the Rhodesian Government. Instead, the white electorate preferred to drop its allegiance to the Crown and in 1970, after a referendum, Rhodesia proclaimed itself a republic.

African Independence. Independence and freedom became the passwords of African nationalists after World War II. Self-government was granted readily in most British colonies by a gradual transfer of power. A fund of goodwill was thereby retained toward the former colonial power. The exceptions were in the colonies of Kenya and Southern Rhodesia where white settlers were unwilling to relinquish their dominant position to Africans on the basis of "one man, one vote." In 1956 the Sudan became an independent republic outside of the Commonwealth. The next year the Gold Coast became (as Ghana) the first sub-Saharan British colony to achieve independence. Nigeria, Uganda, Tanganyika, Zanzibar, British Somaliland, Kenya, and Sierra Leone achieved independence between 1960 and 1963. Under Churchill and Eden British support for African independence was reluctant and passive; under Macmillan the transfer of power was greatly accelerated, and the colonial secretaries readily negotiated the constitutional arrangements necessary for separation.

South African Developments. The United party of Jan Christian Smuts was defeated in 1948, and the Afrikaner Nationalist party under Dr. Daniel F. Malan came to power. The party increased its majority at every election until 1970, and the prime ministership, which passed from Malan to Johannes Strijdom, was held by Dr. Hendrik Verwoerd until his assassination in September, 1966. Thereupon, the Nationalist members of Parliament elected Balthazar Vorster as Prime Minister. The Nationalist party has extended and stiffened the policy of apartheid in a determined effort to maintain the doctrine of white supremacy and racial segregation in a land where there are 3 million whites and 11 million non-Europeans. The Government passed a series of acts to tighten control over all opposition to its policies. Due process of law and freedom of expression were cancelled by the General Law Amendments Acts and the Sabotage Acts. Government control of education increased. The Cape Colored, a mulatto grouping of one million, were placed on separate electoral rolls and can only elect white members of Parliament. Passes must be carried at all times by non-Europeans. At Sharpeville in 1960 a demonstration against the passbooks resulted in the killing of 60 Africans by the police. In the same year a referendum among whites favored making the state a republic; however, the other Commonwealth members condemned Verwoerd's racist policies and opposed his request to remain in the Commonwealth as a republic. As a result South Africa left the Commonwealth in March, 1961, but remained in the sterling area.

Economic Aid. In 1940 Britain reversed its prewar policy against providing economic aid to its colonies, and Parliament passed the first of a series of Colonial Development and Welfare Acts. By 1967 these acts had provided £490 million in grants and loans to underdeveloped areas for large-scale programs. Colonial colleges and universities were established, hydro-electric power developed, soil conservation introduced, and railways and new industries built. To combat poverty and disease in South and Southeast Asia and thereby limit the apeal of Communism, the foreign ministers of Britain, Canada, Australia, New Zealand, South Africa, Pakistan, India, and Ceylon met at Colombo in 1950 to pool their aid in developing the economic resources of the region. By 1965 there were twenty-one nations co-operating in the Colombo Plan. The donor nations were Britain, Canada, Australia, New Zealand, the United States, and Japan. Between 1946 and 1966 Britain extended a total of £1.367 billion in aid to developing countries.

The Suez Crisis, 1956. The withdrawal of western colonial powers from the Middle East and the ensuing Arab-Israeli conflict provided unstable conditions that invited intervention and competition by Communist and western powers for Arab support. In 1955 the United States and Britain outbid Russia's offer of assistance to build the Aswan high dam in Egypt but withdrew the offer the following year. Nasser responded to this rebuff by nationalizing the Suez Canal Company—an act which was contrary to international agreements. When a proposal for a conference in London of twenty-two maritime powers was rejected by Nasser, and recourse to the United Nations Security Council was blocked by a Russian veto, Eden and Selwyn Lloyd met privately with Premier Mollet in Paris on October 16. Apparently the conferees endorsed the Israeli attack on Egypt that was launched on October 29. Nasser rejected the Anglo-French ultimatum to withdraw his forces ten miles from the canal, and the two countries attacked Egypt on October 31. Port Said and a strip of the canal were captured, but thereafter military operations were halted in deference to mounting world opinion against Anglo-French intervention.

The policy of intervention found few supporters either in Britain or in the Commonwealth. The press and the Labor party condemned the action as an assault upon the three basic principles of postwar British foreign policy: solidarity with the Commonwealth, the Anglo-American alliance, and adherence to the Charter of the United Nations. Only Australia supported the attack. The United States, which had not been consulted, denounced it, and the United Nations called for a cease fire. Lester Pearson of Canada helped to arrange a United Nations task force to police the Ghaza strip. The British gained nothing by their military venture: the canal became unusable for shipping; Britain's oil pipeline in Syria was cut; British gold and dollar reserves fell sharply; and Nasser's military defeat by Israel was overshadowed by his diplomatic victory over Britain and France. The Suez remained in Egyptian hands. The only benefits to accrue from the Suez crisis were the submission of two major powers to the will of the United Nations and the establishment of an international police force. Politically, however, the Suez fiasco was a disaster for Eden, splitting his Cabinet and contributing to his resignation in January, 1957.

Defense Policies.   Britain made no attempt to avoid involvement in worldwide trouble spots in the postwar world as she had done in the period between the World Wars. But her active participation in the security of the free world came at a time when she no longer had the power to enforce her will. British spheres of influence were no longer recognized. Realizing that in Europe and in the Far East she no longer could command respect as an independent power, Britain made the critical decision to join NATO and SEATO—permanent military associations for collective security. In 1954 Britain eased French fears and helped terminate Allied occupation of the German Federal Republic by maintaining military contingents on the European mainland. British dependence on the United States for missiles and atomic weapons made the Anglo-American alliance a cornerstone of postwar foreign policy. The support of the fast-growing Commonwealth also became more important as Britain's ability to speak and act with independent authority declined.

In the Middle East the Labor and the Conservative Governments tried to maintain British influence and a favorable power structure to keep the approaches to Africa from falling to hostile powers and assure a steady flow of oil from Iraq and Kuwait. The Anglo-Libyan Treaty (1953), the air bases in Malta, Cyprus, and Aden, the treaty with Kuwait, and the Baghdad Pact were attempts to implement this policy. However, after the Suez crisis British control of the political arrangement in the Middle East was no longer possible, and in 1957 the Eisenhower Doctrine guaranteed American support to this area.

Britain since 1960

The delicate balance of the British economy, crippled by industrial inefficiency and recurring balance of payment crises, remained the most critical problem in the sixties and accounted for the rapid turnover in the post of chancellor of the exchequer. Greater spending in the affluent society on social services and defense raised the old dilemma of how to expand the economy without encouraging inflation. Both major political parties elected new leaders. The election of 1964 ended thirteen years of Conservative Government. Britain's international stature diminished during the sixties as the country became an auxiliary, rather than an ally, of the United States in nuclear and foreign policy. The United States and Russia made momentous decisions without consulting Britain, notably in the Cuban missile crisis of 1962; furthermore France, because of the intransigence of President de Gaulle, was able to frustrate Britain's bid to join the European Economic Community.

Political Changes. By 1959 the two party programs were not far apart. A new political equilibrium had been achieved slightly left of center, as compared to the political alignment in prewar England. Nationalization and doctrinaire socialism no longer stirred much Labor interest, and the trade unions were losing their political consciousness. The Conservatives endorsed the welfare state and accepted the necessity of educational change and economic planning. The death of Gaitskell and the Profumo scandal prompted a change in leadership of the Labor and the Conservative parties.

The Labor Party. The third defeat in succession for Labor at the general election of 1959 left the party disappointed and divided. Gaitskell vigorously opposed the Labor doctrine of earlier years which demanded public ownership of the means of production and fought the doctrinaire Labor members who advocated unilateral renunciation of nuclear weapons. By 1961 his views prevailed and a fresh program was issued urging careful planning for capital expansion and reorganization of education. Before he could lead the party in another election campaign, Gaitskell died suddenly in January, 1963. Labor members of Parliament chose Harold Wilson over George Brown, deputy leader since 1960, as Gaitskell's successor. Wilson was a former lecturer in economics at Oxford before entering the House of Commons in 1945. He had opposed Gaitskell and had become associated with the left wing of the party. However, upon his election to Labor leadership, Wilson achieved harmony by appointing most of his opponents to the shadow cabinet.

The Conservatives. Prime Minister Macmillan's fortune changed after the election of 1959. By 1960 the economic upswing was spent and the balance of international payments was again adverse. In an effort to get the economy moving, Macmillan changed chancellors of the exchequer three times (D. Heathcoat Amery, Selwyn Lloyd, and Reginald Maulding) between 1960 and 1963, raised the bank rate to 7 per cent, and called for a pay pause in all wages and salaries. By-elections in 1962 reflected the declining stock of the Conservatives. In July Macmillan replaced seven members of his Cabinet in a belated attempt to provide fresh ideas and new energy to the Government. The failure at Brussels (1962-63) to gain entry into the Common Market and the scandal of John Profumo, secretary of war, further damaged the Government. Mr. Profumo's improper associations in private life not only resulted in his lying to the House of Commons, but also raised the question of a breach of national security. Although Macmillan survived the parliamentary and press attacks, he resigned in October, 1963, because of poor health. R. A. Butler, Ian Macleod, Reginald Maulding, Lord Home, and Lord Hailsham were candidates for Conservative leadership—the latter two were now permitted to renounce their titles because of the Peerage Act (1963). Since no candidate had a majority among the Conservative members of Parliament canvassed, Macmillan advised the Queen to invite Lord Home, foreign secretary, to become Prime Minister. Once again the quiet, able R. A. Butler, who had held almost every major office, was bypassed for the prime ministership.

Election of 1964. Lord Home renounced his peerage (he became Sir Alec Douglas-Home) and won election to the House of Commons. He formed an able ministry with only Enoch Powell and Ian Macleod refusing to serve under him. The Prime Minister put off an election as long as possible to establish himself and reverse the opinion polls which gave Labor a decisive lead. By September, 1964, the Labor lead had disappeared. In the campaign foreign affairs had little interest for the electorate; the important issues were cost of living, education, and housing. Assisting Labor's prospects were Wilson's obvious talents for party leadership and the feeling that it was time for a change after thirteen years of Conservative Government. The results of the October election gave Labor a thin majority of 4 seats over 304 Conservative and 9 Liberal.

Election of 1966. By March, 1966, Wilson had shown resourcefulness and skill in governing for 17 months with the smallest majority in British parliamentary history. His pragmatic policy in

office was in striking contrast to his earlier support for the doctrinaire left-wing section of the Labor party. With its narrow
majority the Government avoided the controversial 1964 campaign
promise to nationalize steel. On foreign affairs Wilson and Foreign
Secretary Michael Stewart strongly backed American policy in the
Dominican Republic and Vietnam. Wilson's efforts to have Commonwealth prime ministers serve as brokers for a peace conference
on Vietnam achieved no results.

The budget of 1965, which to consumers was one of the most un-
palatable in years, represented an effort to curb inflation, reduce
consumer spending, and promote exports. Encouraged by his success
in halving Britain's trade deficit, Wilson called an election to seek
a more secure majority in Parliament. In the campaign he promised
long-term economic planning to modernize industry and raise productivity—which in 1965 remained almost static in contrast to the
rise in wages and prices. The Conservatives went into the campaign with a new party leader. In 1965 Douglas-Home resigned in
favor of a younger man and Edward Heath, shadow chancellor of
the exchequer, won over Reginald Maulding, shadow foreign secretary, in the balloting by Conservative members of Parliament. The
Conservatives pledged discussion with Ian Smith's Rhodesian government and committed themselves to being the "European party"
in favor of immediate entry into the European Common Market.
In the election of March 31, 1966, the Prime Minister's prestige
abroad and popularity at home, coupled with a continued prosperity, raised the Labor majority in the House of Commons from 3 to 97.

The Wilson Years. Wilson began his first term of office by putting together a Cabinet that included all segments of the Labor
party and talking about "100 days of dynamic action." After two
years he was no more successful than had been Douglas-Home in
solving Britain's chronic economic problems of industrial inefficiency
and economic growth without inflation. By the 1966 election the
earlier "Kennedy style" had been replaced by the "family doctor"
role, as the Prime Minister used television as his most effective
medium to "inspire trust by his appearance as well as by his sooth-
ing words." Once the election was over, Wilson prescribed the
severest dose of economic controls ever imposed during peacetime
in a Western nation in an effort to restore a sick economy.

Winds of Change. Wilson's rhetoric promising a "great crusade"
to confront "the white heat of the technological revolution" was
scarcely matched by his performance in office. The traditional pressures of office, coupled with declining public appetite for novelty

after the fever of political and cultural excitement during the first half of the decade, combined to produce only modest political controversy. Nevertheless, the Labor Government encouraged certain domestic changes at home just as Macmillan and Macleod had accelerated the pace of change abroad from empire to Commonwealth. Under Wilson the first major overhaul of the policies governing welfare services since the Beveridge Report of 1942 was made. The central proposal in the new program was to relate pensions to earnings to provide a pension of 50 per cent of earnings averaged over a lifetime of work. Reflecting its growing orientation toward Europe, the Government passed legislation ending (February, 1971) the quaint, but irrational, British currency and replacing it with a decimal system, and establishing the metric system of weights and measures on or before 1975. Considerable attention was given by Parliament to the younger generation. Imaginative efforts to cope with the growing drug problem were attempted, and in 1969 the voting age was reduced to 18 by the Representation of the Peoples Act. The Parliamentary Commissioner Act created the office of "ombudsman" to serve as a watchdog of the citizens against a growing bureaucracy. The age-old controversy over the dual school system (grammar versus secondary modern) was stirred up by Labor's Education Act of 1970, which passed its second reading in the Commons before Labor went out of office. The bill established a unitary secondary educational system which would join the grammar and secondary modern school into a single comprehensive system. More politically risky—and more essential—were the changes in economic policy.

Economy on Trial. Low productivity, unofficial strikes, and an international crisis of confidence in British sterling plagued Prime Minister Wilson, as they had plagued most of his postwar predecessors. Until July, 1966, the Government continued its stop-go economic policies in a desperate effort to stabilize the inflationary boom of the previous decade. Determined to maintain the illusion of world power, to avoid deflation and unemployment at home, and to save the sterling from devaluation, the Government was finally forced to admit defeat on all three. The July, 1966, voluntary wage-price freeze was changed in November to a mandatory system with fines and prison sentences for violators. This restriction by a Labor Government on the British workers' cherished right of collective bargaining was necessary because workers' wages had risen $2\frac{1}{4}$ times faster than productivity between 1964 and 1966 and exports were being priced out of the world market. The unpopularity of such stringent measures was reflected in Labor losses in municipal and parliamentary by-elections in 1967. Even these sacrifices were insufficient to weather the international run on Britain's slim financial reserves. In November, 1967, the Government was forced to devalue the pound from $2.80 to $2.40, raise the Bank of England's lending rate to 8 per cent, and impose severe restrictions on installment buying. This action staved off the threat of bankruptcy and reassured the international financial community; it also signaled the end of an era. Without the former wealth from invisible trade, and the resources to maintain the illusion of a world power, Britain's diminished post-imperial status became painfully apparent. The drastic budget measures of the Chancellor of the Exchequer Roy Jenkins, between 1967 and 1970, succeeded in curbing consumer spending and stimulating exports. By 1970 Britain enjoyed a strong balance of payments position with a surplus of $1.5 billion.

Immigration. In 1962 the Conservatives passed the first Commonwealth Immigrants Act to restrict entry of Commonwealth ·citizens who were without prospects of employment or means of self-support. The great influx of Commonwealth immigration after 1958, especially from the West Indies and Pakistan (reaching a million by 1968) created social and racial tensions due to their concentration in congested areas of the industrial cities. In 1968 the Wilson Government feared a heavy influx of Kenyan Asians and imposed further restrictions on Commonwealth immigrants, in spite of protests from several Commonwealth countries. At the same time the second Race Relations Act strengthened the 1965 act by banning all racial discrimination in housing and employment within the country.

Biafra. The secession of the Eastern Region under Colonel Odumegwu Ojukwu in 1967 placed the British Government in an awkward dilemma. The massacre of thousands of Ibos by the Hausas in 1966 and their later sufferings in the civil war had made many Britons sympathetic to the Ibo cause and hostile to the Government's support of, and supply of arms to, the Nigerian Federal Government. Foreign Secretary Stewart defended British policy on the grounds that cutting off arms shipments would be tacit support of rebellion against the legitimate government of the country, would lead to increased Soviet influence in Nigeria, and would estrange Britain from other African countries who strongly opposed secessionist tendencies.

Ulster. Submerged sectarian enmity in Ulster surfaced in 1969 when the reform-minded Ulster prime minister, Terence O'Neill, tried to introduce a series of reforms to end religious discrimination against Roman Catholics. Violent clashes in Belfast and Londonderry prodded the Wilson Government to call in British troops to relieve the Ulster police and forced O'Neill to resign from his own Unionist party. His successor, James Chichester-Clark, backed by Westminster, continued with the reform program. The tense situation was polarized further by the election to Westminster in 1969 of Bernadette Devlin as the young heroine of the Bogside Roman Catholics and in 1970 of the Reverend Ian Paisley as the militant spokesman of the Protestant extremists. Miss Devlin served a six-month jail sentence in 1970 after conviction for "incitement to riotous behavior."

Election of 1970. In April, 1970, the polls, which had heavily favored the Conservatives for the past three years, began to swing in Labor's favor. Capitalizing on this popularity and very favorable balance-of-payments figures, Prime Minister Wilson called an election for June 18. The campaign was inward-looking with little attention to issues outside the country. Labor pointed to its rescue of the pound, its defense of social democracy at home, and its pipe-smoking prime minister on television. Conspicuously lacking was the usual Labor emphasis on planning or the radical critique of society offered in 1964. The Conservatives under Ted Heath emphasized practical reforms such as industrial planning, tax and labor union reform, and, above all, pitched the campaign to the housewives' fight against rising prices. Polls predicted an easy Labor victory by a margin of 4 to 12 per cent. Instead, the Tories won by a 4 per cent margin. The final outcome in parliamentary seats was Conservatives 330, Labor 287, and Liberals, under their new leader Jeremy Thorpe, 6 seats.

Britain and Europe. Britain had firmly committed herself through the Brussels treaty and NATO to a full military association with Western Europe, but had remained outside of the European Coal and Steel Community formed in 1951 and the European Economic Community set up by the Treaty of Rome in 1957. Britain feared that the projected economic and political unification of the Common Market countries would conflict with her agricultural interests and sovereignty as well as with her Commonwealth connections. Instead, Britain proposed a looser association and in 1960 joined Norway, Denmark, Sweden, Austria, Switzerland, and Portugal in forming the European Free Trade Association. However, this "outer seven" never matched the economic dynamism of the "inner six" of France, West Germany, Italy, Holland, Belgium, and Luxembourg. After making a candid reappraisal of Britain's diminishing role outside Europe, Macmillan's Government made application for entry into the European Economic Community. The Labor party opposed the application. Early in 1963 the negotiations for entry came to a halt, not on account of Labor or Commonwealth persuasion, but because of the veto of French President de Gaulle, who resented Britain's attachment to the Atlantic Alliance with the United States. A second application was made in 1967 by Wilson's Government after Labor had become a reluctant convert to entry. Again de Gaulle resisted British entry in spite of the support for Britain's application given by the other members. De Gaulle's resignation in 1969 and Heath's victory in 1970 once again made British entry a strong possibility. Heath had served as Britain's chief negotiator for entry in 1963. In 1970 he made Britain's bid to join the European Economic Community a central theme of Conservative economic and foreign policy.

Defense and Disarmament. The rearmament of Britain following the Korean War, along with her worldwide commitments, raised again the old dilemma of "guns or butter" in an economy which could not afford both. Ban-the-Bomb marchers, the Committee on Nuclear Disarmament, and neutralists in the Labor party urged a policy of unilateral disarmament and isolationism. By 1961 the intensity of these sentiments had passed and Gaitskell reversed the Scarborough resolution of 1960 calling for unilateral disarmament. In 1963 Macmillan, "the Champion of Summit Conferences," achieved a bipartisan objective with the nuclear-test-ban treaty signed in Moscow by Britain, the United States, and the U.S.S.R. No comparable success was achieved in the general disarmament discussions which were begun at Geneva.

An independent nuclear deterrent was considered essential to Britain's defense and international stature, but the economy could scarcely sustain the massive expenditures required for such a program. In 1960 research on a British-designed "Blue Streak" missile was abandoned in favor of an American-made "Skybolt." Two years later President Kennedy halted production of the Skybolt and promised, instead, Polaris missiles for British submarines. The United States preferred that Britain support a multilateral NATO nuclear force rather than continue with its independent or Anglo-American deterrent.

By 1967 the Wilson Government accepted the fact Britain was no longer a world power and began to reduce her military obligations east of Suez. This planned withdrawal from Asia underlined the new priority of Europe over Commonwealth and worldwide commitments. Defense Minister Healey (1964-70), through streamlining and economizing, had cut the defense budget by 1970 to less than 6 per cent of the gross national product. The Conservative victory in 1970 meant no change on the importance of Europe, but a commitment to keep a small force east of Suez as part of a Commonwealth unit in Malaysia and Singapore.

The Affluent Society and the Welfare State. Compared to conditions in 1900, poverty in Britain had practically disappeared by 1960. After World War II human welfare was fully accepted as a social responsibility of the state. Real wages had increased 19 per cent from 1949 to 1964. By 1965 nearly five million houses or flats had been built, and for the first time, because of government subsidy, home ownership was possible for the average family. Poverty and economic inequality were no longer controversial public issues. The continuing challenge was how to achieve a satisfactory standard of living while keeping down the cost of living at home and competing successfully abroad. The slowest rate of economic growth since 1945 of any industrial nation, the recurring sterling crises, and rising wages and prices indicated that the affluent British society had not yet learned to stabilize its abundance. Maximizing welfare did not necessarily encourage maximum national production.

Britain's industrial inefficiency results from a combination of circumstances and traditions. Over the past 180 years, Britain has seldom had a favorable balance of visible trade. England prospered from her invisible trade—investments, shipping, banking, insurance —and lost this edge when her investments were diminished by two world wars and war debts, by the dollar's replacing the pound as the staple of world currency, and by banking competition from Zurich, Paris, and New York. Low productivity in industry mirrors the values and habits of British management, education, and trade unions. The cult of the amateur and distrust of the specialist puts British management at a distinct disadvantage in a highly specialized and competitive world. Indifference to efficiency reflects a lack of technical training due, in part, to the humanist tradition of the public schools and "Oxbridge," which produce well-educated gentlemen not likely to be attracted to the technological and vulgar world of business. The trade unions, in turn, with a strong sense of class history, oppose and obstruct any attempt at technological innovation at the expense of manpower. Their restrictive practices and continual strikes—95 per cent of which are unofficial—frustrate efforts by forward-looking companies to compete internationally.

The Labor Government in 1969 attempted to implement a white paper which proposed modest restraints on strike action and additional legal procedures in bargaining. The unions refused to support the reforms and Wilson abandoned the bill. Long-held traditions and class and cultural values continue to clash with the world of technology.

The Queen's Government. Queen Elizabeth II symbolizes the dignity, ceremony, and continuity of British constitutional history. The almost complete concentration of power in the Prime Minister and Cabinet, and the decline in importance of the backbencher and of parliamentary debate, have provoked much discussion of the role and future of Parliament. The changes that have occurred, however, have been largely a result of the extension of the doctrine of popular sovereignty, the growth of party organization, and the influence of the mass media. If the main function of the Government is to govern, it follows that any party in power will arrange the political machinery of the State in order to facilitate this function. No party would risk making arbitrary changes that were obviously against the will or the best interests of the electorate, because such changes would be repudiated at the next election. Change based on continuity has served as the axiom of British constitutional history.

In the House of Lords recent changes included the creation of life peers and peeresses as regular members in 1958, followed in 1963 by the Peerage Act which permitted hereditary peers to disclaim their titles and stand for election to the House of Commons. Viscount Stansgate (Anthony Wedgwood-Benn) and Viscount Hailsham (Quinton Hogg), both prominent politicians, were the first to relinquish the peerages they had inherited. The criticism that only men of means could afford to sit in the House of Commons because of the meager salary was muted in 1964 by the raising of the annual salary from £1,750 to £3,250.

The late Victorian structure of local government which had served its function admirably when instituted in 1888 and 1894 had become inefficient and inadequate by 1945 and made impossible any overall strategic planning between town and countryside. A royal commission on reform of local government under the chairmanship of Lord Redcliffe-Maud in 1969 recommended omnibus unitary authorities to replace the present dual system of county boroughs and county councils. A two-tier system would be retained in the populous conurbation areas.

Contemporary Britain. In 1968 the population of Great Britain was 55 million, of whom 80 per cent were urbanites. The most striking urban development was the growth of conurbation—the peripheral expansion of towns into a single, built-up area with common industrial interests. The human problems resulting from uncontrolled urban growth produced serious efforts at city and environmental planning. Inner cities destroyed by wartime bombing were rebuilt; factories were relocated away from the heart of the city; and such new towns as Stevenage and Crawley were established by statute (1946) as satellites of major cities. American-style "strip" cities along highways have been avoided by "green-belt" legislation. In 1969 the Civic Amenities Act gave additional powers to authorities to preserve or improve standards of environment in town and country.

The biggest postwar social revolution was quietly taking place in education. Between 1938 and 1956 the percentage of 15-to-18 year-old children attending secondary schools doubled. The Labor party endorsed the comprehensive secondary school which offers all types of educational programs and makes no attempt to place students in particular curriculums based upon their performance in national exams. Compared to other industrial nations, Britain is undereducated. The increase in enrollment and the belated effort to catch up in technical education, however, are signs of change. No longer was university education impervious to the social forces already permeating every other institution. University enrollment almost trebled between 1939 and 1970; and new postwar universities, such as the University of Sussex, were founded to accommodate the swelling student population. By 1970 there were over forty universities in Great Britain and the Open University (University of the Air), established in 1969, will make higher education available to another 100,000 through extra-mural studies on television.

Contemporary Britons have higher real incomes, more leisure, and more opportunity for education and a choice of careers than any previous generation; they also suffer a soaring crime rate. The upheaval of traditional values since World War II is reflected in permissive sexual ethics, pop music fads, and a decline in church attendance and influence. Nevertheless, this same skeptical and unconventional younger generation reads more, studies more seriously, protests nuclear disarmament and South African apartheid, and eagerly engages in such humanitarian tasks as Voluntary Service Overseas (V.S.O.).

The British Achievement. Continuity and change, marked by a series of historic compromises, such as the Magna Charta and the Great Reform Bill, have been the hallmarks of the British achievement. Moderation and pragmatism in the pursuit of political and social goals are virtues in British political life. As a result Britain in recent history has been spared much of the violence and rancor that accompany the clash of doctrinaire positions. In times of crisis (as in the Battle of Britain) the love of freedom provided a unity and resilience that was not evident to enemies who mistook mere dissent for debilitating division. Parliamentary government, Common Law, political liberalism, and the English language—and their expansion overseas—have been enduring tributes to Britain and her peoples. Since 1945 Britain's distinctive achievements have been her commitment to domestic social democracy and the successful reconstruction of the Commonwealth to encompass more than a score of largely non-white nations.

Can British institutions and democratic forms adapt to such rapidly changing conditions as the movement toward European unity, nuclear power and competition, and a scientific culture without sacrificing the distinctive qualities and traditions of the British way of life? If the old ideals of parliamentary democracy or the civilizing mission of the British Empire have been either achieved or abandoned, what new ideals, national or international, can provide meaning and purpose for this island nation? How the British people respond to these questions will determine the shape and quality of their future achievements.

BIBLIOGRAPHY OF GENERAL READINGS

Birnie, Arthur, *An Economic History of the British Isles* (1961).
Bullock, Alan, and Shock, Maurice, *The Liberal Tradition from Fox to Keynes* (1956).
Butterfield, Herbert, *The Whig Interpretation of History* (1965).
————, *The Englishman and His History* (1944).
Cam, Helen, *England Before Elizabeth* (1960).
Churchill, Winston, *A History of the English-Speaking Peoples* (4 vols., 1956-58).
Clark, George N. (ed.), *The Oxford History of England* (15 vols., 1937-65).
Cole, George D. H., and Postgate, Raymond, *The British Common People 1746-1946* (1961).
Daiches, David, *A Critical History of English Literature* (1960).
Haskins, George L., *The Growth of English Representative Government* (1948).
Havighurst, Alfred F., *Twentieth-Century Britain* (2nd ed., 1966).
Mackenzie, Robert T., *British Political Parties* (1964).
Maitland, Frederic W., *The Constitutional History of England* (1961).
Morpurgo, J. E. (ed.), *The Pelican History of England* (9 vols., 1950-65).
Rose, J. H., Newton, A. P., and Benians, E. A., *The Cambridge History of the British Empire* (9 vols., 1929-59).
Rowse, Alfred L., *The Spirit of English History* (1945).
Schuyler, Robert L., and Ausubel, Herman, *The Making of English History* (1952).
Smith, Goldwin, *A Constitutional and Legal History of England* (1955).
Somervell, D. C., *British Politics Since 1900* (1953).
Strang, William, *Britain in World Affairs* (1961).
Thompson, Edward P., *The Making of the English Working Class* (1963).
Thornton, A. P., *The Imperial Idea and Its Enemies: A Study in British Power* (1959).
Trevelyan, George M., *History of England* (3 vols., 1926).
Trevor-Roper, Hugh, *Essays in British History* (1965).
Williams, Raymond, *Culture and Society, 1780-1950* (1960).

Selected Readings
and Review Questions

Chapter 1: The Foundations of England

Ashe, Geoffrey, *From Caesar to Arthur* (1960).
Boon, George S., *Roman Silchester* (1958).
Caesar, Julius, *The Conquest of Gaul*, translated by S. A. Handford (1951).
Childe, V. Gordon, *Prehistoric Communities of the British Isles* (2nd ed., 1947).
Clarke, Graham, *Prehistoric England* (1962).
Collingwood, R. G. and Myres, J. N. L., *Roman Britain and the English Settlements* (2nd ed., 1937).
Richmond, I. A., *Roman Britain* (1964).
Tacitus, *On Britain and Germany*, translated by H. Mattingly (1960).

❧❦❧

1. Describe Celtic civilization in Britain and identify the relationship between the Celts in Gaul and in Britain.
2. Compare and contrast the Roman invasions of Britain by Julius Caesar and by Claudius.
3. Explain the operation of Roman administration in Britain. What vas its strength? What were its weaknesses?
4. How did Roman civilization in Britain differ from the Celtic? Which Roman achievements influenced later British developments?

Chapter 2: Anglo-Saxon Supremacy

Bede, *A History of the English Church and People*, translated by J. Sherley-Price (1953).
Blair, Peter H., *An Introduction to Anglo-Saxon England* (1959).
Bryant, Sir Arthur, *The Story of England: Makers of the Realm* (1953).
Crawford, Samuel J., *Anglo-Saxon Influence on Western Christendom* (1966).
Duckett, Eleanor S., *Alfred the Great, the King and his England* (1956).
Garmonsway, George N. (editor), *The Anglo-Saxon Chronicle* (1955).
Hodgkin, Robert H., *A History of the Anglo-Saxons* (1953).
Kendrick, Thomas D., *A History of the Vikings* (1930).
Lindsay, Donald and Price, Mary R., *The Portrait of Britain Before 1066* (1963).

Oman, Sir Charles, *England Before the Norman Conquest* (8th ed., 1937).
Plummer, Charles, *Life and Times of Alfred the Great* (1902).
Stenton, Frank M., *Anglo-Saxon England* (1947).

◄§§►

1. Describe the origins and way of life of the Germanic invaders of the fifth and sixth centuries.
2. What was the heptarchy? What kingdoms did it include? How did a single kingdom achieve paramount power?
3. Trace the growth and achievements of Celtic Christianity.
4. Discuss the judicial courts and methods of trial in Anglo-Saxon England.
5. Identify and describe the administrative units and the officials of local government.
6. Why did the second Danish invasion subdue England whereas the first fell short of this objective? How does Ethelred the Unready enter into this account?

Chapter 3: The French Kings

Barlow, Frank, *The Feudal Kingdom of England, 1022-1216* (1955).
Brooke, Christopher, *From Alfred to Henry III: 871-1272* (1961).
Brown, R. Allen, *The Normans and the Norman Conquest* (1969).
Douglas, David C., *William the Conqueror* (1964).
Green, Alice S., *Henry II* (1888).
Kelly, Amy, *Eleanor of Aquitaine and the Four Kings* (1950).
Maitland, Frederic W., *Domesday Book and Beyond* (1966).
Painter, Sidney, *The Reign of King John* (1949).
Poole, A. L., *From Domesday to Magna Carta* (1951).
Powicke, Frederick M., *The Thirteenth Century, 1216-1307* (1953).
————, *Stephen Langton* (1927).
Sayles, George O., and Richardson, Henry G., *The Governance of Mediaeval England from the Conquest to Magna Carta* (1963).
Stenton, Frank M., *William the Conqueror* (1908).
Stephanson, Carl, *Medieval Feudalism* (1942).

◄§§►

1. Did the Norman conquest differ from earlier conquests? What were the chief contributions of Norman rule?
2. How did the feudal system differ in England from the Continent?
3. Describe the rising political power of the Roman Catholic church. How did it influence the reigns of Henry II and Henry III?
4. Trace the growth of the English legal system from Henry I to Henry III.
5. How do you account for the more rapid advance of constitutional rights and safeguards under poor or weak kings? Give examples.
6. What is unique about English common law? How did it develop?

Chapter 4: Medieval Society

Baldwin, C. S., *Three Medieval Centuries of Literature in England, 1100-1400,* (1946).
Barraclough, Geoffrey, (ed.), *Social Life in Early England* (1960).
Bennett, Henry S., *Life in the English Manor* (1960).
Brieger, Peter, *English Art, 1216-1307* (1957).
Cam, Helen M., *England Before Elizabeth* (1950).
Costain, Thomas B., *The Magnificent Century* (1951).
Coulton, George G., *Medieval Panorama* (1955).
Knowles, Dom D., *The Monastic Order in England, 943-1216* (1949).
Lipson, Ephraim (ed.), *The Middle Ages* (1961).
Moorman, John R. H., *Church Life in England in the Thirteenth Century* (1945).
Pirenne, Henri, *Medieval Cities* (1925).
Poole, Austin L., *Medieval England* (1958).
Sayles, George O., *The Medieval Foundations of England* (1961).
Stenton, Doris M., *English Society in the Early Middle Ages* (1952).

1. How did Christendom respond when challenged in the Middle Ages by another world religion?
2. What relationship did the results of the Crusades have with the original aims?
3. Compare and contrast the begging orders with the monastic orders.
4. What were the economic policies and practices of the business community in medieval towns?
5. What political consequences in England are a result of the rise of towns?
6. Identify the unifying features of medieval life. What forces were at work to modify or destroy them?

Chapter 5: King and Parliament

Barrow, Geoffrey W. S., *Robert Bruce* (1965).
Coulton, George, *Chaucer and His England* (1963).
Harvey, John, *The Plantagenets* (1959).
Haskins, George, *The Growth of English Representative Government* (1948).
Holmes, George, *The Later Middle Ages, 1272-1485* (1962).
Lyon, Bryce, *A Constitutional and Legal History of Medieval England* (1960).
McIlwain, Charles H., *The High Court of Parliament and Its Supremacy* (1910).
McKisack, May, *The Fourteenth Century, 1307-1399* (1959).
Myers, A. R., *England in the Late Middle Ages* (1952).
Oman, Charles, *The Great Revolt of 1381* (1906).
Pantin, William, *The English Church in the Fourteenth Century* (1955).

Perroy, E., *The Hundred Years' War* (1965).
Pollard, A. F., *The Evolution of Parliament* (1964).
Steel, Anthony, *Richard II* (1963).
Trevelyan, George M., *England in the Age of Wycliffe, 1368-1520* (1909).
Workman, Herbert B., *John Wyclif* (1966).

◄§§►

1. Discuss the major legal reforms of Edward I. What was the significance of statute law?
2. How and why did Parliament appeal to the various estates (spiritual and temporal lords, and commons) that composed it?
3. Compare and contrast the forced abdications of Edward II and Richard II.
4. How did the efforts to subdue Scotland affect the political fortunes of the three Edwards?
5. Identify the causes of the Hundred Years' War and relate the original causes to the final outcome of the struggle.
6. Trace the development of Parliament in the reign of the three Edwards.
7. How did the barons attempt to control Richard II? What were the problems inherent in rule by oligarchy?
8. Discuss the growth and significance of the textile industry in the fourteenth century.

Chapter 6: Lancaster and York

Bagley, J. J., *Margaret of Anjou* (1948).
Bennett, Henry S., *The Pastons and Their England* (1922).
———, *Chaucer and the Fifteenth Century* (1947).
Brown, P. H. A., *A Short History of Scotland* (1955).
Chrimes, Stanley B., *English Constitutional Ideas in the Fifteenth Century* (1936).
Gairdner, James (ed.), *The Paston Letters, 1422-1509* (1904).
Green, Vivian H. H., *The Later Plantagenets: A Survey of English History Between 1399-1485* (1961).
Jacob, Ernest. *The Fifteenth Century, 1399-1485* (1961).
Kendall, Paul Murray, *The Yorkist Age* (1961).
———, *Richard the Third* (1956).
Mackenzie, Agnes M., *Robert Bruce. King of Scots* (1956).
Oman, Charles, *Political History of England, 1377-1485* (1906).
Ramsay, James H., *Lancaster and York* (1892).
Salzman, Louis F., *Building in England down to 1540* (1952).
Scofield, Cora L., *Life and Reign of Edward the Fourth* (1923).

1. Discuss the problems Henry IV faced when he won his throne.

2. Describe the circumstances and developments in the reign of Henry VI that led to the Wars of the Roses.
3. Appraise the reign of Richard III. Why is Richard III so often portrayed as the royal villain?
4. What were the consequences of the Wars of the Roses for the nobility?
5. Discuss the developments that took place in fifteenth-century education.
6. What changes took place in Parliament during the fifteenth century? How did Parliament's role differ under the Lancasters and the Yorks?
7. How did the changing economic conditions reflect the decline of feudalism?
8. Describe the efforts of Robert Bruce and James III to achieve independence from England.

Chapter 7: The Early Tudors and the Reformation

Chambers, Raymond W., *Thomas More* (1958).
Chapman, Hester W., *The Last Tudor King: A Study of Edward VI* (1958).
Dickens, A. G., *The English Reformation* (1964).
Elton, Geoffrey R., *England under the Tudors* (1955).
Knowles, David, *The Religious Orders in England: The Tudor Age* (1959).
Mackie, John D., *The Earlier Tudors, 1485-1558* (1952).
Parker, T. M., *The English Reformation to 1558* (1959).
Pollard, Albert F., *Henry VIII* (1951).
————, *Thomas Cranmer and the English Reformation, 1489-1556* (1904).
Powicke, Frederick M., *The Reformation in England* (1941).
Prescott, Hilda F. M., *A Spanish Tudor: The Life of "Bloody Mary"* (1953).
————, *The Man on a Donkey* (1952).
Read, Conyers, *The Tudors* (1936).
Scarisbrick, J. J., *Henry VIII* (1968).
Zeeveld, W. Gordon, *Foundations of Tudor Policy* (1948).

◄§§►

1. How did the Renaissance in Northern Europe differ from the Italian Renaissance? What scholars helped introduce Renaissance thought into England?
2. Describe the problems faced by Henry VII on his accession to the throne and how he coped with them.
3. Compare and contrast the achievements of Henry VII and Henry VIII in establishing an English "nation-state."
4. Why was the confiscation of the monasteries considered such a momentous and revolutionary event? What was its significance for English economic and political life?
5. How did the Henrician Church (Henry VIII) differ from the Edwardian Church (Edward VI)?
6. Examine and appraise Tudor foreign policy in the reigns of the two Henry's.
7. Compare and contrast the protectorships of Somerset and Northumberland.

Chapter 8: Elizabethan England

Bindoff, S. T., *Tudor England* (1950).
Elton, Geoffrey R., *The Tudor Revolution in Government* (1959).
Fraser, Antonia, *Mary Queen of Scots* (1969).
Jenkins, Elizabeth, *Elizabeth the Great* (1959).
Mattingly, Garrett, *The Armada* (1959).
Neale, John E., *Queen Elizabeth I* (1957).
———, *The Elizabethan House of Commons* (1949).
Onions, C. T. (ed.), *Shakespeare's England* (1917).
Read, Conyers, *Mr. Secretary Cecil and Queen Elizabeth* (1955).
Rowse, Alfred L., *The Expansion of Elizabethan England* (1955).
———, *The England of Elizabeth* (1950).
Tawney, R. H., *Agrarian Problem in the Sixteenth Century* (1912).
Williamson, J. A., *Sir Francis Drake* (1951).

◄§§►

1. What was the strength and the weakness of Elizabeth's church settlement?
2. Examine the various responses of English and Continental catholics to Elizabeth from 1558 to 1588.
3. Identify the leading advisers of Elizabeth and examine their influence on her policies.
4. Discuss the problems that Elizabeth faced in order to stay on the throne and describe how she handled these problems.
5. Discuss the role of Mary Stuart in terms of (*a*) the religious developments of Scotland, (*b*) the threat to Elizabeth's throne, (*c*) the politics of Europe.
6. Discuss the causes for, and the significance of, the Elizabethan Poor Law.
7. What role did the Elizabethan House of Commons play in the machinery of Government?
8. Examine and evaluate the methods whereby the Government maintained its contacts and influence with local government.

Chapter 9: King versus Parliament

Ashley, Maurice, *England in the Seventeenth Century, 1603-1714* (rev. ed., 1961).
Bowen, Catherine Drinker, *The Lion and the Throne: The Life and Times of Sir Edward Coke* (1957).
Davies, Godfrey, *The Early Stuarts, 1603-1660* (1959).
Haller, William, *The Rise of Puritanism, 1570-1643* (1957).
Hulme, Harold, *Life of Sir John Eliot* (1957).
Kenyon, John, *The Stuarts: A Study in English Kingship* (1959).
Mitchell, W. M., *The Rise of the Revolutionary Party in the English House of Commons, 1603-1629* (1957).

Notestein, Wallace, *English People on the Eve of Colonization, 1603-1630* (1954).
———, *Winning of the Initiative by the House of Commons* (1925).
Stone, Lawrence, *The Crisis of the Aristocracy, 1558-1641* (1965).
Trevelyan, G. M., *England Under the Stuarts* (1965).
Trevor-Roper, Hugh R., *Archbishop Laud* (2nd ed., 1965).
Wedgwood, Cicely V., *Thomas Wentworth, First Earl of Strafford, 1593-1641: A Reevaluation* (1961).
Willson, David H., *King James VI and I* (1956).

❧❧❧

1. What privileges or "rights" were claimed by Parliament during the reign of James? On what grounds did Parliament base these claims?
2. How did the Thirty Years' War affect the foreign policy of James?
3. Explain how the religious policies of James and Charles affected the settlement of America.
4. The opposition to Charles came largely from what elements or groups? Why?
5. Compare and contrast the foreign policies of James I and Charles I.
6. Examine the growing radicalism of Parliamentary demands from 1624 to 1642.
7. Identify and discuss the religious policies of Archbishop Laud.
8. Explain the importance of the two Bishops' Wars in alienating support for the King.

Chapter 10: Civil War and Interregnum

Ashley, Maurice, *The Greatness of Oliver Cromwell* (1958).
Baxter, Richard, *Richard Baxter and Puritan Politics,* edited by Richard Schlatter (1957).
Brailsford, H. N., *The Levellers and the English Revolution,* edited by Christopher Hill (1961).
Clarendon, Edward Hyde, *Selections from the History of the Rebellion and Civil Wars,* edited by G. Huehns.
Gardiner, Samuel R., *Oliver Cromwell* (1900).
Haller, William, *Liberty and Reformation in the Puritan Revolution* (1963).
Hexter, J. H., *The Reign of King Pym* (1941).
Hill, Christopher, *Puritanism and Revolution* (1964).
Judson, Margaret A., *The Crisis of the Constitution* (1949).
Solt, Leo F., *Saints in Arms: Puritanism and Democracy in Cromwell's Army* (1959).
Taylor, Philip A. M. (ed.), *The Origins of the English Civil War: Conspiracy, Crusade, or Class Conflict?* (1960).
Wedgwood, Cicely V., *The King's War* (1959).
———, *The King's Peace* (1959).

◄§§►

1. Discuss the attack made on royal prerogative powers by the Long Parliament.
2. Explain the circumstances and causes that led to the defeat of Charles in the Civil War.
3. Examine the role of religion in the course of the Civil War and in the peace negotiations.
4. During the Interregnum England had two written constitutions. Indicate how the two constitutions differed from one another. What was the intent of the second constitution?
5. Identify the major features of Cromwell's foreign policy. Why is it considered so successful?
6. Examine the basic dilemma of Puritanism and explain why Cromwell could never find a satisfactory constitutional basis for his Government.

Chapter 11: Restoration and Revolution

Bryant, Arthur, *Restoration England* (rev. ed., 1960).
Burnet, Gilbert, *History of My Own Time*, edited by O. Airy (2 vols., 1900).
Clark, George N., *The Later Stuarts, 1660-1714* (2nd ed., 1955).
Davies, Godfrey, *The Restoration of Charles II* (1955).
Feiling, Keith, *History of the Tory Party: 1640-1714* (1950).
Lee, Maurice, *The Cabal* (1965).
Macaulay, Thomas Babington, *History of England from the Accession of James II* (5 vols., 1887).
Ogg, David, *England in the Reign of Charles II* (2 vols., 1955).
————, *England in the Reigns of James II and William III* (1955).
Pepys, Samuel, *Diary* (2 vols., 1946).
Pinkham, Lucille, *William III and the Respectable Revolution* (1954).
Straka, Gerald M. (ed.), *The Revolution of 1688: Whig Triumph or Palace Revolution?* (1963).
Turner, F. C., *James II* (1950).

◄§§►

1. Discuss the Restoration in terms of the religious and political settlement. How did the Clarendon Code reduce the inclusiveness of the Church of England?
2. What effect did the Treaty of Dover have on Holland and on English catholics?
3. Discuss the rise and fall of the Cabal. How was it affected by the Declaration of Indulgence?
4. Enumerate the ways in which Charles eliminated or reduced the opposition of the Whigs from 1681 to 1685.
5. List the catholicizing acts of James II. How did the Church of England respond to James's policies?

6. Why is the revolution of 1688 described as "respectable" or "glorious"?
7. Discuss the Act of Settlement in terms of its religious and constitutional significance.
8. Compare and contrast William III's consolidation of power in Scotland and Ireland.
9. What limitations were placed on the monarchy by the revolutionary settlement of 1689-1702?

Chapter 12: The Last of the Stuarts

Beer, George L., *The Old Colonial System* (2 vols., 1912).
Butterfield, Herbert, *Origins of Modern Science* (1949).
Churchill, Winston, *Marlborough: His Life and Times* (4 vols., 1958).
Hutchinson, F. E., *Milton and the English Mind* (1948).
Kronenberger, Louis, *Marlborough's Duchess* (1958).
Lever, Tresham, *Godolphin, His Life and Times* (1952).
Mackenzie, Agnes M., *The Passing of the Stewarts* (1958).
Trevelyan, George M., *The England of Queen Anne* (3 vols., 1959).
———, *England Under the Stuarts* (1960).
Westfall, Richard S., *Science and Religion in Seventeenth Century England* (1958).
Willey, Basil, *The Seventeenth Century Background* (1953).

ॐ

1. Discuss the War of the Spanish Succession in terms of (*a*) Marlborough's leadership, (*b*) the arguments for continuing the war after 1708, and (*c*) the settlement at Utrecht.
2. Discuss the circumstances leading to the Act of Union.
3. Appraise the role of Henry St. John in the English ministry of 1710-1714. How was he involved in the succession question?
4. Identify the major political theorists of the seventeenth century and relate their writings to political developments of the time.
5. Trace the major religious developments of the Stuart period. What new ideas or attitudes were in evidence?
6. How was the mercantile theory related to the commercial and colonial policies of Stuart England?

Chapter 13: Georgian Politics—1714-1763

Clement, Mary, *Correspondence and Minutes of the S.P.C.K. relating to Wales, 1699-1740* (1952).
Derry, John W., *William Pitt* (1963).
Marshall, Dorothy, *Eighteenth Century England* (1962).
Namier, Lewis B., *The Structure of Politics at the Accession of George III* (2nd ed., 1957).

Owen, John B., *The Rise of the Pelhams* (1957).
Petrie, Charles, *The Jacobite Movement* (2 vols., 1948-1950).
Plumb, J. H., *Sir Robert Walpole: The Making of a Statesman* (1956).
————, *Sir Robert Walpole: The King and Minister* (1961).
————, *The First Four Georges* (1956).
Robertson, Charles G., *Chatham and the British Empire* (1946).
Sykes, Norman, *From Sheldon to Secker: Aspects of English Church History 1660-1768* (1959).
Williams, Basil, *The Whig Supremacy: 1714-1760*, edited by C. H. Stuart (2nd ed., 1962).

◄§§►

1. Discuss the Jacobite movement from 1714 to 1745.
2. Trace the growing influence of the Cabinet under George I and II. What role did Walpole play in this development?
3. Why did the "Whig Supremacy" emerge in the first years of the Hanoverian era?
4. Trace the rise to power of Robert Walpole. How did the South Sea Bubble crisis contribute to his advancement?
5. Compare and contrast the prime ministerships of Walpole and Pitt the Elder in terms of (*a*) economic policy, (*b*) political management, and (*c*) foreign affairs.
6. Examine Anglo-French colonial and commercial rivalry, 1740-1763. What were the chief areas of conflict?
7. List the major clauses of the Treaty of Aix-la-Chapelle. What controversies were left unresolved in the Treaty?
8. Examine Pitt's management of the Seven Years' War. Why was he so bitterly disappointed with the Peace of Paris?

Chapter 14: England and the American Revolution

Alden, John Richard, *American Revolution: 1775-1783* (1954).
Butterfield, Herbert, *George III, Lord North, and the People, 1779-1780* (1950).
Christie, Ian R., *The End of North's Ministry* (1958).
Coupland, Reginald, *The American Revolution and the British Empire* (1965).
Harlow, Vincent T., *The Founding of the Second British Empire, 1763-1793* (1952).
Mackesy, Piers G., *The War for America, 1775-1783* (1964).
Morgan, Edmund S., *The Birth of the Republic, 1763-89* (1956).
Namier, Lewis B., *England in the Age of the American Revolution* (2nd ed., 1961).
Namier, Lewis B., and John Brooke, *The House of Commons 1754-1790* (3 vols., 1964).
Norris, John, *Shelburne and Reform* (1963).

Pares, Richard, *King George III and the Politicians* (1953).
Parkman, Francis, *Montcalm and Wolfe* (1895).
Reitan, Earl A. (ed.), *George III: Tyrant or Constitutional Monarch* (1964).
Ritcheson, Charles R., *British Politics and the American Revolution* (1954).
Rudé, George F. E., *Wilkes and Liberty* (1962).
Williams, E. N., *Eighteenth Century Constitution: Documents and Commentary* (1960).

❧

1. Explain the circumstances under which Pitt the Elder resigned in 1761.
2. How did the position of the Prime Minister differ in the 1760's from Lord North's prime ministership in the 1770's?
3. Explain the relationship between John Wilkes and parliamentary reform.
4. What steps were taken in the American colonies to unify their protest against England?
5. What were the advantages of a land war in America to Britain?
6. Discuss the contribution made to American independence by the entry of France into the war.
7. Examine the agitation for parliamentary reform at the end of the War of American Independence.
8. What is the significance of the American Revolution in terms of (*a*) changing British colonial policy, (*b*) Irish developments, and (*c*) the power of the King's Friends.

Chapter 15: The Era of the French Revolution

Amann, Peter, *The Eighteenth Century Revolution, French or Western?* (1963).
Barnes, Donald G., *George III and William Pitt, 1783-1806* (1965).
Brown, Ford K., *Fathers of the Victorians: The Age of Wilberforce* (1961).
Cooper, Leonard, *Age of Wellington* (1963).
Creevey, Thomas, *The Creevey Papers*, edited by John Gore (1963).
Feiling, Keith G., *The Second Tory Party, 1714-1832* (1951).
Laprade, W. T., *England and the French Revolution* (1909).
Lecky, W. H., *History of Ireland in the Eighteenth Century* (5 vols., 1893).
Mahan, Alfred T., *Life of Nelson* (2nd ed., 1899).
Nicolson, Harold, *The Congress of Vienna: A Study in Allied Unity, 1812-1822* (1961).
Oman, Charles, *Britain Against Napoleon* (1942).
Rosebery, Earl, *Life of Pitt* (1947).
Watson, John S., *The Reign of George III, 1760-1815* (1960).

❧

1. Explain the connection between the East India Company and the political careers of Fox and Pitt the Younger.

2. Apply the truism that "no government could survive without the good-will of the Sovereign" to Fox and Pitt in 1783 and to Pitt in 1801.
3. Discuss the reforms achieved or attempted by William Pitt in the 1780's.
4. How did the war with France affect England's internal politics?
5. Discuss the major coalitions that Pitt put together against France.
6. What was the Continental System? Explain its significance for (*a*) the satellite countries, (*b*) the United States, (*c*) England's economy?
7. Trace the influence of British sea power on the course of the Napoleonic Wars.
8. Why did the coalition against Napoleon fall apart at the Congress of Vienna?
9. Discuss the failure of the Congress System. Why did Castlereagh's hopes for the alliance fail to materialize?

Chapter 16: Eighteenth Century England

Abbey, C. J., and Overton, J. H., *The English Church in the Eighteenth Century* (1887).

Ashton, Thomas S., *An Economic History of England: The Eighteenth Century* (1955).

Boswell, James, *Life of Johnson* (1953).

George, Dorothy, *England in Transition* (1953).

Kronenberger, Louis, *Kings and Desperate Men: Life in Eighteenth Century England* (1959).

Mantoux, Paul, *The Industrial Revolution in the Eighteenth Century* (1928).

Marshall, Dorothy, *Eighteenth Century England* (1962).

Montagu, Mary Wortley, *Letters and Works* (2 vols., 1887).

Plumb, J. H., *England in the Eighteenth Century* (1950).

Stephen, Leslie, *History of English Thought in the Eighteenth Century* (1902).

Taylor, Philip (ed.), *The Industrial Revolution in Britain: Triumph or Disaster?* (1958).

Turberville, A. S., *English Men and Manners in the Eighteenth Century* (2nd ed., 1957).

Willey, Basil, *The Eighteenth Century Background* (1941).

◄§ᢓᢓᢓ►

1. Compare and contrast the social and economic condition of England in the first and second half of the eighteenth century.
2. Discuss the influence of preferment by Government appointment on the church and universities.
3. Appraise the significance of the Wesleyan Movement in England.
4. How does Burke's philosophy run counter to Locke and Smith? How does Smith relate the "natural laws" of the Enlightenment to economics?
5. How did the Industrial Revolution force improvements in transportation?
6. Explain the relationship between the agricultural and industrial revolutions.

7. Discuss the acceleration of inventions in the textile industry to meet recognizable needs.

Chapter 17: Repression and Reform, 1815-1841

Arbuthnot, Harriett, *The Journal of Mrs. Arbuthnot, 1820-1832* (1950).
Aspinall, A. (ed.), *Letters of George IV, 1812-1830* (3 vols., 1938).
Brinton, Crane, *English Political Thought in the 19th Century* (1962).
Cecil, David, *Melbourne* (1955).
Greville, C. C. F., *Journal of the Reigns of King George IV, King William IV and Queen Victoria* (8 vols., 1888).
Halévy, Élie, *A History of the English People in the Nineteenth Century*, Vol. II (*The Liberal Awakening, 1815-1830*) and Vol. III (*The Triumph of Reform, 1830-1841*), (1961).
Jackman, Sydney (ed.), *The English Reform Tradition, 1790-1910* (1965).
Maccoby, Samuel, *English Radicalism* (4 vols., 1955).
Newman, John H., *Apologia Pro Vita Sua* (1964).
Temperley, Harold W. V., *The Foreign Policy of Canning, 1822-1827* (1925).
Trevelyan, George M., *Lord Grey of the Reform Bill* (1929).
Ward, Stephen G. P., *Wellington* (1963).
Woodward, E. L., *The Age of Reform* (1958).

❧❧❧

1. What grievances were expressed by the workers in England following the Napoleonic Wars?
2. Compare and contrast the foreign policy of Canning and Castlereagh.
3. What were the arguments used against the passage of the Great Reform Bill?
4. Compare and contrast the ideas of Owen and Bentham. Why was Bentham more influential in influencing legislation?
5. Identify the leadership in the colonial office in the postwar years. What were the opposing points of view on colonial policy?
6. Examine the circumstances leading to and the significance of the Durham Report.
7. Discuss the Oxford Movement in terms of (a) leadership, (b) church-state position, and (c) relationship to the Roman Catholic church.
8. Trace the political-constitutional developments of 1834-1841 which conclude with the establishment of responsible government in the British parliamentary system.

Generation (1964).

Cecil, Algernon, *Queen Victoria and her Prime Ministers* (1953).
Checkland, Sidney, *The Rise of Industrial Society in England, 1815-1885* (1965).
Dodds, John Wendell, *The Age of Paradox; a biography of England, 1841-1851* (1952).
Gash, Norman, *Politics in the Age of Peel* (1953).
Greville, Charles C. F., *The Greville Memoirs, 1827-1860*, ed. by Roger Fulford (1963).
Guedalla, Philip, *Palmerston* (1950).
Hammond, J. L. and Barbara, *Lord Shaftesbury* (1969).
Houghton, Walter E., *The Victorian Frame of Mind, 1830-1870* (1957).
Hovell, Mark, *The Chartist Movement* (1950).
McCord, Norman, *The Anti-Corn Law League, 1838-1846* (1958).
Roberts, David, *The Victorian Origins of the British Welfare State* (1960).
Rostow, Walt W., *The British Economy of the Nineteenth Century* (1948).
Southgate, Donald, *The Passing of the Whigs, 1832-1886* (1962).
Thompson, Edward P., *The Making of the English Working Class* (1964).
Vincent, John, *The Formation of the British Liberal Party, 1857-1868* (1967).
Webster, Charles K., *The Foreign Policy of Palmerston, 1830-1841* (1951).
Woodward, Ernest L., *The Age of Reform, 1815-1870* (2nd ed., 1962).
Young, George M. (ed.), *Early Victorian England, 1830-1865* (1934).

◆§◆

1. Compare and contrast the Tory party under the leadership of Peel and of Derby-Disraeli.
2. Trace the steps which led Peel to support free trade and abandon the Corn Laws. What were the consequences for his party?
3. Appraise the significance of the extra-parliamentary pressure groups in the 1840's.
4. Explain the loose party alignments of the mid-Victorian years. How did this circumstance affect Cabinet policies?
5. Discuss the domestic and foreign policies of Russell's first administration.
6. Why is Palmerston frequently considered the embodiment of the Mid-Victorian Compromise? How did his attitude differ on domestic and foreign policies?
7. Examine England's economic growth during the years 1840-70. What was the significance of England's title, "Workshop of the World"?
8. Identify the basic themes of British foreign policy in the nineteenth century and describe their application under Lord Palmerston.
9. Explain the causes and the consequences of the Indian Mutiny.
10. Examine Anglo-French relations in the period 1830-65. What "triumphs" did Palmerston achieve over the French?

Chapter 19: Gladstone and Disraeli, 1865-1886

Ausubel, Herman, *John Bright: Victorian Reformer* (1966).
Bagehot, Walter, *The English Constitution* (rev. ed., 1933).
Blake, Robert, *Disraeli* (1966).

Clark, G. Kitson, *The Making of Victorian England* (1962).
Cole, George D. H., and Filson A. W., *British Working Class Movements: Select Documents, 1789-1875* (1951).
Cruise O'Brien, Connor, *Parnell and His Party, 1880-1890* (1957).
Ensor, Robert C. K., *England, 1870-1914* (1936).
Hammond, John, *Gladstone and the Irish Nation* (1964).
Longford, Elizabeth, *Queen Victoria: Born to Succeed* (1965).
Magnus, Philip, *Gladstone* (1954).
Mill, John Stuart, *Autobiography* (1958).
Monypenny, W. F., and Buckle, G. E., *The Life of Benjamin Disraeli, Earl of Beaconsfield* (rev. ed., 1929).
Seton-Watson, Robert W., *Disraeli, Gladstone and the Eastern Question* (1962).
Somervell, David C., *Disraeli and Gladstone* (1929).
Winks, Robin W. (ed.), *British Imperialism: Gold, God, Glory* (1963).

⮞⮜

1. Discuss the circumstances surrounding the passage of the Second Reform Bill. What was the political significance of the bill?
2. Compare and contrast the administrations of Gladstone and Disraeli in the following areas: party organization, the "Irish question," and political reform.
3. Examine Gladstone's first administration, 1868-74. What were its major achievements?
4. How did the two parties accommodate themselves to the increasing role of the State in society?
5. Discuss the new imperialism of the 1870's. How did Gladstone and Disraeli differ on the merits of imperialism, British influence in Africa, and Anglo-Turkish relations?
6. How did foreign affairs contribute to the outcome of the elections of 1880 and 1885?
7. How did Disraeli's philosophy of social reform reveal itself in social legislation, 1874-80?
8. Appraise Gladstone's Irish policy in terms of his legislative program, its effectiveness, and the results for the Liberal party.
9. Relate the extension of the vote to the developments in party organization, 1865-85.
10. How did the political philosophy and party program of Gladstone and Chamberlain differ?

Chapter 20: Democracy at Home—Empire Abroad

Clapham, John H., *An Economic History of Modern Britain*, Vol. III (2nd ed., 1938).
Cross, Colin, *The Liberals in Power* (1963).
Dangerfield, George, *The Strange Death of Liberal England, 1910-1914* (1961).

De Kiewiet, Cornelius W., *A History of South Africa, Social and Economic* (1941).

De Mendelssohn, Peter, *The Age of Churchill: Heritage and Adventure, 1874-1911,* (1961).

Fulford, Roger, *Votes For Women* (1961).

Garvin, J. L., and Amery, Julian, *Life of Joseph Chamberlain,* (4 vols., 1932-1951).

Jenkins, Roy, *Mr. Balfour's Poodle* (1954).

Kennedy, A. L., *Salisbury* (1953).

Magnus, Philip, *King Edward the Seventh* (1964).

Nowell-Smith, Simon H. (ed.), *Edwardian England, 1901-1914* (1964).

Pelling, Henry, *The Origins of the Labour Party, 1880-1900* (2nd ed., 1965).

Spender, J. A., and Asquith, Cyril, *The Life of Herbert Henry Asquith, Lord Oxford and Asquith* (2 vols., 1932).

Webb, Beatrice, *My Apprenticeship* (1926).

◆§§◆

1. .What consequences did the Irish Home Rule bill of 1886 have on (a) the Conservative party, (b) the Liberal party, and (c) social legislation?
2. Discuss the origins of the Labor party. Why did the Liberal party fail to hold the labor movement?
3. Examine Anglo-Irish relations, 1886-1905. What important bills were passed by Parliament relating to Ireland?
4. Explain the landslide Liberal victory of 1906. How did the Liberal Government attempt to implement their mandate?
5. Trace Anglo-Indian relations, 1876-1909. To what extent did constitutional changes follow those occurring in the white settlement Dominions (Canada, New Zealand, Australia, South Africa)?
6. Discuss the origins of the Boer War.
7. Explain the relationship between the passage of the Parliament Act and the Third Irish Home Rule bill. Give the highlights of each bill.
8. Examine the political and constitutional situation of 1910-13. How did developments jeopardize the Liberal ideals of the 19th century?

Chapter 21: England in the Nineteenth Century

Arnold, Matthew, *Culture and Anarchy* (1932).

Briggs, Asa, *Victorian People* (1965).

Brinton, Crane, *English Political Thought in the Nineteenth Century* (1962).

Chadwick, Owen, *The Victorian Church* (2 vols., 1966, 1970).

Clapham, J. H., *Economic History of Great Britain* (3 vols., 1927-1938).

Clark, G. Kitson, *The Making of Victorian England* (1967).

Halévy, Élie, *History of the English People in the Nineteenth Century* (2nd ed., 1949).

Jackman, Sydney W. (ed.), *The English Reform Tradition, 1790-1910* (1965).

Rostow, Walt W., *British Economy of the Nineteenth Century* (1948).
Strachey, Lytton, *Eminent Victorians* (1963).
Trevelyan, George M., *British History in the Nineteenth Century and After, 1782-1919*, (2nd ed., 1937).
Willey, Basil, *Nineteenth Century Studies* (1949).
Young, George M., *Victorian England: Portrait of an Age* (2nd ed., 1953).

᠁᠁

1. What were the merits of Victorian Liberalism? Why was it diminishing by the beginning of the twentieth century?
2. How was nineteenth-century faith in progress revealed in Victorian thought?
3. Identify nineteenth-century scientific progress in physics, chemistry, and medicine.
4. Compare and contrast the characteristics and values of early and late Victorianism.
5. What influence did Darwin's hypothesis have on religion and ethics?
6. How did John Stuart Mill anticipate the liberal socialism of the twentieth century? Why did he turn away from laissez-faire economics?
7. Appraise the changing role of the monarchy in the nineteenth century.
8. What changes in the judiciary took place under Victoria? Why were they necessary?

Chapter 22: The Great War

Beaverbrook, William M. A. (Lord), *Politicians and the War* (2 vols., 1928).
————, *Men and Power, 1917-1918* (1957).
Buchan, John, *Pilgrim's Way* (1963).
Churchill, Winston S., *The World Crisis* (6 vols., 1931).
Falls, Cyril, *The First World War* (1960).
Grey, Edward, *Twenty-Five Years* (1937).
Hurwitz, Samuel, *State Intervention in Great Britain, 1914-1919* (1949).
Jones, Thomas, *Lloyd-George* (1951).
Liddell Hart, Basil, *The Real War, 1914-1918* (1930).
McKenna, Stephan, *While I Remember* (1922).
Riddell, Lord, *War Diary* (1933).
Taylor, Alan J. P., *Politics in Wartime* (1965).
Tuchman, Barbara, *The Guns of August* (1962).
Wells, H. G., *Mr. Britling Sees It Through* (1916).

᠁᠁

1. Identify the crises leading up to World War I and how they contributed to Entente solidarity?
2. What steps did Austria and Russia take after the assassination of Archduke Ferdinand that contributed to the outbreak of world war?

3. Identify the Schlieffen plan. Why did it fail?
4. Discuss the leadership and war administration of Lloyd George.
5. Examine Britain's position in the world and at home at the end of the war.
6. What was the relationship of Lloyd George to the Liberal party, 1916-18? Why did he favor the Coupon election?
7. To what extent did the Treaty of Versailles follow or violate the Fourteen Points?
8. Discuss the controversy over reparations and evaluate the decision that was finally reached.

Chapter 23: Britain Between the Wars

Beaverbrook, William M. A., *The Decline and Fall of Lloyd George* (1963).

Blake, Robert, *The Unknown Prime Minister: Bonar Law* (1955).

Carr, Edward H., *The Twenty Years' Crisis, 1919-1939* (1954).

Churchill, Winston S., *The Gathering Storm* (1948).

Eden, Anthony, *Facing the Dictators: Memoirs, 1931-1938* (1962).

Feiling, Keith, *Life of Neville Chamberlain* (1946).

Gilbert, Martin, and Gott, Richard, *The Appeasers* (1963).

Graves, Robert, and Hodge, Alan, *The Long Week-End: A Social History of Great Britain, 1918-1939* (1963).

Keith, Arthur B., *Speeches and Documents on the British Dominions, 1918-1931; from Self-Government to National Sovereignty* (1932).

Lewis, W. Arthur, *Economic Survey, 1919-1939* (1949).

Masterman, C. F. G., *England After War* (1922).

Medlicott, William N., *British Foreign Policy Since Versailles* (1968).

Mowat, Charles L., *Britain Between the Wars, 1918-1940* (1955).

Nicolson, Harold, *King George V: His Life and Reign* (1958).

Raymond, John (ed.), *The Baldwin Age* (1961).

Taylor, Alan J. P., *English History, 1914-1945* (1965).

Woodward, Ernest L., *Short Journey* (1942).

◀ॐॐ▶

1. Examine the economic problems faced by Britain after the war and the steps the Government took to deal with them.
2. Compare and contrast the imperial arrangements made with Ireland and India between the wars.
3. What developments and circumstances contributed to the Conservative political hegemony, 1918-38?
4. Compare and contrast the foreign policies of the Conservative and Labor parties, 1922-31.
5. Trace the history of disarmament efforts between the wars.
6. What steps in social welfare were taken between the wars?
7. Why did the National Government of 1931 come into existence? What was the strength and weakness of this Government?

8. Explain how Dominion developments evolved after World War I into the Balfour Report.
9. Discuss the collapse of collective security in the thirties. What action or policy would have been essential to stop Hitler?
10. Explain Chamberlain's foreign policy in the context of his times and his assumptions.

Chapter 24: The Second World War

Beveridge, William, *Power and Influence* (1953).
Churchill, Winston, *The Second World War* (6 vols., 1948-1953).
Collier, Basil, *The Battle of Britain* (1962).
Feis, Herbert, *Churchill, Roosevelt, Stalin* (2nd ed., 1967).
Hancock, W. Keith, and Gowing, Margaret M., *The British War Economy* (1949).
Sanson, William, *Westminster at War* (1947).
Snell, John L., *The Meaning of Yalta: Big Three Diplomacy and the New Balance of Power* (1956).
Snyder, Louis L., *The War: A Concise History, 1939-1945* (1960).
Titmuss, Richard M., *Problems of Social Policy* (1950).
Waugh, Evelyn, *Men at Arms* (1952).
Webster, Charles, and Frankland, Noble, *The Strategic Air Offensive Against Germany* (4 vols., 1961).
Woodward, Ernest L., *British Foreign Policy in the Second World War* (1962).

ᕳᢢᢢᕥ

1. Discuss the events and circumstances that prompted the resignation of Prime Minister Chamberlain in May, 1940.
2. "The United States stretched its neutrality legislation to provide assistance to Britain and her allies before the United States was a belligerent." Discuss.
3. What were the military objectives of the Germans in 1941 and how successful were they in winning these objectives?
4. Axis advances were halted on three fronts in 1942 and successful Allied counteroffensives undertaken. Identify the three theaters and the turning point in each.
5. Why was the location of a Second Front a subject of controversy between Churchill and Stalin?
6. Why was Stalin in such an excellent bargaining position at the Yalta Conference? What decisions were reached by the Big Three at the Conference?
7. To what extent did the idea of systematic military planning also apply to social and economic planning within Britain during the war?
8. Explain the Labor landslide in the election of 1945.

Chapter 25: Contemporary Britain

Boyd, Francis, *British Politics in Transition, 1945-1963* (1964).

Dalton, Hugh, *High Tide and After: Memoirs 1946-1960* (1962).

Harrod, Roy, *The British Economy* (1963).

Havighurst, Alfred F., *Twentieth-Century Britain* (2nd ed., 1966).

Hopkins, Harry, *The New Look: A Social History of Britain in the 1940's and 1950's* (1964).

Lindsey, Almont, *Socialized Medicine in England and Wales: The National Health Service, 1948-1961* (1962).

Mansergh, Nicholas, *Survey of British Commonwealth Affairs: Problems of Wartime Co-operation and Postwar Change, 1939-1952* (1958).

Middleton, Drew, *The Supreme Choice: Britain and Europe* (1963).

Morrison, Herbert, *An Autobiography* (1960).

Perham, Margery, *The Colonial Reckoning* (1963).

Sampson, Anthony, *Anatomy of Britain Today* (1965).

Seton-Watson, Hugh, *Neither War nor Peace* (1960).

Titmuss, Richard, *Essays on "The Welfare State"* (1958).

Woodhouse, C. M., *British Foreign Policy Since the Second World War* (1962).

◄§§►

1. Compare and contrast the achievements of the Labor and the Conservative Governments in extending social services since 1945.
2. Describe the objectives and the operation of the National Health Service.
3. Identify the major problems faced by the Labor Government in economic reconstruction after the war and tell what measures were applied to alleviate the problems.
4. Trace the political fortunes of the Conservative party, 1950-1964. Identify and explain the changes in party leadership.
5. Assess the success of Britain in relinquishing her empire in Asia and Africa after the war. Why did ex-colonies elect to continue in the Commonwealth.
6. Discuss the purpose and scope of the Colonial Development and Welfare Acts.
7. Examine the increasing subordination of British defense policies to American leadership. How has the nature of this Atlantic alliance changed in the two decades since World War II?
8. What were the issues that divided the Labor party in 1960? How did the Labor party platform change in the sixties?

Review Examinations

Part I

Britain to 1714

1. Identify and state briefly the significance of each of the following.
   (1) Synod of Whitby
   (2) Heptarchy
   (3) Elizabethan Poor Law
   (4) Babington Plot
   (5) Dr. Bonham Case
   (6) Court of the Star Chamber
   (7) Domesday Book
   (8) *Piers Plowman*
   (9) Earl of Clarendon
   (10) *Absalom and Achitophel*
2. Discuss the obstacles to strong royal Government that existed in Anglo-Saxon England.
3. "Religious nationalism reached England before political nationalism." Identify the events, attitudes, and individuals that promoted religious nationalism in the fourteenth and fifteenth centuries.
4. Geoffrey Templeman writes that "Parliament can no longer occupy the foreground of the [Medieval] picture. Instead the scene is dominated by the King and his Council jointly controlling an already elaborate judicial and administrative organization, which was steadily developing its own complicated procedure." Drawing upon pre-Tudor history, support or criticize this thesis.
5. Compare and contrast the achievements of Henry VII and Queen Elizabeth I in establishing an English nation-state.
6. "The radical religious reformation in England took place in the Civil War and Interregnum rather than under Henry VIII and Cranmer." Do you agree with this assertion? Why?
7. Identify the most significant economic and commercial developments during the reigns of Elizabeth I and James I. How did these developments affect the political scene?
8. Compare and contrast the foreign policies of Cromwell and Charles II.
9. Clyde Grose writes, "Restorations usually bring ills in their train and merely defer necessary solutions to problems. That of 1660 was no exception. But among restored monarchs Charles II was an unusually good one. He got in the way less than most of them do." Why was the Restoration so successful—at least temporarily? What problems were not really resolved by the Restoration?

10. "Freedom versus authority" was a major theme in Seventeenth Century England. Discuss this theme in terms of the literature of the period.

Part II

Britain since 1714

1. Compare and contrast the prime ministerships of Robert Walpole and William Pitt the Younger in terms of (*a*) economic and fiscal policies, (*b*) foreign affairs.
2. Taking the three Enlightenment themes of reason, natural law, and progress as your standard, observe their application in the religion, literature, and historical writing of eighteenth-century England.
3. Victor Hugo claims that "There is nothing more powerful than an idea whose time has come." Trace the influence of Adam Smith's free trade idea on English politics between 1776 and 1861.
4. Compare British imperial policy in the treatment of the Thirteen Colonies before 1783, and the Canadian colonies after 1783.
5. Identify the major interests of British foreign policy in the nineteenth century and describe their application under Lord Palmerston.
6. Discuss British imperialism in the last half of the nineteenth century. What bearing did the extension of the franchise and foreign industrial competition have on British imperial policies? Use Africa as the area of specific example.
7. Explain the changing fortunes and decline of the Liberal party from Gladstone's second ministry in 1880 to the end of World War I.
8. Compare and contrast the politics and problems of England following World War I and World War II.
9. Discuss Britain's foreign policy since World War II in terms of relations with (*a*) the United States, (*b*) Europe.
10. Examine the rise of Irish nationalism. Identify the leaders and the various issues and developments that culminate in the creation of the Irish Free State.

Sovereigns of England and Great Britain

Anglo-Saxons and Danes

Kent
Ethelbert, 560-616

Northumbria
Ethelfrith, 593-617
Edwin, 617-633
Oswald, 635-642
Oswy, 642-670
Ecgfrith, 670-685

Mercia
Penda, 626-655
Ethelbald, 716-757
Offa II, 757-796
Cenulf, 796-821

Wessex
Ine, 688-726
Egbert, 802-839
Ethelwulf, 839-858
Ethelbald, 858-860
Ethelbert, 860-866
Ethelred I, 866-871
Alfred the Great, 871-899
Edward, 899-924
Ethelstan, 924-939
Edmund, 939-946
Edred, 946-955
Edwig, 955-959
Edgar, 959-975
Edward, 975-978
Ethelred II, 978-1016
Edmund, 1016
Canute, 1017-1035
Harold I, 1035-1040
Harthacanute, 1040-1042

Edward the Confessor, 1042-1066
Harold II, 1066

Normandy

William I, 1066-1087
William II, 1087-1100
Henry I, 1100-1135

Blois

Stephen, 1135-1154

Plantagenet (Anjou)

Henry II, 1154-1189
Richard I, 1189-1199
John, 1199-1216
Henry III, 1216-1272
Edward I, 1272-1307
Edward II, 1307-1327
Edward III, 1327-1377
Richard II, 1377-1399

Lancaster

Henry IV, 1399-1413
Henry V, 1413-1422
Henry VI, 1422-1461

York

Edward IV, 1461-1483
Edward V, 1483
Richard III, 1483-1485

Tudor

Henry VII, 1485-1509
Henry VIII, 1509-1547

Edward VI, 1547-1553
Mary, 1553-1558
Elizabeth I, 1558-1603

Stuart

James I, 1603-1625
Charles I, 1625-1649

Interregnum (Commonwealth
and Protectorate)

Council of State, 1649
Protectorate, 1653
Oliver Cromwell, 1653-1658
Richard Cromwell, 1658-1659

Stuart

Charles II, 1660-1685
James II, 1685-1688

William III and Mary, 1689-1702
Anne, 1702-1714

Hanover

George I, 1714-1727
George II, 1727-1760
George III, 1760-1820
George IV, 1820-1830
William IV, 1830-1837
Victoria, 1837-1901

Saxe-Coburg

Edward VII, 1901-1910

Windsor

George V, 1910-1936
Edward VIII, 1936
George VI, 1936-1952
Elizabeth II, 1952-

Prime Ministers of Great Britain

Robert Walpole, 1721-42
Lord Wilmington, 1742-44
Henry Pelham, 1744-54
Duke of Newcastle, 1754-56
Duke of Devonshire, 1756-57
Duke of Newcastle, 1757-61
Duke of Newcastle, 1761-62
Lord Bute, 1762-63
George Grenville, 1763-65
Lord Rockingham, 1765-66
William Pitt, Earl of Chatham, 1766-68
Duke of Grafton, 1768-70
Lord North, 1770-82
Lord Rockingham, 1782
Lord Shelburne, 1782-83
Duke of Portland, 1783
William Pitt, the Younger, 1783-1801
Henry Addington, 1801-04
William Pitt, the Younger, 1804-06
Lord Grenville, 1806-07
Duke of Portland, 1807-09
Spencer Perceval, 1809-12
Lord Liverpool, 1812-27
George Canning, 1827
Lord Goderich, 1827-28
Duke of Wellington, 1828-30
Earl Grey, 1830-34
Lord Melbourne, 1834
Sir Robert Peel, 1834-35
Lord Melbourne, 1835-41
Sir Robert Peel, 1841-46
Lord John Russell, 1846-52
Lord Derby, 1852
Lord Aberdeen, 1852-55

Lord Palmerston, 1855-58
Lord Derby, 1858-59
Lord Palmerston, 1859-65
Lord John Russell, 1865-66
Lord Derby, 1866-68
Benjamin Disraeli, 1868
William E. Gladstone, 1868-74
Benjamin Disraeli, 1874-80
William E. Gladstone, 1880-85
Lord Salisbury, 1885-86
William E. Gladstone, 1886
Lord Salisbury, 1886-92
William E. Gladstone, 1892-94
Lord Rosebery, 1894-95
Lord Salisbury, 1895-1902
Arthur J. Balfour, 1902-05
Henry Campbell-Bannerman, 1905-08
Herbert H. Asquith, 1908-16
David Lloyd George, 1916-22
Andrew Bonar Law, 1922-23
Stanley Baldwin, 1923-24
James Ramsey MacDonald, 1924
Stanley Baldwin, 1924-29
James Ramsay MacDonald, 1929-31
James Ramsay MacDonald, 1931-35
Stanley Baldwin, 1935-37
Neville Chamberlain, 1937-40
Winston Churchill, 1940-45
Clement Atlee, 1945-51
Sir Winston Churchill, 1951-55
Sir Anthony Eden, 1955-57
Harold Macmillan, 1957-63
Sir Alec Douglas-Home 1963-64
Harold Wilson, 1964-1970
Edward Heath, 1970-

Normandy and Plantagenet (Anjou)

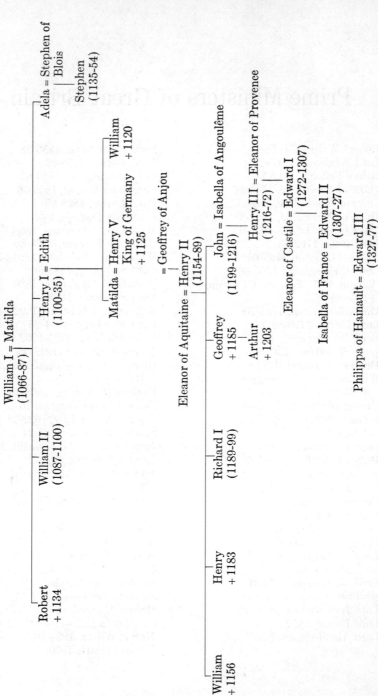

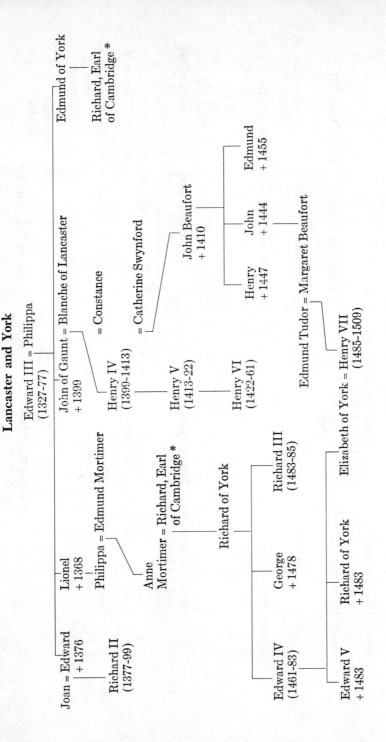

Lancaster and York

* Richard, Earl of Cambridge, son of Edmund of York, married Anne Mortimer.

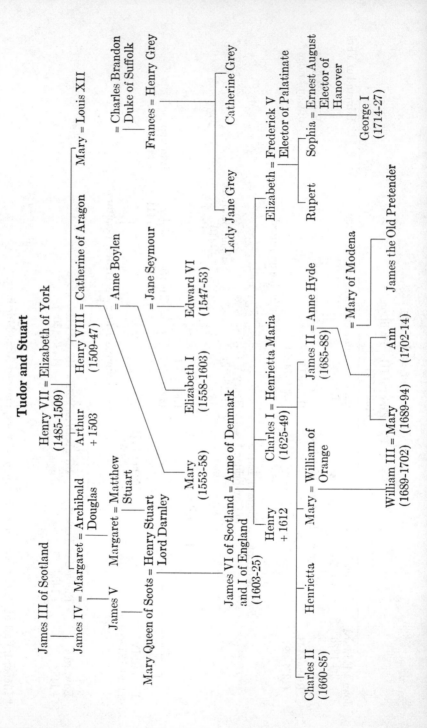

Tudor and Stuart

Hanover, Saxe-Coburg, and Windsor

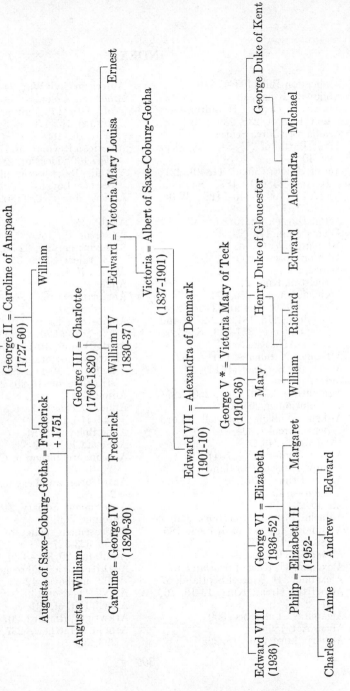

* In 1917 official name of royal family became Windsor, superseding Saxe-Coburg.

INDEX

Abdication Bill (1936), 319
Abdullah, King, 350
Aberdeen, George Hamilton-Gordon, Earl of, 235, 239, 240
Acadia. *See* Nova Scotia
Acre: Battle of (1798), 185; siege of, 40
Act of Union: Canada (1840), 221; Ireland (1800), 187; Scotland (1707), 66, 140-141; Wales (1536), 77
Acton Burnell, Statute of, 47
Adams, John, 175
Addington, Viscount, 187
Addison, Joseph, 200
Aelfric, 20
Aethelstan, King, 21
Afghanistan, 252, 256, 271
Africa, 8, 136, 354; and British colonialism, 175, 181, 272-275; and independence, 351-353. *See also* North Africa
Afrikaner Nationalist party, 352
Agincourt, Battle of (1415), 54
Agricola, 6
Agriculture, 27, 97, 147, 250, 287; revolution in, 205-206
Aitken, William Maxwell (Lord Beaverbrook), 304, 319
"Alabama," 243, 248
Albany Conference (1754), 161
Albany, Duke of (Scotland), 68
Albert, Prince, 226, 250
Albigenses, 40
Alcuin, 20
Aldhelm, bishop of Sherborne, 20
Alexander I, Czar of Russia, 185, 188, 189, 193-195
Alexander II, Pope, 24
Alexander II, King of Scotland, 67
Alexander III, King of Scotland, 67
Alfred the Great, King, 14-16, 20, 21
Algerciras Conference, 300
Aliens Act, 186
Althorp, Lord, 216, 218, 225

American Civil War, 242-243
American Colonies: establishment of, 110, 148; imperial policies toward, 167-170; in Seven Years' War, 162-165
American Revolution, 170-173, 175-177, 199; ideas of, 289; and Ireland, 186; lesson of, 221, 268. *See also* Loyalists
Amiens, Treaty of (1802), 185-186, 187
Anabaptists, 81, 89
Anderson, Sir John, 329
Angevin: empire, 32-33, 34, 37, 44, 73; rulers, 23, 29, 55
Angles, 10-12
Anglesey, 6
Anglican church. *See* Church of England
Anglo-Irish Treaty (1921), 312, 322
Anglo-Saxon Chronicle, 16, 20
Anglo-Saxons, 10-11, 15-22; literature of, 20; origins of, 10; settlement by, 10-11; society and institutions of, 16-20, 25-27
Anjou, 33
Anne, Queen, 137, 138, 139, 140-143, 150, 156
Anne Boleyn, 79, 81
Anne of Cleves, 82-83
Anselm, archbishop of Canterbury, 28, 40, 43
Anti-Corn-Law League, 227, 230, 231-232
Anti-Slavery Society, 218
Antonine Wall, 6
Appeasement, policy of (1931-39), 320, 323-327
Aquitaine, 29, 34, 48-49, 53
Architecture: eighteenth-century, 202; medieval, 42-43
Argyll, Duke of, 143
Argyll, Earl of, 131
Arkwright, Richard, 207
Arnold, Matthew, 237, 288, 289, 293, 294